AF361295

After Images

After Images

Photography, Archaeology, and Psychoanalysis and the Tradition of Bildung

ERIC DOWNING

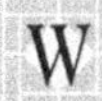

WAYNE STATE UNIVERSITY PRESS

DETROIT

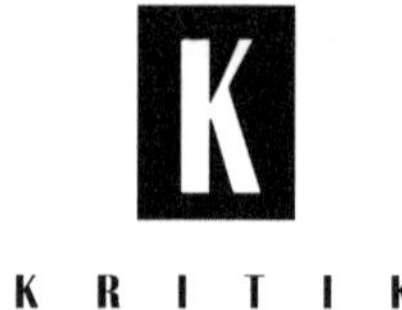

KRITIK

German Literary Theory and Cultural Studies
Liliane Weissberg, Editor

*A complete listing of the books in this series
can be found online at wsupress.wayne.edu*

ISBN-13: 978-0-8143-3301-3   ISBN-10: 0-8143-3301-X

LIBRARY OF CONGRESS CATALOGING-IN-PUBLICATION DATA

DOWNING, ERIC.

AFTER IMAGES : PHOTOGRAPHY, ARCHAEOLOGY, AND PSYCHOANALYSIS

AND THE TRADITION OF BILDUNG / ERIC DOWNING.

P. CM. — (KRITIK, GERMAN LITERARY THEORY AND CULTURAL STUDIES)

INCLUDES BIBLIOGRAPHICAL REFERENCES AND INDEX.

ISBN 0-8143-3301-X (CLOTH : ALK. PAPER)

1. MANN, THOMAS, 1875–1955. ZAUBERBERG. 2. JENSEN, WILHELM, 1837–1911. GRADIVA.

3. BENJAMIN, WALTER, 1892–1940. BERLINER CHRONIK. 4. SUBJECT (PHILOSOPHY) IN

LITERATURE. 5. LITERATURE AND PHOTOGRAPHY. 6. ARCHAEOLOGY AND LITERATURE. I. TITLE.

II. SERIES: KRITIK (DETROIT, MICH.)

PT2625.A44Z3236 2006

830.9'353—DC22

2006012993

For Nancy and Jes

Contents

CONTENTS

3.

Bildung and the Archaeology of Images in Walter Benjamin's *Berlin Chronicle* 167

Epilogue (Nachbildung): Bildung, Archaeology, and Photography in W. G. Sebald 271

Acknowledgments

In writing this book, I have incurred many debts. The most important of these is owed to Jim Porter, who has been a first reader of almost everything I have written, and one could not ask for a more critical, incisive, and original reception. Over time, his voice has migrated into my brain as a kind of daimon variously haunting and guiding my thought, and for those who have ears to hear, I am sure it is still audible in many of these pages. One of the joys of this project has been that it brought my work back into the orbit of our shared interests in German and classical studies, and both this book and I have benefited incalculably from his intellectual and personal friendship.

It seems almost reckless to have assumed similar debts to another friend. Christopher Wild was my *Gesprächspartner* on many walks, commutes, and days on campus, who listened patiently to the stutterings of this work in progress, helped transform them into articulate ideas, and gave invaluable feedback on their written form. Writing can be a solitary enterprise, but such a friend assured that it was never only that.

Much of the groundwork for this project was laid during my years at Harvard, and I have former colleagues and graduate students to thank for their input and support. Dorrit Cohn, Judith Ryan, and Maria Tatar were all extremely generous with their time, wisdom, and unflagging goodwill. Margret Guillemin was always the kindest reader; Kevin McLaughlin made sure Benjamin was always part of the picture. Among the at-that-time graduate students, I want especially to single

ACKNOWLEDGMENTS

out Catriona MacLeod, Joe Metz, Bill Donahue, and Peter McIsaac, all of whom have since become valued colleagues in their own right and all of whom read parts of the manuscript and provided much appreciated comments. At the University of North Carolina at Chapel Hill, I have been wonderfully supported by Alice Kuzniar, Clayton Koelb, John McGowan, and Jim O'Hara, each of whom contributed to this book in ways both great and small: the same must be said of my colleague at Duke, Thomas Pfau. Heather Klomhaus Hrács is to be thanked for her help in tracking down elusive references, and Will Taylor for his in compiling the bibliography. And from a completely different part of the world, my thanks to Gordon Turner for responding to e-mail queries about his former colleague W. G. Sebald.

Audiences at the Johns Hopkins, Columbia, and Rutgers universities and several GSA and ACLA conventions all heard parts of this study and provided useful criticism. I am especially grateful to those individuals whose invitations made those occasions possible. I also thank three colleagues who did not live to see this project completed but all of whom read large parts of it in manuscript and provided cherished insights: George Avery, Bianca Theisen, and Ken Weisinger.

Finally, my thanks to my family. To my mother, Chris, who first introduced me to Mann and Freud and who shares my love of classical studies. And to Nancy and Jessica, the rock of my world. And thanks to Emma too.

Some portions of the first chapter have already appeared in print in different form. A version of the first nine sections appeared in *Deutsche Vierteljahrrschrift* 77, no. 1 (2003), and a version of the tenth in *Germanic Review* 76, no. 2 (2001). I gratefully acknowledge these journals and their editors for their permission to include these pieces in revised form in the present study. I would also like to express my gratitude to the Institute for the Arts and Humanities at the University of North Carolina at Chapel Hill, where a fellowship allowed for a semester's leave to work on the manuscript at a crucial point in its development: I am particularly beholden to Ruel Tyson, Lloyd Kramer, and Mary Sheriff for their support during that time. And, of course, special thanks to Liliane Weissberg in her role as editor of the Kritik series, as well as to the three anonymous readers who reviewed my manuscript for the Wayne State University Press. Their advice was very useful, and this book is clearly better for it.

A Word about Translations

Excellent translations of almost all the primary texts used in this study are readily available in English: John E. Woods's of Thomas Mann's *The Magic Mountain;* James Strachey's of Freud's *Gradiva* essay in *The Standard Edition of the Complete Psychological Works of Sigmund Freud;* Edmund Jephcott's of *A Berlin Chronicle* in Michael Jennings, Howard Eiland, and Gary Smith's edition of *Walter Benjamin: Selected Writings;* and Michael Hulse's and Anthea Bell's respective translations of works by W. G. Sebald. I have based the translations used here on these editions, although the exigencies of my argument have sometimes called for more literal renderings of the German to secure my point, in which instances I have emended their translations with my own. Nonetheless, for the English-only reader of this book, I have included references to these English editions alongside my references to the German texts in my citations, even when the English translation provided might not precisely coincide with that found in the reference. My practice has been to present an English version of the given citation first, followed by the original German in parentheses and then to reference the German text first, followed by the English (German text/English translation).

Introduction

This study has its origins in the Smyth Room, which is the reading room and library for classical studies at Harvard University, occupying its own special corner on the second floor of Widener Library. The room is always locked, and to get in one needs a key, and to get a key one needs special permission from the classics department. The room itself exudes the same sense of privilege hinted at by that locked door. Thick Persian rugs cover the floor. Long oak reading tables stretch out most of the room's length, with the occasional graduate student sitting quietly, almost reverently, over a classical text. Several marble busts set on pedestals are scattered about the room, gazing down on the students at their books—whether gods, emperors, or philosophers I never determined but certainly all male, in keeping with the nineteenth-century ambiance of the room as a whole. At one end of the room is a long glass case where various archaeological artifacts are displayed; behind it are the holding shelves for all books placed on reserve for that semester's seminars. Bookcases of the same dark oak as the reading tables run around three walls, and like a frieze above them are pictures of all the previous chairmen of the Department of the Classics at Harvard, beginning with engravings but soon giving way to black-and-white photographs. All these men look down on the students at the tables with the same still gaze as the marble busts, gravely enforcing the continuance of the same classical educational ideal.

As a newly arrived faculty member in the German department, it was far from easy for me to get into the Smyth Room. Only after several phone calls from my home institution attesting to my comparatist and classicist credentials did I finally obtain my key. But once I got it, I used to like to go there, though not just to "do" classics. I often went to the Smyth Room to prepare my German courses, partly because I knew I wouldn't run into my German colleagues there and partly because I took perverse pleasure in defying, as it were, the disciplinary mandate that the room with its classical books, busts, and photographs represented. On one particular day I was working on Thomas Mann's *The Magic Mountain* for my seminar on the Bildungsroman, when I saw a copy of Heinrich Schliemann's *Ilios* on the shelf behind me. Picking it up and putting down Mann's novel, I began to read the story of Schliemann's childhood that prefaces the account of his archaeological work at Troy, a story I knew mostly for its well-known influence on Sigmund Freud.

I soon discovered that, in many ways, the story conformed to the generic contours of the Bildungsromane I was teaching in my German seminar. It was a rich, psychologically cast account of certain formative childhood experiences that ultimately determined the life choices of Schliemann as an archaeologist—although one also suspected it to be the construction of a childhood, and psychology, meant to provide a legitimating origin for Schliemann's belated career, a fabricated link between his German childhood and his Greek excavations that would justify his somewhat unwelcome and uncouth intrusion into precisely the classical *Bildungskultur* represented by the room in which I read. I was particularly struck by his account of an early encounter with Jerrer's engraving of Aeneas escaping Troy with his father on his back, seen in a copy of *Die Weltgeschichte für Kinder* given him by his own father, an image that, he said, inspired his lifelong dream of excavating Troy. The picture clearly functioned in much the same way as the many childhood pictures, or *Bilder,* in the fictional *Bildungsgeschichten* of Goethe, Novalis, Stifter, Keller, and now Mann read for my seminar, and not at all unlike the marble busts and photographic portraits watching over me, all of which worked to impose their specific model of *Bild-ung* onto the subject in psychologically inculcated ways. It also clearly adumbrated the numerous engravings of finds from Troy that come later in *Ilios,* the evidence, as it were, of the realized dream initially attached to that childhood *Bild*.

The more I thought about it, the more surprised I was to find Schliemann using engravings rather than photographs to illustrate his work. The portraits above the bookcases attested to a shift in image technology during the nineteenth century—the same shift, I realized, found in Mann's novel, where painted portraits were similarly giving way to photographic ones, indeed to X-ray photographic ones. Schliemann's engravings seemed unexpectedly conservative, even archaic in a way. I knew that photography had entered the cultural space previously occupied by painting at close to the same moment as archaeology entered that traditionally occupied by texts in classical studies. Both seemed to have radically changed the image culture of the time, and both seemed to have had similarly radical effects on the culture of Bildung—in the one case on the Bildungsroman and in the other on classics. And as I sat there considering the increasingly conspicuous connections between the two strains of Bildung spread out before me—the one German, the other classical (but no less German for that)—and the related influence that photography and archaeology had on both Bilder and Bildung entering the twentieth century, I returned to my thoughts about Freud and his more or less contemporary invention of psychology, which had its own obvious links to both Schliemann's text and Mann's novel—indeed to Bildung as well—and I realized I had the beginnings of a project. I had come to the Smyth Room to relish my relative freedom from the cultures of both German and classical studies; I left enthralled by their mutual entanglements.

This book, then, explores the intersections of photography, archaeology, and psychoanalysis and their effects on conceptions of the subject and his formation, or Bildung, in the literature and cultural theory of the late nineteenth and early twentieth centuries. All three disciplines emerge out of the same basic historical context; both photography and archaeology had major influences on psychoanalysis and how it came to conceive of the subject, his memory, and the formation of his identity, and psychoanalysis had an equally major effect on how contemporary authors came to think about these same things. The resultant changes in their thinking about Bildung in both its more individual, novelistic and institutional, classical strains is the especial concern of what follows. I have chosen to focus on three major writers of the late realist and early modernist period who register the impact on Bildung of all three of these fields: Thomas Mann, Sigmund Freud, and Walter Benjamin. I begin by considering these themes severally. Chapter 1 concentrates on photography, psychology, and Bildung in Mann's *The Magic Mountain*, chapter 2 on archaeology, psychology, and Bildung in Freud's reading (and my own) of Wilhelm Jensen's *Gradiva*. Chapter 3 then brings together photography and archaeology and looks at their influence on psychoanalysis and Bildung in Benjamin's *Berlin Chronicle*. An epilogue explores the fate of my constellated themes in the postmodern work of W. G. Sebald. I would like to follow a similar procedure here in the introduction, outlining some of the more general ways that photography and archaeology affected both psychology and Bildung before addressing two more specific issues raised by this study: its engagement with a constellation of themes rather than a single topic and its focus on archaeology and photography as discursive regimes rather than either concrete practices or abstract metaphors. More extensive discussions of the theoretical underpinnings to the study will be found in the book itself, mostly in the form of introductions to the individual chapters; here I wish to provide a thematic overview for the work as a whole.

Let me give a few summary examples of how photography altered conceptions of the subject and his formation, or Bildung, in the time period under consideration. It is an oft-noted historical fact that the fields of photography and psychoanalysis arose in close proximity with one another and that the latter was frequently influenced by the former in the formulation of its leading concepts. Freud's theory that the mind consists of two distinct states, one unconscious and the other conscious, is well known, as is his proposal that we have certain experiences in childhood that enter the unconscious and remain stored there and only manifest themselves much later in life. What is less well known is how, in his writings, Freud often explained this new conception in terms of the apparatus of photography, where an impression can be made on the "negative plate" of the unconscious as a result of some early exposure and then remain stored there for many years before being developed into a positive, visible print. Michel Foucault called this principle of latency and the specific conception of memory and development it entailed the most decisive factor in the nineteenth century's reformulation of subject identity; without any direct influence from Freud, the same basic model appears in the works of many other contemporary authors and thinkers, who also frequently evoke the same parallel with the photographic process. Oliver Wendell Holmes famously described photography as a "mirror with a memory" in 1859; these later authors, however, were turning the trope around and elaborating a model for memory as a form of photography. And one of the guiding assumptions of this study is that photography functioned not simply as a trope that reflected these writers' new mode of thinking but also as a decisive factor in shaping that mode of thinking to begin with.

Another example derives from the influence that photography had on conceptions of negative and positive values. The early nineteenth century was dominated by a tendency toward oppositional thinking. It tended to conceive of cultural issues in starkly contrastive terms, such as enlightened reason versus dark passion, truth versus error, body versus consciousness, or subject versus object, all, especially in Germany, reflecting the powerful influence of Hegelian thought. But after William Henry Fox Talbot—a classicist, by the way, and one of the original decoders of cuneiform script—devised the negative/positive process in the early 1840s, photography gave new meaning to such oppositions, one that insisted on a basic shared identity. A photographic negative was, of course, very much the same "thing" as its positive, was in fact an indispensable part of that positive. Rather than a strict opposition, the negative/positive process of photography introduced an oscillating relation based on a specific procedure that, by reversing light values, converted the one into the other—a procedure that could always be repeated going back again the other way. And such a reconception of the relations between opposites had its decisive echoes in other fields as well, perhaps most famously in the work of Friedrich Nietzsche, who reformulated the relations between truth and fiction, good and evil, and so on, in ways that stressed the shared basis of each term in the other and the processes of value reversals through which the one became the other. By the turn of the century, such thinking had led to the radically altered world of modernist literature and thought, which dispensed with the stable verities and secure distinctions of the previous period and introduced instead complicated schemata of ambiguity and equivocation—schemata not infrequently described by the novelists and thinkers themselves in terms of the photographic relations just mentioned. As we will see, one of the most provocative instances of the application of these newly conceived "photographic" relations to the matter of modern subject formation comes in respect to the perplexed issues of gender identity and sexuality in the works of several key modernist figures, each of whom deployed the photographic schema of negative and positive to portray the oscillation he associated with his subject's gender and sexual identity—and again, I suggest that photography was functioning as much more than just a metaphor in the formation of their conceptual apparatuses.

Let me offer two more examples of how the introduction of photographic technology altered conceptions of subjectivity. As Walter Benjamin famously insisted, one of the great innovations of photography relatively unknown to the previous era was the phenomenon of reproducibility. Once one had a negative, the so-called master plate, or *cliché*, one was able to produce a theoretically endless number of positive prints or copies. The finished photograph as a work of art lost the sense of unique identity that had previously adhered to particular visual representations; the identity of a photograph was from the start always intimately related to its more or less uniform reproducibility. Proust was inspired by this model to reconceive the notion of erotic love in its image. He claimed (and Freud had much the same idea) that a person always somehow loved the same woman or man, but successively, that a master plate—or image—was imprinted in the subject's unconscious and he would seek its reproduced form in every one of the many loves he encountered in his life. Others applied the model more directly to the subject himself. Charles Darwin and Francis Galton in England, Alphonse Bertillon in France, and August Sander in Germany all enlisted photography in the service of various systems of typology for individual identity. Nancy Armstrong has laid out some of the major effects of such photographic templating for the representation of character in British fiction of the realist period.[1] The effects are even more acute in the case of German letters in the modernist period, where issues of typology penetrated the spheres of both psychology and politics in ways that were mutually reinforcing and, in the 1930s, became dangerously implicated in the rise of fascist ideology, a movement almost unthinkable apart from the actual technology that both supported and inspired it.

My last example might seem more trivial, but in fact it proved equally important and disruptive of received paradigms of the subject. As Siegfried Kracauer and others noted, unlike paintings, or more particularly painted portraits, photographs had an alarming way of appearing out-of-date almost immediately. They revealed something about the way a person was at just that instant; they could be interrogated for clues about what the unguarded moment might have discovered about him or her, but to know what the person was like before or after that moment, another photograph was needed. Unlike that of a painting, the truth value of a photograph seemed a fleeting one indeed, without much staying power, and it tended to produce a correspondingly ephemeral sense of history and, more pointedly, self-image. The subject too was no longer thought of as a single, sustained, or constantly true identity; it became a series of possibly disconnected and always changing images or truths. And this incredibly diminished sense of the durative value of personal truths and identities, the dizzyingly accelerated pace at which they became outmoded, this too was both a reflection and residue of the impact of photography, and it too made its mark, both formally and thematically, on the thought and writing of the modernist era.

The changes wrought by photography on the conception of the subject had an equally profound effect on the field of Bildung, and in particular on the tradition of the Bildungsroman. Ever since Goethe's seminal novel, *Wilhelm Meister's Apprenticeship* (*Wilhelm Meisters Lehrjahre*), pictures, or Bilder, had played a major, even defining role in the Bildung of the protagonist. This can be seen throughout the nineteenth century, from Novalis's *Heinrich von Ofterdingen* to the realist works of Stifter's *Indian Summer* (*Der Nachsommer*) and Keller's *Green Henry* (*Der Grüne Heinrich*), all of which engage paintings as indices and instruments for the psychological, aesthetic, and social development of their protagonists. With the beginning of the modernist era, however, and particularly with Mann's *The Magic Mountain* (*Der Zauberberg*), photography began to insinuate itself into the thematic space traditionally occupied by paintings in these novels, and the new regime of Bilder changed notions of the subject's Bildung. Foucault notes how the new nineteenth-century principle of latency created an equally new space for regulatory intervention or supervision, what in psychological terms is known as "analysis" and in photographic ones as "development"; both figure prominently in the pedagogical, socializing project of the modernist Bildungsroman. The sense of oscillation and equivocation that came with the new understanding of positive and negative values affected pedagogical attempts to fix and determine the identity of subjects, rendering especially problematic the achievement of manliness (*Männlichkeit*) as the intended telos of the protagonist's education. The new notion of psychological templating gave new, potentially disturbing significance to the traditional ideal of Bildung as at once the realization of the subject's individuality and his assimilation into a generic social normativity—even as the greatly increased sense of almost instant obsolescence eroded the faith in the durative value and effect of the Bildung project itself. And as we will see, all of these photographic effects manifested themselves not only thematically, in the presentation of Bildung within the modernist novel, but also formally, in the representative strategies of the Bildungsromane themselves.

Psychoanalysis emerged in close historical proximity not only with the practice of photography but also with that of archaeology. The connections among the three fields are multiple, including those between photography and archaeology. As mentioned, William H. F. Talbot, the English inventor of photography, was a notable classicist involved in deciphering the cuneiform script recently unearthed by archaeologists at Nineveh. And when Louis Arago made his famous plea for the French government to purchase the patent for Daguerre's photographic process, one of the major benefits he foresaw was for the budding field of archaeology. Photography did indeed have a major impact on archaeology, contributing to the elaboration of archaeology's own program of typology—its dominant conceptual framework in the nineteenth century and its most influential one outside its own field—as well as to archaeology's widespread popularity throughout Europe at this time.[2] And together with photography, archaeology contributed greatly to a new privileging of images over texts as the standard bearers of the true and the real and to a fundamental blurring of the lines between the aesthetic and nonaesthetic realms. Indeed, in this respect photography and archaeology combined to have a significant influence on the rise of a realist aesthetic in the latter half of the nineteenth century.

My primary interest in this study, however, is not in the direct connections between photography and archaeology but rather in more indirect ones, beginning with each one's connection with the field of psychology. For just as with photography, archaeology had a profound effect on conceptions of the subject; just as with photography, archaeology was both introjected into the subject as a model for memory and psychic identity and associated with the analyst as a model for his disciplinary activity. This is true not only of Freud, whose lifelong interest in, and even identification with, Schliemann is well known, as is his frequent recourse to archaeological analogies. It is true too of Carl Jung, another would-be archaeologist, of the *Lebensphilosoph* Ludwig Klages, who tried to map Bachofen's prehistorical schema onto the psychic sphere, and of Benjamin, who like these others combined archaeological frameworks with notions of dark, buried Bilder that were at once archaic and vaguely mythical. In fact, as we will see, archaeology had a way of pushing psychology into the somewhat suspect realm of nineteenth-century mythicism and vitalism, even as photography pushed it into that of contemporary spiritualism. Both yielded Bilder that seemed to challenge established realist doctrines even as, in other ways, they helped to set them.

In any case, for all their overlap, there were ways in which the introjection of archaeology proved a quite different enterprise from that of photography. To begin with, archaeology—or rather, classical archaeology—was associated with a somewhat different strain of the Bildung tradition. Whereas photography became incorporated into the tradition of the Bildungsroman, a more or less unofficial and privately staged program, archaeology was incorporated into classical studies, or *Altertumswissenschaft,* which since the beginning of the nineteenth century had formed the foundation of the official, institutionally enforced program of education in German-speaking lands. *Altertumswissenschaft,* and archaeology as part of it, was explicitly involved in the state's process of socialization and particularly in the formation of a new kind of bourgeois class, the so-called *Bildungsbürgertum.* The alliance of classicism and classism led to far more disconcerting effects for the introjection of archaeology than for that of photography and the Bildungsroman. Class ideology and subject psychology became complicit in rather more troubling ways.[3]

The questionable collusions of archaeology and psychology were even more pronounced in respect to the relations they established between national identity and personal identity during this period, particularly in Germany in the work of figures such as Jung and Klages, whom Benjamin quite justifiably came to identify with fascist tendencies. Archaeology has always been somewhat problematically involved in the task of forging an anterior basis for the present national group. This was as true in nineteenth-century England and Europe as it is today, for example, in the states of Israel or Mexico. But in Germany the task was exacerbated by at least two factors: first, by the dissemination of racial doctrines by archaeologists within Germany's own borders and, second, by the staging of this nation-building project outside of Germany's borders, in Mediterranean lands. The first led to the overlaying of increasingly racist typologies onto notions of German identity and, with their introjection by psychology, onto psychic identity as well. The second was more complicated, and inseparable from the German investment in classical studies as the basis of Bildung. Unlike the majority of its powerful European neighbors, Germany was more or less excluded from the extensive imperialist enterprise of colonization of Africa, Asia, and the Americas during the nineteenth century. In its stead, through its immense investment (both financial and cultural) in archaeology, the Germans opted, as it were, to colonize the past—the Mediterranean past—and in the process to ride as roughshod over the culture of the present inhabitants as their European neighbors were doing in more concrete and conspicuous a fashion. As Martin Bernal and others have insisted, from the late eighteenth century on, German national identity had been formed through the detour of Greece, and in the nineteenth century archaeology played a decisive and disturbing role in shaping that detour, imparting an overtly political cast to the project—from the founding of the Second Reich up into that of the Third, German archaeology abroad was always a state-funded and directed undertaking. The classical world it sought out, and sought to take away from the local peoples and for itself, was inextricably implicated in the formation and legitimation of the German state. To this extent, the so-called tyranny of Greece over Germany was always more properly the other way around.

Even as archaeology engaged in the production of an anterior origin for purposes of national identity formation, so too did contemporary psychology for purposes of personal identity formation. Where the archaeologist practiced a virtual form of imperialist colonization of the past and the so-called cradle of civilization, the psychologist practiced a strictly similar form of colonization of the "unconscious" and childhood. And by introjecting the one field into the space of the other and pressing the discursive homology between the two, psychology almost unavoidably imported into its practice many of the most questionable and compromised aspects of archaeology's own, insofar as it inevitably engaged archaeology not as a mere abstract and politically pristine metaphor but as a concrete, culturally specific, and often quite dirty historical enterprise. The resultant coordination of the two fields yielded many effects worth interrogating—for example, how an archaeologically conceived German psyche provided legitimation for imperialist colonization abroad, insofar as the Germans were only, after all, reclaiming what was properly, psychically, their own anyway or, conversely, how in Freud and (especially) others, the quasicolonial violence of archaeology in foreign lands became interiorized as a new kind of sexuality and ideal masculinity. As we will see, all this rebounded on the field of Bildung, in both its more private and public strains, for whereas the Bildungsroman had also, ever since Goethe, pursued a connection between personal and national identity formation, as had Germany's official program of classical education, the connection forged by the melding of psychology and archaeology had a way of materializing and sullying the project in entirely unprecedented ways.

Of course, the role of archaeology in the cultural imaginary was never quite so one-sided. Even as in the case of photography and the Bildungsroman, so archaeology worked both to support and to challenge the discursive foundations of Bildung and its accompanying psychologies. At its simplest, archaeology was from the outset uncovering material evidence of a common, often primitive world that contested the Germans' self-reflecting, projected ideals of a glorious, *glänzend* classical past, and as the national agenda availing itself of that idealized past became ever more problematic in the early twentieth century, so too did the impulse to deploy archaeology's deidealizing tendencies against it. Let me offer just two related examples of this, both of which also emphasize some further intersections of archaeology and photography.

As mentioned, archaeology shared with photography in the radical transformation of visual culture in the late nineteenth and early twentieth centuries. Not only did both participate in promoting a new standard of quasidocumentary truth associated with Bilder and a new relation of such images to the extra-aesthetic "real"; they also participated in the proliferation of a new culture of virtuality, of inauthentic images and simulacra. For photography, this was part and parcel of its quality of endless reproducibility, its widespread dissemination of copies, and its concomitant devaluation of originals; of the capacity of photographs to be falsified or aestheticized, touched up, or distorted in ways more or less irrelevant to paintings; and, more tightly joined to archaeology, of the capacity of photographs to steal images, to take them away from their original context and, in a quasi-imperialist way, traffic in them as virtual artifacts, as appropriated trophies. For archaeology proper, the participation in the new, simulacric economy was part of the nineteenth century's traffic in classical facsimiles, whether ancient Roman copies of even more ancient Greek originals or modern buildings reproducing classical motifs or, more modestly, contemporary plaster casts of classical museum pieces, whether we are speaking of faithful, almost academic reproductions, of crassly commercial or politically inspired copies, or even of outright forgeries.

The problem of forgeries and fakes had always haunted archaeology, an almost inseparable companion to its own thievery. It was there, for example, in the suspicions that persistently surrounded Schliemann's "discovery" of Priam's Treasure, the lingering allegations that certain items were manufactured and then buried by him so as to then be "found" at Troy.[4] But it was also there in the mimetic project of classicism itself, which from the beginning of the century—from Weimar classicism on—in as diverse fields as literature, statuary, and architecture, had always hovered in its identity somewhere between a reverential traditionalism and tasteless modern kitsch. Archaeology readily played its part in this simulacric world, flooding its imaginary cultural economy with both original and copied artifacts that reinforced the ideals of German classicism, which in turn furthered (hugely) the project of Bildung, both educationally and politically. But archaeology also, in its material, deidealizing impulse, provided the model for a counter impulse, an impulse to break through the questionable, counterfeit constructions of classicism and *Bildungskultur* and to expose the common, deglamorized aspect of all this—its dirt and debris, as it were—and this was as true of the attitude toward the constructions of the public political sphere as it was toward those of the private, psychological sphere, where the suspicions of falsely unearthed "archaic images" found in Schliemann reappeared in relation to the discoveries of Freud, Jung, and others as well.

The place of archaeology within the simulacric image economy of classicism in the nineteenth century, as both ancillary support and undermining rival, was one of the chief ways that the archaeological was brought to bear on the modern period itself. Another way can be seen in relation to the culture of instant obsolescence that emerged at this same time. As mentioned, photography introduced, or participated in, a radically accelerated pace at which things became outmoded, in which the durative value of images, truths, and identities increasingly gave way to a sense of the ephemeral, of serial replacement. In part, this was symptomatic of broader trends in technology in general, where the rate of change and accompanying abandonment of cultural artifacts was seemingly creating as many superseded eras in the nineteenth and early twentieth centuries alone as had accrued in the several millennia preceding them. But in part it was also symptomatic of the new, changed modes of perception of the past—including the most recent past—that photography itself inaugurated, for as I said, photography had a way of making things seem almost immediately past in unprecedented ways. Given this new, distinctly modern culture of the more or less instantly outmoded and discarded, archaeology acquired a new and only quasimetaphorical role: as an archaeology of the modern, just past age itself—an archaeology, let it be said, in which photography played a major part as the unearther and preserver of rapidly disappearing historical Bilder.

This archaeology of modernity was pioneered by the French surrealists, by photographers such as Eugène Atget, and further pursued by figures such as Benjamin. Through the influence of Foucault, it has continued to be a major part of cultural studies today—and, through the work of writers such as Sebald, of literature too. In the modernist period, this new archaeology proved a potent means for dissecting the more traditionally conceived practice of archaeology both at home and abroad, for challenging the inherited, nineteenth-century project of Bildung, both personal and national, and for critiquing its more ideologically suspect (and archaeologically grounded) models of psychology. Alongside the "archaeological" excavation and critique of modernity's fixation on a mythical, classical, or archaic past, this new archaeology could explore and critique more directly the creation of the modern period itself, including its own embeddedness in apparently archaic, mythical forms. It could break down the faith in the present permanence of the culture of the *Bildungsbürgertum,* revealing its own supersededness and so too indirectly dissolve the sense of *durée* linking the classical past and the German present on which both German national identity and its cultural project of Bildung were based. And finally, in focusing on a notably socio-historical setting as opposed to the quasimythical, prehistorical sites of archaeology proper—which, as we will see, included elaborating a distinctly social typology as opposed to archaeology proper's racial and mythical ones—this modern archaeology also provided quite a different model for psychological introjection, moving away from the grandly mythical and archaic images associated with archaeology proper (not only Jung's archetypes but even and also Freud's Oedipus or Klages's *Naturbilder*) and toward shaping images far more quotidian, recent, and factual, indeed material, in a word, photographic.

Such, then, are some of the intersections of photography and archaeology with the fields of psychology and Bildung and, inevitably, with each other that are explored in this study. And as this brief overview should make clear, a defining characteristic of this book is that it does not so much address a single, unified topic as a set of interacting themes whose precise arrangements and orders of hierarchy are often shifting. Although still somewhat unusual, such an approach has come more and more to the forefront of literary and cultural studies in recent years, offering a new paradigm for the comparatist project. It draws on the model of what Benjamin called a configuration or constellation (*Sternbild*) of concepts as the basis for an idea; what Foucault defined in terms of emergence, or *Entstehung*, as the new, and newly hegemonic, arrangement of inherited discourses at a given historical moment; what the cultural theorist Stuart Hall has called a conjuncture of numerous contending forces within the social field, whose elements and relations become differently articulated in different contexts and periods; or what Stephen Greenblatt has described as the negotiations between multiple, culturally demarcated zones, "a subtle, elusive set of exchanges, a network of trades and trade-offs."[5] Like all these critics, I am concerned with something that, while firmly tied to concrete points of reference, looks more to the imaginary connections that organize but do not determine their grouping, grouping that is neither compulsory nor completely arbitrary. Like them, I place particular emphasis on the historical background against which these concepts, discourses, forces, and zones appear. I consider how, as they emerge together at a particular cultural moment, these fields—photography, archaeology, psychology, Bildung—subtly and reciprocally influence each other's discursive character and cultural role in ways inflected by issues of social power and contest and how, as the historical moment or even program changes, these fields alter their arrangements and the nature of their cultural work. And also like these critics, I am especially interested in the relations or movement between my chosen fields, in how concepts and image systems are shifted, shuttled, moved from one zone to another, generating a sense both of cultural unity, where the mirroring repetition of similar elements in different discourses creates a network of mutual support, and of inevitable conflict, where elements assume different and often competing characters when placed in different roles or spheres.

The emphasis on a so-called constellation of themes is one reason for the sometimes slippery nature of this book's project. Another has to do with the nature of the themes themselves. This study approaches the fields of photography and archaeology neither as simply empirical practices nor as simply metaphorical repertoires but rather as elements that partake of both but can be reduced to neither. It approaches them as discursive, or symbolic, structures within the given cultural imaginary, something that is always at once both phantasmatic and historically specific. On the one hand, I resist treating the appearance of photographic or archaeological references in the fields of psychology or Bildung as mere metaphors, as many critics before have done, especially in regard to psychology; but photography and archaeology are far too much actual, historically embedded disciplines or practices for that, not only exerting their own shaping force on the concepts and practices of psychology and Bildung, but also, necessarily, bringing with them all the cultural dirt of their own enterprises when they are imported and introjected into the field of subject identity and formation.[6] The need to recognize the never *just* metaphorical status of a given author's or era's dominant tropes and to see instead their specific historical grounding is a task that various critics have recently taken to heart. It motivates my own overview, at the beginning of chapter 2, of nineteenth-century archaeology to prepare the reader for my analysis of Freud and Jensen; and, in chapter 3, it motivates my discussion of actual debates about photography and specific technological innovations within it as part of my analysis of Benjamin's use of photography as a model for both memory and the writing of a *Bildungsgeschichte*.

On the other hand, the aspects of photography and archaeology in which I am most interested are not so much connected with their empirical practices and histories within their own discrete fields as with their more abstract, elusive existence in the cultural imaginary of the modernist period, with the cultural representations of these fields. It is, after all, in their character as what I variously call metaphorical regimes, discursive fields, or aspects of the cultural imaginary that both photography and archaeology absorb the ideals, obsessions, and compulsions of their time and place in a way that permeates their cultural meaning;

similarly, it is in such a figurative or symbolic form that archaeology and photography are transported out of their proper spheres to pass into other, apparently unrelated ones. I do not intend, that is, to make the kind of argument that theorists such as Friedrich Kittler or Jonathan Crary have elaborated for photography and other technological media, that the actual physical training and concrete discipline of their mechanisms exercised a compulsory influence on the formation of modern subjects. An exclusive appeal to such a technological determinism is far from my goal. Indeed, the pairing of photography with archaeology, about which no such argument can be made but whose determination of modern subject identity is incontestably no less central, is at least in part motivated by a desire to dispel such a position from the start. Rather, I am concerned with something far more indirect and insubstantial: with the force of given hegemonic image systems on the imaginary of a given culture and the imaginations of its major authors in thinking about subjects, their psyches, and their socialization. It is for the same reason that I focus throughout this study on the field of literature, even when discussing Freud and Benjamin, for throughout the modernist period, literature functioned as the privileged site for a staging of the major discursive regimes of the cultural imaginary in both the social and the psychological spheres in ways that most directly confronted their symbolic significances. Only by close and patient readings of such literary, imaginative texts can the full impact of photography and archaeology on notions of subject identity and formation be adequately registered. So let us begin.

1

Photography, Psychoanalysis, and Bildung in Thomas Mann's *The Magic Mountain*

The death of the soul through the mechanism becomes doubtful at the moment the mechanism becomes ensouled.

Der Tod der Seele durch den Mechanismus wird zweifelhaft in dem Augenblick, wo der Mechanismus sich beseelt.

Thomas Mann, Rede Über das Theater[1]

The English translation of Thomas Mann's *The Magic Mountain* by John E. Woods is accompanied by two different photographs of the author.[2] The first was taken in 1925, shortly after Mann had completed the novel, and serves as the frontispiece. The photograph shows Mann in three-quarter profile, with his eyes turned away from the camera and viewer, posed much like Settembrini during the duel, when he turns politely to one side in offering himself to Naphta's shot—or perhaps better, like Behrens's wife in her husband's photographs, graciously conforming to the genteel imperative not to look directly at the camera. In any case, obliquity as a stance, as a posture of culture. The second photo was taken in 1955, on the occasion of Mann's eightieth birthday. It is placed on the back of the translation's dust jacket. It depicts the aged author in the same three-quarter profile but with his eyes now directed straight ahead. The gaze seems to convey at once a sense of satiety and authority.

The relationship between the two photographs is a suggestive one and no doubt intentionally so. The second, much later photo seems positioned as somehow the telos, the consummation, of the earlier one, but in that format gently mocked by Siegfried Kracauer in his early

17

essay on photography: "The Faces of Famous People: This Is How They Were—And This Is How They Are Today!" Kracauer's complaint about this practice—"Marx as a youth and Marx as the leader of the Center Party, Hindenburg as a lieutenant and as our Hindenburg"—is that one can neither guess the later image from the earlier one nor reconstruct the earlier image from the later, that nothing links the two images in a manner that accounts for their relation and, presumably, for the person the one has become and the other had been.[3] However, in the present case of the two Mann photographs, that link does seem to be provided, or at least suggested, by the substantial pages of the Bildungsroman that they frame—as if the book itself and the drawn out story of its hero's maturation could somehow account for the author's maturation as well, posing that final photograph, with all its satiety and authority, as the completion not only of the first image but also of the interceding Bildung work. On the other hand, it also seems significant that this last photo is on the dust jacket and so implicitly dispensable, not even really part of the book—almost as if the intended course of maturation and edification implied by the two photos was itself not really part of the book either.

My interest in this added dimension of meaning to the novel—in how these two photographs might offer new access to its significance, truth, and trajectory—no doubt seems an eccentric approach and certainly not a long sustainable one. Let me reformulate it in more modest and manageable terms, terms more obviously intrinsic to the work itself. I want to piece together an argument for how *The Magic Mountain* is a Bildungsroman and is not one and how it is rather an *Entwicklungsroman*, that is, a novel of development; and I want to try to account for these distinctions in terms of the insinuation of photography into the thematic space traditionally occupied by painting within the Bildungsroman genre. How, I want to ask, does the introduction of the discursive or metaphorical regime of the photograph fundamentally alter the project of Bildung, including the characteristic engagement of *Bilder* (pictures) in its program?

Preparing Our Plate

Even this approach might seem somewhat surprising and eccentric, especially in its inaugurating claim that the status of the novel as a Bildungsroman needs to be questioned. After all, in his "Introduction to *The Magic Mountain*" (1939) Mann himself links his work with the tradition of Goethe's *Wilhelm Meister* (1795–96), and elsewhere he frequently refers to both the novel and the tradition in terms of the Bildungsroman, though usually coupled with the term "Entwicklungsroman" and with warnings of a special kind of modernist decomposition (*Zersetzung*).[4] Moreover, the traditional critical literature on the Bildungsroman genre has had far less trouble accepting Mann's work within its folds than it has with other perennial contenders, such as Novalis's *Heinrich von Ofterdingen* (1802), Stifter's *Indian Summer* (*Der Nachsommer* [1857]), or even Keller's *Green Henry* (*Der Grüne Heinrich* [1879–80]), all authors whom Mann was reading, the latter two for the first time, during the writing of his novel.[5]

However, much recent criticism has tended to shift the descriptive focus and to foreground slightly different features of the Bildungsroman from those previously privileged by critics and even by Mann himself as constituting its defining characteristics, and this new focus and definition allow us, indeed require us, to revisit the question of *The Magic Mountain* as a Bildungsroman. The revised model for Bildung, developed by scholars such as Friedrich Kittler, Gerhard Kaiser, and Jochen Hörisch, tends to concentrate on the inculcation of certain familial, psychological structures into the (male) protagonist as the decisive tactic for his socialization, for his joint movement toward individualization and assimilation into society, and for his accompanying realization of a certain prescribed ideal of *Männlichkeit,* or masculinity.[6] The tactic is sometimes conveniently referred to as the protagonist's "Oedipalization," but the peculiar insistence of the new Bildungsroman criticism—indeed, that which marks it as a critique of Bildung—is the claim that the process is not naturally or psychologically inherent but socially and ideologically installed. The bourgeois cultural regime, which is of course always also a patriarchal regime, inscribes the male subject of Bildung with a regulatory Oedipal mechanism for the production of those desires that will successfully navigate him toward his assigned social role—hence the apparently wondrous harmony between the individual's driving desires and society's normative expectations, the posited agreement between personal individuation and social assimilation that grounds the course of Bildung.

The classic example of this installation process comes in Goethe's *Wilhelm Meister,* with the painting, or Bild, hung in Wilhelm's playroom as the guardian of his childhood. Much like a tableau out of Schiller's *Don Carlos,* the painting depicts a sickly prince secretly yearning for the queen, who stands nearby but with the boy's father-king positioned between them. The Bild imprints its Oedipal scenario on Wilhelm's psyche, providing, as it were, the prescriptive narrative for his subsequent Bild-ung. It is later supplemented by Wilhelm's theater exercises, such as the repeated slaying of Goliath by David, which similarly inscribe, or build, Oedipal patterns into his education. Wilhelm's successful completion of his Bildung is then signaled by the reappearance of this same Bild at the end of the novel, thus securing the classic connection between Bildung and Bild for the genre; and reinforcing this same association, the narrative of Wilhelm's education secretly composed by his mentors and presented to him at the moment of his assimilation into their (patriarchal) company is also referred to as his Bild, or *Porträt*. Although I will not elaborate on them, similar connections between Bildung and Bilder can also be shown for the works of Novalis, Stifter, and Keller.[7]

There are, of course, features of *The Magic Mountain* that seem conducive to interpretation according to such an Oedipal model. For example, as Hörisch points out, there is the pencil that figures so prominently in the relation between Hans Castorp and Pribislav Hippe and then again between Hans and Clawdia Chauchat, something of a not-so-subtle phallic symbol that Hans must get to succeed at his erotic, educative venture.[8] With the pencil or, more accurately, with the shift of the partner in the pencil exchange from Pribislav Hippe to Clawdia Chauchat, there is a move from male to female "other" and thus the anticipated progress toward sexual differentiation, capped by Hans's acquiring the "phallus" from Clawdia, who is then properly deprived of it. Moreover, with Clawdia there are also vague (and not so vague) Oedipal structures apparent in the novel, especially in two places: in "Walpurgisnacht" with its triangulated contest between Hans, Clawdia, and Ludovico Settembrini, itself shadowed by that between Hans, Clawdia, and Hofrat Behrens, and then again in the Mynheer Peeperkorn chapters, where the Oedipal structures, gestures, and outcomes seem even more insistently asserted.

Despite the undeniable presence of such features, I still find most such readings of Mann's novel somewhat forced and distorting. They seem to secure a certain structural and semantic stability for the novel, especially for its psychological, gender, and Bildung thematics, that the novel itself is unable or unwilling to support. They work *too* well, too clearly, in a novel-world in which nothing works particularly well or clearly anymore; they achieve their order, their picture, only by leaving out everything that seems deliberately to undermine and obfuscate it. Mann's personal skepticism toward simplistic, that is, unqualified Freudian readings of his work, in particular of *The Magic Mountain,* is well known.[9] What seems to be called for is an exploration of those elements that complicate the picture.

Let me begin to describe what I take to be the apparent breakdown in the generic conditions of Bildung and Oedipalization by focusing on what might be called the primal scene of Hans Castorp's childhood, namely, the chapter "The Baptismal Bowl" ("Von der Taufschale") and its description of Hans's family and of his grandfather's *Kabinett.* What we note right away about Hans's family background is that Hans is portrayed as almost immediately orphaned of both parents and so too as situated in a family that is decidedly nonnuclear and is, instead, distanced, decentered, avuncular, and almost exclusively male. The only female presence of note is the Tienappels' servant, Schalleen, and even she seems but a belated replacement for the grandfather's more colorful, memorable, and erotically suggestive male servant, Fiete. What cohesion the family does possess is secured by two factors: by the baptismal bowl, or *Taufschale,* which presents an ordering that is again all male and widely extended, although in this case the extension is backward, and by disease, whose regular recurrence unites the family even as it destroys it—or in other words, whose patterning dissolves the traditional social relations in the course of imposing its own. All of this underscores how, almost uniquely among Mann's bourgeois fictions, the protagonist of this novel is set within a pointedly non-Oedipal family. The base conditions for Oedipal socialization, so prominent in the eighteenth- and nineteenth-century Bildungsromanen, are no longer clearly dominant in this twentieth-century modernist text, which seems itself orphaned, as it were, from its nineteenth-century family origins, which stand, so to speak, a distant, grandfatherly generation removed.

The significance of disease, of the recessive familial thematics, even of the almost exclusively male cast to Hans's household as introduced in this primal scene, has long been recognized by critics, including their various corrosive effects on traditional Oedipal structures. However, almost all critics seem to overlook the accompanying context within which these several features are introduced: the description of the contents other than the baptismal bowl and plate in the grandfather's *Kabinett*. The *Kabinett* itself occupies a dual status as both a *Kunstversammlung*, or art collection, and a family archive; as such, it reproduces a central topos within the Bildungsroman tradition. It is the functional equivalent of the grandfather's art collection in *Wilhelm Meister*, which includes the painting of the sickly prince; analogous collections also appear in both *Indian Summer* and *Green Henry*, and function similarly in providing models for the protagonists' subsequent Bildung. What is new to the family archival collection in *The Magic Mountain* is, noticeably, technology: a broken barometer with figurative wooden carvings, a model ship, a little mechanical Turkish doll, an album of daguerreotypes, and "way at the bottom, a rattrap no less" ("ganz zu unterst sogar eine Rattenfalle" [35/20]).

Each item in this list has its suggestive significance for Hans's subsequent Bildung; as Geoffrey Winthrop-Young remarks, if Mann seems sometimes to treat ideas as gadgets, he tends also to treat gadgets as ideas.[10] We note right away the album of daguerreotypes, precisely there where previously one would find miniature paintings, such as we encounter in the mid-nineteenth-century world of Mann's *Buddenbrooks* (1901); the album serves immediately to place this novel within a new, more modern representative regime, associating the earlier stages of Hans's family with those of photography itself. We also note the model ship that so clearly anticipates important aspects of Hans's future, including his exceptional—indeed, career-determining—childhood drawings of ships, with all their technical details inscribed behind the surface watercolors; it also adumbrates the technical manual on ocean steamships that accompanies Hans as his sole reading (or Bildung) material on his trip up the Magic Mountain. Even the rattrap deserves attention, with its comical but also slightly ominous resonances as the last item in the list, a sum figure denoting both past decay and, once sprung, future violence.

What proves the most provocative item in the collection, however, is that little Turk, "hard to the touch beneath its bright silk costume, with a mechanism in its body" ("hart anzufassen unter seinem buntseidenen Anzug, mit einem Uhrwerk im Leibe" [35/20]). The exotic oriental exterior resonates with motifs, especially erotic ones, that become of increasing importance as the novel progresses; think, for example, of Behrens's Turkish coffee set, bestowed on him by his Egyptian princess, or of Clawdia Chauchat's "Oriental" disposition. But the mechanical interior also resonates, the engineered apparatus that occupies an otherwise spiritual, psychological, and erotic space; indeed, it presents us with something of a miniature icon for the new, modern self at issue in the novel and hence also for the new, modern subject of Bildung. This penetration of technology into the sphere of Bildung and its consequences have only recently begun to attract the interest of Mann scholars.[11] But it is not without significance that, for all its initial parody and subsequent seeming de-emphasis, the protagonist here is a would-be engineer and not, as in *Wilhelm Meister,* a would-be actor or, as in other Bildungsromanen, a painter or artist. The technological medium has come to displace not only the inner psychological but also the outer aesthetic domain as the decisive arena of Bildung.

What I believe we need to focus on, then, is how this new dimension of technology alters the operations of Bildung—including its mechanisms for identity formation, erotic self-realization, gendering, and social assimilation—and, as part of that, how it alters the format of the Bildungsroman. As I said, my primary interest is in the effects of the regime of photography on practices of Bildung and the novel, but this regime needs to be situated within the broader domain of technological innovation, or intervention, per se. So let me momentarily widen our focus.

Friedrich Kittler was among the first German literary critics to insist upon the importance of the radical change that occurred in the late nineteenth century as a result of the introduction of technology into the various aesthetic media.[12] Kittler's example for illustrating the general character of this shift is not the photograph but rather the typewriter, the earliest of which did not allow the operator to see what letter he or she had just formed. As Kittler argues, the typewriter fundamentally altered our relation to writing—indeed to Being itself—by taking language "out of our hands," away from the present subject, and introducing a gap or spacing between the self and its articulation or representation. This space, or blind, which somehow precedes conscious manifestation, introduced a split in the self between the hidden and the revealed, the latent and the manifest, and this space, gap, or mediation is filled by technology itself.

The "spacing" opened up and occupied by the new technology is evident not only in the case of writing but in that of most all the other major media as well, with the result that, as Jonathan Crary observes, technology became an almost compulsory site for the reconception of socio-cultural reality in general and of the individual subject in particular.[13] So, for instance, in *The Magic Mountain*, Settembrini comically and yet still insightfully insists that morals, ethics, indeed the entire apparatus of normative social ideals, has become a matter of technology. So too has his own field of pedagogic "enlightenment," arguably the underlying ideology of Bildung proper—after all, every light on the Magic Mountain is now an electric one. Similarly, through the pervasive technologization of medical discourse, the whole body, and especially the diseased body, has become in a sense technologized, has, that is, been reconfigured in technical terms (as well as subjected to technical interventions). And as we will see, desire and sexuality also become saturated or mediated by this new dimension or space. Although Hörisch does not mention it, the all-important pencil that Hans Castorp borrows from Pribislav Hippe and Clawdia Chauchat is emphatically a mechanical one; even the similarly significant cigars Hans smokes and exchanges with Hofrat Behrens are, notably, *Fabrikate*.

Of course, the issue of technological mediation in Mann's oeuvre is not thematized in terms of a Kittlerian typewriter nor, for that matter, even in terms of writing. Rather, Mann tends to turn to writing's sister arts, to those concerned not with words but with sounds and sights. He is, for instance, openly interested in the technologization of music, a subject he explores in several critical essays as well as in *The Magic Mountain*, where the gramophone is famously celebrated as "the German soul up-to-date" ("die deutsche Seele up-to-date").[14] And he was also quite taken with the entirely new medium of film, which he discusses in several essays—mostly critically but not without noting its significant parallels with his own narrative art—and which he also evokes as an (admittedly somewhat caricatured) *mise-en-abîme* for *The Magic Mountain* itself in the figure of the Bioskop theater.[15]

However, like many other modernists, Mann ultimately seems less involved with these up-to-date media and more preoccupied with the metaphorical potentialities of photography for representing the effects of the new technologization on culture, psychology, and narrative. As a medium, of course, photography rose to prominence during the nineteenth century, and perhaps more than any other marked the radical shift noted by Kittler; as Roland Barthes says, "It is the advent of the Photograph which divides the history of the world."[16] But it was primarily in the early twentieth century that photography began forcefully to assert itself as an aesthetic medium with significant implications for the other arts and with suggestive, even insistent implications for conceiving the modern world and subject. As in so many other instances, the case of photography reminds us to look for the roots of modernism in the nineteenth rather than simply in the twentieth century—a caveat especially applicable to a consideration of Mann, whose modernism always seems peculiarly embedded in the still emergent discourses of the nineteenth century.

We see Mann's interest in photography expressed in several places, perhaps most directly in his review essay of Albert Renger-Patzsch's book *The World Is Beautiful* (*Die Welt ist schön* [1928]).[17] Published in 1929, shortly after the completion of *The Magic Mountain*, the essay staunchly defends the still controversial technologization of art represented by photography against the objections of humanistic prudery (*humanistische Prüderie*), exclaiming, "Technologization of the aesthetic—it certainly sounds bad, it resonates with decay and the downfall of the soul. But what if, even as the soulful falls victim to the technical, the technical becomes ensouled?" ("Technifizierung des Künstlerischen—gewiss es klingt schlimm, es klingt nach Verfall und Untergang der Seele. Aber wenn nun, in dem das Seelische der Technik anheimfällt, die Technik sich beseelt?" [10:902]). The essay goes on to elaborate on certain advantages of photography over painting for the psychological rendition of character as well as on its parallels with Mann's own representative practices. I will have more to say about this admittedly obscure essay later on. A far better known example of Mann's interest in its subject matter comes in the *photographische Apparat* that appears so provocatively at the end of *Death in Venice* (*Der Tod in Venedig* [1913]), written just before the composition of *The Magic Mountain*. Poised on its tripod stand (*dreibeinigen Stativ*) and apparently unattended (*scheinbar herrenlos*), this photo apparatus is left fairly underdetermined as to its precise significance. But it does seem to suggest that high ideal of Apollonian objectivity abandoned by Aschenbach although still, apparently, championed by the novella's narrator. That is, like Mann's review essay, it draws connections between photography and both art and psychology. It suggestively positions the camera as an embodiment of the work's own operant aesthetic ideal or representative practice, and of the subject-position intended for, but vacated by, its protagonist.

Mann seems to make a self-conscious allusion to this instance from *Death in Venice* early on in *The Magic Mountain* when, after his first evening meal in the dining hall at Davos, Hans Castorp notices some optical instruments in the salon. As with the gadgets in the grandfather's *Kabinett,* each of these instruments has its suggestive significance. There is a stereoscope, that favorite device of the late nineteenth century that, as Crary shows, contributed greatly to a reconception of *aesthesis,* both by bringing binocular vision into play as an operation for constituting its single Bild out of two apparently distinct ones and by promoting a certain isolated privatization of perceptual experience (both points of obvious importance for *The Magic Mountain*).[18] Positioned beside this toy Hans also finds a kaleidoscope, another nineteenth-century invention: celebrated by Charles Baudelaire as the avatar of modern, multiplicitous consciousness, it was also critically apprised by Karl Marx and Friedrich Engels for its "bourgeois" reduction of the aesthetic to a mere mirror trick of endlessly proliferated equivalented forms (and Mann's novel is as easily the one as the other).[19] Finally, Hans also finds what is apparently an up-to-date version of a phenakistiscope, or possibly a zootrope, into whose revolving drum one inserts a cinematographic strip and then peers through a slotted opening as it whirls about—a device that, by incorporating the element of time into the visual realm, very much resembles that described by Henri Bergson in "The Cinematographical Mechanism of Thought" ("Le mécanisme cinématographie de la pensée") for illustrating the relation between the objectively discrete units of experience and the subjective illusion of its continuous flow.[20] Given the arguably disciplinary nature of all three of these instruments, it seems appropriate that among the things Hans can see in the last of them is a schoolmaster disciplining a boy ("ein Schulmeister einen Knaben züchtigend")—although given his always ludic relation to such training, it seems equally telling that it also shows an almost Nietzschean tumbling tightrope dancer ("springender Seiltänzer" [120/82]).

But the first such toy Hans picks up and peers through—and it is worth emphasizing how often throughout the novel Hans's vision, whether engaged in reading, desiring, or what he calls playing king (*regieren*), seems mediated by optical instruments, from magnifying glasses to telescopes—is the stereoscope. He inserts the photographs provided behind its lenses and sees, of all things, a Venetian gondolier. This sly, half-playful self-allusion of the type Mann so delighted in, shrewdly linking the final photo apparatus of *Death in Venice* with the first one in *The Magic Mountain,* would suggest a certain continuity between the representative role of photography in the two works. And by extension it would lead us to expect a detectable affinity between the aesthetic ideals embodied by both works (and both apparatuses), an evocation of the same kind of Apollonian objective realism so often associated with photographic pictures, as well as with Mann's novella. And one would also anticipate a similar subject position, or psychology, to correspond with the evoked apparatus, a similar investment (and that includes, of course, erotic investment) in the lucid images of the apparent world.

In fact, however, and despite the allusion, Mann seems to be doing something quite different and new with photography in *The Magic Mountain*, something decidedly more attuned to the thematics of modernism and of Bildung—although here too we are forced to observe distinctions. Other authors, most notably Walter Benjamin and Susan Sontag, have marked the importance of photography for modernist poetics;[21] still others, such as Kittler and Crary, have described the actual physical training and regulation to which such technological innovations subjected the modern individual. But while Benjamin and Sontag focus on the elements of instantaneity and infinite reproducibility introduced by the photograph, as well as on the problematics occasioned by the unparalleled one-to-one correspondence between the "reality" and its representation, Mann's interest—like that of many other modernists—is far more in the technology or medium *behind* or *before* the image, in what most radically distinguishes the photographic regime from that of the surface world of painting, and so too in what most consequently distinguishes modernism from any form of realism, Apollonian or otherwise. Similarly, while Kittler and Crary both concentrate on the concrete disciplinary practices, mechanisms, and effects of the photographic medium on the modern subject, Mann's interest seems characteristically invested in a far more nebulous field: in the discursive impact of what I call the metaphorical regime of the photograph on the traditional conceptual territory of Bildung, including its rendering of the subject, his socializing cultivation, and the always complicitous practice of representation. In all these various ways, the role of photography in *The Magic Mountain* would appear to be far more extensive and shadowy than anything we would expect either from Mann's earlier novella or from these other theorists' investigations.

Our exploration, then, of Mann's suggestive incorporation of the new metaphorical field will no doubt take us into some foggy, treacherous, and difficult-to-chart territory—such is the terrain of the Magic Mountain, and were it anything else we would know we were on the wrong track. But let me stake out three general paths that, while often crossing and even doubling back, our investigation can follow, paths that correspond with three major features of the photographic field. First, there is the process of *Entwicklung,* development, or more precisely, of exposure and development; I wish to follow how this Entwicklung comes to inform and even supersede traditional Bildung and in the process alters the model of the subject and his training. Second, there is the photographic relation of the negative and positive, an increasingly complicated and implicated relation of supposedly opposing values; I wish to follow how this relation comes to confound the traditional "painterly" Bildung model of a single, present Bild and in the process radically reconfigures the role of both gender and sexuality in the subject's formation. Finally, there is the photographic need for a fixative, a new requirement of this metaphorical system quite foreign to the earlier vocabulary of Bildung and Bilder; I wish to follow how this feature too alters and even perverts the traditional course of Bildung, perhaps even in ways that prove unexpectedly and unprecedentedly impossible to sustain.

Photographic Memory and Development

On his first evening at the Berghof sanatorium, after dining in the restaurant with his cousin Joachim, Hans Castorp is introduced to Edhin Krokowski. We hear of Krokowski's incredibly pale, almost white pallor, set off against his black eyes and brows and even more against his black suit and shoes. And we hear of a peculiar feature of this suit, "a soft floppy collar such as Hans Castorp had seen only once before, on a photographer in Danzig, and indeed it did impart something of the studio to Dr. Krokowski's appearance" ("ein weich[er] überfall-ende[r] Halskragen, wie Hans Castorp ihn bis dahin nur bei einem Photographen in Danzig gesehen hatte und welcher der Erscheinung Dr. Krokowski's in der Tat ein ateliermässiges Gepräge verlieh" [29/16]). The identification of Krokowski as a photographer, whom we soon discover to be something of a psychoanalyst, happens only this once, when he is first introduced. It is, however, enough, especially since Mann never ceases to describe him in such (photographically) black-and-white terms; nor does the doctor ever stop wearing his photographer's outfit.

Walter Benjamin reminds us that the advent of psychoanalysis coincides with that of photography—Jean-Martin Charcot was the first to appoint a hospital photographer, and, with the young Sigmund Freud looking on, he took pictures of his hysterical patients—and however parodied in the figure of Krokowski, we also know that psychoanalysis in *The Magic Mountain* remains one of the more important sites both for a reconception of the subject and, more pressingly, for the imposition of an interceding practice of social supervision for the production of the "truth" of the individual, which is to say, for his Bildung, his Entwicklung.[22] Moreover, Krokowski is hardly alone in his association of the photographic with such mechanisms of social supervision and subject formation; as we will see, in one way or another, each of Hans Castorp's primary pedagogical influences is situated within the metaphorical field of photography and its model of Entwicklung. The question provoked, then, both by the initial description of Krokowski and by the subsequent situation of Hans's mentors and his Bildung within the new discursive field, is this: how exactly does photography figure in this refiguring of both the conception of the subject and the practices of Bildung?

Perhaps the best place to look for an answer is to focus on the narrator's initial reference to Hans as "this unwritten page" ("dies unbeschriebene Blatt" [55/35]). As we know, the tabula rasa had been a rather set trope for the subject of Bildung at least since Locke in the seventeenth century, and it well suited the eighteenth- and early-nineteenth-century conflation of Bildung and Bilder, the characteristic depiction of subject formation as a kind of surface inscription in which writing and painting seamlessly merge. In a slightly later chapter in *The Magic Mountain,* however, Settembrini revises and improves upon the trope in a highly revealing way. He says,

> The gifted young man is no unwritten page [or "unpictured surface"] but rather one on which everything has been inscribed, so to speak, with invisible ink, the good with the bad. And it is the educator's task decisively to *develop* the good but forever to obliterate the false that would come forth.

> Der begabte junge Mensch ist kein unbeschriebenes Blatt, er ist vielmehr ein Blatt, auf dem gleichsam mit sympathetischer Tinte alles schon geschrieben steht, das Rechte wie das

Schlechte, und Sache des Erziehers ist es, das Rechte entschieden zu *entwickeln,* das Falsche aber, das hervortreten will . . . auf immer auszulöschen. (142/98, my emphasis)

Settembrini reformulates the basic premises of the image of the subject as a tabula rasa in terms that are recognizably photographic; that is, the newly emergent medium seems to have in-formed the conventional topos and simultaneously to have altered its traditional representation of both the self and its Bildung. The blank page, or *Blatt,* of the self has been refigured as much like a photographic plate, or *Platte;* the clean slate, or *tabula,* has become, so to speak, the only seemingly opaque tablet (*Täfelchen*) of a photographic negative, with all its invisible "script" (see 540/382). As such, the subject, rather than being simply inscribed or painted (*gebildet*), is to be developed (*entwickelt*) or, more precisely, having first been "exposed" and taken on, or in, its impressions from the outside world—and in this respect we must understand the sustained emphasis on Hans Castorp as "receptive" (*aufnahmelustig* or *aufnahmefähig*)—the subject is then to be developed, brought out, and, finally, potentially, "fixed," or *befestigt* (see 139/96).

The new notion of character—and, implicitly, of memory—suggested by Settembrini's reformulation of the tabula rasa motif and its relation to the field of photography is hardly unique to Mann. Rather, many of his modernist contemporaries were similarly engaged in rethinking the model of the psyche and its mnemonic apparatus, often focusing on precisely those same new properties of the "plate" introduced by Settembrini and doing so even more explicitly in terms of the new technological medium. In fact, Kracauer is more or less alone among the major figures of modernism in contrasting the domains of photography and memory, continuing instead to associate the latter with the domain of painting and, not incidentally, with a Goethean ideal of character as a cumulative, selectively fashioned truth.[23] Far more representative of the period is the approach taken by Ernest Hello in *L'Homme* (1872), which, as J.-K. Huysmans points out, was among the very first works to explore "the many interesting comparisons that can be established between the processes of photography and memory" ("les intéressantes comparaisons qui peuvent s'établir entre les opérations de la photographie et celles du souvenir"), beginning with its description of photography as "the symbol of memory . . . a mirror that remembers" ("le symbole du souvenir . . . un miroir qui se souvient").[24]

Hello contrasts photography with unmemorylike painting and specifically associates the former with the newly emergent subject of the nineteenth century. He depicts memory as a kind of photographic plate (*la plaque*) or glass (*le verre*), onto which "the image deposits itself while exposed to the fullness of day . . . however, this image does not catch sight of itself. It is there, yet invisible" ("l'image se dépose sur elle, pendant qu'elle exposée au grand jour . . . [Mais] cette image ne s'aperçoit pas. Elle est là, mais elle est invisible").[25] In order to make it appear, memory must conjure or develop the stored image in (and out from) the darkness, through the application of its chemical solvent (*l'acide*). The highly suggestive inclusion in the photo metaphor of the chemical agent and its analytic, caustic contribution to memory's development is mostly left unexplored by the later tradition (except, I will argue, by Mann and Proust); otherwise, Hello's model seems to have set the basic points of connection between photography and the psyche for many of the most important (French) modernists, including Huysmans, Bergson, Proust, and Benjamin.

There is another figure whose thinking of the self and its psyche as a form of photographic plate proves especially rich and especially useful for an analysis of Settembrini's reformulation of the tabula rasa motif: Freud. Marshall McLuhan has shrewdly observed, "The age of Freud is above all the age of the photograph"—not only because, as mentioned, so many of his contemporaries were engaged in thinking together the models of the psyche and of photography, but also because Freud's own model of psychology explicitly draws on the field of photography for its conceptual apparatus, often focusing on precisely those same new properties of the tabula introduced by Settembrini.[26] Without anything resembling a direct connection, and despite the known skepticism toward Freud expressed by Mann, both Mann and Freud—like their French contemporaries—found themselves similarly registering the impact of this new recording, or *Datenverarbeitung*, system on their conception of the subject. Indeed, the lack of direct influence, even the noted resistance to influence on Mann's part, underscores all the more powerfully how photography itself functions as a decisive factor in occasioning their respective conceptions to begin with.

Perhaps the most basic property and far-reaching aspect of the (relatively) new apparatus of photography attributed by Freud to his equally new psychical apparatus is what he famously calls latency, or *Nachträglichkeit*.[27] For example, in *Moses and Monotheism* (*Der Mann*

Moses und die monotheistische Religion [1939]), Freud describes the "uncomfortable discovery" that

> the strongest compulsive influence arises from impressions which impinge themselves upon a child at a time when we would have to regard his psychical apparatus as not yet completely receptive. The fact itself cannot be doubted, but it is so puzzling that we may make it more comprehensible by comparing it with a photographic exposure which can be developed after any interval of time and transformed into a picture.

> die stärkste zwangsartige Beeinflussung von jenen Eindrücken herrührt, die das Kind zu einer Zeit treffen, da wir seinen psychischen Apparat für noch nicht vollkommen aufnahmefähig halten müssen. An der Tatsache selbst ist nicht zu zweifeln, sie ist so befremdend, daß wir uns ihr Verständnis durch den Vergleich mit einer photographischen Aufnahme erleichtern dürfen, die nach einem beliebigen Aufschub entwickelt und in ein Bild verwandelt werden mag.[28]

This model of latency and the specific conception of belated personal development it entails clearly presents a challenge to the sequential unfolding and historical continuity of the subject traditionally assumed by Bildung—what D. A. Miller calls the nineteenth century's "genetic" notion of both narrative and character—as well as to its assumption of its subject as always somehow (even if ever increasingly) evident.[29] Instead, the new model introduces a potentially radically staggered, nonsequential and nonevident model for subject formation, or, as Freud puts it, for a "compulsive influence" exercised on the subject's identity. Moreover, the model clearly corresponds quite closely with that elucidated by Settembrini in the passage cited earlier. Each involves a similar, new dialectic of the latent and manifest that opens up a temporal gap between the negative, unconscious plate of the self and its eventual manifest representation—precisely that gap into which the process of development inserts itself.

Freud also invokes photography to elucidate several other aspects of the psychical apparatus that are of importance for Mann's novel. For example, in "A Note on the Unconscious" ("Einige Bemerkungen

über den Begriff des Unbewußten in der Psychoanalyse" [1912]),
Freud deploys photography to describe the two distinct states of mind
presumed by his model, the unconscious and the conscious, as well as
the process or activity whereby the one becomes the other. There are
obvious overlaps with the passage cited from *Moses and Monotheism*,
but newly added considerations also come to the fore:

> A rough but not inadequate analogy to this supposed rela-
> tion of conscious to unconscious activity might be drawn
> from the field of ordinary photography. The first stage of the
> photograph is the "negative"; every photographic picture
> has to go through the "negative process," and some of those
> negatives which have held good in examination are admitted
> to the "positive process" ending in the picture.

> Eine grobe, aber ziemlich angemessene Analogie dieses sup-
> ponierten Verhältnisses der bewußten Tätigkeit zur unbe-
> wußten bietet das Gebiet der gewöhnlichen Photographie.
> Das erste Stadium der Photographie ist das Negativ; jedes
> photographische Bild muß den "Negativprozeß" durch-
> machen, und einige dieser Negative, die in der Prüfung gut
> bestanden haben, werden zu dem "Positivprozeß" zuge-
> lassen, der mit dem Bilde endigt.[30]

Two aspects of this description are of special interest to us. First, we
note how it further defines the split in the self between its unconscious
and its conscious manifestation in terms of a relation between two opposite fields or processes, the negative and the positive. Second, we
note how Freud's description of the "first stage of the photograph"
leaves crucially unclear just where the "picture" comes from—much as
in Settembrini's account of the "page on which everything has already
been inscribed, so to speak, with invisible ink," where we are left igno-
rant as to where the "writing" came from. The first Freud passage cited
does make clear that the relevant impressions originate from the outside, just as in photography, through a prior moment of exposure. But
the property of latency, which distances the "negative" from its original exposure, also imbues the negative with a sense of autonomy, as if
the impression, or Bild, actually originates in the negative, or unconscious, itself—whereas in fact this photo-psychic paradigm remains as

fundamentally distinct from a Platonic model of innate ideas as it does from the Lockean one of a blank slate. Nonetheless, the confusion wrought by such a photographic latency proves most useful to a traditional ploy of Bildung, insofar as Bildung has always sought to disguise as inherent what is actually externally installed, and this is but one of many instances where the new apparatus of Entwicklung reconfigures but also improves upon the earlier mechanics and practices of Bildung proper.[31]

Finally, Freud returns to the photographic in a passage from "Resistance and Repression" in the *Introductory Lectures on Psychoanalysis* ("Widerstand und Verdrängung" in *Vorlesungen zur Einführung in die Psychoanalyse* [1917]) in order to account for the issue that is most personally central to Settembrini's reformulation, namely, the matter of selection, the idea that certain scripts, impressions, or images get developed and others do not. Freud writes:

> Let us assume that every mental process . . . exists to begin with in an unconscious stage or phase, just as a photographic picture begins as a negative and only becomes a picture after being turned into a positive. Not every negative, however, necessarily becomes a positive; nor is it necessary that every unconscious mental process should turn into a conscious one.

> Nehmen wir an, daß jeder seelische Vorgang . . . zuerst in einem unbewußten Stadium oder Phase existiert und erst aus diesem in die bewußte Phase übergeht, etwa wie ein photographisches Bild zuerst ein Negativ ist und dann durch den Positivprozeß zum Bild wird. Nun muß aber nicht aus jedem Negativ ein Positiv werden, und ebensowenig ist es notwendig, daß jeder unbewußte Seelenvorgang sich in einen bewußten umwandle.[32]

This is, I would say, a notion of the self and its Entwicklung that is essentially alien to the notion of the self and its Bildung supported by the single or simple Bild vocabulary of painting, a notion more in keeping with the potential multiplicity of the self assumed by modernism. And while the extent to which the strategy of selection actually holds for the case of Hans Castorp—that is, the success of Settembrini's efforts at discriminatory exclusion—must remain undecided, the new metaphorical regime here certainly stresses how Entwicklung, or development, is always somehow a matter of repression: not the simple additive or expressive procedure of Bild-ung but rather necessarily subtractive and censorious. Or to draw the distinction less radically, we might say that the photo analogy graphically presents a facet of Bildung always implicit but unexpressed by the previous pictorial parallel, that the desired manifest image-of-the-self is not simply a positive product, nor for that matter a release of a potential but oppressed and occulted self, but is rather itself somehow a negative product, a matter of repressive (non)production.

The Developer

As Settembrini's description of the subject of Bildung as "no unwritten page (or unpictured surface)" makes clear, the newly figured topos also provides room for a developer, for a new position of pedagogical intervention intimately related to the new conception of the modern self. For once memory and its mechanisms for subject formation have been reconceived in photographic terms, it seems almost inevitable that the supervisory tactics of Bildung would also become refigured in the same way.[33] And Settembrini, or rather Mann, is not alone in recognizing and exploiting this new regulatory space; other contemporary authors also sought it out. For example, in *Absalom, Absalom!* William Faulkner describes how Charles Bon takes Henry Sutpen to New Orleans and actively seeks to shape and control his companion's impressions:

> I can imagine him, the way he did it: the way in which he took the innocent and negative plate of Henry's provincial soul and intellect and exposed it by slow degrees to this esoteric milieu, building gradually toward the picture he desired it to retain, accept . . . watching the picture resolve and become fixed . . . the plate docile . . . he (Bon) stroking onto the plate himself now the picture he wanted there . . . the exposures brief . . . the plate unaware of what the complete picture would show, scarce seen and yet ineradicable.[34]

Interestingly enough, Faulkner determines on a slightly different moment in the photographic process to stage his formative interference than does Mann. Whereas Settembrini tends to privilege the later moment of actual development and its transferred fixing of the already stored latent image as a positive manifest print, Bon concentrates on manipulating the initial moment of exposure and the transferred fixing of its impression on his charge's negative plate. But for both authors, the new field of photography and its concomitant new conception of the self also allow for a new conception of the practices and importance of the external, supervising, manipulating agent, a new conception that decisively transforms traditional Bildung into Entwicklung.

As I mentioned before, each of Hans Castorp's primary pedagogical influences is situated within the metaphorical field of photography, and each one's mediating intervention into Hans's development decisively transforms Bildung by virtue of its photographic character. Perhaps more than any other, Hofrat Behrens's supervisory practices stage the gap that has opened up between photography and painting and hence too between modernist Entwicklung and traditional Bildung; the X-ray photographs of his patients that so graphically challenge the truth value of their picturesque (*malerisch*) appearances intervene to impose a different truth—a hidden or latent one—for the subject and hence too a different regime of prescribed behavior or identity. Similarly, Krokowski's psychoanalysis, or *Seelenzergliederung,* as it is frequently called, proves a photographic mode of Entwicklung opposed to traditional Bildung. The basic similarity of his mediating apparatus with that of Behrens is brought out by the pairing of his "psychic" and Behrens's "organic" illumination chambers (*Durchleuchtungskabinette*); indeed, for all its characterization as illicit and somehow deviant, Krokowski's mode of truth production—which is to say, of character formation—is far more obviously complicit with the newly dominant technologies for the intervention into and hence regulation of the subject's inner life than is, for example, Settembrini's more licit and "proper" mode. Like Behrens's, Krokowski's edification of the subject takes place behind or before the visible—in the dark, hidden, latent, and negative reaches of the soul—which it then works to develop and bring forth. But the self it would bring forth, into the picture, so to speak, is of course quite different from the self already "positively" pictured there. This is one aspect in which Krokowski's photo-psychoanalytic Entwicklung of his subject differs from traditional Bildung. Another is in how its development of the subject is, however paradoxically, at the same time his or her disintegration (*Zergliederung*). Even as the development of a photographic plate is fundamentally a process of decomposition, of breaking down the (seemingly blank) exposed surface through the application of corrosive, literally analytic chemical solvents that thereby reveal or release the hidden picture, just so does Krokowski's psychoanalysis develop the subject by dissolving it. This is, I would say, symptomatic of a peculiarly modernist notion of the subject, one that seeks at once its articulation and its vanishing, a notion radically opposed to a painterly model of Bildung but very much in keeping with a photochemical one of Entwicklung.[35]

The place of Settembrini's humanism within the photo field is also fairly obvious—although given his pronounced allegiance to the tradition of Bildung, it too is fairly ambivalent. He is, of course, the one who brings light, taking full advantage of Hans's receptivity and developmental potential; indeed, in respect to its siting within the photographic domain, Settembrini's humanistic enlightenment pedagogy very much resembles Krokowski's psychology. Both operate within the same inaugurating division of the field of Bildung into black and white, dark and light, and negative and positive values, both attract the metaphor of bringing to light, and both work to develop the latent ideational "scripts" of Hans's soul. But as the well-known moment at the beginning of the chapter "Sudden Clarity" ("Plötzliche Klarheit") illustrates, Settembrini's enlightening practices are also potentially destructive forces, as inimical to Hans's Entwicklung as a bright overhead light suddenly switched on in a darkroom. In this respect at least, the requisite conditions for photographic Entwicklung are radically opposed to those of Settembrini's more traditional efforts at Hans's Bildung.[36]

Finally, we should note how even the narrator's relationship with Hans Castorp can be situated within the photographic field, insofar as he too develops his subject, articulates his thought, and brings out the hidden writing, working to expose and develop the preconscious into manifest consciousness. This is one of the many parallels between the mediating function of Mann's narrator and Proust's, which emphatically places both in the same modernist regime. Consider the following passage from Proust:

One experiences, but what one experiences is like those negatives which show nothing but black until they are held up

before a lamp, and they, too, must be looked at from the reverse side; one does not know what it is until it has been
held up before the intelligence. Only then, when one has
thrown light upon it and intellectualized it can one distinguish—and with what effort!—the shape of what one has
felt.

On éprouve, mais ce qu'on a éprouvé est pareil à certains
clichés qui ne montrent que du noir tant qu'on ne les a pas
mis près d'une lampe, et qu'eux aussi il faut regarder à l'en-
vers: on ne sait pas ce que c'est tant qu'on ne l'a pas approché
de l'intelligence. Alors seulement quand elle l'a éclairé, quand
elle l'a intellectualisé, on distingue, et avec quelle peine, la figure de ce qu'on a senti.[37]

As Dorrit Cohn describes it, Proust uses the photographic metaphor
and the image of dark and light (and I would add of acidlike analysis or
dissolution) here to depict the distinction between the merely sensed
and nonverbally experienced and the intellectually and belatedly developed (and then graphically re-presented).[38] Cohn shows this distinction
and its transformative mechanism to define the relation between Marcel as narrator and as character. It might also be taken to define much
of the relation between Mann's narrator and his protagonist, especially
the kind of Entwicklung of Hans that we see in such chapters as "Ex-
cursus on the Sense of Time" ("Exkurs über den Zeitsinn"). Here we
see how the narrator deploys his rather formidable mediating technology, which (like Proust's) is always at once an operation of enlightening exposure and analytical breaking down, in order to give developed,
finished representation to ideas Hans has only more or less been "impressed" by, bringing to bear his whole sophisticated, supervisory apparatus in order to develop the individual's latent experience—and yet
also of course, and simultaneously, to assimilate it to a more generalized, socialized, discursive realm. This double process, whereby the
narrator's development brings Hans simultaneously closer to a state of
both self-manifestation and generic assimilation or representation, is of
course something that keeps his Entwicklung firmly within the realm of
Bildung, but as we will see, it also keeps it within that of the photograph in ways that subtly change both the process and its final product.

CON/TEMPLATING THE SUBJECT

One of the most notable qualities of the teaching Settembrini expounds is that it is not an *Originalphilosophie* (142/98), and as he explains in describing Hans Castorp as "no unwritten page (or unpictured surface)," the clichéd quality of his pedagogical discourse is very much in keeping with the model of development he sees himself facilitating. We note a similar quality in the narrator's development of his character, which (as just mentioned) is most often directed toward assimilating Hans Castorp's thought to gnomic generalizations and his experience toward more archetypal, representative patterns—as if behind his individual character there lurked, shadowlike, a more master template, out of which his experience emerges as a particular copy.

The implication, of course, of both Settembrini's and the narrator's practice is that the hidden writing on Hans's tabula is not truly original either and that the process of development consists in large part in exposing or bringing out the impersonal, unconscious, archetypal basis of self-identity. This feature is also an important manifestation of the photographic metaphor, one brought out particularly well by the French designation of the negative plate as a "cliché."

The relation between the one master plate, or *cliché*, and its copy is, of course, central to Benjamin's reading of the new model of art and reality ushered in by photography. It occasions a condition of endless reproducibility that negates the earlier aesthetics of auratic originality that adhered, for example, to the unique portrait and, by extension, to its unique subject. By contrast, the identity of the photograph and its subject are from the start caught up and characterized by the inherent possibility of more uniform, interchangeable, successively produced and proliferated copies. As Roxanne Hanney notes, this condition is centrally represented by Proust's reconception of the erotic field in photographic terms such that "it is almost as if all the women to whom one man is attracted in the course of his lifetime have come from the same negative plate."[39] Although not presented in explicitly photographic terms, Freud's notion of a repetition compulsion betrays a similar importation of the new conditions of standardized reproduction into the sphere of individual psychology.

Mann himself often explored a related aesthetics and psychology of reproducibility, already in *Death in Venice,* and far more consequently in his later works *Doctor Faustus* and, especially, *Felix Krull*. In *The Magic Mountain*, however, he seems to work a different conception of the negative as stereotype, a different interplay of photography and psychology. Barthes hints at something of this second connection when he writes, "the Photograph sometimes makes appear what we never see in a real face, a genetic feature, the fragment of oneself or of a relative that comes from some ancestor. The Photograph gives a little truth, but this truth is not that of the individual, who remains irreducible; it is the truth of lineage."[40] It is this aspect of photography qua psychology that Mann himself explicitly foregrounds in the essay I mentioned before, "The World Is Beautiful" ("Die Welt ist schön") and he contrasts it favorably with the earlier art of painting. He writes, "The development of photographic portraiture in the direction of the psychological, of character and type studies, is patent, and it benefits from a circumstance that is of little use to human painting" ("Die Entwicklung des photographischen Porträts in der Richtung des Psychologischen, der Charakter- und Typenstudie ist augenfällig, und sie zieht Vorteile aus einem Zustande der Malerei, der menschlicher Bildniskunst wenig günstig ist").[41] In the formulations of both Mann and Barthes (and Kracauer describes much the same effect), the *cliché*, the stereotypical quality of the photograph, comes to inhere and to manifest itself in the individual example, almost as if the template character of the master photographic negative expressed itself as a psychological truth in the positive print. Darwin—who has a shadow presence in Settembrini's rhetoric of Entwicklung—also took note of this peculiar quality of the new photographic medium and exploited it for the presentation of his own new notion of the human subject and his psychological development. His *On the Expression of the Emotions in Man and Animals* avails itself of numerous photographs and "Heliotype Plates reproduced from the original negatives" in order to illustrate the typical expressions that are his subject. He explains how photos "are much superior for my purpose to any drawing, however carefully executed," his purpose being scientific and modern, very much distinct from the earlier regime of physiognomy, which Darwin links to the earlier psychology and practice of painting.[42] Darwin's cousin, the eugenicist Francis Galton, took this stereotypical quality of the photograph to its logical extreme in the *Mischphotographie* of his family portraits, which sought to bring out hereditary likenesses by photographing several faces on the same negative plate, an example that Freud would use repeatedly to explain his model for how images are composed, stored, and reproduced in the unconscious memory.[43]

In *The Magic Mountain,* Mann's adaptation of the negative *cliché* and positive copy relationship in terms of this second connection is most evident in two examples: the relation between Hans Castorp and his grandfather and that between Clawdia Chauchat and Pribislav Hippe. Hans's grandfather, the senator Hans Lorenz Castorp, is significant to us in many respects, not least because he represents the first portrait in the novel. Senator Castorp is explicitly described as the picturesque personality in the family ("die malerische Persönlichkeit in der Familie") and his admirable portrait (Bild) dominates the entrance of the *Repräsentationsräume* of Hans's childhood home. We are told that the painting is tastefully executed in the style of the old masters, reminiscent of certain late medieval Dutch pictorial practices. Significantly, however, the relation between the model and copy here is hardly a straightforward one of the kind normally associated with Dutch realist portraiture nor, for that matter, with realist photography. Rather, the portrait presents a certain clichéd, stereotypical image of the grandfather, which for Hans represents his true, or authentic, identity. The grandfather himself, in his apparently irreducible particularity, is only a slightly marred, somewhat ineptly turned individual copy of the original Bild, or template of the portrait, but a copy that nonetheless retains and manifests certain perceptible features of that (his own) "true" *cliché* (41/24–25).

There is, then, this initial discrepancy or space between the picture and its subject, and as we soon learn, the grandfather himself only gradually "develops" into the picture, only becomes the authentic Bild through the workings of time and the chemical changes brought about by the moment of his death. Even more than the initial, partial manifestation of the clichéd Bild in the particular grandfather, this subsequent development of the latter into the former seems to confirm an observation made by Benjamin, that the earlier medium of painting is not so much (or not only) positioned in opposition to photography as it is remapped or refigured in terms of photography.[44] More immediately important for us, however, is that a process of development almost identical to the one that takes place between the grandfather and his portrait takes place again between Hans Castorp and his grandfather. We are told Hans Castorp finds that "the image of the grandfather was imprinted much more deeply, clearly, and significantly in him than that of his parents" ("daß das Bild seines Ältersvater sich ihm viel tiefer, deutlicher, und bedeutender eingeprägt hatte als das seiner Eltern" [38/22]), an imprint, or *Gepräge,* which is preserved as a memory picture, an *Erinnerungsbild.* Hans's memory is, again, recognizably photographic. And as with all photography, this memory also goes through its negative-to-positive process: even as the supposedly forgotten memories of his parents suddenly "re-presented themselves precisely, instantaneously, and piercingly in their incomparable particularity" ("sich genau, gleichzeitig, und durchdringend in ihrer unvergleichbaren Eigentümlichkeit wieder her[stellten]" [43/26]) at the moment—we might say, with the shock, or "flash"—of his grandfather's death, so does the Bild of his grandfather sink into a negative, unconscious state until Hans's arrival on the Magic Mountain, where it reappears in the corporeal form of Hans's sudden development of his grandfather's trembling of the chin. Even as the grandfather develops into his Bild through the chemical metabolic workings of death, so too does Hans develop into the same Bild by the chemical metabolic workings of the Mountain, which brings out the resemblance to the grandfather through an Entwicklung of one of Hans's stored unconscious impressions (or "scripts"), recasting the present image through the background negative *cliché.* Again, what is at issue here is clearly a logic of reproducibility newly intrinsic to representation in the wake of photography. But rather than this reproducibility being extended spatially or successively, as in Benjamin's model, it is kept diachronic and internal, as in Barthes's (or Galton's). And we note how neatly it thus furthers and refigures the traditional program of Bildung, as through the development of such previously installed memory images (*Erinnerungsbilder*), the subject moves simultaneously closer to a moment of self-realization and one of generic assimilation or representation.

The second example of Mann's adaptation of the *cliché* and copy relationship is similar but more pointed. It comes in the way Hans Castorp finally finds the negative *Urbild* (169) for Clawdia Chauchat in the *Erinnerungsbild* of Pribislav Hippe. Even more emphatically than in the case of the grandfather, this memory image is structured according to the schema of what Henri Bergson, in *Matter and Memory* (*Matière et Mémoire* [1896]), calls spontaneous recollection ("le souvenir spontané"), a form of memory he explicitly distinguishes as photographic ("le faculté de photographie mentale") in its manner of both storage and retrieval.[45]

Hans's spontaneous recollection of the *Erinnerungsbild* of Hippe and his pairing of it with the present image of Clawdia occurs in the same chapter—indeed at the same moment—in which he also develops the trembling chin, or *cliché,* of his grandfather. Mann makes the connection of the former with the photo thematics more or less explicit later on, when Hans returns to the scene of his memory image (*Erinnerungsbild* [540/382]) and in connection therewith (*im Zusammenhange damit* [540/382]) takes out and contemplates his photographic negative of Clawdia. But the connection is more or less implicit from the outset. We are told that the figure, or Bild, of Hippe "emerged imperceptibly out of the fog into his life, slowly taking on ever greater clarity and palpability, until that moment when he was most near and materially present, there in the schoolyard, stood there in the foreground for a while, and then gradually receded and vanished again into the fog, without even the pain of farewell" ("unmerklich aus Nebeln in sein Leben getreten war, langsam immer mehr Deutlichkeit und Greifbarkeit gewonnen hatte, bis zu jenem Augenblick der größten Nähe und Körperlichkeit, auf dem Hofe, eine Weile so im Vordergrunde gestanden hatte und dann allmählich wieder zurückgetreten und ohne Abschiedsweh in den Nebeln entschwunden war" [172/120]). Benjamin has quite beautifully described the "fog" out of which, he says, photography arose and more specifically back into which all early photographs (unless hermetically sealed) eventually faded.[46] Such seems the early fate of Hippe's Bild as well.

But while the positive, manifest image fades, the Bild is nonetheless retained in the "negative" space of Hans Castorp's unconscious, where it remains stored, latent, awaiting, like the memory image of the grandfather, its subsequent development and duplication. And it finds this not only in Hans's spontaneously produced, flashlike vision of Hippe but also, and even more importantly, in the figure of Clawdia Chauchat. Interestingly, Hans's early perceptions of Clawdia are always portrayed as somehow undeveloped, not fully formed; only once he has retrieved and worked up the negative, unconscious *Urbild* of Hippe does the figure or image of Clawdia Chauchat emerge in all its clarity. Thus, even as Hans Castorp here—precisely here—develops into the Bild of his grandfather, succumbing to a certain logic of reproducibility, of belated reproduction of the unconscious *cliché*, so too does Clawdia Chauchat develop out of the negative unconscious *cliché* of Pribislav Hippe, reproducing in her image the generic features of the master template (or nonoriginal script). And as in the case of the grandfather and Hans, as the *Erinnerungsbild* develops and reappears, the subject (Clawdia) moves closer to a moment of both self-manifestation and generic assimilation or representation. Thus memory qua photography, and self-formation qua Entwicklung, come doubly to further and to refigure the traditional thematics of Bildung.

The example of the photo relation between Pribislav Hippe and Clawdia Chauchat is, in fact, even more deeply embedded in the metaphoric logic of the new medial field than that between the grandfather and Hans, and in two distinct ways. First, the negative/positive relation between Hippe and Clawdia is conceived as just that, as a relationship of opposite or reversed values: not only of a male as opposed to a female figure, and so too of a homoerotic as opposed to a heteroerotic attraction on Hans's part, but also of death as opposed to life and a whole slew of other such motivic binaries. Second, however, the relationship between Hippe and Clawdia is also conceived in terms even more challenging to the standard mimetic relation of model and copy than that posed by the grandfather and his Bild, terms that again draw on the photo relation of negative and positive but in such a way as to challenge their oppositional relation. That is, there is an emphatic sense in which Hippe and Clawdia are the *same* figure, the same image with the identical blue-gray or gray-blue Kirghitz eyes, and so on, and similarly, a sense in which there is no stable or secure way of fixing on one as the source or prior term for the other, at least not in a way that would discount a further reversal. Both of these relations and their seeming contradictions and complications are, of course, intrinsic to the photographic domain, and both have major repercussions for Bildung.

The Black and White
of Sex, Gender, and Subjectivity

As Naum Gabo insisted in his "Realist Manifesto" of 1920, the *Weltanschauung* promulgated by the photographic medium was profoundly black and white. The emergence of the X-ray, understood at that time as simply the latest extension of the photographic regime, further confirmed the conviction that the "real" and "true" only came to us in such monochromatic, starkly contrastive hues.[47] And despite Hans Castorp's innovative but disappointing forays into color photography near the end of the novel, the same basically holds true for the world of *The Magic Mountain* as well. Its world is fundamentally conceived in black-and-white terms, in polarized terms of dark and light, shadow and substance—such as the materialist Behrens's white coat and the spiritualist Krokowski's preferred black smock; Settembrini's "enlightened" and positive doctrines of humanism, rationality, and progress and Naphta's dark and negative principles of mysticism, unreason, and reactionism; or the ruling oppositions between East and West, classicism and romanticism, democracy and tyranny, reason and instinct, or life and death, between which Hans's Bildung is poised.[48]

At the same time as what Barthes calls the "original truth of the black-and-white photograph" imposed such a binary model on the world, however, I would suggest it also contributed to a radical reconception of the fundamental relations between the opposing poles of the model as an inevitable consequence of the new understanding of the relation between negative and positive values associated with photography.[49] We get an early example of what I mean here in the lecture delivered by our photo-psychoanalyst Krokowski and heard by Hans immediately after the chapter "Hippe." The lecture manifests the photographic in the doctor's discourse in two apparently competing ways. First, as Hans is somewhat shocked to discover, the lecture works to bring the dark, hidden, and private subject of sexuality out into the broad daylight (180/124), to transform the unspoken or unspeakable into the graphic print of language. This is the primary thrust of Krokowski's "Entwicklung" of his topic (181/126), a mode of development and enlightenment (see 179/124) that, as noted, ironically aligns Krokowski's psychoanalysis with Settembrini's humanism and so too perpetuates the basic oppositional model—of dark and light, negative and positive, and so on—that the Italian pedagogue in particular imposes and propagates throughout the novel.

But as Hans Castorp discovers, the lecture also elaborates a rather different relation between the dark and the light, the negative and the positive, one essentially opposed to the Settembrinian but still (and even more) within the photographic domain. The lecture not only describes how the process of development moves its stored ideational material from the dark to the light, the negative to the positive; it also describes how it moves it in the other direction, from the positive to the negative. Indeed, it describes the positive and the negative as simply different stages, or rather, as reversed values of the same "thing." The subject is love and illness, and in Krokowski's account the negative of disease is simply an almost mechanical inversion of the positive of love. Psychoanalysis in turn promises a re-reversal, a *Wiederverwandlung,* of the latent/negative of illness into the manifest/positive of healthy eros (183/127).[50] Even as the photographic medium introduces a representational model that requires a serial process of transformative reversals in which the notions of original and copy, cause and effect, even positive and negative become vertiginously interchangeable and endlessly extendable, so too does Krokowski's psychoanalytic discourse pose for the relation between the positive and negative values of the interior life.

The new relations between the negative and positive, the dark and the light, and so on, suggested by the photographic medium and reproduced by Krokowski's psychoanalytic model has major consequences for the operation of Bildung in Mann's novel. And as one might anticipate after Krokowski's conflation of photography and the erotic—a not-infrequent association in modernist thought—this is especially the case for those structures of desire that I mentioned at the outset as among the privileged mechanisms through which the socialization of the protagonist is traditionally accomplished in the Bildungsroman, namely, those structures that properly direct (indeed construct) the protagonist's impulses toward the ideal of manliness that marks the completion of both his personal and social Bildung.

The consequences of this new set of relations for Hans Castorp's Bildung are most evident in respect to the figure of Clawdia Chauchat, in terms of her place within both the erotic and photographic thematics of the novel, and this in turn is most evident in terms of her relation to Settembrini, who, as the chief of the many male figures who undertake the more overt Bildung or Entwicklung project of Hans's acculturation, provides the decisive context for an understanding of Hans's erotic adventures and Clawdia's photographic character. For as is typical of the genre, Mann's central character seems subjected to two concurrent educations: one by men who cultivate his public, social, cultural, and even political intellectual development and another by women or, rather, a woman who cultivates his more private erotic development. The critical task is, as always, to determine the role of the latter within the former.

Mann himself makes clear the need to consider the figure of

Clawdia Chauchat—and her place within the photo thematics in general and the negative/positive thematics in particular—in conjunction with Settembrini and his education of Hans Castorp in the passage alluded to above, in which Hans brings the *photographische Negativ* of Clawdia to the picturesque (*malerisch*) place where the memory image of Pribislav Hippe first and so photographically appeared to him and where he now contemplates the transparent image of the human body ("das transparente Bild des Menschensleibes") as part of his self-appointed task of playing king (*regieren*). Hans holds in his hand "a little plate, which when held parallel to the ground seemed black, reflective and opaque, but when held up to the heavens grew light and revealed humanistic things" ("ein Täfelchen, das, wenn man es in gleicher Ebene mit dem Erdboden hielt, schwarz-spiegelnd und undurchsichtig schien, aber, gegen das Himmelslicht aufgehoben, sich erhellte und humanistische Dinge vorwies" [540/382]), and in connection therewith ("im Zusammenhange [da]mit"), he specifically conjures up Settembrini and the many conceptual binaries he has exposed Hans to—form and freedom, spirit and body, and so on. The contemplated Bild, so starkly divided between its dark, earthly character and its enlightened, uplifted one, would seem to inscribe a certain fundamental opposition onto the figure of Clawdia, even as, through the implicit imposition of Settembrini's mode of oppositional representation onto her X-ray photograph, it would seem to inscribe a certain gendered doubleness onto the image, a joining of male and female principles distinct from that already and also suggested by the pairing of Clawdia and Hippe. In any case, the image confirms that an understanding of Settembrini is essential to one of Hans's fascination with Clawdia or, rather, with her photograph.

As mentioned, one of the basic enabling gestures of Settembrini's pedagogic, humanistic desire to bring things to light is his essentially metaphysical division of the world into two opposing states: one dark and one light, one negative and one positive, and so on (and on). This gesture is clearly evident in Hans Castorp's manipulation of Clawdia's photographic image here, but as Alexander Nehamas argues, it is also a gesture whose basis and motives are very much at issue and opened to question in the novel.[51] In the case of Settembrini—its prime if hardly sole practitioner—the gesture seems clearly indicative of a strategy of repression. Unable to accept himself or the world for what they wholly are, he deploys a metaphysical apparatus that consigns all the conditions and forces he most fears to the "darkness" and embraces everything that leads away from them as his "positive." The apparatus is not only applied in the more or less external domain for the production of those social, cultural, and political "humanistic" ideals that make up the traditional program of Bildung that Settembrini constantly holds up to Hans; it is also implemented in the more internal realm for the manufacture of that subject-ideal that similarly supports the traditional picture of Bildung. Unable to accept his own sensual, internal nature, Settembrini systematically disavows the erotic and material as part of himself and poses his self instead as a purely rational, cultural being that is ideally free of relation to such dark, negative, opposing forces. And it is worth emphasizing that, despite initial appearances to the contrary, the exact same apparatus is wielded by Settembrini's seeming competitor in Hans's Bildung, namely, Naphta, who similarly identifies himself only with a positive, spiritual ideal that projects itself out and away from the low, material, negative base, which is subsequently left out of the picture (literally) of the ideally realized self. Moreover, with minor modifications, the same can be shown to hold true for Hans's other male educators, Behrens and Krokowski, even Peeperkorn and Ziemßen, all of whom wield a similar positive/negative, black-and-white model for the articulation of their ideal (male) subject.[52]

Hans, however, clearly resists making the choice between the negative and positive, the dark and light, or any of the other many binary terms produced by Settembrini, precisely that choice so central to the subject formation of traditional Bildung. He also resists choosing between the various images (*Hochgebilde* [540/383]) of the ideal subject proffered by Settembrini and Naphta or by any of his other male mentors. Rather, all are similarly opposed, because all would separate and eliminate one half from the whole picture-making process, from the full (photographic) truth. Instead, Hans increasingly comes to insist on a more complete logic—a photographic logic—of ongoing inversion and exchangeability. He comes more and more to learn to take together the dark and the light, the negative and positive—the physical and intellectual, the erotic and cultural, the personal and political, and so on—to learn that, for all their (potentially endless) opposing transformations, they are not even or ever truly distinct or separable to begin with.

As I said, this has major consequences for our understanding of Clawdia Chauchat, her photographic Bild, and their place within the novel's Bildung thematics, primarily because it establishes what is at stake in our reading of the oppositions associated with her figure and Bild. On the one hand, one could surmise from Hans's handling of the plate of her X-ray photograph that Clawdia just represents the dark opposed to Settembrini's *humanistisch* light, the body-erotic opposed to the spiritual-intellectual or the female opposed to the male. In this reading, Clawdia would simply seem a perpetuation of the ruling oppositions of the bourgeois patriarchal system of Bildung, wherein, as Theodor Adorno says, "The feminine character is a [negative] imprint of the positive of male domination. But therefore equally bad" ("Der weibliche Charakter ist ein Abdruck des Positivs der Herrschaft. Damit aber so schlecht wie diese").[53] On the other hand, one could also surmise from the same evidence that Clawdia represents instead the dark *and* light, earthly and intellectual together—after all, the dual-natured Bild is of her alone—which would represent her as a rather different challenge to the humanist's Bildung model. It would represent her in opposition to his system of opposition; indeed, in true photographic fashion, it would represent an insistence on the equally implicated and inseparable relations of opposition and identity between any of the black-and-white values to any given ideal image, or *Hochgebild,* of the subject.

Let me mention another, perhaps clearer example of Clawdia's place within the dark and light logic of the novel: Hans's description of his boat ride at twilight (*Kahnfahrt im Zwielicht*). The topos is first introduced as Hans listens to Settembrini's portrayal of his (Settembrini's) grandfather, whose world Hans takes to be so radically different from that of his own grandfather: his comparison of the two worlds reminds Hans of his boat ride on a lake one evening, when he sat poised between the day and night, the setting sun and rising moon, shuttling his enraptured attention rapidly and repeatedly between the two (218/150). At the end of the same chapter, the narrator informs us that Hans has been conscientiously heeding Settembrini's educative discourse on patriotism, the dignity of man, and beautiful literature only in order to license his thoughts in another, *opposite* direction ("seinen Gedanken und Träumen wieder in anderer, in *entgegengesetzter* Richtung" [226/157, Mann's emphasis]), namely, in the direction of Clawdia: when he thinks of her as Settembrini talks, he is again reminded of his day-bright/moon-night experience. One reading—a valid one, I believe—might take the topos as opposing Clawdia to Settembrini, her misty eastern night sky to his clear western daylight, with

Hans poised between them. But a second reading (also valid) might note that the entire topos is actually applied to Clawdia alone, who is made to encompass and include both poles, both worlds, much as was the case with her contemplated photograph. That is, she is the opposite (*die Entgegegensetzte*) of Settembrini in not accepting opposition—or, rather, opposition that denies and excludes from itself half its terms. And this includes not accepting the gender and erotic distinctions that traditionally accompany such oppositions and on which Bildung traditionally depends.

THE X-RAY AND THE PORTRAIT

The same implication in and dismantlement of oppositions that we see in the application of the twilight topos we see again in the two motifs most closely attached to Clawdia in the novel's first half: the X-ray photograph and the painted portrait. Both are produced by Hofrat Behrens, arguably the representative authority of the Magic Mountain; together they forcefully place Clawdia at the center of the novel's photo thematics, especially at the center of its contested (and complicitous) relation between photography and painting, and so too between Entwicklung and Bildung.

The X-ray is, of course, one of the most dominant and overdetermined features of *The Magic Mountain,* and it represents a peculiar kind of photograph. On the one hand, it still clearly belongs within the discursive regime of photography, and X-rays are routinely referred to as photographs, and even portraits, throughout the novel. On the other hand, the X-ray also and just as clearly disrupts that regime, or, rather, it accentuates that aspect of photography most at odds with simple (portrait) painting and so breaks with that aspect still most aligned with painting, its truths, and its model for the subject. I will have more to say about this in a moment. For our immediate concern with Clawdia Chauchat and the negative/positive dimension of our topic, the most important aspect of photography as X-ray is the decisive emphasis it places on the negative. X-rays are one of the few forms of photography where the negative is the acknowledged primary form of the image, where—as Behrens's laboratory with its red-lit darkness confirms—the negative is contemplated directly, without any transformation into a final positive print, into one of the pretty pictures (*fidelen Bilder*) of lightened day (303/213). Or rather, because that is not quite accurate, let me phrase it somewhat differently: the X-ray is a form of photography where the distinction between the negative and the positive folds, where, for example, Clawdia's X-ray image can be interchangeably referred to as a "Negativ" and "[Dia]positiv."

It is not of course only through her actual X-ray *Porträt* that Clawdia is drawn into this thematic cluster. Rather, the "Bild" of Clawdia, which frequently presents itself to Hans Castorp even before he acquires his "Souvenir," is itself decidedly X-raylike. For instance, we are told that Clawdia's "Bild" appears to Hans as he sits in his dark room (also equipped with a red light), wringing from him the cry, "My God!" ("Mein Gott!" [289/203]), the same cry wrung from him by his viewing of his cousin Joachim's X-ray (during which Clawdia herself sits waiting in the next room [305/215]). This is, we remember, the "Bild" Hans is picturing when Settembrini walks in and suddenly turns on the overhead electric light, effectively ruining the image and so too reinforcing the opposition between the two regimes and figures, marking Hans's fascination with Clawdia's "Bild" as one with the dark, negative state of things—with death, disease, and asocial desire—so contraposed to Settembrini's enlightened values of humanistic Bildung.

However, even as through her X-ray image Clawdia is associated with the negative plate of death, disease, and Hans's asocial desire, through her painted portrait she is also placed at the more positive pole of life, flesh, and Hans's socializing desire. As mentioned earlier, both the X-ray and Clawdia's portrait are produced by Hofrat Behrens, which is one way the relation between them is established. Another is in how, much as the novel's other portrait, that of the grandfather, was seen to be affected by the new competing field of photography, so too is this portrait of Clawdia affected by the most recent form of photography, the X-ray. As Behrens proudly explains, its visible features are rendered from below the surface, based on what is not to be seen ("was nicht zu sehen ist"), and the resulting scientific realism ("wissenschaftliche Realität" [360/254]) contributes to a technologization of the body every bit as much as the X-ray with its depiction of the interior skeletal engineering of the human form (see 390/275–76). In this respect the portrait, in its collapse of surface and depth, seems also to blur the novel's operant oppositions even as the X-ray does in its collapse of negative and positive, inside and out.

For the most part, however, and despite this complication, the painting is presented as the opposite of the X-ray, as an "outer" as opposed to the X-ray's "inner" portrait. After all, the site of its representation is almost obsessively depicted as the skin, which is precisely what an X-ray photograph sees through and misses. More important, the opposition between the X-ray and the painted portrait also extends into the novel's Bildung thematics. Whereas the X-ray, and the Clawdia Chauchat associated with the X-ray, seems to lead Hans Castorp away from the regular, regulating course of Bildung—its public regimes, its ideals of responsibility, edification, and so on—the portrait seems to lead him, in both his intellectual and erotic inclinations, back into the traditional byways, which is to say that the painted Bild fulfills its customary function of facilitating Bildung. We see this in Hans's conversation with Behrens in the latter's apartment, where Hans first encounters the portrait and, carrying it about with him, works always to bring it more into the light (362/255, 363/256). Whereas in the earlier encounter with Behrens the X-ray incited Hans's negative obsession with death, in this encounter the portrait stirs up his positive interest in "life." It instills in Hans an enthusiasm for medicine, physical nature, and traditional aesthetics and notions of beauty, even extending, in typical Hans Castorp fashion, to jurisprudence, philology, and theology—in short, to the traditional humanistic callings (*die humanistischen Berufe*), the well-nigh Faustian bases of "formaler Bildung" (362/256). Moreover, these callings (or rather, the portrait that evokes them) direct Hans in the following chapter to *books*—apparently his only extended foray into this most traditional of educative domains—and so channel his intellectual interests into more or less socially viable discursive fields and ends.[54]

This juncture between Clawdia Chauchat and her portrait and the traditional, "positive" humanistic orientation of Bildung is perhaps best captured in the association of both with what Hans calls "die Plastik" (363–65/256–58). Hans associates Clawdia with this traditional aesthetic category, which includes both sculpture and painting and which, with its customary resonances of the malleable and fashionable, encompasses much of the traditional metaphoric field of associations adhering to Bildung (see 385/272). *Plastik* is, after all, one of the primary concepts associated with Settembrini, and especially with his characteristic desire to bring everything to the surface, to the bright, fashioned, graphic state of fully and sharply focused articulation—much like a finished, positive photographic print, which, in isolation from the rest of its regime, was often assimilated to this same traditional aesthetic domain. We can see, then, how the *Plastik* of Clawdia and her painted portrait come to embody Settembrinian principles, humanistic principles: not the fundamentally distinct relations (*grundverschiedene Verhältnisse*) suggested by the opposition of Clawdia's X-raylike Bild and Settembrini's overhead light, but rather modifications of one and the same general concern ("Variationen von ein und demselben allgemeinen Interesse" [362/255]), which is to say humanism—which is to say the pedagogic program of Bildung.

The "positive" of the portrait also has its effect on the more general, abstract Bild of Clawdia that sometimes appears to Hans, and transforms it for the first time into a truly photographic Bild, one that continually oscillates between the negative and positive values separately maintained by her X-ray and painted Bilder. We see this especially in the chapter in which Hans purchases his textbooks and, in the red-lit darkness, engages in his most formal experiments yet in personal cultural development; and there appears to him the image of Life ("das Bild des Lebens" [385/272, 398–99/281]). The "Bild" is clearly recognizable as that of Clawdia Chauchat and is just as clearly related to the "Bild" Hans contemplated of her before, until interrupted by Settembrini. But whereas the previous "Bild" was an X-raylike negative associated with Hans's dark attraction to death, this one is more like the portrait and associated with his fascination with life (and books, and Bildung)—a "Bild" that allows Hans to stop at and dwell on all the minute details of the surface, the skin, *matt-weisslich.* "Das Bild des Lebens" is, at it were, the positive to that previous negative but still very much the *same* "Bild," with reversed values, and so the "Bild" of Clawdia becomes equally, at once and by turns, negative and positive, set in opposition to Settembrini's pedagogic regime both as its negative opposite *and,* insofar as it too encompasses a positive state, as not supporting its exclusive oppositional structure.

PENCIL AND PICTURE: PHALLUS AND PHOTO

Exactly how the photographic character of Clawdia Chauchat and of Hans's attraction to her impacts on his Bildung is no doubt best seen in the chapter "Walpurgisnacht," the early culminating experience of Hans's erotic education. Significantly enough, the chapter is placed firmly under the sign of the photograph, not only through the prominent place occupied by both the X-ray portrait and the painted one in Hans's and Clawdia's presented conversation, but also and more famously through the traded "Souvenirs" in their occluded tryst. Sexual consummation is signified by photographic acquisition and exchange.

I am going to argue that the photographic nature of the encounter fundamentally affects and even determines its erotic nature or structure, and that includes its function in Hans's development or Bildung. But I should emphasize that an initial reading of the chapter seems rather to confirm the continued operation of the traditional mechanisms of erotic Bildung, for until the arrival of Mynheer Peeperkorn, no moment more clearly evinces an Oedipal structure, and, in keeping with this, no moment more clearly facilitates Hans's coming at once into his own and into the social sphere. The Oedipal is foremost. The requisite triangulation is conspicuously supplied by the relations between Hans, Settembrini, and Clawdia, with Hans clearly situated as child between the other two: as problem child (*Sorgenkind*) vis-à-vis Settembrini and *petit bourgeois* vis-à-vis Clawdia and as famili-arly *perdu* vis-à-vis both. The anticipated moment of aggression against the Father is most realized in Hans's leave-taking from Settembrini, his first truly rebellious act against his fatherly mentor as he, Hans Castorp, turns to lay claim to the forbidden, feminine domain. Moreover, Hans's "Oedipal" action yields the characteristic paradox that the apparent attack against the patriarchal power and reveling in the illicit erotic nonetheless represents an assimilation into the patriarchal and an advancement of its lawful, regulating order. Hans succeeds, as it were, to the position of the dominant (not-quite-father) himself, assumes and confirms his proper male and heterosexual identity, and simultaneously assumes an ever more responsible role in the social and cultural sphere, as evidenced, for instance, in the playing king he begins in the chapter immediately following. That is, in typical Oedipal fashion, the moment of apparently transgressive rupture turns out to be a mechanism for the protagonist's assimilation and acculturation, and, in classical fashion, the seemingly competing erotic education of the subject turns out to serve the more public program of his Bildung proper.

The linchpin to an Oedipal reading of the scene is usually taken to be Hans's acquisition of that little mechanical pencil from Clawdia, a maneuver that, significantly, repeats a ploy practiced years earlier by Hans on Pribislav Hippe. For example, Hörisch, who perhaps anachronistically points to a Freudian text for support, stresses two related aspects of the pencil's phallic function in the Oedipal scenario.[55] First, it acts as a phallus proper, one that—mobile in good Lacanian fashion—is transferred from Clawdia ("klein aber dein" ["little but yours"]) to

Hans. The transfer rids Clawdia of her dominant, masculine identity (suggested both by her possession of the pencil and her conflation with Hippe) and allows her to become a properly submissive, castrated woman. At the same time, the transfer wins for Hans the symbol of dominant male identity, an acquisition which signals the culmination of a traditional erotic education, namely, the attainment of his manliness (*Männlichkeit*). Second and equally important, Hörisch stresses the significance of the pencil as pencil, that is, as a writing (or drawing, *bilden*) instrument. In strict coordination with Hans's obtainment of sexual power and male identity comes his rising control over meaning and inscription, precisely the linkage insisted on by the reading model of Oedipal Bildung.

For all its persuasive strength, however, there is a problem with this reading, one recognized by Hörisch himself, though he works hard to avoid its consequences. The problem is that Clawdia gets the pencil back, indeed gets it back precisely then, at the occluded moment of sexual consummation (in the dark room, as it were). That is, rather than becoming attached to Hans Castorp, the phallic pencil retains its (more than good Lacanian) character as exchangeable or reversible, and in this, I would propose, it becomes subsumed in its significance to the regime of the other exchange accompanying the moment of sexual consummation, namely, that of the photographic plates.

Let me explain what I mean. That Clawdia first possesses the (phallic) pencil and then gets it back alerts us to a rather obvious circumstance that an Oedipal reading would overlook or even repress: that Hans's relationship with Clawdia Chauchat remains in a very meaningful way a homoerotic one. This is true not only because Hans's attraction to her remains somehow one to Pribislav Hippe: the same eyes, the same voice, the equivocal causal relation between the two. But it is also true because, as Hans himself observes, his attraction to Clawdia Chauchat as the embodiment of disease, death, and sterility renders it functionally, essentially homoerotic: "Because for a man to be interested in a sick woman was certainly no more reasonable than . . . well, than for Hans Castorp to have pursued his silent interest in Pribislav Hippe" ("Denn daß ein Mann sich für eine kranke Frau interessierte, dabei war doch entschieden nicht mehr Vernunft, als . . . nun, als seinerseits bei Hans Castorps stillem Interesse für Pribislav Hippe gewesen war" [182–83/127, Mann's ellipses]). As Hans's infamous seduction speech at the end of "Walpurgisnacht" underscores, a good part of his attraction to Clawdia is as an embodiment of this negative value, and the X-ray negative, as the double sign of the Hippean and diseased nature of Clawdia's character, subtly brings this homoerotic aspect to the fore, or, rather, it brings the scene itself under the sign of the homoerotic and so too out from under that of the strictly heterosexual regime of Bildung.

The homoerotic nature of Hans Castorp's attraction to Clawdia can be seen as photographic in a further, more consequential sense as well: not only in the sense that Roxanne Hanney, for instance, describes for Proust's work, where homosexuality is understood as the "inverted" negative of the positive state of heterosexuality ("inversion" being the preferred term for homosexuality in the modernist era), even as Hippe seems the inverted figure of Clawdia, or the deathful Clawdia the reversed negative of Settembrini's positive enlightened Bild-ung, but also in the sense suggested by the previously mentioned topos of twi-light (*Zwielicht*) already associated with Clawdia and her photographic character.[56] Interestingly enough, the topos itself is not original to Mann but comes from Goethe: and besides its role in *The Magic Mountain,* it also figures prominently in Mann's 1925 essay "Concerning Marriage" ("Über die Ehe"), where it is cited as part of Mann's personal definition of the homoerotic, which clearly cannot be reduced to a simple matter of same sex attraction nor to a simple inversion of heterosexuality.[57] Rather, as the *Zwielicht* image insists, Mann defines the "homo" in the same epicene sense that, for instance, Barthes attributes to the "neutral," as "a back and forth, an oscillation, the converse of an antinomy," where the homoerotic represents not so much the opposite, negative, or inverted form of the heterosexual as the inclusion of both by turns and the unending, enormously erotic oscillation between them—the oscillation between a same-sex and heterosexual attraction to the *same* figure, the endlessly reversible negative and positive forms of one's one desire.[58] It is of course just such a model of the homoerotic that dominated the cultural milieu of the early part of the century, especially in Germany: from Ulrich's notion of *der Urning* and *die Urningin,* sexual beings whose identities oscillated between the "poles" of male and female, female and male, to Hirschfeld's notion of the third sex (*das dritte Geschlecht*) to Fließ's and Weininger's theories of bisexuality, and even Freud's claim that for the homosexual, or invert, "the sexual object is not the same sex, but rather a joining of the characteristics of both sexes, something like a middle course between one impulse that desires a man, and another that wants a woman" ("das Sexualobjekt ist nicht das gleiche Geschlecht, sondern die Vereinigung beider Geschlechtscharaktere, der Krompromiß etwa zwischen einer Regung, die nach dem Manne, und einer, die nach dem Weibe verlangt").[59] It is just such an oscillating and invertible "homo" figure that is represented in the negative/diapositive figure of Hippe/Clawdia, or rather, in the Clawdia of the X-ray and painted pictures combined. And it is just such a figure that defines the new photo-erotic regime of Hans's Entwicklung.

The breakdown of the heterosexual Oedipal regime through the complementary inclusion of the homoerotic dimension also results in a breakdown of the gender regimes on which both the Oedipal and Bildung processes depend. While both Bildung and Oedipalization aim at the realization of a special ideal of manliness, to be achieved through the distinct but complementary guidance of men and women, this particular Bildung scene is notably dominated by images of gender reversals, most prominently in the many "women in men's apparel and, conversely, the men who had put on women's clothing" ("Damen in Herrentracht; [und] Herren, umgekehrt, die Frauenroben angelegt hatten" [454/320]). In respect to the two principals of the scene, the gender-blending figures in regard to both Clawdia *and* Hans. We see it for Clawdia, not only in her dual character as both Clawdia and Hippe, but more importantly for the Bildung thematics in her character as both the requisite female opposite of Settembrini's male mentorship and as somehow Settembrinilike herself, speaking and philosophizing in ways that clearly violate the conventional distinctions between the male and female educative functions ("Tu parles comme Monsieur Settembrini" [475/336; see also 473/334]). And we see it for Hans too, who adopts not only the masculine position in this scenario but also a feminine one. We recognize the latter, not only retrospectively, with the return of Clawdia's pencil (or even later, with Hans's adoption of the role of Margarethe in the Faustian subtext that also underlies this chapter), but also in the scene itself, where Clawdia transfers to Hans both her pencil *and* her paper triangle hat (*Papierdreispitz*), which connotes the feminine as patently as the other does the masculine (478/338, 474/335; see also 386/272, 477/337).

The double androgyny of Clawdia and Hans and the complex way it figures in their erotic relationship fully justifies why the exchange of that single phallic drawing pencil—the instrument of *bilden*—should give way to the double exchange of (dia)positive/negative photographs, as the token not only for the operant mode of sexuality directing Hans's subject formation but also for that of cultural meaning, and power, governing the novel in general.[60] The photographs suggest the double nature of both figures and their relation: as Mann puts it in the essay noted earlier, "It is about an equalization between the sexes in matters of Bildung" ("Es handelt sich um einen Ausgleich zwischen den Geschlechtern . . . in Dingen der Bildung") and an increasingly realized bisexuality on the part of both sexes that subtly alters, shifts, and realigns both the ideal form of sexual and social identity and the balance or modality of cultural power.[61] Far from asserting some definitive final, singular control or Bild, this bisexual, photographic system of representation insists on the continued, shuttling, back-and-forth reversibility of all its engaged values, whether man or woman, light or dark, reason or erotics. Photography and androgyny—a combination already apparent in the passage we started with, wherein Hans, with his dual-natured photograph of Clawdia in hand, undertakes his *regieren* conspicuously surrounded by androgynous flowers—photography and androgyny together have seriously altered the traditional model of Bildung posed by Settembrini and his logocentric, phallocentric world.

X-Rayed Endings

I said earlier that I would return to the matter of X-rays, and now, as we begin to approach the end and the question of endings, I would like to do just that. I noted how X-rays are routinely referred to as photographs (and even portraits) throughout the novel, but how they also accentuate that aspect of photography most at odds with simple painting and so too with its model of the subject. This is partly because X-rays see through things or, more precisely, through bodies. In the process, they accentuate the gap between the often picturesque appearance of the many Berghof patients and their quite different, decaying interiors: they weaken the common, pictorial faith in the veracity of the evident, in the visible as the privileged site for knowledge, for the determination of truth, and for the manifestation of self-identity. But the most radical transformation occasioned by X-ray photography, with the greatest effect on the conception of both the Bildungsroman and the subject of Bildung, comes from a slightly different displacement of truth in the novel. It has to do with death, and it has to do with endings.

X-rays not only move the notion of truth away from the apparent surface of things; they also move it away from the end. And they do the same to the notion of death. As Benjamin argues in "The Storyteller" ("Der Erzähler" [1936]), the moment of truth in an individual's life was always associated with his or her moment of demise, in the sense that who he or she was at the moment of death, the manner in which death presented itself to him or her, had a tremendous interpretive, retrospective authority over the meaning or truth of that individual's preceding life.[62] This common association of truth and death had a determinative effect on the structure, trajectory, and significance of the traditional nineteenth-century novel, including, as Benjamin stresses, the Bildungsroman, whose truth is also teleologically determined; that is, the condition of the protagonist at the novel's end—its (and his) symbolic death—provides the material point for determining all that precedes, determining it, in fact, as a goal-oriented unfolding toward that final point: as Bildung.

The X-ray photograph, however, dissociates both the moments of truth and of death from the end point and relocates them, along with their joint authority, elsewhere and earlier on (and on). The decisive, even revelatory interpretive moment now occurs when the doctor—in this case Behrens—presents the evidence of his X-ray photo, the ghostly image that confronts the patient in the midst of seeming life with the hard fact of his or her mortality (see 261/183). Death is no longer appointed as a terminus, imparting a structure of analeptic closure to a life. The interpretation or imposition of the subject's life significance (*Sinn des Lebens*) is abrupted forward—or, if you will, is simply taken away. This is, as it were, an intensification of the "crisis of death" that Barthes associates with the advent of photography in general, a crisis in which what perishes, what "has been but is no more," becomes at once more fixed and more flat, leaving one waiting with "nothing to say," and it has rather particular consequences for both the sense of self and the regime of Bildung in Mann's novel.[63] As Settembrini notes, the X-ray photo becomes "a kind of identification, like a passport or membership card" ("wie ein Ausweis sozusagen, ein Pass oder eine Mitgliedskarte" [337/238]), an identification paper comparable to the narrative scroll Wilhelm Meister receives at the end of his novel, the scroll that consigns Wilhelm's identity, marks his Bildung, and signals his assimilation into the select social group of the Tower Society. But in contrast with Wilhelm's scroll, Hans's X-ray is issued much earlier on in his story and somehow evades the authoritative nexus of Bildung. As one of the key exchanges between Settembrini and Hans about X-ray photography underscores (275/193), there is a conspicuously antagonistic relation between the traditional truth regime of humanistic pedagogy and that of the *photographische Platte,* such that Hans senses the latter refutes the former in both its political and literary pretensions ("sogar die Republik und den schönen Stil"). And I would say this is not only because of the hard facts of the photograph, which cut through the flattering, shaping illusions of Bildung, but also because the X-ray deprives Settembrini's program of its equally illusory truth in endings, its teleologically secured authority over the issues of self, society, and even narrative (leaving one with "nothing to say," even as Settembrini himself is here reduced to silence ["zum Verstummen gebracht"]).

There is a further ramification of this dissociation from the end of both truth and death that is of equal importance for the notion of the subject, the role of Bildung, and the form of the Bildungsroman in *The Magic Mountain.* For in the course of weakening the regime of truth in endings—that is, weakening the functioning of endings, a hallmark of modernist texts plainly evident here—X-ray photographs also and inseparably therefrom transform both truth and death, for all their hard and clear objectivity, into something far more evanescent, momentary, fleeting, mutable, and questionable, and not only from the face-saving vantage of a Settembrinian skepticism. The truth of an X-ray, far from being able to determine and shape a life, a self, is soon outdated: all the patients on the Magic Mountain need regularly to have their X-rays retaken, and no one, patient and physician alike, can long depend on the truth of any given photo (see 294/207). Truth fades and is almost dead on arrival.

This is an aspect of X-rays that falls again within the photographic field but one normally opposed to painting. It was the custom with painted portraits, as for example with that of Hans's grandfather, that only one needed to be produced of a person. It could then be scrutinized for revealing details about that figure's personality, past, and even future prospects, because, as with Hans's grandfather, the painting was taken to represent the authentic, abiding, auratic self—indeed, one of the crucial relations between the realm of death and the otherwise lifelike, life-affirming world of painting is the sweeping interpretive authority each is able to impose on the preceding life, a relation more than just patent in the case of Senator Castorp. Moreover, we see something extremely similar in the case of the Certificate of Apprenticeship (*Lehrbrief*) Wilhelm Meister receives at the end of his training, a record of his life that is, revealingly, referred to as "his picture outside of himself, not of course as in a mirror, a second self, but as in a portrait, another self" ("sein Bild ausser sich, zwar nicht, wie im Spiegel, ein zweites Selbst, sondern wie im Porträt, ein anderes Selbst").[64] This "Porträt"—the only such narrative produced of Wilhelm—is subsequently scrutinized by Wilhelm for clues about his past self and durative identity and is even employed by him to interpret and represent himself to himself and others. The Bild is, at it were, the shaping representation of his Bildung, the durative, cumulative, and singular truth of his authentic self.

Unlike painted portraits, however, photographs are characteristically never singular, and throughout *The Magic Mountain,* from Hans's very first days (see 67/43) until very near the end, photos—and not only X-rays—are being taken and distributed among the patients and doctors. For all their increased claim to true representation, their representation is never true for long; another photograph is always needed. This fleeting truth of the photograph, including the X-ray, tends to produce a correspondingly ephemeral sense of self-image, which is no longer conceived, portraitlike, as a single, sustained, and constantly "true" identity but rather as a series of possibly disconnected and always changing truths. And this changed notion of the self—whose incredibly diminished sense of durative value and dizzyingly accelerated pace of obsolescence exists side by side with the new notion of data storage and master templating also introduced by photography—also effects the project of Bildung, not least in its loss of a goal, of faith in cumulative progress and the staying power of its fixed ideals.

THE PROBLEM OF THE MISSING FIXATIVE

The loss of durative value and the advent of momentary truths that accompanies the insinuation of photography into the thematic space traditionally occupied by painted Bilder in the Bildungsroman reflects a paradox marveled at by Barthes: the photographic regime not only newly allows the abiding, affective preservation of "what has been" as never before; it also abolishes the reign of, the belief in, permanency, fixedness. As Barthes says, the age of the photograph is not only that of extended historical consciousness but also of "revolutions, contestations, assassinations, explosions, in short, of impatience, of everything that denies ripening."[65] And this is yet another avenue by which the photograph enters the realm of death and changes it: the emergence of the reign of the ephemeral, the presence of death itself less as monument and more as fleeting moment.

There is an additional aspect of the photograph that also contributes to the assertion of the evanescent: its natural tendency to dissolve away. Early photographs in particular had a marked tendency to succumb to what Benjamin calls fog: the quality of the image soon faded, weakened, even vanished. This tendency gave added poignancy to one of the most famous early photographs, depicting the deathbed scene of an adolescent girl and titled *Fading Away* (1858)—for such was the recognized fate not only of the human subject but of her photographic record as well.[66] There were two known ways for postponing this process—postponing but not negating, for the fading away, vanishing, even dying of the photograph can only be deferred, not denied: either the photographic image could be hermetically sealed and stored, or a chemical fixative could be applied. Such a fixative was, moreover, also needed for another part of the photograph, the negative, which was also prone to a progressive deterioration, albeit of a different kind. Without the timely, interceding application of a fixative, the negative plate would continue to be sensitive to both light and the developing, corrosive or etching chemical solvent, such that the Entwicklung would continue unchecked, and the stored image would, as it were, self-consume.

While the process of hermetically sealed storage receives abundant attention in Mann's novel, there is, of course, no mention of this other aspect of photographic fixing. But it is nonetheless interesting to me that its problem makes itself felt in ways that further confirm the place of the novel within the age of the photograph. Indeed, it presents itself in or as its absence, as the problem of the missing fixative, and in both its applications. So, for instance, the apparent Oedipal triumph achieved in "Walpurgisnacht" at the end of the novel's first half proves to lack staying power, to be unable to keep itself fixed, and so it needs to be repeated, to be retaken, first in the remarkable vision of the chapter "Snow" ("Schnee"), and then again in the late encounter with the blurred (*verwischt*) figure of Mynheer Peeperkorn. Each of these scenes repeats, or updates, the lesson and tableau of "Walpurgisnacht," with

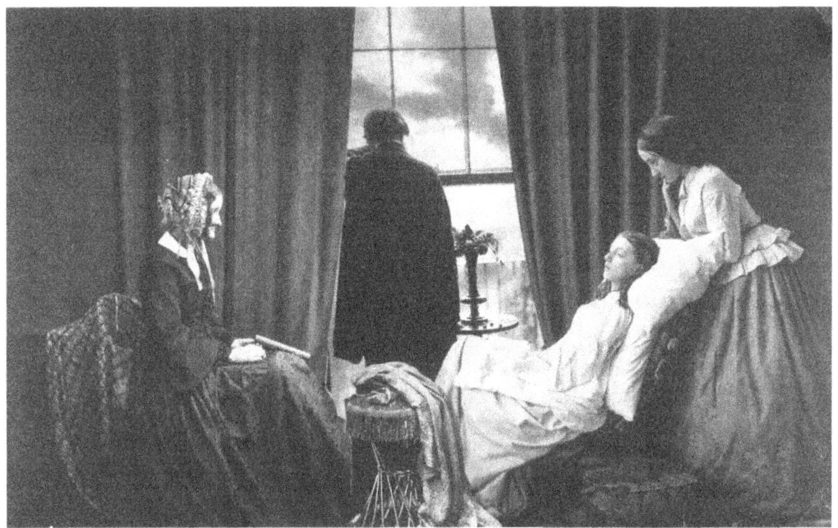

Henry Peach Robinson, *Fading Away*. Combination albumen print, 1858. Courtesy George Eastman House, Rochester, New York.

the latter especially marked both as rather exemplarily Oedipal (also again with evasions, in fact the same evasions) and as rather unusual in its felt need to introduce a new major character and a by and large redundant scenario so far into the narrative (758/538). But the retake is required precisely because of the fleeting character of the previous takes, perhaps most evidently so in "Snow." Hörisch argues—persuasively, as usual—that Hans's mountain epiphany proves itself the most Oedipal moment in the novel, retaking many of the same figures and subjects earlier depicted in "Walpurgisnacht."[67] And yet I would argue that it also proves—again in ways that impact the apparatus of Oedipal Bildung—one of the most photographic, at least in the sense addressed here, in terms of Barthes's paradox. Not only does Hans's classical vision evidence the abiding, affective preservation of what has been, the certain assertion of the far-distant past (in all its particular *and* generic features)—somehow stored on the negative *cliché* of Hans's unconscious memory plate, and now developed, made manifest and incontestably visible and present—it also evidences the loss of permanence, the inevitable fading away of all the phantasmatic spectacle. Hans experiences that fading away as surely and centrally as he does the vision itself. It is soon paling ("im Verbleichen begriffen" [688/489]), just as the memory image of Pribislav Hippe "gradually disappeared again into the fog" ("allmählich wieder . . . in den Nebeln entschwunden war" [172/120]) or, in a subsequent scene, as the spirit Holger's poem is no sooner heard than its details and revelations begin to fade from consciousness, impossible to hold fast, "so that the poem would now inevitably fade into forgetfulness, in fact was already fading into forgetfulness, due to a certain incapacity to hold it fast" ("so daß nun das Gedichtete unfehlbar in Vergessenheit geraten werde, ja, leider allergrößtenteils schon in Vergessenheit geraten sei, vermöge einer gewissen Unhaltbarkeit" [923/655]), or as Hans himself at the novel's end simply disappears from our sight into the rain and dusk ("in dem Regen, der Dämmerung, kommt er uns aus den Augen" [994/706])— fading away, even dying, without leaving a permanent mark or trace, his Bild and Bildung simply dissolving amid the "impatient" explosions of the First World War.

The second aspect of the problem of the missing fixative, which results in the continued, unchecked exposure or sensitivity to both light and applied chemicals of the photographic negative, such as ultimately to destroy its stored distinctions between light and dark values and so dissolve its Bild in a moment of overexposure and self-consumption, is also suggestively present in the novel, in the "negative" figure of the corrosive Naphta, whose very name means "solvent" and whose *ätzend* (517/366) effect is such as to destroy all the imprinted distinctions of Settembrini's intended development of Hans Castorp's tabula—indeed, to destroy all distinctions between Settembrini's positive and negative values—and so to render both Hans's and the novel's own development out of control, excessive, destructive of its own ground. This effect is especially evident in Naphta's lengthy debates with Settembrini, which threaten not only to dissolve Hans's imprinted values but also (as most readers will attest) to consume the very form of narrative representation—a mode of photographic violence that seems to anticipate the raging social decomposition of the novel's end, so different from the standard Bild of social integration and stability previously associated with the conclusion of Bildung and the Bildungsroman.

OUTSIDE THE FRAME: PARAPHOTOGRAPHY
AND THE ENT-WICKLUNG OF BILDUNG

No doubt the strangest and most consequential instance of the transformative introduction of photography into the traditional schema of Bildung in the novel, including the erotic schema, comes in the late chapter, "Highly Questionable" ("Fragwürdigstes"): "the strangest hours our hero's young life had ever known til then, and . . . they remained the strangest hours he would ever experience" ("die sonderbarsten Stunden, die unseres Helden junges Leben bis dahin aufzuweisen hatte; und die . . . die überhaupt sonderbarsten blieben, die er erlebte" [939/667]). The chapter presents the séance in Edhin Krokowski's dark chamber, where, through the medium Elly Brand, there develops the manifest image of the departed Joachim Ziemßen. Richard Koc points out the link between this produced image and the previous ones of Hippe and in "Snow," whose photographic character has already been discussed.[68] But the role of photography here proves far more thoroughly implicated and decisive, not only for the scene in particular but also for the novel as a whole.

The chapter comes, we should note, immediately after and in some ways as the culmination of two others that are of particular importance to our general focus. First, in "The Great Stupor" ("Der grosse Stumpfsinn"), Mann couples the sudden rage for *Liebhaberphotographie* (amateur, or lit. "lover's," photography) and its concomitant point of honor, to develop oneself ("Ehrensache, selbst zu entwickeln" [872/619]) with Hofrat Behrens's experiment of extracting bacteria from Hans Castorp and exposing them on a culture plate, bacteria that belatedly ("nachträglich" [882/626]) develop and are then reinjected into Hans Castorp himself. The affinities between the fields of tuberculosis and photography are many, especially in regard to their common processes of exposure and development, and these affinities are shrewdly elaborated during the course of Mann's novel.[69] But what is most at issue here is how in both cases those processes that had previously remained almost exclusively internalized and within the properly psychological are momentarily externalized, brought outside of Hans Castorp. As we will see, the same externalization is also centrally on display in the parapsychological experiment of the séance, where the normally internal is also brought momentarily (and somewhat abominably) outside, or "para."[70]

"The Great Stupor" is followed by "Fullness of Harmony" ("Fülle des Wohllauts"), the chapter just before "Highly Questionable." It is here that the technologization of aesthetic media—and of the human subject—reaches its most pointed thematic representation since the X-ray of the novel's first half, in the form of the gramophone and its black plates (*schwarze Platten*) that, like those of photography, invisibly store and then reproduce their data. As Behrens says, the gramophone represents "the German soul up-to-date" (885/628), a technologization of the modern *Geist* analogous in almost every way to that occasioned elsewhere in the novel by the photograph.[71] The particulars of this chapter have been well analyzed by others. For our purposes we need only secure one general point, namely, the overall trajectory of the chapter. It begins with the narrator's vocal, and unusually foregrounded, enthusiasm for the new technology, "the truly musical in its modern mechanical form" ("das treusinnig Musikalische in neuzeitlich-mechanischer Gestalt" [885/628]), and develops toward his troubled analysis at the end of its counterpart, Schubert's "Lindenbaum," the paradigm of "artificial folksongs, if one may put it that way without impugning their in-timacy with the word 'artificial'" ("künstliche Volkslieder, wenn man so sagen durfte, ohne durch das Wort 'künstlich' ihrer Innigkeit zu nahe zu treten" [889/631])—in other words, also "the truly musical in its modern mechanical form," a technologization of the *geistig* and aesthetic, much like the gramophone itself (a technologization also evident in the abstract technical language the narrator deploys to describe Schubert's "Kunstgesang"). It is this technologized manifestation of the original folk-song that makes it seem, much as Mann also describes Bildung and the Bildungsroman, something especially, indeed exemplarily German ("etwas sogar besonderes und exemplarisch Deutsches" [903/640]) but that also makes it seem deathful and violently threatening.[72] Indeed, as we soon learn, Schubert's "Kunstgesang" is depicted as foreboding the disastrous venture of the coming war—the first fully mechanized war—which is thus posed as the almost logical consequence of the convergence of the German soul and its technological development or, in other words, of Bildung in its modern mechanical form.

These two chapters provide the immediate, larger context within the novel for a reading of "Highly Questionable." But we need also to situate it within the still larger context of the Bildungsroman tradition itself. I would like to suggest that the séance scene occupies the same functional position in the narrative of Hans Castorp's Bildung as does Wilhelm Meister's initiation into the secret realm of the Tower Society in Goethe's original Bildungsroman, *Wilhelm Meister's Apprenticeship,* wherein Wilhelm is ushered into a dark and mysterious chamber and initiated into the esoteric practices, magical manipulations, and well-nigh cabbalistic beliefs of this select group, after which (or through which) Wilhelm's apprenticeship is effectively brought to completion.[73] Two aspects of Wilhelm's culminating experience are of special importance for us. First, Wilhelm here receives the script or scroll of his own narrative that is subsequently described as "his picture outside of himself, not of course as in a mirror, a second self, but as in a portrait, another self."[74] This portrait "Bild" signals for Wilhelm a sense of self-recovery and revelation, a sense of the restoration of what was lost or hidden and yet nonetheless archeteleologically aimed at. It represents perhaps the clearest instance of the conflation of Bild and Bildung so central to Goethe's novel and its nineteenth-century descendents. The conflation, its centrality, and its signaled sense are further underscored by the unexpected mention here by the Tower Society of the long-lost painting of the sickly prince, which, along with the narrative scroll, is then presented to Wilhelm. Like the scriptive portrait "Bild," this Bild has also been secretly shaping and scripting Wilhelm's Bildung all along toward this culminating moment. It too maintains the crucial correlation of Bild and Bildung.[75]

Second, it is during this same initiation scene that Wilhelm Meister becomes, as it were, a father. He is presented at the final moment by the Tower Society with the boy Felix and is assured that Felix is indeed his son—underscoring the ironic and perverse but also crucial point that, in the Bildungsroman, paternity is granted only by patriarchy. These two features, then—the ascension to the position of father and the acquisition of (in some ways the recovery of) his Bild—are presented as the twinned conditions for the completion of Wilhelm's Bildung.[76]

"Highly Questionable" does not, of course, initiate Hans Castorp into the esoteric machinations of an eighteenth-century secret society but rather into those of a quite topical and recognizably twentieth-century one, one that famously occupied such figures as Conan Doyle, Houdini, Yeats, Rilke (and even, let it be said, Freud): spiritualism or, rather, "mediumistic studies." In fact, Conan Doyle and Houdini both attended séances featuring the well-known medium Eva C., who was the special protégé of Dr. Freiherr Albert von Schrenck-Notzing, a Munich-based doctor of sexual pathology whose forays into spiritualism and parapsychology Mann also knew, both through personal experience—he too attended several sessions during 1922 and 1923—and through a reading of von Schrenck-Notzing's quite popular book *Phenomena of Materialisation* (*Materialisationsphänomene* [1912/1923]).[77] Mann based his séance chapter in *The Magic Mountain* on the work of von Schrenck-Notzing (or, rather, as with his procedure in *Felix Krull,* Mann chose to juxtapose the high culture discourse of the Goethean Bildungsroman with such a low, somewhat ill-reputed popular text). But Mann also wrote about both his personal experiences and von Schrenck-Notzing's parapsychological writings in several other places besides *The Magic Mountain,* most notably in his 1924 essay "Occult Experiences" ("Okkulte Erlebnisse"). Clearly, von Schrenck-Notzing's work was deeply important to Mann's thinking in ways that linked it firmly to major preoccupations of his day.

For our purposes, von Schrenck-Notzing's work is significant in both a general and a more particular way. In general, his work registers the event of the technologization of this cultural discourse as well. Over and again, von Schrenck-Notzing is at pains to evoke the advances in science leading to new conceptions—advances such as X-rays and (color) photography, energy physics and the philosophy of Bergson—in order to mark the shift between traditional spiritism and his new mediumistic studies. The highlighted technologization of the parapsychological manifests itself both conceptually, in the terminology and explanation systems he deploys, and practically, in the apparatus and procedures he mobilizes to produce, monitor, and record the "spiritual" phenomena. In regard to the former, we should remark how certain equivocal overlaps between the emergence of psychoanalysis and nineteenth-century occultism have long been noted, and certainly one of the more significant of these overlaps is the quite similar reconception of the spiritual realm in terms of recent technological innovations. What the one does for the interiorized, the other does for the exteriorized *Geist.*

In particular, von Schrenck-Notzing's research stakes its own peculiar contribution to the scientificization of mediumistic studies on its unprecedented implication of the technology of photography. (This claim is no doubt exaggerated, as the connection between photography and twentieth-century occultism is rather broad.)[78] In any case, the implication of photography takes two distinct forms in von Schrenck-Notzing's practice. Overtly, he undertakes to employ photographic cameras for the objective registration (*objektive Registrierung*) of his occult phenomena, for the provision of positive proofs (*positive Beweise*) of what was observed during his séances.[79] To this end, he set up cameras in the séance room (his book includes close to two hundred supporting photographs); indeed, he began to replace human participant observers with his photographic recorders, gradually working up to nine such devices, including several stereoscopic cameras, elaborate flashing magnesium lights, and even something called a veroscope. Meanwhile, the number of human subjects present was reduced to as few as three. The ostensible logic motivating this substitution was that human senses were the less reliable and the more easily deceived. Photography became the operant standard of truth, and its mechanical devices replaced their *geistig* equivalents (human eyes, etc.).

Von Schrenck-Notzing's overt implication of the technology of photography furnishes the background for a more covert but no less important one. Photography provides not only the concrete technology that is to establish the objective truth of the objects under study but also the metaphorical regime, the conceptual framework for the production of the objects themselves. For instance, the séance room itself was converted by von Schrenck-Notzing into a photographic darkroom called the Laboratorium, replete with the red light and other appropriate accoutrements. Ostensibly, or at least in the first place, the conversion was meant to accommodate the cameras and flash lights, that is, to provide the conditions required by the newly introduced, objectively recording photo technology. But this reconception of the room also yielded a reconception of the occult phenomena themselves, which, we are told, only develop (*entwickeln*) in feeble red light and darkness and would be destroyed by bright white lights. In other words, the traditional spiritist requirement of the darkened room becomes refigured in terms of the new instruments of evidence: it is admitted that the phenomena themselves require certain conditions ("daß die Phänomene selbst gewisse Bedingungen fordern"), which are justified by a scientific analogy: "Do not certain chemical combinations require to be formed in darkness in the laboratory? Do not photographic plates also require a red light?" ("müssen nicht gewisse chemische Verbindungen im Dunkel der Laboratorien hergestellt werden? Verlangen nicht auch die photographischen Platten Rotlicht?").[80] My

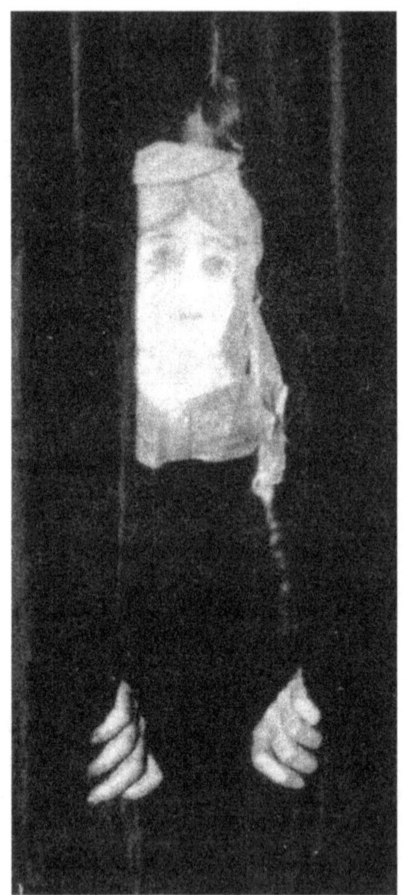

Albert von Schrenck-Notzing, *Figure 107: Author's Third Flashlight Photograph, 5 August 1912.* Note the medium's head, viz hair-part, behind the teleplastic image. From *Phenomena of Materialisation,* 180.

point would be that the parallel with photography is not a mere metaphor illustrating the mode of occult appearances but is instead a decisive factor in determining that mode to begin with, that the veracity of the concerned phenomena is anticipated by their appearing in the form of the very technology that is to establish their truth.

We see the basis for this claim in a number of details besides the instance of the newly conceived requirements for the traditional lighting conditions. For example, we see it in the infamous black chamber (*schwarze Kabinett*) in which the medium was enclosed during the séance. In some ways, the black chamber simply doubles the darkroom-like condition of the larger room, but in other ways it tends also to turn the medium him- or herself into a kind of camera—a camera obscura, so to speak. This latter effect was reinforced by the black curtains hung over the front opening of the *Kabinett/camera,* which would quickly be opened and shut and through whose aperture one saw the flashlike (*blitzartig*) appearance and disappearance of the so-called teleplastic images, in strict coordination with the *blitzartig* flashing of the magnesium lights and opening and shutting of the real cameras' shutters.[81] And the impression was even more powerfully reinforced by the requisite all-enveloping, or coating, black dress of the medium who was placed in the cabinet, an outfit described by von Schrenck-Notzing as an apparent necessity for the development of the teleplastic images, insofar as only against such a black surface could the hardly visible material images be seen ("heben sich bereits die kaum sichtbaren materialistierten [Gebilde] ab"), transforming the medium inside the "camera" into something closely resembling a negative photographic plate.[82] As Kittler says, a medium is a medium is a medium.[83] But consider how curious and significant the setup of the entire room has become. We have a red-lit darkroom equipped with up to nine cameras, all in place of human observers, and these cameras are all focused on the similarly dehumanized, black-coated medium enclosed in a black box with its aperture of quickly opened and shut curtains—one cameralike apparatus mimicking the other, with the refiguring of the human, or *geistig,* as camera in both cases.[84] This is, as it were, exactly the same chiastic arrangement as that just mentioned for the photograph's "truth" apparatus over and against the photolike production of the images they are to prove. Indeed, the former is the concrete realization of the latter and contributes mightily to the latter's persuasive effect.

Von Schrenck-Notzing's refiguring of the medium in photographic terms is not, however, limited to his or her external trappings and props. Rather, as he repeatedly emphasizes, the medium him- or herself must be refigured as a technological *Instrument,* and this is accomplished through the correct training (*richtige Heranbildung*), education (*Erziehung*), and development (*Entwicklung*) of the medium.[85] In general, this pedagogic development involved the gradual displacement of the medium's own traditional spiritistic conceptualization of his or her activity by a more scientific, instrumentalized one. In particular, it involved von Schrenck-Notzing's gradual development of the medium's innate gift for imagistic production by a suggestive education (*suggestive Erziehung*) that worked on his or her enhanced impressionability and sensitivity and a gradual training and adaptation to von Schrenck-Notzing's wishes to enable her or him better to differentiate her or his products, make them sharper and more plastic, and to expose them longer to light.[86] In other words, the pedagogic Entwicklung was intended to transform the occult medium more purely into a high-quality, high-resolution photographic medium so as to form a firm empirical basis for the study by photographic means ("um ein möglichst umfassendes empirisches Fundament zur Beurteilung [der Teleplastie] durch zahlreiche photographische Aufnahmen zu schaffen"), to transform him or her *within* into something of a camera.[87] Again, a medium is a medium is a medium.

Finally, and as already implicit in all that precedes, the very ideo- or teleplastic images themselves, the parapsychological phenomena produced by the cameralike medium inside the cameralike box in the darkroomlike room—these images also partake of the photographic in such a way as greatly to contribute to their effective truth value. The teleplastic images are explicitly and repeatedly said to develop (*entwickeln*), indeed to pass through several stages of development.[88] More specifically, they are said to develop out of images stored subconsciously on the medium's memory and into manifest figures that form outside of the medium's body (*blitzartig*, and only under the appropriate conditions, in the darkroom and with a trained developer such as von Schrenck-Notzing)—in other words, an externalization of a normally interior psychological mechanism. Von Schrenck-Notzing makes the connections between memory, photography, and his materialization phenomena appear directly in his description of so-called middle stages on the way to full-blown teleplastic images, stages wherein he obtained on prepared photographic plates impressions that corresponded to the medium's thought pictures (*Gedankenbilder*), in much the same way as another cited experimenter had developed his medium's ability to transfer such thought pictures directly onto blank pieces of paper.[89] Von Schrenck-Notzing calls this phenomenon "Gedankenphotographie," or thought photography, and signals the factors of externalization and objectification as of the greatest importance for an understanding of materialization phenomena ("von grösster Tragweite . . . zum Verständnis der Materialisationsphänomene").[90] Clearly, photography provides the decisive link for media-ting the transition between the normal, interior psychology of memory (à la Hello, Freud, Bergson, et al.) and the paranormal, external parapsychology of teleplastic images. But in providing that link, photography just as clearly reveals the essential affinity between the extraordinary processes of teleplastic development and formation and the ordinary processes of Bildung qua Entwicklung that have been our concern throughout. For the complicated (deceitful, yet effective) chiastic fashion in which the external, objectively determining technology of von Schrenck-Notzing and his photographic apparatus are metaphorically installed inside the medium as a psychological apparatus, which then in turn produces or develops into an objective, externalized form that can present itself to the "final link" and confirming authority of von Schrenck-Notzing and his attendant cameras, closely parallels the manner in which, for example, the painting of the sickly prince is installed in Wilhelm Meister's psyche (as an Oedipal exemplar) and then figures his Bild-ung toward the fully realized subject who presents himself to the final authority of the Tower Society and their Bilder. And this confirms how the mechanism for truth production deployed by von Schrenck-Notzing's occult parapsychology, far from being something eccentric, falls instead centrally within the orbit of the interacting spheres of photography and Bildung followed by Mann throughout his novel.

I still need to mention one more crucial component of the constellation of forces at work in von Schrenck-Notzing's séance sittings. His efforts at the development of both the medium and his or her materialized images not only bring together the regimes of photography and Bildung but also, inevitably, these with that of sexuality. The implication of the erotic, and especially the feminine erotic, in the occult practices of the nineteenth century is, of course, well established[91]—in their subtle linkage and release of illicit subconscious forces or, less generously, in their similar invitation to credulous seduction—and so it is hardly incidental that, although famous for his work in parapsychology, von Schrenck-Notzing began his career as a sexual pathologist.[92] But what concerns me is how his technologization of mediumistic studies reconfigured or affected the erotic involvement as well. There should be no surprise in learning that the instrumentalization of the medium and setting in no way lessened the operant eroticism. Instead, in some respects at least, it increased it. For instance, ostensibly in the interests of controlling possible fraud, the medium was not only undressed and then redressed but all of his or her bodily cavities were regularly probed, including the rectum and, for women, the vagina—out of both of which, interestingly enough, the Bilder were said to develop or be (re)produced.[93] This (usually digital) probing was always done at the insistence of the supervising authority, that is, our good doctor von Schrenck-Notzing, but it was also frequently done at the request of the medium him- or herself, sometimes after as well as before each sitting. Moreover, von Schrenck-Notzing also remarks on a point I will be expanding on, namely, the similarity of the medium's production pains to those of childbirth—with the result that metaphors of engendering (*erzeugen*) and conceiving (*empfangen*) become at times almost interchangeable with those of developing.[94]

The technologization, or scientificization, of the occult practices sustains and changes the significance of the sexual character of the practices. This is apparent in respect to both of the instances just mentioned, and in both the changes are most emphatic in respect to gender, which in each case is subject to the technology's characteristic "neutralizing" effect. So, for example, because the disrobing and digital probing were supposedly nonsexual, they could be, and were, practiced with the same moral (or cultural) impunity whether the medium was a young boy or a young girl, and similarly whether the appointed *Kontrolleur* was a man or a woman. Thus, while seemingly (and perhaps also actually) perpetuating a certain gendered model of power— man over woman, man over machine[95]—the new practice also broke down such a model, permitting a certain otherwise illicit homoeroticism or, rather, a certain erotic equivocation, an oscillation, or *Schwanken,* between the human and the instrument. Similarly, because the birthing was not biological but technological—indeed, photographic—the birthing parent(s) could be interchangeably male or female. In this case, the equivocation between the natural and the mechanical yields something potentially both erotic and disconcertingly monstrous—but more on that in a moment.

Many of the details and much of the rhetorical structure of von Schrenck-Notzing's *Phenomena of Materialisation* find their way into Mann's work, including the crucial implication of the fields of photography, sexuality, and Bildung. The first two are most foregrounded in the essay "Occult Experiences." Mann mentions the distinctions between spiritualism and the new "scientific" occultism, including its new vocabulary and conceptual apparatus. He meticulously describes the

Laboratorium setting for the séance, outfitted with "a red-shaded lamp [and] cluttered with photographic apparatus and such as needed for magnesium flash-lights" ("ein rotverhülltes Lämpchen [und] unordentlich angefüllt mit photographischen Apparaten und solchen für Magnesium-Blitzlicht"), such that the séance room resembled a photographic studio ("einem photographischen Atelier glich").[96] The black chamber is noted (though not actually used in the ensuing session), as is the medium's all-enveloping black body stocking. The medium himself, the famous Willi S. (as opposed to Eva C., the primary medium in Schrenck-Notzing's book), is presented as a delicate organic instrument (*heikel-organisches Instrument*) through which the teleplastic images become *entwickelt*. And the images themselves are presented as objectified externalizations of unconscious images stored in the medium's memory (and are subsequently described as techno-organic formations ["eine organisch-technische Ausbildung"]).

Mann also dwells on the clearly erotically charged mechanics of the production. He lingers over the undressing and then reclothing of Willi's brown, boyish body and the discretely exchanged or averted glances of the men and women present. Mann himself was assigned (but later abdicated) the privileged role of supervisory *Kontrolleur.* He describes the probing of Willi's provocatively proffered (oral) cavity; indeed, in the separately published debriefing reports delivered back to von Schrenck-Notzing himself, Mann even brings up Willi's erections and ejaculations ("Erektionen und selbst Spermergüsse") during the séance proper, apparently while being closely held by said *Kontrolleur.*[97] Moreover, as in von Schrenck-Notzing's own work, the sexual dimension to this paraphotographic process is further captured through the evocation of childbirth, although childbirth of a doubly unnatural kind: as Mann exclaims, "A masculine maternity ward in red-lit darkness!" ("Eine männliche Wochenstube im Rotdunkel!"),[98] with both qualifiers, the all male agents and the photographic conditions, converging to engender the erotic anomaly. Finally, let us also note that this convergence here of the homoerotic and photographic is actually somewhat more involved, although in just that way we have observed in Mann before. The ghostly spirit for whom Willi is the "plastic" presence is a woman, Minna, and the resultant equivocal, oscillating doubleness or neutralizing of Willi's gender—itself coupled with the oscillating doubleness of "his" status between human and machine—is a decisive feature of both his homoerotic attraction and his photographic identity.

Again, many of the details from both von Schrenck-Notzing's book and Mann's own essay find their way into the chapter "Highly Questionable" in *The Magic Mountain,* including the crucial implication of the fields of photography and sexuality, but both these fields have also been somewhat transformed by their own implication in the novel's especial thematic concern with Bildung. The references to photography are numerous, although, as I will elaborate in a moment, perhaps not as numerous as we might expect. The sessions are supervised by the psycho-photographer Krokowski and are presented as the logical, even necessary culmination to the development of his lectures, that is, his interest in the "hidden activities of love and transformation back into conscious affect" ("verkappter Liebesbetätigung und Rückverwandlung in den bewußt gemachten Affekt" [908/644]). At the end of the first session in which he takes part, Hans Castorp finds Clawdia Chauchat's X-ray negative/diapositive "apported" into his lap, the final issue of this test run, as it were, for the séance proper. Hans Castorp's subsequent decision to participate in the séance and to call forth the image of Joachim Ziemßen is based on Hans's recollection of his X-ray visit with his cousin, where he viewed Joachim's ghostly, photographic interior—an experience that already, through the evocation of the clairvoyant great-aunt (*seherische Urtante* [306/215; see also 913/648]), linked together the occult and this most recent innovation in photographic technology. And the parallel with the X-ray is consistently maintained throughout the chapter (e.g., 931/661, 936/664).[99]

The indices of photography are also evident in the setup. Krokowski's ordination room (*Ordinationszimmer*) with its adjoining *Kabinett* has been revamped, furnished with the requisite red lights and black curtains over the windows, in ways that deliberately recall the improvised darkrooms described in "The Great Stupor." Again, the opposition to the destructive effect of the overhead electric light is clearly signaled. As Krokowski explains, the special lighting conditions are not to be understood in the sense of mystification, a mere matter of setting the mood ("im Sinne der Stimmungsmache und Mystifikation"), but instead as the necessary practical conditions for this scientific (*wissenschaftlich*) process: "The nature of the forces at issue and under investigation were such that they simply could not develop in white light" ("Die Natur der hier in Frage stehenden und zu studierenden Kräfte bringe es nun einmal mit sich, daß sie bei Weisslicht sich nicht zu entwickeln . . . vermöchten" [935–36/664]. Mention is made earlier of the complete "Bildung" of a spiritual limb [929/659]).

Finally, the convergence here of the vocabularies of photography, Bildung, and parapsychology—all with the proleptic implication that the final product of the séance, the ideoplastic Bild of Joachim, be understood in these same terms—also appears in relation to the medium herself. The glasslike, clear, and pure ("gläsern-keusche, klare") Elly Brand no sooner appears in the picture ("auf der Bildfläche" [910/645]) than Krokowski himself is in the picture ("im Bilde" [912/645]) in order to discipline her to the requirements of scientific mediumicity (914/648–49, 927/658, 929/659), to transform her more properly into a despiritualized (and dehumanized) medium, "to develop the possibilities latent within her" ("die in ihr schlummernden Möglichkeiten zu entwickeln" [914/649]) and in particular to develop her ideoplastic, image-producing capabilities and products (929/659). That is, as in von Schrenck-Notzing's work, both the medium and her ectoplastic images are configured in more or less photographic terms and at the same time assimilated into the thematics of Bildung qua Entwicklung.

The sexual and erotic dimension of the séance scene is as conspicuous as its photographic one, if not more so. Hans Castorp describes his anticipation as much like on an occasion years before, when, a bit tipsy, he had joined some companions and set out for the first time to visit a brothel in Sankt Pauli ("als er sich, etwas bekneipt, mit Kameraden zum erstenmal angeschickt hatte, ein Mädchenhaus in Sankt Pauli zu besuchen" [932/661]).[100] Then, as he sits with the seductively clothed Elly's legs clasped tightly between his knees, and she whispers her "Ja" caressingly into his ear, Hans experiences the gooseflesh whose erotic properties were laid out earlier, in "Humanioria." And the conception of the séance's manifestation in terms of childbirth is so explicit as not to need comment. In fact, the chapter seems almost more about this metaphor than its actual subject. But we should at least mention how the childbirth here, which is to say the production of the teleplastic image, is still equally kept under the metaphor of the photographic, as the description of "this maternity ward in red-lit darkness" ("dieser . . . Wochenstube im Rotlicht" [940/667]) again underscores.

It is the sexual, and especially the sexual metaphorical, dimension of the chapter that most forcefully pulls it into the orbit of the Bildungsroman tradition, aligning it in particular with the moment where Wilhelm Meister receives his fatherhood from the Tower Society. In fact, in the complicated thematic cluster that renders the apparition of Joachim Ziemßen here simultaneously a child (Hans's child) and a "Bild" (out of the lost past and yet also a proleptic image of Hans Castorp himself, an other self ["ein anderes Selbst"]), the culmination of this chapter manages to combine the twinned conditions of completed Bildung in *Wilhelm Meister:* the acquisition of paternity and the restoration of his "Porträt" (or alternatively, of the painting of the sickly prince).

The evocation of this Goethean pre-text, or *Vor-bild,* however, is probably less likely to suggest the similarities between the two moments of completed Bildung than it is to define their differences, differences that in many ways point to something gone conspicuously awry in the present case.[101] These differences strike me as of special significance for determining what has happened to the course of Bildung in its modernist manifestation, and in order to get at these differences, these aberrations, we can take the detour of describing the differences between the séance in "Highly Questionable" and that in its more immediate textual *Vorbild,* Mann's "Occult Experiences." The differences between the two Mann texts can, I believe, be attributed to the Bildung thematics of the novel, that is, both its alignment with and deliberate reworking of the generic conditions of Bildung. Thus, the differences between these two texts should help us to specify the terms of those between the other two texts, that is, between the Goethean *Vorbild* and *The Magic Mountain.*

There are three points at which Mann's two séance scenes differ that jump out at the reader, especially the reader intent upon following the photographic and erotic thematics of both scenes. In *The Magic Mountain,* the medium is described as wearing not the black bodystocking but instead a dressing gown–like robe of white crêpe ("ein schlafrockigen Gewand aus weissem Crêpe" [934/662–63]); the gender of the medium has been switched from the male Willi S. to the female Elly Brand; and there is no camera apparatus in evidence—indeed, the photographic is left conspicuously implicit rather than explicit throughout the scene. The first of these I consider relatively insignificant. The shift in the medium's gender identity is clearly a more important and consequential point than that of the coloring of the medium's clothing.[102]

One could, I suppose, speculate that Mann wished here to avoid the more or less overt homoeroticism of his actual sitting with Willi S., and moreover to avoid it for extratextual, social-political reasons rather than aesthetic ones. But we should also note that the engagement of a female medium allows Mann to situate and elaborate the séance scene more fully in terms of the novel's, and the tradition's, Bildung thematics, and in particular in terms of the Bildung thematics of paternity. Indeed, in arguing that the gender shift is motivated by the desire to make the moment more "properly" conform to the demands of Bildung, we could also account for the other essential feature of the shift, the figuring not only of the medium Elly Brand as female but also of her spirit, Holger, as male. For even as the former seems calculated to foreground the traditional, requisite conditions for the (metaphorical) production of Hans's paternity, so too the latter. As we recall from *Wilhelm Meister,* paternity is always the gift of the patriarchal powers in Bildung, always a rendering of the feminine as only the ventriloquistic vessel of male authority. In this respect, Holger's claim to be a poet becomes all important. And again, this reproduces the terms not only of *Wilhelm Meister* but also of much of *The Magic Mountain* itself, in particular of two crucial Bildung qua Oedipalization scenes, the "Snow" episode and "Walpurgisnacht," from both of which numerous details are composited into the present séance scene. For "Snow," Hans Castorp's Arcadian vision that culminates in his gory epiphanic visit into the forbidden but sacred feminine realm of the Mothers, is nonetheless all presented under the so-called name-of-the-father, that is, scripted according to the dictates of the novel's *Vorbilder* in Goethe (both *Faust* and "Et ego in Arcadia"), Nietzsche (*The Birth of Tragedy* [*Die Geburt der Tragödie*]), Stifter (*In the Bavarian Forest* [*Im Bayrischen Walde*]), and so on. Perhaps the paternity—or paternal society—of no other chapter is so patent. So too in "Walpurgisnacht," Hans's illicit encounter with Clawdia Chauchat remains under the inscriptive dictates of patriarchal figures, most notably of Settembrini with his Faustian script and of Hofrat Behrens with his Circean tableau. In each of these earlier instances, Hans Castorp's venture into both the feminine and deviant (or extraordinary) proved instead to be but a further initiation, or *Ordination,* into both the patriarchal and the normative. And the same argument could be made here for "Highly Questionable," bolstered by the observed gender shift of the medium, a shift that increases both the normative and male-dominated nature of this only ostensibly para-normal and il-licitly erotic experience.[103]

The shift and exchange of gender roles between the medium and her communicating spirit does not, however, only have the effect of re-inforcing the traditional Bildung structuration of the scene. They also clearly serve to dismantle it, to *ent-wickeln* it. For again, very much as with Clawdia Chauchat in "Walpurgisnacht," the erotic engagement of Hans Castorp with Elly Brand here remains an undeniably homoerotic one, and not only (or even) in that, as Hans is reminded, it is Holger whose knees he clasps between his knees and whose whispered "Ja" arouses his, Hans's, gooseflesh and confused erotic feelings—such that one might be tempted to argue that the overt heterosexual and norma-tive scenario merely covers the more important, and deviant, homosex-ual satisfaction. But the homoerotic character is also (or rather) asserted in how Elly Brand comes to assume the oscillating, double-gender na-ture that renders the meeting at once hetero- and homosexual in pre-cisely the manner that, we have seen, Mann designates as the homo-erotic. It is just this to-and-fro doubleness that motivates Elly Brand's association with the epicene "neutral" of *das Medium*—or with the whisper of "a sweet young thing" ("ein junges Blut" [938/666])—and that also motivates the portentous appearance of Clawdia's negative/di-apositive as the heralding token for the séance proper. Elly too repre-sents the same constantly and rapidly alternating arrangements of oppo-sition and identity, of hetero- and homorelation, between female and male, manifest and latent, life and death, and so on, as did Clawdia, or rather, as did the pairing of Clawdia and Hippe. In this case as well, it is just such a photo-homoeroticism that determines the operant erotics (incremented, as I will argue, by a homologously homoerotic quality to Elly's double, oscillating identity as human and as *Apparat*) and so too undercuts the Bildung dynamics or program of the scene. Despite all the marshaled apparatus of the patriarchal order and the decisive effort to fashion Hans as a properly Oedipalized, paternal "man," the picture of his desire remains resolutely double, indeterminate, unfixed: photo-graphic.

The gender doubleness and its challenge to the formative pro-gram of Bildung is not limited to the figure of Elly Brand; Hans Cas-torp's own gender proves decisively "neutral" as well. The doubleness to Hans's identity is not, to be sure, signaled by the token of a photo-graphic plate but instead by the other, similarly apported black plate in the scene, the record album of Gounod's *Margarethe*.[104] As the previous chapter, "Fullness of Harmony," has prepared, the record clearly positions Hans here in a feminine role—or, rather, because other topoi do not cease to function, it positions him in both a masculine and feminine role, as at once father *and* mother of the final, decisive Bild and child of the scene, which cannot appear until this other, second black plate is activated—which is to say, until Hans's own "feminine," reproductive and mediumistic quality is engaged. In this way, the apported black plate of the Margarethe album furnishes the needed complement to the apported X-ray black plate of Clawdia and so too the full complement of the operant system of reproduction activated to produce the teleplastic image of Joachim. For just as in "Walpurgisnacht" the photographic regime was represented not by Clawdia's X-ray alone but rather by an exchange of X-ray *Platten* between her and Hans, so here the system of representation stays double, involving both Elly/Holger and Hans/Margarethe. And the result of this added gender and technological dimension is a neutralization of both the reproductive process and its product, which seriously complicates the issue of paternity and manhood at stake in this culminating moment of Bildung qua Entwicklung. (It also helps motivate the important detail that Hans clasps Elly's knees inside his own: Hans is the one opened up here.)

The third and final point of difference between the essay "Occult Experiences" and the chapter "Highly Questionable" is undoubtedly the most significant one for our inquiry. Despite the numerous contextual indices to the pervading photographic regime—in the setup of the room, the depiction of the medium, the manner of the teleplastic phenomena, and especially the culminating appearance of the image of Joachim Ziemßen—there is no camera in the room; it is conspicuous in its absence. And yet, as my mention of the black plate of Gounod's opera already suggests, while there is no photographic apparatus per se, there is its functional equivalent in the phonographic apparatus. And I submit that, if we are fully to understand the role played by the record machine in the scene, it must be understood in its role as a photo machine, as a mechanical device for storing and reproducing not a song but an image.

Mann himself had already established the functional equivalence and exchangeability of the visual and acoustic instruments in the chapter that first introduced the gramophone. The new machine ("the German soul up-to-date") was depicted first as the technological successor to the several optical devices Hans took up during his first week at the sanatorium (883/627), and then, in its system of inscription, storage, and (diminutive) reproduction, it was described by an extended analogy with the visual field (886/628). Moreover, as the reference to the German soul underscores, the phonograph was implicated in the same technologization of the human subject occasioned elsewhere in the novel by the photograph. In particular, it furnishes a similar, and similarly new model for both memory and representation (*Datenverarbeitung*). Kittler has discussed the many important historical relations between the two medial apparatuses that conspired together in the refiguring of cultural notions about the subject and that also facilitate their functional equivalence, or exchange, in *The Magic Mountain*'s séance scene; and Mann's own narrow descriptive focus in the scene on the *Apparat* (933/662, 945/670–71, etc.) and its black *Platten* serves to secure and sustain the intended parallel.[105]

More important for us, the phonographic *Apparat* in "Highly Questionable" functions in a strict equivalence with the photographic *Apparat* in von Schrenck-Notzing (and "Occult Experiences") in providing the technological parallel for the medium and her activity, the parallel medium underwriting, as it were, the conditions of mediumistic (re)production and of its end product—the image to be produced as somehow the image already recorded or stored. As such, the phonograph furnishes—much like the camera in the earlier instance—the implicit metaphorical basis for asserting the credible "truth" of Elly as the operant productive mechanism. Insofar as the veracity of the gramophone's reproduction is accepted, it assures the acceptance or veracity of the medium and its image, Elly and her reproduction. Mann underscores the parallel between the two mediums verbally, by mentioning how Krokowski "had confiscated the child [Elly Brand] for science" ("hatte das Kind mit wissenschaftlich Beschlag belegt" [914/649]), and then soon after how the gramophone similarly was confiscated ("wurde mit Beschlag belegt"), again for Krokowski's "scientific" purposes (927/658). But Mann underscores it thematically as well, and to far more consequence, in how the Entwicklung, or childbirth, of Joachim's teleplastic image is jointly accomplished through the media of Elly Brand and the *Apparat*. The trancelike, medium state of Elly Brand is always coextensive with the operation of this other apparatus—the one begins, pauses, and begins again with the other, and both together always in the same darkened room with the extinguished overhead light and red-lit darkness (see 943/669). The need for the ap-ported black plate of the record album—and again, the parallel with the similarly apported black plate of Clawdia's X-ray photograph should be kept in mind—is explained in words that deliberately echo those used to explain the need for red lights if Elly's images are to develop (*Stim-mungsmache/Stimmungssache* [935/664, 944/670]). And finally, the reproduction of the stored musical "memory" and of the "child" are equated as well. It is, we are told, Hans Castorp's wish (*Wunsch*) that the phonograph produce the song (943/670), even as it was his wish that Elly produce her "child" (940/668). Both reproductive processes converge in the labor production of the wished-for Bild. The Bild of Joachim is every bit as much the Entwicklung or child of the one medium as the other, and the common ground uniting them, in both their mode of operation and their final product, is the only seemingly absent term of photography.

But how, we ask, does the presence of this other instrument effect the role of Hans Castorp in the scene, and equally importantly, how does it effect the issue of his Bildung, his Entwicklung? Two points seem to me of special importance, both concerning Hans's paternity, which is so key to the assimilative project of traditional Bildung. First, although in many ways the phono *Apparat* merely parallels and repli-cates the role of Elly, in others it clearly disrupts and perverts it, and this directly impacts on Hans and his Bildung. Like Elly, or rather, like Holger, the gramophone seems to represent the well-nigh invisible pa-triarchal powers that grant Hans his paternity. The record is specifically masculine ("And it began manfully" ["Und männlich begann es" {945/671}]): like the poet Holger, it too represents a dominant system of cultural inscription, and the fact that it is so baldly technological a system of power simply makes manifest the normally hidden, apparatus-like nature of even the most traditional of Bildung orders, such as Goethe's Tower Society. But far more explicitly than with Elly/Holger alone, the phonographic *Apparat* also forces—or loosens—Hans out of his own traditionally assigned masculine role and into a feminine one. As mentioned, this is most forcibly signaled in how the record positions Hans as Margarethe, but Hans's new, feminine role is even more exten-sive than just this. Insofar as the teleplastic Bild—the child—only ap-pears once the record's black *Platte* is activated, and insofar as the Bild—like that of Hippe, or of Hans's Arcadian vision—is something actually stored on the plate of *Hans's* unconscious (see Holger's poem;

also the earlier photo of Joachim studied by Hans), one could argue that it is not until Hans's own reproductive, mediumistic quality is engaged that the image of Joachim can come forth. The result of this added gender and technological dimension—where Hans becomes not only somehow feminine but also (and even because he becomes) himself a mechanized data-storage and reproductive medium, himself oscillating not only between the masculine and feminine, the paternal and maternal, but equally between the human and machine—the result is a neutralization inherent in the very technologized nature of both the process and its product, which seriously complicates the issue of paternity and "manhood" at stake in this culminating moment of Bildung qua Entwicklung.

The second point of importance regarding the changed status of Hans's paternity, or *Vaterschaft,* comes with the final, photolike image product of this technologized process of Entwicklung and childbirth. It is an outcome decidedly more troubling than that in the analogous, *vorbildlich* scene of *Wilhelm Meister.* The product, the child, the Bildung or Entwicklung, is not, as there, the smiling promise of Wilhelm's Felix, who gaily appears at the end of the secret ceremony, but rather the sad and serious, ghostly portent of the dead Joachim. And to reiterate, Joachim's image here is not only the securing "child," marking the culmination of Hans's social, patriarchal maturation, but also Hans Castorp's own "image outside of himself, as in a portrait, his other self" ("Bild ausser sich, wie im Porträt, [s]ein anderes Selbst"), marking the end product of the novel's own system of development or inscription. Joachim appears not in his familiar military dress but in the still unfamiliar uniform of a World War I German soldier, the uniform in which we last see Hans as he disappears into the battlefield, the final, culminating Bild of his Entwicklung. The startling, disturbing quality of the séance's final Bild does not, then, lie only in its ghostlike, phantom nature, a nature long associated by critics such as Kracauer, Benjamin, and Barthes with the photographic domain. It also lies in its foreshadowed, embodied violence, a violence inseparable from the new mechanization and mediation of the human realm that reached its early, modern apex in the mechanical warfare of the First World War, "the product of a perverted science" ("das Produkt einer verwilderten Wissenchaft" [993/705]).[106] Even as Hans's Entwicklung has yielded this final Bild, so too has the same, altered Bildung regime yielded this final war—both the product of the same development of technology, the same technology of development.

Of course, such a concluding negative image is significantly not other than the positive image we have also seen, the positive development perhaps especially manifest in matters of sexuality, in the escape from the compulsions of both the patriarchal and the heterosexual regimes, but also in all matters of culture, self-identity, even novelistic representation that we properly celebrate as modernist. The devastation of the war is not other than the breakdown and reconfiguration of tradition by modernism in response to the emerging cultural technologies, the scattered body fragments of barely mature young men not other than the attack on the image of a single, cohesive, unified subject.[107] Even the tragedy of "there lie two men—they were friends, they had lain themselves together in their need: now they are commingled" ("dort lagen zwei—es waren Freunde, sie hatten sich zusammengelegt in der Not: nun sind sie vermengt" [993/705]) is not other than the "wild" release of same-sex desires into Hans's experience and development. And Mann is perhaps most Mann in leaving us with this final truth, this final image of the process and project of Entwicklung as essentially situated in both its negative and positive states, or rather, in the neutral oscillation between them—as homoerotic, as photographic.

2

Archaeology, Psychoanalysis, and Bildung in Freud and Wilhelm Jensen's *Gradiva*

1
Split Images: Nineteenth-Century Archaeology

The intersections of archaeology with the fields of photography, Bildung, and psychoanalysis are manifold. To begin, archaeology as a distinctly modern discipline arises out of basically the same historical moment as photography, and to some extent, together with photography. Although there is not quite so exact a point as for the emergence of photography out of the earlier visual media technologies, the transformation of the earlier tradition of antiquarianism into the newly "scientific" discourse of archaeology is still generally attributed to the same post-Romantic, mid-nineteenth-century moment in European history, indeed even more or less to the same decade. Lyell's *Principles of Geology* appeared in 1833, establishing the principle of uniformation that allowed for the stratigraphical analysis of sites; at roughly the same time, paleontologists in England and France discovered bones and tools of human beings buried in the same layers of earth as long extinct animals. In 1836 the museologist Christian Thomsen published his guidebook to the Danish National Museum, *Ledetraad til Nordisk Oldkynighed*. It introduced both the method of seriation for classifying material artifacts and the so-called Three Age system, which for the first time allowed for a recognition of temporal depth to prehistory far exceeding anything previously assumed by Bible-based cultures, and equally important, it did so without any required reliance on written records. Thomsen's student, Jens Worsaae, brought the Three Age system to bear on actual fieldwork in 1842 and pioneered the so-called typological method; he was subsequently appointed the first professor of archaeology at the University of Copenhagen in 1855.

In the more specialized field of classical studies, the 1830s and early 1840s were also key for the emergence of archaeology out of antiquarianism. In 1829 the Prussian Institut für archäologische Korrespondenz (IfAK) opened in Rome, the forerunner of the Deutsches-Archäologisches Institut (DAI).[1] In 1830 K. O. Müller published his *Handbook for the Archaeology of Art* (*Handbuch der Archäologie der Kunst*), which established the (quasi-nationalist) disciplinary model for the study of Greek artifacts that dominated the rest of the century. Martin Bernal in particular credits Müller with revolutionizing the field, replacing the eighteenth century's Romantic understanding of the ancient world with a newly "scientific" archaeological approach.[2] In 1839–40 Müller made the trip to Greece, which marked a first contact between the abstract, academic discourse of Hellenism and the possibility of actual fieldwork; he was joined there by Ernst Curtius, the future head of the Germans' first major dig at Olympia.

Certainly photography played a part in the emergence of archaeology out of antiquarianism, both indirectly and directly, and it continued to do so throughout the period of archaeology's cultural hegemony, which, like photography's, basically lasted until the waning of modernism after World War II. Indirectly, photography became a new, even dominant method of "collecting" artifacts, especially in foreign, colonial territories. Antiquarianism had never been far from thievery and grave-robbing and had always been filled with copies, both facsimiles and forgeries. Photography continued this tradition in a more virtual fashion; its pursuit of images, its appropriation of virtual artifacts from ancient and aboriginal cultures, competed and colluded with the traffic in plaster cast copies, fakes, and, of course, original items back to the European nations. In 1852 Maxime Du Camp published a volume of 122 photographic prints of his voyage to the Middle East with Gustav Flaubert.[3] In 1858 Francis Frith achieved huge commercial success in England with his photographs of ancient Egyptian monuments, as did Robert Macpherson with his of Rome. At about the same time, Roger Fenton was hired as the official photographer of the British Museum and charged with photographing its store of artifacts.[4] Farther afield, Désiré Charnay brought back photographs of the pre-Columbian ruins of Mexico in 1857, and in the 1860s Félix Bonfils and William Stillman each photographed the Acropolis in Athens, beginning a tradition that would continue through to the work of Walter Hege in the 1930s.[5] All of these works—there were many more—focused primarily on monumental artifacts and sites known to Europeans through texts, and all of them prosecuted a kind of imperialist agenda that implicated equally the fields of archaeology and photography and indirectly contributed to the popularity of both in the cultural imaginary of the nineteenth century.[6] Together, they occasioned a radical transformation of the visual culture of the time.[7] Like photography's virtual artifacts, archaeology's circulated stores of material artifacts vastly expanded the evidentiary range and truth value of the visual, especially over and against the textual, while photography also contributed greatly to an aestheticization of archaeology's objects and sites in ways that supported their ever-increasing idealization, and abstraction, in the European imagination.

Photography also contributed more directly to the development of nineteenth-century archaeology. It was in good part the newly available supply of circulated photographic copies of pottery and other artifacts that allowed scholars and museologists to develop the "scientific" system of classification known as typology. This rise of typology in archaeology paralleled a similar trend in the field of photography itself, as we see, for instance, in the work of Galton and Bertillon; together they contributed to the emergence of the racial systems that would dominate both the political and psychological realms by the century's end.[8] Photography was also important in transforming archaeology into a science in the field. Alexander Conze at Samothrace in 1873, Curtius at Olympia in 1875, and Wilhelm Dörpfeld at Schliemann's dig at Hisarlik (Troy) in 1882 were among the first to pioneer the use of onsite photography.[9] They used photographs to record not only the specific location of particular finds but also the progress of the dig, preserving the evidence of each stratum as it was removed, a preservation not only of the found objects but of the discarded dirt. It was in no small part this added, preserved record of a site's layers and topography that helped transform mere treasure-hunting antiquarianism into the modern discipline of archaeology.[10]

The intersections of archaeology and Bildung are even more pronounced, and more determinative. This was the case for archaeology in general, whose proffered model of ever-advancing technological progress greatly reinforced the basic ideals and vision of development on which Bildung depended. A sure index of this comes in the inclusion of archaeological collections in the Exposition Universelle of 1867 as part of its staged narrative of the nineteenth century's material and cultural advancement.[11] But it was even more particularly, and differently, the case for classical archaeology, which, especially in Germany, was quickly assimilated to the discursive domain of philhellenism that had been inaugurated by Winckelmann, expanded by Goethe and Schiller, and remained dominant in German culture through to Werner Jaeger's highly influential *Paideia* in the 1930s. This particular dominance of the classical ideal in Bildung was grounded on the conviction that Greece in particular, and Greco-Roman culture in general, represented the origin or foundation of European ideals of both the subject and community. Although the same basic belief also extended to the biblical lands (including Egypt) and to the aboriginal tribes of Europe itself, these latter archaeological fields long remained both subordinated to and isolated from the discourse of classical archaeology, whose dominance in the cultural imagination was in no small way dependent on just that sense of autonomy and unity this isolating gesture invested in the model of both the individual and the community (which is to say, nation and, increasingly, race).

In any case, unlike the Goethean tradition of Bildung we traced through Mann's *The Magic Mountain*, a tradition centered on private life and enforced by decidedly eccentric, unofficial means—whether erotically by women or pedagogically by self-appointed male mentors— the Bildung tradition associated with classicism, although also in some sense a Goethean one, was first and foremost an official, institutional one for Germans in the nineteenth century. This began with Alexander Humboldt's school reforms in 1809–10 when, in the aftermath of the Napoleonic Wars, a program of Bildung based on *Altertumswissenschaft* (classical studies) was instigated to provide the Germans with a renewed basis of unity for their damaged and fragmented sense of self-identity. The program was enforced by the newly founded *Gymnasien*, which throughout the nineteenth century devoted almost half their class hours to classical language instruction, and then again (with greater specialization) in the research seminars of the University of

Berlin, also founded by Humboldt, which trained the future mentors of the *Gymnasien.* The eventual institutional prestige of this system had a major impact on the educational practices in Austria, France, and especially England, where the field of classical studies followed a similar course of institutionalization of the educational ideal.[12] In all these countries, the study of Greek and Latin culture functioned as the official, prescribed basis of bourgeois socialization, the sine non qua for the emergent *Bildungsbürgertum,* and in Germany in particular, it functioned as the prescribed basis not only for individual and class culture but for national culture as well.

Although archaeology as a whole, including local European archaeology, long remained isolated from this institutional setting, classical archaeology was quickly assimilated to its pedagogical program. It was state-supported almost from the outset and was incorporated as the handmaiden of classical education. From the very start, however, it also proved a troublesome servant, and in two different ways. First, *Altertumswissenschaft* was dominated at the time by philology and the study of texts, which were considered the foundation of the classical "inheritance." Archaeology was initially utilized to illustrate and complement this written—and largely aesthetic—tradition: "ut poetas pictura," so to speak. It tended to concentrate on the acquisition, interpretation, and display of statues, inscriptions, public monuments, and the like, material that supplemented the vision of the ancient world conveyed by the textual tradition and that could in turn be interpreted and understood on the basis of that tradition. The coordination was such that archaeology was even conceived as a form of *Sachphilologie* (thing philology), in a fully complementary relation to the *Sprachphilologie* (lingual philology) of the textual field.[13]

Soon, however, archaeology began to uncover and construct a quite different image of the ancient world, not least through its ever-growing supply of everyday and decidedly nonclassical objects, with little relation to high culture and the image of Greece transmitted by its canonical texts. In this respect, archaeology clearly shared with photography in the vast expansion of visual culture that threatened to erase the line between the aesthetic and nonaesthetic realms in the nineteenth-century imagination, and so too to threaten with their "realism" the exclusive dominance of the classical ideal within the aesthetic domain. And as the field of archaeology became less and less related to the historical sources of the classical world, it began a fundamental refiguring of the relations between the visual and textual realms, which came more and more to seem fundamentally distinct, if nonetheless cohabitant, spheres, different discourses occupying and competing for control of the same cultural space, aggravating the increasing split within nineteenth-century *Altertumswissenschaft* itself between historicizing and banalizing impulses on the one hand and aestheticizing and idealizing ones on the other. This led to a growing challenge on the part of classical archaeology to the text-based construct of the Greek world on which Bildung was originally founded, a challenge that threatened to dilute its serviceability as an aestheticized, imitable ideal for an aspiring bourgeoisie and nation.

Second, and intimately related, a key part of this challenge was archaeology's increasing tendency to focus on a *pre*historical world, on artifacts that predated, for example, the Homeric world. This was most obviously the case with Schliemann's work at Hisarlik that uncovered a Mycenean civilization far older than, and different from, anything suggested by the *Iliad* or *Odyssey*.[14] This had the unsurprising, but no less insidious, effect of undermining the very assumption on which classical Bildung was based, namely, that ancient Greece was itself the origin and foundation of European civilization. It turned out not even to be the origin of itself. Moreover, the discovery of this prehistorical world, widely dispersed throughout the Mediterranean lands, significantly weakened the sense of autonomy and exclusivity that had formed the basis of classical Greek identity, threatening the usefulness of the concept of the Greeks as a unique people or nation, which was also central to Bildung.[15] A more subtle, but no less important effect was how archaeology's focus on prehistory led to an association of the nonverbal, the imagistic, with the *pre*verbal, the ab-original, the well-nigh preconscious or even nonconscious, a configuration of cultural/psychic space with major implications for nineteenth-century politics and psychology, not least in the growing sense of the vast expanses of primal, archaic human experience (within "us") that were not to be encompassed by the more advanced, civilized ideals of classical Bildung.[16]

But by far the most troubling aspect of archaeology for our understanding of Bildung comes not in its challenge to but in its furtherance of the institutional and official function of Bildung, namely, its critical implication in the ideological formation of the German nation and its sense of self-identity. This role of archaeology in the emergence of nineteenth-century German nationalism has implications not only for the model of the community but also for that of the subject; for one of the implicit assumptions of Humboldt's pedagogic program was always that the sense of national identity would be produced at the site of, and in the form of, the individual subject of Bildung. As we will see, the nineteenth century's "invention" of the nation and the individual are inseparable, and problematically so.

The role of archaeology in the elaboration of national identity was fundamentally twofold during the period under consideration, divided between the archaeology practiced abroad and that practiced within the country's own borders, however porous and contested these latter often were. Perhaps surprisingly, particularly in the case of Germany, it was the former—archaeology abroad—that proved the primary site for the manufacture of national identity, at least for most of the nineteenth century. In matters of both social prestige and institutional standing, archaeology at home was consistently subordinated to that abroad. In fact, throughout most of the one-hundred-year period with which we are concerned, archaeology within Germany was actually under the jurisdiction of its Foreign Ministry.[17] As we will see, each of these sites (home and abroad) suffered its own further division or split, with decisive consequences for the project of nationalism in particular and for the metaphorical regime of archaeology in general. Let us begin abroad.

The investment of archaeology abroad in the national identities of other European nations, particularly England and France, was, of course, fairly concrete. Concomitant to their political involvements in both Egypt and the Ottoman Empire, archaeology for both France and England was inextricable from their imperialist enterprises. For example, the twenty-three-volume *Description de l'Egypte* (1809–28) can be said to have accomplished discursively the same appropriation of Egyptian culture as Napoleon's troops sought to achieve militarily. Edward Lane's *Account* (1836) similarly reinforced British imperial domination of the Mideast.[18] Both were the discursive complements to the many actual digs and appropriation of artifacts each of these nations engaged in in their all-but occupied territories. The many tales (both amusing and horrifying) of the competition and mutual subterfuge of the archaeologists of these two countries illustrate the somewhat paradoxical situation of nationalist competition for a supposedly common past. No matter how universalist and pan-European the classical, biblical, or Egyptian past might have been represented to be, that universalism was always also intended to support the universalist claims of quite particular imperial nations.[19]

Although the Germans did follow the British and French in their archaeological forays into Egypt—Müller's student Richard Lepsius hoisted the Prussian flag over the pyramid of Cheops in 1842 and helped fill the new Egyptian museum with collected artifacts by 1859—most of their archaeological enterprises were invested in the Greco-Roman sphere, to which Egyptology and its Orientalism remained safely subordinated and discursively separated, a separation especially important for the nineteenth century's growing elaboration of racial ideologies.[20] Of course, unlike the British and the French, the Germans were by and large shut out from any direct imperial presence in the Mediterranean lands. This had a twofold result. First, institutional archaeology itself became a major vehicle for the (indirect) realization of Prussian Germany's imperial ambitions, playing a far from subordinate role in establishing and maintaining the German presence in the Ottoman Empire and other Mediterranean lands, often helping to engineer some of its more overtly political designs. One result of this was that archaeologists would always be suspected (sometimes correctly) of being agents or spies of the German government. Second, the Germans came to occupy—or, better, to colonize—more the imaginary historical-cultural past of this region than its political-cultural present, even subtly to detach the two and so dispossess the latter of the former in a most subtle way, investing much of their national-imperialist identity in the conquering and acquisition of this past imaginary realm, and in such a way as to intersect only obliquely, and often oddly, with their more present political interests. This quasi-colonial dimension to German archaeology was not hidden, just discreet and "civilized." The absence of direct political advantage allowed for the perpetuation in this field of the imaginary identification of the Germans as particularly benign and enlightened colonialists that Russell Berman has argued was such a crucial part of the Germans' national self-image at this time.[21]

Both of these tendencies (archaeology as vehicle for national ambitions abroad and the focus on colonizing not the present but the past) can be observed in the founding of the forerunner to the DAI, the Institut für Archäologische Korrespondenz in Rome. Almost from the start funded by the Prussian state and the private discretionary funds of the kaiser, it served as a cultural, ambassadorial outpost representing the German nation abroad.[22] It was situated in Rome as the conceived center of the Greco-Roman world, which since Winckelmann had remained a fairly abstract and idealized construct for the Germans: there were few actual trips to Greece taken by the major figures of philhellenism and even fewer actual digs begun. The Greco-Roman archaeological past was more or less still an imaginary discursive realm for these *Dichter und Denker,* and so the IfAK was happily at home in the simulacric world of Rome, with its copies and museums—one thinks of Freud at the beginning of the next century and his avoidance of Greece, fueled by the unacknowledged suspicion of the disjunct between the image and the actuality and assiduously safeguarding the image.

By mid-century, however, German interests came to focus more directly on Greece. This was at least in part in keeping with the self-conscious rise of German nationalism, which led to a self-distancing from the Roman, Italian, and French world and a more exclusive investment in ancient Greece alone as the original model for modern German Bildung and identity. This in turn led to a new, or newly reopened, split in the former imaginary of the Greco-Roman that privileged the Greek as original and disparaged the Roman as falsely derivative, very different from the orientation of Winckelmann and Goethe. Nietzsche's *The Birth of Tragedy* (*Die Geburt der Tragödie* [1872]), published just after the Franco-Prussian War and the founding of the new Reich, furthered this distancing of everything Greek and German from the Romanic world.[23] This reorientation corresponded to the transformation of the IfAK into the Deutsches-Archäologisches Institute, an official organ of the new Reich, and a self-conscious shift in the language of classical archaeological scholarship from Italian (and French and Latin) to German.[24] The moment of the founding of the new Reich was also the occasion for the opening up of a new branch of the DAI in Athens, which quickly became the launching point for most of Germany's archaeological projects and for the beginning of Germany's "big dig" at Olympia—a dig on a scale only conceivable with major governmental investment. Olympia seems especially symptomatic of the harnessing together of archaeology and the imperial ambitions that came with the expansion of Germany's new political order. Hitler's staging of the 1936 Olympics and Leni Riefenstahl's famous film are residual effects of the powerful link forged between this particular archaeological project and Germany's sense of self-identity.

The shift toward a more exclusive focus on Greece was also, of course, inseparable from the Greek War of Independence and founding of the modern Greek state in the nineteenth century: a popular cause throughout northern Europe but particularly for the philhellenic Germans and their volunteer forces.[25] As many scholars have noted, the German involvement was fueled far more by their ideal of ancient Greece and a projection of their own rising nationalism and self-determination onto the site of "Greece" than by any interest in the actual modern issues. In one of the most revealing of ironies, the first king of modern Greece was Otho I, a Bavarian prince.[26] The Germans' attitude was very much in keeping with their more general archaeological tendency to disregard everything of the more modern Hellenistic or Roman period, everything that formed a bridge to the more recent past, as so much debris or decadence. Both were part of an implicit, albeit rarely articulated, strategy for detaching Greece from its own history.[27] The same could be said from a slightly different vantage of the tendency to imagine modern Greece as a European nation in the midst of the Ottoman Orient. Here too we see the impulse to distance Greece from its contemporary context and at the same time to claim it for one closer to the Germans themselves.[28]

This singling out and privileging of Greece as an autonomous cultural site was, of course, a tricky and precarious feat for the Germans, perhaps especially given the conceivable tension between a model of democratic Athens and the reality of Bismarck's decidedly nondemocratic Prussia. But the stakes at issue are made all the more conspicuous by that, not only in the differentiation of Greece from the more general Greco-Roman cultural inheritance, nor only that of Greece from the Ottoman Empire and its Oriental identity, but also more generally in the continued differentiation of classical archaeology from Mediterranean archaeology in general, the ruthlessly noncomparative approach and discursive isolation of "Greek culture."[29] But again, this was driven by the need for a distinct and pure origin of culture, of Bildung, and ultimately, of Germanness.

As the nineteenth century progressed, however, the unique status of Greece in the cultural politics of the German state took on an added dimension as its complex relation to the rest of the Ottoman Empire unfolded. As culturally invested as the Germans were in Greece, including the modern Greek state, they were also politically invested in helping the Ottoman Turks, that is, in upholding the fragilely controlled

Ottoman Empire, which, as the "sick man of Europe," had long been conceived as a site of immense chaos and lawlessness, not unlike Freud's ever-looming, ever-threatening unconscious.[30] Bismarck became the major player in the Berlin Congress of 1878 that renegotiated the treaties of the Ottomans with Europe and Russia (much to the chagrin of Russia); under the directorship of Georg von Siemens, the Germans began building their Baghdad railway (much to the chagrin of France and Britain); and the new kaiser, Wilhelm II, personally wooed the sultan, reassuring him of Germany's ongoing commitment to the Ottoman state.[31] The new crop of German archaeologists—not a few of whom were part of the railroad company and so not necessarily philologically trained—became more and more interested in non-Greek, nonclassical dig sites and actively pushed the German government to support their projects, often directly competing with the classicists for state funding, and, given the political leanings of both Bismarck and the kaiser, often succeeding. The result was that, as the nineteenth century proceeded, the earlier pairing of Greek and Roman came more and more to be replaced or, rather, overlaid by the pairing of Greece and Asia Minor, with a whole different set of fissures coming to define the relationship that defined "Greece"—and through Greece, Germany. The new binaries pitted the Greeks against the Ottomans and Europe against the Orient, a small isolated island of civilized rationality against a vast surrounding realm of nearly lawless chaos and arbitrary will, a world of conscious recorded history against a buried prehistorical one of silent ciphers, and so on.[32] Certainly, the role of "Greece" in the national and cultural imaginary of Germany became newly textured by Germany's complex political involvement with the Ottoman Empire, and archaeology's divided commitment to classical and prehistorical enterprises became more and more overlaid with its equally divided commitment to Hellenic and more Orientalized sites.[33]

While the cultural and national imaginary was being (re)fashioned abroad along this new set of fault lines, archaeology was fostering a similar set of divisions for the national consciousness at home—indeed, in such a way that the foreign/colonialist and local/nationalist discursive fields came more and more to resemble one another, even to overlap and reinforce a common split image. Of course, local archaeology was almost from the first implicated in discourses of nationalist identity, and not only in Germany; the English sought out their Druids and ancient Britons and the French their Celts and Gauls every bit as eagerly as the Germans their Goths, Teutons, and Aryan tribes.[34] But in Germany, and especially after the racist theories disseminated by Gustav Kossinna at the beginning of the twentieth century, local archaeology played a particularly central and virulent role in manufacturing notions of German identity.[35] Even so, and again bespeaking the peculiarities of the Germans, it is critical that we remember how archaeology at home was always subordinated to its foreign and, especially, classical counterparts, both politically—as mentioned, local archaeology was under the administrative authority of the Foreign Ministry, and the DAI, after opening up its second branch in Athens, opened up a third in Germany itself—and discursively. The amateur practice and status of those devoted to indigenous archaeology was always contrasted with the professionalism of classical archaeologists, who were both better funded and better trained. The lesser distinction was reinforced by the designation of the homeland practice as *Altertumskunde* (the study of antiquity) as opposed to the *Altertumswissenschaft* (the science of antiquity) of the classicists. It was further reinforced by museological practices, which not only assigned the finds of the two fields to two different kinds of museums but also granted far greater prestige and funding to the classical collections than to the so-called ethnographic ones (to which, incidentally, Schliemann's nonclassical prehistorical finds were also relegated).[36] All this reminds us that, for most of the nineteenth and early twentieth centuries, local archaeology played a greatly subordinated role in the cultural imaginary of the Germans.

But back to the split. In part, the split within German archaeology at home was occasioned by the same nationalist and institutional forces that were at work in archaeology abroad, namely, the increasing self-distancing from the Romanic world as part of the tendency toward German self-assertion and needed self-identity. Archaeologically speaking, Germany was a divided territory, separated by a wall long before the Berlin Wall: the *limes* that marked the borders of the ancient Roman Empire, placing on one side the Rhineland and Bavaria and on the other, Brunswick, Prussia, and the other north German states, the split between so-called Germania romana and Germania libera. The geographical split was fraught with ideological issues of German identity that permeated archaeological theory and practice: whether Germany was to be identified with the former, and so assigned a European identity, seen as part of the great Western tradition of the Greco-Roman past, and forming a secure barrier against the barbarism to the East, or with the former, and so invested with a uniquely and uncontaminated German racial identity, with an aboriginal past untouched or vitiated by decadent Western civilization, and so on.[37]

The geographically enforced cultural split corresponded to a similar split within the field of archaeology. On the one side were the classically trained and invested archaeologists who wished to control and define the domestic field, keeping it under the aegis of the DAI and the Foreign Ministry. They tended to concentrate on Germany's shared European heritage and, like the newly founded Reichslimeskommission, on the archaeology of Roman (which is to say, historical) fortifications and artifacts and generally looked down on the amateur efforts of those engaged in purely German, prehistoric archaeology as semi-barbaric. On the other side were the usually amateur practitioners of *Altertumskunde,* who based their bid for controlling and defining the archaeological field more purely on nationalist claims. They wished to subordinate and assimilate archaeology to a more or less exclusive *Heimatskunde,* to have it devoted to the discovery of a uniquely German racial past. Interestingly, the nationalist ambitions of *Altertumskunde* and its concentrated focus on Germania libera as the locus of German identity coincided with the imperialist ambitions of Prussia, Wilhelm II, and Bismarck, not least in their common ambition to dominate over Germania romana. This had the hardly unexpected result that the state-funded archaeologists working in Bavaria and the Rhineland, like their counterparts abroad, were often considered spies of the Prussian state. Certainly the practices of *Altertumskunde* and of Bismarckian unification were more and more difficult to separate, one extending a common Germany through time, the other through territory.[38]

Interestingly too, this vision of archaeology seems to have rested on a more or less opposite imaginary principle from that regulating archaeology abroad, especially in Greece and the Middle East, a principle programmatically formulated by Kossinna, a major figure in the eventual Nazification of German archaeology. For while the implicit practice was, say, in Greece, to divorce the ancient past from the present regional inhabitants, even to discard as debris all the sedimented strata connecting the past to the particular present and thus manufacture a nonparticular, universal "inheritance" to connect with the German (or more broadly, the European) present, at home the practice was to assume that the uncovered past had a unique and uninterrupted connection with the present nation. As Kossina stated, "Cultural areas that are sharply bounded archaeologically always coincide with completely different people or races."[39] This principle eventually became the basis for claims that territory previously occupied by prehistorical Germanic tribes in, say, Poland by rights belonged to the present German people. It was also extended by figures such as Carl Schuchhardt and Adolf Furtwängler, who came to argue that Mycenean civilization was the creation of Aryan invaders from the north and so the ancient Mediterranean world was a part of the Germanic past.[40] This led to something of a reversal of the earlier imaginary construction of ancient Greece while retaining all the justification for its colonial exploitation in the present. At the beginning of the nineteenth century, Greece had been considered the origin of German identity; by the beginning of the twentieth, Aryans were considered the origin of the Greeks. By a "commodius vicus of recirculation," the archaeologists at home had worked to make their triumph over the Greco-Roman world complete.[41]

The relationships between the similarly split discursive fields of archaeology abroad and at home proved complex and contradictory for the common ideal of archaeological identity, even apart from the increasing tendency toward the interpenetration and collapse of the two arenas themselves. On the one hand, the self-distancing of Germanic *Altertumskunde* from the Romanic and European world positioned Germania libera in much the same role as that allocated to classical Greece in its detachment from the supposedly derivative and degenerate Roman Empire: each as an original and unique center or source of national culture, in such a way as to confirm the identity of Germany with Greece, and leaving it to the classicists to play the spoilers in arguing for a necessarily mixed German identity (and for that matter, Greek identity). On the other hand, and I suspect far more disconcertingly, the distancing from the classical world per se seemed to place Germania libera in much more the role allocated to Ottoman lands over and against the Western tradition in such a way as strangely to commingle many of the features of the Ur-Germanic self and its Oriental counterpart, yielding a shared prerational, mystical identity: the I as the Other. This overlap was institutionally reinforced by the common opposition of local and Ottoman-located archaeology to academically based classical archaeology, methodologically reinforced by the anthropological approaches of those at home and in the nonclassical lands as opposed to the philological orientation of the classicists, topically reinforced by the focus on prehistorical life (*Leben*) as opposed to historical (written and rational) culture as the genuine "origin" of contemporary culture, and politically reinforced by a similar confluence of interests, with the more or less explicit cultural alliance of *Altertumskunde* and Bismarckian Prussia's ambitions at home lending support to the privileging of Germany's political alliance with the Ottoman Empire over and against both Greece and the other European nations abroad. To support Prussia was to support an identity neither Greek nor European but decidedly Other. In a most unusual fashion, to identify an otherness as the source of identity came to further the ideal of self-identity for the Germans at this time.

Such, then, were some of the major contours of the discursive or metaphoric field of archaeology in Germany during the mid-nineteenth through to the early twentieth century, nurtured by both classical Bildung and national politics. It is, of course, hardly surprising that archaeology should prove so open to the projection of such imaginary constructions, and not only to those promoting national identities. As Bruce Trigger points out, archaeologists do not observe the behavior or, like historians, have direct access to the thoughts as recorded in written texts of the people they are studying. Instead, they simply infer human behavior and ideas based upon their present understanding of how human beings act.[42] This means that archaeological interpretation is always susceptible not only to the influence of such specific cultural-historical factors as the rise of Prussian power or the shifting alliances of Germany's foreign policy but also to that of broader cultural schemas for conceptualizing human beings and their history, whether biblical notions of a common human origin, Enlightenment notions of a common trajectory of technological progress, Darwinian or Marxist notions of social evolution, or racial notions of fundamentally discrete cultures expanding ever outward.[43] Each of these schemas seeks to establish the relationship of the human past to the human present, and each in turn proves equally projectable onto archaeological material. Indeed, archaeology seems unusually dependent on such borrowed schemas, arguably (though no doubt overstated) having none of its own—hence its inevitable involvement with other discursive fields such as biblical or classical studies, ethnography, or anthropology. In fact, one of the dominant paradoxes of archaeology as a dominant imaginary site is its essential blankness, its inherent "weakness" that leaves it open to imprinting by other "strong" fields.[44] And I suspect that in large part this hermeneutic blankness supported rather than frustrated the seductive materiality of the field for the nineteenth- and early-twentieth-century imagination. The concreteness of archaeology's practice, its sites, its found objects, and its evidence (but evidence of what?) contributed to a unique blending of materiality and *nothing else* that made it unusually attractive as a site for cultural—and national—projection of its own values, its own concerns.[45]

My primary interest, however, is not so much in how archaeology proved such an important site for the cultural projection of various schemas for conceptualizing "man" as in how its metaphorical field proved a privileged site for cultural introjection as well, for a reconception of the human subject as himself an archaeological site and project, with archaeology figuring as a model both for memory/storage and for the practice of memory's retrieval, reconstruction, and display.[46] It is here that the intersections of archaeology with the fields of Bildung, photography, and psychoanalysis prove most pronounced, for along with photography, archaeology contributed significantly to the emergence of psychoanalysis at this time, including its reconfiguration of the individual subject of Bildung. Archaeology may not have been the "compulsory" site for a reconception of the subject that Jonathan Crary and others have described technology to be, but as we have seen, it was still very much a privileged, historically and culturally valorized site for the north European nations, and especially for the Germans.[47] And as we will see, archaeology offered some of the same metaphorical elements as photography for psychoanalysis to draw on, such as the contrast between the hidden and exposed, the dark and light, the typical and specific, or the securely preserved but then quickly fading, while also adding more elements for reconceiving both the subject (as site) and his emergence or extraction.

An archaeological metaphor for the individual subject and his subsequent extraction and interpretation was already emergent in the Romantic period, in the writings of authors such as Schlegel and Novalis, with their combined interest in notions of interiority, hidden depths, and death, and can still be found in the postmodern period, most conspicuously (and problematically) in Foucault's early work on "man."[48] For the most part, however, the metaphor is to be found during the late realist and modernist periods, precisely the period of archaeology's own hegemony. This is no doubt most famously the case in the field of psychoanalysis. Freud's privileging of archaeological metaphors is perhaps even better known than his use of photography, as is the collection of artifacts that kept company with the photographs in his study. Freud's most influential follower, C. G. Jung, also drew heavily on archaeological discourse to elaborate his notion of the subject and, again like Freud, displayed a direct interest and involvement in the field as well. But its use was hardly limited to psychoanalysis alone. As I hope to show, the archaeological conception of the subject was prominently in place in literature and other cultural fields during this period as well.

Some of this, especially the archaeological metaphor in Freud's writing, has been considered before. But as Derrida insists, such "metaphors" must be tirelessly questioned, and perhaps not least in respect to what is meant by their metaphorical status.[49] For while the appropriation of archaeology to figure the interiority and analysis of the individual subject is in the most basic sense metaphorical, it is nonetheless the appropriation of a field that—as the preceding discussion has sketched out—brings with it its own specific historical contours and conflicts, its own dirt and debris: its own cultural-historical imaginary investments and issues, and chief among them its privileged and problematical role in forging national identities and supporting official Bildung. That is, we need to take *seriously* the discursive, metaphorical field of archaeology and not approach it either over-formally or over-generously. We must not divest it of its concrete, historically and ideologically acquired parameters; nor can we afford to leave unquestioned its valorized, and valorizing, imaginary status. Instead, as with our discussion of subject formation and photography, we need to insist that in the case of subjectivity and archaeology, the latter functions not merely as a reflective analogy but as a formative force in determining the new form of psychological thinking to begin with, and unlike with photography, we need also to consider the effects of archaeology's place in official Bildung and national politics on its "metaphorical" place in the Bildungsroman and psychology.

What I would like to explore in what follows, then, are a number of fairly simple questions: What are the consequences of the insinuation of archaeology into the traditional field of Bildung, that is, of conceptions of the subject and his (sometimes her) disciplined formation? What in particular are the consequences of the mutual investment in archaeology of the discourses for fashioning national identity and psychological identity? Is psychological identity somehow also an introjected replotment of national identity, with all its questionable consequences? In his essay on Freud, Mann famously underscored Freud's "colonialist" impulses and ambitions: Is psychoanalysis an introjected form of colonialism? Of nationalism? Of both?[50] Or, more generously, what interventions into the archaeological discourse and politics of national identity does its appropriation into the field of the individual subject, whether in literature or psychology, make possible? How can the discourse of the archaeological subject be tactically deployed within the discourse of archaeology at large?

To explore these questions, I choose to concentrate my discussion on a reading of two—or, rather, three—texts. In the rest of chapter 2, I focus on Wilhelm Jensen's *Gradiva* and Freud's well-known essay on the novella, his first sustained venture into linking the fields of psychoanalysis and archaeology and, for that matter, those of psychoanalysis and literature. My intent is to reconsider the role of classical archaeology in Jensen's work in terms of the late-nineteenth- and early-twentieth-century imaginary mix of Bildung and politics outlined above and thereby to inaugurate a new consideration of Freud's reading and, more generally, of the complicity of psychoanalysis and archaeology his reading entails. In chapter 3, I will look at Walter Benjamin's *Berlin Chronicle* (*Berliner Chronik*) and its interweaving of archaeology, Bildung, and politics. This work allows me to consider Benjamin's own pairing of not only archaeology and psychology but also, picking up on chapter 1, photography and psychology. Between them, Jensen's and Benjamin's works offer examples of a thematization of archaeology abroad and at home, of *Altertumswissenschaft* and *Altertumskunde*, respectively, with all their own imbrications of the foreign and the national, the classical and the German, and between them, they offer a sense of the changing fortunes of archaeology in both Bildung and psychology, in large part due to changes in the political fortunes of Germany between the founding of the Second Reich in the late realist, early modernist period and the adumbrated rise of the Third Reich in the Weimar years of high modernism following the Great War. This was a period critical not only to changing conceptions of the subject but also to the reformation of German national identity, and as we will see, archaeology played a dominant role in both fields.

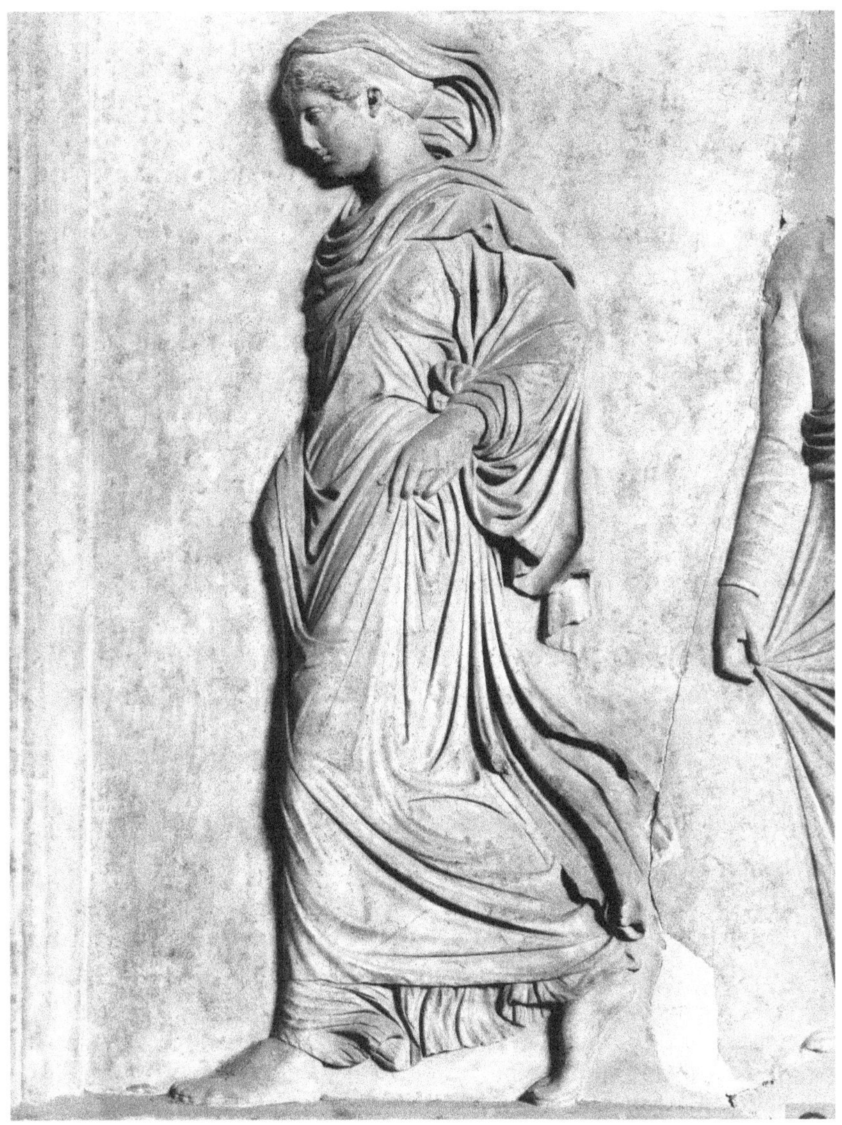

Relief fragment of *The Seasons* (aka *Gradiva*). Vatican Museums,
Vatican State. Photograph from the Fratelli Alinari Society,
Florence, Italy/Art Resource, New York.

2
Classical Dirt (Gradiva)

Archaeology is a topic of increasing importance for German literature during the late nineteenth century. For example, already in 1874, Theodor Storm's *Viola tricolor* has as its protagonist an archaeologist whose writing desk is covered "with all the apparatus of a learned archaeologist; bronzes and terra cottas from Rome and Greece, small models of ancient temples and houses and other things risen up out of the debris of the past filled almost the entire top of it," including "a small bronze lamp from Pompeii that he had just recently acquired and, as an experiment, had filled with oil."[51] In 1883 Paul Heyse (primarily remembered now as an early theorist of realism) published *Unforgettable Words* (*Unvergessbare Worte*), whose protagonist was again an amateur archaeologist, and in 1893 Theodor Fontane published *Frau Jenny Treibel,* which has two of its main characters, the archaeologist Marcell and his wife—herself the daughter of a Gymnasium professor of German and classics—going off on a honeymoon that is to culminate with their joining Heinrich Schliemann and his wife at Mycenae or, perhaps, Tiryns.

The potential affinities between archaeology and the reigning literary movement of the period, namely, poetic realism, centrally represented by all these authors, have been noted by several critics. For instance, Suzanne Marchand emphasizes the common devotion to a certain de-aestheticization of their respective cultural domains, a shared focus on the more quotidian and prosaic details of everyday life—a de-Romanticization of the cultural imaginary, which, for archaeology, entailed a diluting of the Winckelmannian inheritance with the addition of a more "sober" and large-scale praxis that focused on not only art objects but also artifacts of a more mundane nature.[52] As part of this, both archaeology and poetic realist literature were also engaged in expanding the culturally accepted range of artistic styles beyond the dominant classical paradigm, an effort that in the case of archaeology potentially challenged its own philhellenic ideal and in that of poetic realism, its own reputed commitment to "transfigured" (*verklärte*) representation. Other critics have explored the impact of photography and its new technovisual regime on the practices and assumptions of both spheres, and still others have underscored their common complicity in the *Realpolitik* of Bismarckian nationalism.[53] To all these important points of contact we might also add their common investment in "place" as an organizing principle for defining identities and action.

However, the relationship between archaeology and realism was not only complicitous; it was also contentious. Thus, as the archaeological domain became of increasing importance to literature—in the 1890s—the realist regime began to give way to the new forces of what would eventually organize itself as modernism. As we will see, archaeology challenged some of the most basic tenets of realist poetics, not least its privileging of the present—or, more accurately, of the most recent past—as the site of the real and its confidence in the visibly present, the ground immediately under one's feet, as it were, as a solid basis for representing the world. Archaeology changed that sense of presence, and this yielded corresponding changes in literary practices of representation.[54] But it should also be said that realism, in its ceaseless questioning of contemporary social discourse, also often challenged some of the most basic tenets of archaeology, not least its privileging of the past as the ground for nationalism as well as its confidence in its own praxis (its own ground, as it were) as objective, "real," and removed from the impinging pressures of social, psychological, and even "poetic" forces. For all these reasons, the encounters between archaeology and literature during the last years of the nineteenth century and early years of the twentieth century proved especially rich in both collusion and conflict.

The richness of these mutual encounters is perhaps most evident in the works of two relatively late realists, Wilhelm Jensen and Wilhelm Raabe. Both were amateur paleontologists with extra-literary interests in archaeology. Both were northern German and ardent nationalists at the beginning of their literary careers, before the triumph of Bismarck's peculiar vision of the German nation. And both wrote works that combined their interests in archaeology, national identity, and literature, works that began to push literature beyond the borders of realism while still sustaining a characteristically realist critique of their subject matter. They were, moreover, close friends, even best friends, who paid continued attention to each other's artistic endeavors.

It was a friendship characterized not only by shared interests but also by notable, defining differences, both in regard to literary reputation—with Jensen broadly popular during his lifetime and Raabe toiling away in comparative obscurity—and in regard to literary subject matter, even in regard to their common ground in archaeology. Walter Benjamin has perceptively noted, "'When someone goes on a trip, he has something to tell about' goes the German saying, and people imagine the storyteller as someone who has come from afar. But they enjoy no less listening to men who stayed at home, making an honest living, and who know the local tales and traditions. . . . Indeed, each sphere of life has, as it were, produced its own tribe of storytellers."[55] Jensen stems from the first tribe, Raabe from the second, and the archaeology that figures in their work is correspondingly divided between abroad and home. Raabe focused on *Altertumskunde,* archaeology at home: already in 1865 with his comic short story "Celtic Bones" ("Keltische Knochen" [1864–65]) and then in two of the masterpieces of his later mature work, *The Odin Field* (*Das Odfeld* [1888]) and *Fatso* (*Stopfkuchen* [1891]). Jensen, on the other hand, wrote about *Altertumswissenschaft* and archaeology abroad: his present reputation rests almost exclusively on his novella *Gradiva* (1903), a love story between a young archaeologist and a bas-relief set in Pompeii and famously read by Freud as a parable for the connections between archaeology, the psyche, and the practice of psychoanalysis. In recent years, the critical fortunes of Raabe and Jensen have begun to shift, with Raabe's now on the rise and Jensen's all but fallen. For all the justness of Raabe's growing repute, however, the neglect of Jensen is unwarranted, and so I have chosen to follow Freud and revisit the *Gradiva,* which I believe will amply reward renewed attention.[56] Let us begin.[57]

Site Prep (Auszug)

Although Jensen's novella was composed rather late in the realist period and is moreover designated as a Pompeiian fantasy (*pompejanisches Phantasiestück*), it nonetheless grounds itself in a relatively early (German) model of the classical world and its accompanying conception of archaeology. It is centered on the Greco-Roman model with the decisive weight on the Roman, with its imitative and simulacric base, much as we find it at the turn of the preceding century with Winckelmann and Goethe, easily the most heavily aestheticized version of the classical world in the repertoire of the German imaginary. The novella focuses on Pompeii, itself an early dig, begun already in the eighteenth century (1748) and sporadically continued since, and a decidedly recent burial, placed underground by an eruption of Vesuvius in 79 C.E., a moment at the extreme modern edge of the classical world—in some ways requiring a concerted imaginative effort to associate it with the earlier (and even so still historical) classical period of Periclean Athens and Augustan Rome.

For all its hearkening back to an early, well-nigh eighteenth-century classical model and archaeological setting, Jensen's use of both is decidedly still contemporary, or *zeitgemäß*, in its literary elaboration and is even fairly original in its focus on Pompeii. This was, after all, a dig from which the Germans had been almost completely excluded, and interest in it as a dig seems to have been fairly minimal for the German imagination in the century before *Gradiva* was published. For example, Goethe in his *Italian Journey* (*Italienische Reise* [1816–17]) visits Pompeii but gives it extremely short shrift. He writes, "The mummified city left us with a curious, disagreeable impression," and is in a hurry to get away: his interests and attention are far more invested in Vesuvius, its rock formations and its living fauna and flora, and on the "houses, habits, tastes, amusements, and style of living" of the contemporary inhabitants.[58] Similarly, Nietzsche describes "the vulgarity [*Gemeinheit*] that one discovers as one walks through Pompeii" and is far more fascinated with the image of Vesuvius—admiring and identifying with it, as also with the contemporary inhabitants who dare to live near it.[59] In the years just after Jensen's work, Walter Benjamin describes the dead city (*die tote Stadt*) as colorless, uniform (*einförmig*), hot, and deserted, inspiring anxiety, disorientation, and almost paranoiac isolation, while at the same time as the site of a crass commercial culture of plaster imitations and swindling baubles aimed at the foreign tourist; he is far more attracted to nearby Naples, with its teeming and colorful, intricately interwoven local life, so different from that of any north German city.[60] Even Freud, whose interest in archaeology and Jensen's novella might suggest otherwise, had no real purchase on Pompeii. Although he poured over maps and tourist guides through the long Viennese winters, in all his trips to Italy he apparently spent at most one day at Pompeii before hurrying on to other, more inviting locations.[61]

But what fascinated Jensen at the turn of the twentieth century was, apparently, what pushed the others away, what they found lacking or all-too-present: the odor of death and the dislocation from surrounding Italian life, the pervading sense of an encroaching *Gemeinheit,* and perhaps especially the all-too-easy transformation of Winkelmann's simulacric, Greco-Roman classical ideal into a crassly commercial, contemporary culture of counterfeits and keepsakes, of maps and guides for the foreign German visitor. Where the others all seem anxious to flee both Germany and Pompeii, Jensen chooses to stay in Pompeii—and not least, I will argue, because he wants to return to Germany.

Let me begin with a brief summary of the *Gradiva,* in order to draw out both its archaeological and literary thematics. The story takes as its male protagonist, Doktor Norbert Hanold, a docent of archaeology in a large north German city. He is the only son of a university professor and archaeologist (*Altertumsforscher*), and he has devoted himself from earliest childhood on to continuing the family "business," a business that has yielded considerable property ("beträchtlichen Vermögensbesitz"). After passing his exams in classical philology (with a specialization in graffiti, as we subsequently learn), Hanold makes the prescribed study trip to Italy ("die vorschriftsmäßige Studienreise nach Italien"), where he seeks out the originals of those ancient sculptural artworks ("alte plastische Kunstwerke") that he had first known through their reproductions, or *Nachbildungen.* Upon his return to Germany, he immerses himself completely in his discipline. He retreats to his study, his books, and his Bilder, without need of any other inter-course—indeed, there are suggestions made throughout the story that, in a sense, Norbert Hanold never leaves his study, his books, and his Bilder in his north German setting. We are told, "for his feelings marble and bronze were not dead minerals, but rather the only really living thing; . . . the female sex was for him only a conception in marble or bronze" ("für sein Gefühl waren Marmor und Bronze nicht tote Mineralien, vielmehr das einzig wirklich Lebendige; . . . das weibliche Geschlecht war . . . für ihn nur ein Begriff aus Marmor oder Erzguß" [31/26]).

One particular artwork especially attracted the archaeologist on his Italian journey, a bas-relief (*Reliefbild*) he discovered in a large antique collection in Rome that depicted a Roman virgin (*römische Virgo*) in the act of walking. Returning to Germany, he acquires a copy, a plaster cast (*Gipsabguß*) that he hangs on the wall of his study where it will be illumined by the evening sun. He gives it a name, Gradiva, "die Vorschreitende," She who walks forth (derived, we are told, apparently incongruously but still rather ominously, in association with the war god going to battle). It soon becomes the privileged object of the young German's archaeological fantasizing and, as such, becomes subject to two distinct but curiously complementary displacements. First, although in fact a Roman genre image ("im Grunde ein römisches Genrebild"), Hanold imagines it to incorporate and reproduce something—though not in a low sense—humanly commonplace, rather "contemporary" ("etwas im nicht niedrigen Sinn Menschlich-Alltägliches, gewissermaßen 'Heutiges'" [23]), a "something" intimately connected in his thoughts with its "rest in motion" (*Ruhe in Bewegung*), that is, its embodiment of an identifiably contemporary German classical ideal. Second—and again, despite its Roman identity—Hanold fantasizes the Bild out of the frame of the great, noisy city of Rome ("der Rahmen der großen, lärmvollen Stadtwelt Roms" [24]) and, with the aid of his archaeological knowledge ("unter Beihilfe seiner Altertumskenntnis" [25]), into the site of his own, earlier archaeological studies at Pompeii (apparently the only practical fieldwork he knows). Then, almost without transition, he decides, with sufficient grounds ("ausreichender Begründung"), that it must be not Roman or Latin but Greek ("nicht von römischer oder lateinischer, sondern von griechischer Art" [25]). The fantasy culminates in a dream in which Hanold finds himself in old Pompeii, on August 24 of the year 79; he watches as the Gradiva, whom he sees walking in front of him, grows pale, as if changed into white marble ("wie wenn [sie] sich zu weißem Marmor umwandle" [28]), before disappearing beneath the raining ash of Vesuvius, as if a Northern winter snowfall buried the figure under a smooth, even cover ("auch wie ein nordisch-winterliches Flockengestöber die ganze Gestalt unter einer gleichmäßigen Decke begrub" [28]).

Guided (albeit half-unknowingly) by his dream and supported by his inheritance, Norbert Hanold departs for Italy in the company of many other Germans, all making their prescribed honeymoon trips (*vorschriftsmäßigen Hochzeitsreisen*) to take in the classical antiquities, Baedekers in hand. After brief, aborted stays in Rome and Naples, Hanold arrives in Pompeii, where all the guests stay in one of two hotels, the Dioscuri pair (*Dioskurenpaar*) of the Hotel Suisse and the Hotel Diomede—despite the (modern) Teutonic name of the one and the argive lineage (*argivische Abkunft*) of the other, we are informed they are actually identical, not least in their common store of counterfeit antique splendors (*antiken Herrlichkeiten*). Hanold stays in the Diomede. The next day, as he sits alone among the archaeological ruins at the intersection of Vicolo di Mercurio and Strada di Mercurio (the god of business and death), Hanold succumbs to a professional crisis that, significantly enough, is experienced as a language crisis. He forgets in what language he had communed with his science, archaeology ("in welcher Sprache er überhaupt mit ihr [d.h., seiner Wissenschaft, der Archäologie] verkehrt habe" [41]). The site has meantime become completely silent and vacant, because it is noontime, in whose ghostly hour life must be silent and suppressed, because during it the dead awake and begin to talk in toneless spirit-language ("in deren Geisterstunde das Leben verstummen und sich niederdrücken müsse, weil die Toten in ihr aufwachten und in tonloser Geistersprache zu reden begannen" [44]), and suddenly Hanold imagines he sees the Gradiva walk out of the Casa di Castore e Polluce—that is, of the Dioscuri—cross the Strada di Mercurio, and enter into the Casa di Meleagri. He immediately engages in some complex mythological-literary historical-archaeological (*mythologisch-literarhistorisch-archaeologisch*) juggling with the name Meleager that manages in two ways to displace it from the Roman into the Hellenic sphere: first by reassigning the reason for its association with this villa from a painting on one of the walls to a minor Greek poet he imagines to have lived there, then by replacing as his literary model Ovid's Meleager with Homer's. He enters the house and sees the Gradiva sitting silently with a sketchbook (and poppy) on her lap. He addresses her, asking after her origin, first in classical Greek and then in Latin. She replies, "If you wish to speak with me, you must do so in German" ("Wenn Sie mit mir sprechen wollen, müssen Sie's auf deutsch tun" [51]). The young (German) archaeologist is not at all surprised or *befremdet*. Such is the language of the dead, the spirit-world, and classical archaeology: German.

Such is Hanold's first encounter with his beloved plaster cast come to life, or what amounts to (almost) the same thing: with the dead woman he imagines having perished—and been preserved—along with the rest of Pompeii almost two millennia before. In any case, subsequent encounters introduce an added dimension. The Gradiva becomes a real woman, not (just) the *Reliefbild* Hanold fantasizes nor the dead woman from ancient Pompeii but a German woman named Zoë Bertgang from Hanold's own past and his own north German hometown. The rest of the narrative might be described as a contest between Hanold's fantastic desire to impose on the woman the identity of the Gradiva (in its dual status as artwork and dead woman, as both aesthetic and archaeological artifact) and her own desire to assert her own independent, authentic, and "real" identity, to have Hanold desire her as her immediate self and not as representation—except that there really is no contest. Not only does the German woman willingly enter into the fantasy and assume the identity of the Gradiva, even to the extent of reenacting its pose in the novella's last line; her own "real" identity also proves the ideal fulfillment of Hanold's fantastic desire: as Zoë Bertgang, the Roman *Reliefbild* is (literally) translated by Hanold into something at once German and Greek, living, ideal, and his own. He translates her Greek first name as Life (*Leben*) and—unexpectedly expert in not only classical but also Germanic philology—her last name as meaning the same thing as Gradiva and signifying "She who is splendid in walking" ("mit Gradiva gleichbedeutend und 'die im Schreiten Glänzende' bezeichne[nd]" [82]), converting the Latin into German, and at the same time reconciling his language crisis and his statue fixation, as Zoë becomes the happy embodiment not only of the artwork but also, in a sense, of language, of the satisfactory restoration of philology in Hanold's life.

DIGGING FREUD

The preceding synopsis might well, indeed should, call to mind two other "plots." First, it should suggest the significant similarities in story and theme that Jensen's novella shares with a specific strain or tradition of narrative: perhaps most readily represented by Mann's *Death in Venice,* which shares the displacement to Italy, the obsessive artifaction of the beloved by the protagonist's classicizing gaze, and the crucial linkages of the aesthetic, the erotic, and death. But it is equally properly associated with the subgenre of Poe's "Ligeia," Storm's *Viola tricolor,* Nabokov's *Lolita,* and Hitchcock's *Vertigo,* all of which retain the gender of the beloved as female and also add to the protagonist's aestheticization of the living beloved his attempt to have her somehow become, or be replaced by, a previous, dead beloved woman—an attempt that almost always requires the death of the second, living woman.[62] I will have more to say about *Gradiva*'s elaboration of this narrative tradition, and its so-called Ligeia impulse, as we go along. For now, I want merely to identify it and to note how Jensen's novella both employs a variant wherein the woman seemingly survives the Ligeia impulse and uniquely implicates the basic story in a tale about archaeology.[63] We will want especially to consider the consequences of the latter, particularly in its contribution to the former.

The second "plot" that my synopsis should call to mind is, of course, the plot summary of *Gradiva* presented by Freud at the outset of his essay "Delusion and Dreams in W. Jensen's 'Gradiva'" ("Der

Wahn und die Träume in W. Jensens 'Gradiva'" [1907])—not the content, which is actually somewhat different, but the tactic, the common strategic move of beginning with a representation of the story. Freud's summary of *Gradiva* is altogether remarkable and an indispensable aspect of his argument; twenty-five pages long, it comprises close to a third of his entire essay, which is itself almost exactly the same length as Jensen's novella.[64] Given the overriding importance of Freud's essay to any later reception of the novella, it is worth quoting in full the paragraph with which Freud introduces his *Reproduktion* and considering in detail what is at stake in his first step:

> And now I really need to ask all my readers to lay aside this book and to replace it for quite some while with the *Gradiva* that appeared in bookshops in 1903 so that in what follows I can refer to what is familiar. But for those who have already read the *Gradiva*, I will recall to memory the content of the story through a short summary, and I shall expect their memory to restore for itself all the charm of which the story is thereby deprived.

> Und nun müßte ich eigentlich alle meine Leser bitten, dieses Heft aus der Hand zu legen und es für eine ganze Weile durch die 1903 im Buchhandel erschienene "Gradiva" zu ersetzen, damit ich mich im weiteren auf Bekanntes beziehen kann. Denjenigen aber, welche die "Gradiva" bereits gelesen haben, will ich den Inhalt der Erzählung durch einen kurzen Auszug ins Gedächtnis zurückrufen, und rechne darauf, dass ihre Erinnerung allen dabei abgestreiften Reiz aus eigenem wiederherstellen wird. (93/10)

Of course, Freud's summary, or *Auszug*—literally a "marching out," as when Jensen glosses "Mars Gradivus" as "der zum Kampf ausziehende Kriegsgott," the god of war marching out to battle: in other words, Gradiva—is anything but short. Instead, and despite the express wish that readers replace his book with Jensen's, it seems clearly to seek to rival or replace the original with its reproduction.[65] It does so in part by a mechanism of reputed recollection: Freud wants his summary to recall or reproduce the stored memory of the tale, as if his Gradiva replica represented something already there, latent, in the psyche. The point is important because it exposes the almost uncanny parallel between Freud's formal strategy and his (subsequent) thematic analysis of the novella proper. He will argue that Jensen's story revolves around a repressed erotic childhood memory (Hanold's, of Zoë) that finds itself reproduced in or as the Gradiva. The *Reliefbild* simply represents something already there, latent, in Hanold's psyche. The equation, or *Gleichstellung*, between Jensen's *Gradiva* and Freud's *Auszug* is made to adumbrate that between the figure of Zoë and the bas-relief. The one set of similarities secures and implicates the other.

The point is a tricky one, not only because we have similarities similar to similarities, in a relation of resemblances that draws Freud's method of analysis into the subject matter of Jensen's text, nor only because in fact, and despite its often verbatim detail, Freud's summary proves a rather questionable, even fantastic replication of that text. Rather, the particularly precarious "trick" to Freud's proposed equation is its temporal, or logical, reversal of terms. Even though his *Auszug*—his Gradiva—is manifestly a subsequent, secondary copy of Jensen's *Gradiva,* it nonetheless poses itself as the original, essential reality *behind* Jensen's fiction; which is to say that while we might want to identify Freud's summary with Hanold's plaster cast copy of the Gradiva, it itself would wish to be identified with the figure of Zoë. Even as, for all her subsequent appearance, Zoë is proposed as the hidden reality behind Hanold's archaeological Gradiva fantasy, so too is Freud's psychoanalytical précis, for all *its* subsequent appearance, proposed as the hidden reality behind Jensen's "Pompeiian fantasy." As Bernd Urban and Johannes Cremarius point out, Freud's recounting of the text is one of the chief means by which, as Jensen wrote to Freud, "here and there you do in fact slip something into [lit., 'lay something under'] the story" ("hie und da legen Sie ihr in der Tat einiges unter") and more than anything else, what Freud "lays under" is the prior, repressed erotic memory of Zoë as the origin of the story.[66] In fact, Freud seems to operate here much like the innkeeper in the tale who tries to sell Hanold a supposedly antique and just recently excavated brooch. Although manifestly a recent reproduction (or fake), the innkeeper claims that behind it lies an ancient love story: On the day of Pompeii's destruction, a young couple had died in firm embrace; the innkeeper himself had been present when they were found and their preserved bodies brought to the light of day. The brooch is produced as authentic proof of the story, which in turn secures the genuineness of the brooch. The logic is deeply flawed, but it is essentially the *same* logic that is deployed by Freud to argue that an ancient love story lies behind the bas-relief, a love story that he himself helped bring to light—and all this in a story that, like the anecdote of the brooch, seems instead to direct us to consider the problem of simulacra without originals and leaps in logic that produce "originals" where, in fact, none are to be found.[67] But in thus presenting his *Auszug*—his Gradiva—as the same as Jensen's *Gradiva,* indeed as the essential reality behind the latter's "fantasy," Freud further implicates his reading in the thematics of the text, and especially in its involved concern with appropriative identities and the troubling exchanges between the fictional and the real, the copy and the original, and the prior and the subsequent.

For our purposes, the most important of the appropriative identities that Freud's reading proposes are those between psychology and archaeology, in regards both to Freud's own methodology and to his reading of the relation in the story between Hanold's psychological motivations and his archaeological profession. In respect to the former, it is not only a matter of Freud's well-known general understanding of psychoanalysis as a kind of archaeological dig and the psyche as an archaeological site, indeed as a peculiarly Pompeiian site; it is also a matter of how, more specifically, Freud uses the archaeological metaphor as a means for securing the priority (which is to say, the prior identity) of his psychoanalytical version of Jensen's tale over the literary text itself.[68] At the point where Freud confronts the revelation that the woman taken to be the Gradiva turns out to be Hanold's north German neighbor and former childhood companion, Freud exclaims, "We are threatened by the disappointment of a shallow solution that seems unworthy of our expectations" ("Uns droht es wie eine Enttäuschung durch eine *seichte* Lösung, die unserer Erwartungen nicht würdig ist"), only to counter, "But it adds an essential depth when we realize that this childhood relationship can explain so many details" ("Es trägt aber doch wesentlich zur *Vertiefung* bei, daß uns einfällt, dies Kinderverhältnis erkläre . . . so manche Einzelheit" [110/30, my emphasis]). Freud's repressed childhood memory, which is the "same" as Jensen's "shallow solution," is nonetheless deeper, buried, and for just this reason more essential (*wesentlich*) and weighted with illuminating, explanatory, and unifying force. Much, of course, is at stake here, and not only how the archaeological metaphor secures the required identity nor only how it imbues Freud's psychoanalytic reading with its own underlying force, with the "buried" as the more original and the more original as causal. It also shows us a slightly different function for the archaeological qua psychoanalysis that will become more important to us, namely, how it is meant to save or rescue the story from the "shallow," the surface, the insipid, from far too simple or ordinary a relation to itself—to eliminate what Nietzsche calls commonness (*Gemeinheit*) by re-storing what Freud calls a lost charm (*Reiz*) and to do so through the mechanism of a recovered memory.

The similarity or equation between psychology and archaeology that Freud posits for Hanold in the story is equally involved, and equally involved in the proposed relation between Zoë and the Gradiva. Freud remarks, "The author had good cause to linger over the valuable *similarity* that his fine sense detected between a particular psychic process in the individual and an isolated historical event in the history of mankind" ("Der Dichter hatte ein gutes Recht bei der wertvollen *Ähnlichkeit* zu verweilen, die sein feiner Sinn zwischen einem Stück des seelischen Geschehens beim Einzelnen und einem vereinzelten historischen Vorgang in der Geschichte der Menschheit aufgespürt" [118/40, my emphasis]). Although Freud will argue elsewhere for phylogenetic connections between the individual psyche and the ancient past (see 153–54/84–85), here his reading of the relation between the two is grounded in his concept of repression and its corollary notion of compromise. Quite simply, Freud argues that Hanold's own childhood love life (*Liebesleben*) is both repressed and reproduced by his archaeological studies, specifically by his obsession with the *Reliefbild*. On the one hand, archaeology is understood as the anti-erotic, the anti-fantastic rational and conscious pursuit by which Hanold denies or disavows his original feelings for Zoë (see 113/34, 123/45–46). On the other, it becomes itself the so-called compromise that allows the original to reappear. The classical historical past "covers" the personal childhood past and allows the latter to reemerge, fantastically, and play itself out *as* the former without the conscious knowledge of the subject, Hanold. Hanold's obsession with the *Reliefbild* is his economical means to pursue both his conscious scientific and his unconscious erotic interests at once—although for Freud, always with the implicit understanding that they are fundamentally different and that the latter is the causal, original real and the former the merely manifest, supplementary available material for the former's representation or, as he also puts it, that the one is superficial, the other buried beneath it (128/52).[69]

117

Fantastic as Freud's reading is, it seems to depend on a number of fantastic assumptions. The first assumption, indeed the ground of his analysis, is that there is an anterior erotic memory, a childhood "love life," that is repressed by Hanold and that the fascination with the Gradiva represents and restores. But as Freud is forced to admit, Jensen's fiction itself neglects to motivate any such repression, that is, it does not provide support for the so-called repressive hypothesis nor for any anterior "love life" and, hence, no connection between psychology and archaeology in the sense proposed—no repression, no unconscious (126/49; see also 124/47). Instead, I think we need to consider the possibility that, rather than the *Reliefbild* being for Norbert Hanold a displaced fantasy fulfillment for the anterior/original childhood Zoë, perhaps it is the notion of an original/anterior childhood Zoë that is for Freud (and not only Freud) the displaced fantasy fulfillment for the *Reliefbild,* suggesting a rather different conflation of archaeology and psychology: both as somehow always projecting a past to support themselves.

A second and related assumption is that, for all their "compromised" conflation, Hanold's erotic and his scientific interests are fundamentally distinct; in other words, his fantasy life and his archaeological profession are essentially separate from one another, such that the former has its ground in the eros-driven psyche of the individual subject and simply invades the sober science of the latter cultural enterprise. The assumed separation of fantasy (*Phantasie*) and science (*Wissenschaft*) is inseparable from Freud's analysis. It determines his understanding not only of Jensen's story but also of the nature of literature in general and, ultimately, of the relation between literature and psychoanalysis. Very early on in his plot summary, Freud writes, "The author, who called his story a 'fantasy,' nonetheless found no occasion for explaining to us whether he wanted to leave us in our world, governed by the laws of science, or lead us into another, fantastic world" ("Der Dichter, der seine Erzählung ein 'Phantasiestück' benannte, hat ja doch keinen Anlaß gefunden, uns aufzuklären, ob er uns in unserer . . . von den Gesetzen der Wissenschaft beherrschten Welt belassen oder in eine andere phantastische Welt führen will" [99/17]). That is, Freud insists on a strict, genre-defining division between a fictional world grounded in the real—here identified with the "laws of science"—and one grounded in the purely imaginary or fantastic.[70] His claim at the end of his synopsis, "that we would make no objection were the *Gradiva* to be called not a 'fantasy' but a psychiatric study" ("daß wir keinen Wider-spruch äußern würden, wenn die Gradiva nicht ein Phantasiestück, son-dern eine psychiatrische Studie hieße" [119/41]), expresses his conclu-sion that the story conforms to the laws of science—his science—and hence is not governed by "fantasy"; this conclusion is in turn based on his claim that Hanold's fantasy is a delusion, or *Wahn,* that merely dis-torts the otherwise objective realm of his science. In a most subtle way, Freud has discarded at once fantasy and archaeology as motivating forces in the tale and replaced them with *Wahn* and psychology, respec-tively; in doing so, he has also (and again) replaced Jensen's "Pompei-ian fantasy" with his own, supposedly identical, "psychiatric study." But as Michael Rohrwasser points out, Freud's substitution of "Wahn" for "fantasy" is not supported by the text, and I would add neither is the substitution of "psychiatric" for "Pompeiian" (or "archaeological") as the source for the fantasy.[71] Rather, Jensen's text seems to suggest a quite different relation between science and *Phantasie,* one that insists on their inseparability and on a reversal of priority in the accompanying relation between archaeology and psychology. That is, it seems to sug-gest that Hanold's archaeological science can, perhaps, produce its *own* fantasy, its own imaginary desires and logic that the story unfolds—a fantasy and set of desires that are then reproduced as an interiorized eroticism on the part of the individual protagonist. And since Freud's own reading has linked together the fate of science in Jensen's tale with that in his own field of practice, we might add that it indirectly suggests that Freud's science might similarly (precisely "similarly") prove capa-ble of producing *its* own fantasy, a fantasy it produces as an anterior "truth" behind and within its individual subject, in this case, Jensen's fiction.

There are, Freud says, only two points at which it proves difficult, indeed almost impossible, to account for Jensen's *Gradiva* in strictly psychoanalytic terms and hence to replace the fiction of the one with the reality or "scientific laws" of the other. These are, however, the two most crucial points to the story, and observing where Freud stumbles can help, I think, to set us more surely on our own way. The first premise (*Voraussetzung*) that Freud's "ground of the laws of reality" ("Boden der realen Gesetzmäßigkeit") cannot cover is that the young archaeologist finds "an undoubtedly antique bas-relief that imitates in every detail a person living long afterward" ("ein unzweifelhaft antikes Reliefbildnis . . . welches . . . in allen Details . . . eine so viel später lebende Person nachahmt" [119/41–42]). The second is that Hanold encounters "the living woman precisely in Pompeii, whither his fantasy alone has displaced the dead one, while it was precisely through the journey to Pompeii that he distanced himself from the living woman" ("die Lebende gerade in Pompeji, wohin nur seine Phantasie die Verstorbene versetzte, während er sich eben durch die Reise nach Pompeji von der Lebenden entfernte" [119/41–42]). Of course, the first is only a problem if one assumes that the imitation, or *Nachahmung,* is more or less an exact one and that it is the bas-relief that imitates the living woman and not the other way around, and the second is only a problem if one assumes that the "living woman" was the beloved before she was encountered in Pompeii. In any case, Freud addresses these two difficulties in reverse order, and as I will explain in a moment, I find his rhetorical strategy of chiasmus itself significant, even key to his proposed solutions.

In considering why Hanold should find his beloved in Pompeii, Freud offers three different explanations. He first proposes it may be explained by more or less common chance, *Zufall,* which nonetheless mirrors "the fate that has determined that it is precisely through fleeing that one delivers oneself up to that which one flees" ("das Verhängnis, welches bestimmt hat, daß man gerade durch das Mittel der Flucht sich dem ausliefert, vor dem man flieht" [120/42]). The explanation is extremely weak, not only because it reduces to mere chance one of the two central conditions of the story, but also because the fate it sees reflected is so underdetermined. While perhaps (but perhaps not) explaining why Hanold must flee Germany, it does not at all address why specifically he must go to Pompeii. Yet surely, the chosen site of Pompeii for Hanold's finding Zoë-Gradiva seems hardly coincidental or unimportant. Somewhat later on, Freud proposes a slightly different explanation that, albeit indirectly, does acknowledge something of the necessity of Pompeii. He writes, Norbert Hanold "displaces his fantasy to Pompeii, because, in his science, there is to be found no better analogy to the remarkable condition in which he has, through an obscure knowledge, traced the memories of his childhood friendship" ("versetzt seine Phantasie nach Pompeji, weil sich in seiner Wissenschaft keine bessere Analogie mit dem merkwürdigen Zustand finden lässt, in dem er durch eine dunkle Kundschaft seine Erinnerungen an seine Kinderfreundschaft verspürt" [127/51]). He finds Zoë-Gradiva here because, by analogy, this is where he buried her. Pompeii becomes, as it were, merely appropriated metaphorical material, a manifest content for the latent childhood desires of Hanold—without any recognition that this material might be desirable to appropriate for its own sake, capable in fact of being the object of desire proper. This recognition is ultimately allowed by Freud, although only in his final paragraph, where he brings up the primary wish ("der erste Wunsch") that is fulfilled by Hanold's fantasy, the wish, comprehensible to every archaeologist ("der bei jedem Archäologen begreifliche Wunsch" [161/93]), to have witnessed the destruction of Pompeii, a wish that he then links with the erotic wish to see the beloved laid out "to sleep." It quickly becomes apparent why Freud should have deferred this insight for as long as possible. It leads to a complete reversal of his argument. Freud presents a desire, a motivating drive that originates within a common *social* imaginary of archaeology itself, and even intimates that the peculiarities of the (subsequent) erotic desire—for the dormant beloved—are in a sense a reenactment, or restatement, of the "Pompeiian" one: a cultural, scientific fantasy behind the find in Pompeii, not an individual psychological one, not a fleeing from but a going to, not the Gradiva and Pompeii as invented analogies for Zoë and Hanold's childhood memory but the (chiastic) reverse.

The second stumbling point that Freud (chiastically) addresses— "the first premise, on which all that follows depends, the so far-reaching similarity or resemblance between the sculpture and the living girl" ("die erste Voraussetzung, welche alle weiteren Begebenheiten trägt, die so weitgehende Ähnlichkeit des Steinbildes mit dem lebenden Mädchen" [120/42; see also 142/70])—proves much more recalcitrant to conventional psychoanalysis. It is, of course, a problem of Freud's own making, his own *Voraussetzung,* as Jensen pointed out in a letter to him.[72] But it does inspire in Freud the temptation "to allow the play of our own fantasy to forge a link with reality" ("Hier zur Anknüpfung an die Realität die eigene Phantasie spielen zu lassen" [120/42]). Freud's own fantasy is far and away the most remarkable passage in his essay, not least because its very presence so clearly calls into question the distinction between science and *Phantasie* that he has insisted on throughout. It too is worth quoting in full:

> The name *Bertgang* might indicate that the women of this family had already in ancient times been distinguished by such a peculiarity of their graceful gait, and through the suc-

cession of generations the German Bertgangs were connected to that Greek tribe from which a woman had once caused an ancient artist to capture the peculiarity of her stride in sculpture. Since, however, the different variations of the human form are not independent of one another and since in fact even in our own midst the ancient types that we encounter in art collections reappear again and again, it would not be completely impossible that a modern Bertgang would reproduce the figure of her ancient ancestress in all other features of her body as well.

Der Name *Bertgang* könnte darauf deuten, daß sich die Frauen dieser Familie schon in alten Zeiten durch solche Eigentümlichkeit des schönen Ganges ausgezeichnet haben, und durch Geschlechtsabfolge hingen die germanischen *Bertgang* mit jenen Griechen zusammen, von deren Stamm eine Frau den antiken Künstler veranlaßt hatte, die Eigentümlichkeit ihres Ganges im Steinbild festzuhalten. Da aber die einzelnen Variationen der menschlichen Gestaltung nicht unabhängig voneinander sind, und tatsächlich auch in unserer Mitte die antiken Typen auftauchen, die wir in den Sammlungen antreffen, so wäre es nicht ganz unmöglich, daß eine moderne *Bertgang* die Gestalt ihrer antiken Ahnfrau auch in allen anderen Zügen ihrer körperlichen Bildung wiederholte. (120/42)

Freud's reasoning here is clearly not logical, is indeed quite fantastic. Just for that reason, however, it helps lay bare the fantastic logic—not of his unconscious but of the archaeological imaginary, indeed of the same archaeological imaginary behind Jensen's story. We note first that Freud's account assumes a matrilineal descent to the name, or tribe, of Bertgang, which in itself, and in terms of the story (where Zoë conspicuously has no mother and is instead very much her father's daughter), seems an inexplicable misstep—unless perhaps Freud is being led on by a Bachofean schema that projects a matriarchal world behind the classical.[73] Second, and in an even more apparently illogical misstep, Freud posits a more or less direct biological (even racial) connection between the German and the Greek. Why this should explain what is specifically described by Jensen as a *Roman* artwork ("ein *römisches* Genrebild") is, of course, an important question. Freud seems inadvertently (almost ineluctably) to follow Hanold in his explicitly ungrounded fantasy of the Gradiva as somehow Greek, and Freud's English translators have responded by replacing his original "Griechen" with "Roman." But Freud's own replacement of the Roman with the Greek seems significant and seems also to be part of the same logic that directly connects the German and the classical Bild. *Why* the German and Greek races should be imagined as connected and why this should facilitate the replacement of the Roman artifact with a living German "original" certainly seem questions worth directing not only at Freud's reading but also at Jensen's novella.

Third, there is a puzzling but again revealing ambiguity to Freud's depiction of the succession of generations (*Geschlechtsabfolge*) he posits to explain the identity between Zoë and the sculpture (*Steinbild*). In the imaginary connection between the German and the Greek, it remains profoundly unclear in Freud's reading which comes first, that is, which is the "original" race from which the other descends. One reading, perhaps less alien to our contemporary sensibilities, is that Freud is asserting that the German stock of Bertgang derives from an archaic tribe (*Stamm*) of Greeks. But the peculiarities of the late-nineteenth-century archaeological imagination also suggest that Freud might well be arguing the opposite. Carl Schuchhardt and many others rather successfully promoted the theory that the classical Greeks were themselves descendents of invading Aryans from the north—that an original German race lies behind the aesthetic culture of the classical Greek artists—and perhaps Freud is conflating this preclassical German race with Bachofen's preclassical matriarchal order.[74] Freud's syntax makes it impossible to know which of these connections was intended, but in either case I think we need to wonder what kind of wish is being fulfilled by his fantastic assertion and how Jensen's novella might support or exploit it—or, rather, how both Freud's reading and Jensen's novella might facilitate this racial fantasy, and to what end. We should also just note the persistent presence of this seemingly discrete racial fantasy throughout Freud's analysis, which repeatedly refers to Hanold's fantasies and the Gradiva Bild and name as "descendents" of his repressed memories ("Abkömmlinge seiner verdrängten Erinnerungen") of the German/Greek Zoë.[75]

Finally, we note the role of the aesthetic in Freud's *Phantasie*. On the one hand, there is the implicit assumption that every sculpture, the

Gradiva included, must have a real life original that it represents ("a woman had caused the ancient artist" ["eine Frau hatte den antiken Künstler veranlaßt" {120/42}]). In this respect, Freud's psychoanalytical reading seems to depend on a simplistic realist aesthetic that sees art as always the mimesis or reproduction of some anterior reality. Only on the basis of this (easily discredited) principle can Freud imagine the relation of similitude between Zoë and the bas-relief: as the living image, she must be the prior original. On the other hand, Freud makes the explicit and far more extraordinary assumption that "in fact even in our own midst the ancient types that we encounter in art collections reappear again and again," that somehow contemporary reality is itself a copy or reproduction of classical models, a claim that seems significantly opposed to the preceding one.[76] Freud's second claim points us in a different direction from his first: not life into art but art into life, not peculiar individuals into statues but idealized aesthetic "types" into individuals—which at the same time entails the transformation of classical art into modern-day German reality.

Let me just briefly sum up some of the main finds we have unearthed from our discussion of Freud's plot summary, psychoanalytic reading, and archaeological *Phantasie* that can help us find our way back to Jensen's novella. First and most important, we have discovered a rather simple mechanism that works to produce a rather complex set of reversals and replacements of originals and copies, a mechanism of retrojection that is also at times one of introjection. Freud himself identifies and evokes this mechanism to describe how Hanold replaces life with art, erotic desire with scientific interest, and the German Zoë with the Roman Gradiva. But in the simulacric world of Jensen's text (and Freud's copy of it), which draws the very notion of originals into question, the same mechanism that Freud uses to secure and reconstruct Jensen's novella serves also to inhabit and deconstruct his own narrative. We see how Freud replaces present art with anterior "reality," a public archaeological fantasy with a private psychological delusion, and the Romanic setting with a German-Greek racial connection—all the while suspecting that in reality it might be completely the reverse ("daß es sich in Wirklichkeit ganz umgekehrt verhält" [129/53]).

Second, we discover that Freud's reading, whether consciously so or not, seems as embedded in a strategy of disavowal as he himself attributes to Hanold's delusion (*Wahn*), and we need to expose this strategy if we are to understand not only Freud's reading but also Jensen's novella. Freud's reading denies any imaginary impulse to the "science" of classical archaeology, which leads him to attribute all "fantasy" to erotic psychology. This allows him to remain blind to a crucial aspect of Jensen's text: its exploration of how archaeology might well be a somewhat curious science in its own right ("die Archäologie an sich eine etwas kuriose Wissenschaft sein mochte" [32]), in other words, the story's exploration of the dreams and desires of a more broadly conceived imaginary regime, that of classical archaeology itself—in Jensen's own words, that it actually is a "Pompeiian fantasy." And Freud himself, in his own archaeological *Phantasie,* reveals what is most disconcertingly at stake here and so too what is most in need of staying unseen or forgotten (think of that poppy in the lap). Classical archaeology is deeply invested in the project of manufacturing, or "discovering," a specifically German, and specifically modern, national, even racial, identity. Behind the tale of Hanold's unearthing of his private past lies another, the tale of Germany "unearthing" its national past; behind Hanold's "recovery" of Zoë's true personal identity through the Gradiva lies the story of Germany's invention of its own (hardly true) racial identity through classical archaeology. Freud might well profess puzzlement over why Hanold should encounter Zoë in Pompeii or how Zoë should be "identical" to the antique Bild in his psychological approach to the novella as grounded in "our world, governed by the laws of science" ("unserer von den Gesetzen der Wissenschaft beherrschten Welt" [99/17]). I believe we will be able to explain both these puzzles with an approach that focuses less on psychological realism and more on cultural fantasy and with a quite different understanding of the idea of a world ruled by the laws of science.

Third, we have raised some suspicions that the role of psychoanalysis in relation to this archaeological imaginary is not just one of disavowal. Nor is it just a matter of denying the fantastic drive to archaeological science as a way of ignoring the fantastic drive to psychoanalysis's own. Rather, in a complex way, psychoanalysis seems actually to be complicit in the archaeological project of forging a national identity (and so Freud's "fantasy" is not so unconnected to his "science" after all). As we will see in what follows, psychoanalysis facilitates a projection, that is, an *introjection* of the archaeological imaginary into the psyche (the "interior") of the individual subject. The mechanism for the production of a national racial identity becomes relocated as a mechanism for constructing an individual sexual identity. In other words, the project of forging a national identity is to a disconcerting degree *achieved* by being realized at the site of individual (erotic) identity: it is made real, psychologically real. Thus the equation of archaeology and psychoanalysis that is so celebrated by Freud should, I believe, give us pause, at least insofar as psychology thereby becomes a kind of introjected nationalism—and indeed, in its journey to Italy, of introjected colonialism or imperialism. And so we will need to watch for just those points in Jensen's text where the archaeological seems to pass over into the personal and tirelessly question what is at stake in this metaphorical equation.

GRADIVA (RELIEFBILD)

Let me begin my own reading of the novella with a detailed, leisurely, even obsessed consideration of the *Reliefbild* itself. This is, after all, where the story begins and where Jensen himself says it originates. In a letter to Freud, Jensen explained, "The idea for my little 'fantasy' arose out of an ancient bas-relief that made an especially poetic impression on me. I possess it multiply in an excellent reproduction from Nancy in Munich (whence also the frontispiece), and although for many years I sought for the original in the Museo Nationale in Naples, I never found it" ("Entsprungen ist die Idee des kleinen 'Phantasiestückes' aus dem alten Reliefbilde, das auf mich ein besonders poetischen Eindruck machte. Ich besitze es mehrfach in einer vortrefflichen Reproduktion von Nancy in München [daher auch das Titelbild], suchte jedoch jahrelang vergebens in Museo Nazionale in Neapel nach dem Original, habe dies auch nie gefunden").[77] As we know, Freud tries to improve upon Jensen's efforts by successfully locating the "original," whether conceived as Hanold's childhood memory of Zoë or—as he triumphantly proclaims at the end of his essay—as the original artwork *he* found in the Vatikan Museo Chiaramont.[78] But I believe we will do better to stay with Jensen, his reproduction, and his necessarily futile search as our own "original" starting point and to follow how the novella develops from there.

The fact that the *Reliefbild* Hanold possesses and on which he fixes his fantasy is a copy, a German copy, is undoubtedly its most important feature. It immediately associates the Gradiva with the world of inauthentic simulacra that Hanold will discover in Pompeii: in the counterfeit "antique splendors" seductively displayed for sale in both the Hotel Suisse and the Hotel Diomede, in the artificially patinaed brooch and its accompanying story foisted on Hanold by the innkeeper at the Albergo del Sole, and even in the watered down, doctored wine that was apparently passed off by the innkeeper's ancient counterpart in old Pompeii.[79] Less immediately, but no less significantly, the Gradiva's status as a copy associates it with the many German tourists' tendency to encounter the classical world only through the mediation of their Baedeker guidebook, approaching each item in their Italian travels only as a confirmation, or reproduction, of its simulacric description; or again, with Zoë's sketchbook and its penciled reproductions of the Casa di Meleagro, which again suggest a mindset that can only experience the Italian past (and present) secondhand, at an aesthetic remove.[80]

Especially these second two examples—of the Baedeker and sketchbook—hint at something mildly aggressive and appropriative about this copy culture. They also seem to indicate something specifically or, rather, broadly German about it. Indeed, in a remarkable passage, Jensen describes how Hanold first makes his way into Pompeii. We are told, "before and behind him wandered the population of the two hotels in little troops commanded by official guides, armed with red Baedekers or their foreign cousins, lusting after secret excavations of their own" ("Vor ihm und hinter ihm wanderte in kleinen, von den Zwangsführern befehligten Trupps, mit rotem Baedeker oder ausländischen Vettern desselben bewaffnet, die derzeitige, nach heimlichen eigenen Ausscharrungen lüsterne Bevolkerung der beide Gasthöfe" [42]). The unmistakably militaristic language, exuding its own violently tinged eroticism, is telling: "armed" with their Baedekers and its representation of what they have not yet seen (but already know), the troops lust to make Pompeii their own, through secret, *heimlich* excavations—as, in a sense, they already have, through their Baedekers themselves (see 35, 37). This latter point is driven home by the seemingly casual phrase "or their foreign cousins," the implication being that, in Italy and Pompeii, the German Baedeker is not foreign but native, original. Even with no other German than Hanold in sight, the German *copy* reigns supreme, even over the original Italian city before him. In any case, as an "excellent" German reproduction, the *Reliefbild* that Hanold possesses and that fixes his fantasy introduces into the novella an entire culture of simulacra that brings with it questions of both possession and fixing fantasies.[81]

A second feature of the *Reliefbild* worthy of consideration is its status as a *Gipsabguß,* a plaster cast, which introduces some peculiar qualities to its more general character as a reproduction. To begin, the *Gipsabguß* occasions a slight shift in the identity of the original of which it is a copy. This original is not the Roman bas-relief itself but rather the manufactured mold into which the plaster is poured, a mold designed to produce not a single unique copy but a multitude of reproductions. We might think of Jensen's claim to possess his reproduction multiply (*mehrfach*) or of the way copies of the Gradiva came to be disseminated throughout the Freudian community almost as a badge of belonging.[82] In any case, the mold/copy relation thus doubly removes the image from the culture of origins and places it instead as part of the modern media culture perhaps most associated with photographs ("whence also the frontispiece"), with their dual model of a master template and endlessly reproducible copies, both of which reinforce a sense of the generic, or stereotypical, inhabiting the individual instance.[83] Every individual image is shot through with the general mold or template, and this general, in some sense original, model is still never the original itself but also a copy—and in this case, a German copy.

The *Gipsabguß* resembles a photograph in another respect as well. The positive print of its appearance is the product of a negative, the mold itself, in which all the features of the "original" (and final copy) are inverted and reversed. In chapter 1, I discussed some of the ramifications of this negative/positive relationship for photography and the psychology to which it gave rise, and as my earlier discussion here of Freud has suggested, reversals and inversions are also crucial to the production of the image of the Gradiva. However, in at least one crucial respect, the role of the negative and positive prints suggested by the *Gipsabguß* in Jensen's novella is quite different from that in photography. The positive print need not be a faithful reproduction. Julianne Vogel has shrewdly called attention to Jensen's anecdotal history of the "Villa des Diomedes" and the exact print of the neck, shoulders, and beautiful breasts of a young girl found here ("der hier aufgefundene genaue Abdruck des Halses, der Schultern und des schönen Busen eines jungen . . . Mädchens" [77]), a negative print, or *Abdruck,* that invites each viewer to fill it in and out with his or her own fantasy of its original—where the positive image will always, of course, resemble less some unknowable prior original and more the projected needs and desires of the subsequent knower.[84] The point has equal relevance to the identity of the Gradiva *Abguß* and Hanold's obsessive fantasy of it. After all, it is her *foot* that fascinates him most, and he travels to Pompeii "in order to discover whether he could find traces of her—and indeed in a literal sense, since, given her unusual way of walking, she must have left a print of her toes in the ashes that was distinct from all others" ("um danach zu suchen, ob er hier Spuren von ihr auffinden könne. Und zwar im wörtlichen Sinne, denn bei ihrer besonderen Gangart mußte sie in der Asche einen von allen übrigen sich unterscheidenden Abdruck der Zehen hinterlassen haben" [47]). It is the Gradiva as *Abdruck*, as *Abguß*, that fixes Hanold's imagination, precisely because it invites a projective reconstruction of an original in, or as, his own image.

Certainly the significance of the plaster cast as print (*Abdruck*) or tracks (*Spuren*) gives us one way of understanding its most pronounced characteristic, the one after which it is named: that it is the image of a woman walking. However, there are other ways of grasping the importance of this feature as well. When Hanold first imagines the Gradiva living in ancient Pompeii, we are told, "In just this way he saw her putting one foot over the gap between two stepping stones, while the other stood poised to follow" ("So sah er sie, wie ihr einer Fuß sich über die Lücke zwischen zwei Steinen hinübergesetzt, während der andere im Begriff stand, nachzufolgen" [25]). The idea of Gradiva walking as bridging a gap, or *Lücke*, is indeed a dominant one from the beginning of the story until its closing lines; but crucially, the overstepping of gaps at stake in the story is always Hanold's own. The motif of "feet" and "walking" is one maintained and extended throughout the narrative, and it is consistently applied both to the Gradiva and, more intriguingly, to the "steps" and "bases" of Hanold's imaginative constructions. Hanold initially imagines the Gradiva to have lived in Rome, then imaginatively displaces her to Pompeii, and proceeds to decide she is Greek. Jensen is remarkably ingenious about couching Hanold's fantasizing the static image into narrative (and life) in terms of walking. He bases one conclusion on the "feet" of another; his ideas "proceed," constantly stepping over logical gaps and so going from the "foot" of objective observation to the "foot" of fantasy, and so on (25, 32, 42). More than anything, Hanold seems fascinated with the Gradiva's stepping image because it is the image of the steps of his fascination.[85]

Nor is this self-reflecting projection something entirely innocent. When Hanold first arrives in Pompeii (after which everything happens on foot) and seeks to apply his scientific philological training to the ruins, we are told, "one saw that the now illegible inscription inlaid with mosaic on the sidewalk before the shop was worn away by many feet" ("man sah, die nicht mehr lesbare, mit Mosaiksteinchen eingelegte Inschrift auf der semita vor dem Laden war von vielen Füßen abgetreten" [45]). The original significance of the place has been worn away and effaced by all the subsequent "feet" that have passed over it. But a moment later, when Hanold steps over into a more openly dreamlike and fantasizing state, feels "master of his feet" ("Herr seines Fußes"), and approaches the threshold of the Casa di Meleagro, where he is about to encounter his Gradiva, we are told, "the inlaid greeting, 'Have,' still discernible, looked back at him" ("von deren Schwelle [sah] ihm, noch erkennbar, der eingelegte Gruß 'Have' entgegen" [49; see also 60]). English-speaking tourists have been chattering in his ears all morning; now, when Hanold looks to his feet and prepares to step into the place where the Gradiva will begin to speak German, he "master"-fully and "dream"-fully finds the invitation to "Have." The old original inscription might have disappeared underfoot; the imperative of appropriation takes its place.

Another important and revealing connection between the image of the walking Gradiva and Hanold's manner of imagining has to do with the matter of direction. When Hanold first attributes the name Gradiva to his plaster cast, the Latin is immediately translated as "die Vorschreitende," She who is walking forth (24). The *Vor* is, notably, an over-translation; it attaches a notion of forward motion to the stepping, or overstepping, of the *Reliefbild*. Why this directionality should be imaginatively added to the image—or perhaps better, to its German translation—is a crucial question, one certainly related to its corporeal reproduction (*körperhafte Wiedergabe*) of something contemporary (*etwas Heutiges*). But before we can even satisfactorily pose this question, we need first to note how actually, according to the left/right conventions of Western (scriptive) culture, the Gradiva of the frontispiece seems to be walking *backward*—a circumstance rendered all the more worthy of our contemplation by the placement of the image *before* the beginning of the scripted tale. How backward should become forward or, alternatively, why "She who steps forth" needs to step back is thus the more complete version of our question, and I believe we can already surmise its affinities with the issues of reversal raised before.

But to capture fully the force of the added "forward" here—and its suppressed "backward"—we need, I think, to link it with Hanold's other over-translation of the same term. Near the end of the story, Hanold claims that "Bertgang means the same as Gradiva and signifies 'She who is splendid in walking'" ("Bertgang mit Gradiva gleichbedeutend ist und 'die im Schreiten Glänzende' bezeichnet" [82]). Even as the first German translation of "Gradiva" is supplemented with *vor*, so is this second with *glänzend*. Somehow, by becoming German, by proceeding forward, the Gradiva has been *verklärt*, rendered radiant, as it were. But as the backward/forward reversal of the Bild itself might suggest, the added attribute seems to work in the other direction too. The German also becomes invested with an extra splendor by being translated "back" into the classical (Latin). And just how, by progressing backward, Hanold's imaginative construction of the Gradiva Bild yields the "splendor" to be added to the forward dimension is important to see. As mentioned, Hanold's fantasy takes *two* steps back from the present *Reliefbild,* displacing it (that is, its anterior original) first to Pompeii and then, and even more emphatically, "back" into a Hellenistic descent. Both steps aim at a recognizable ennoblement and idealization. The first has her transformed into the daughter of a *nobilis* ("die Tochter eines Nobilis"); the second imbues her with Greek Bildung ("mit griechischer Bildung") and a refined spirituality ("etwas fein Durchgeistigtes"). In a complicated but I believe already apparent way, by proceeding backward, Hanold's fantasy of the Bild idealizes it, but the ultimate target of the idealization is, as he quite rightly indicates, the *Vor,* the present German Gradiva, who will become She who is splendid in walking. The broader issues at stake in this backward/forward play and its concomitant gain in splendor will need to be further elaborated, but we should already note the metonymic chain that links the forward idealization of Hanold's "stepping" with the image of the god of war striding out to battle (24). Idealization, especially in its dynamic of temporal displacement, seems inseparable from a kind of violence, almost an act of war.

One final feature of the Gradiva walking that is crucial to our understanding of Hanold's possession of and fascination with the bas-relief was briefly touched on in my earlier summary, namely, its corporeal figuration of perhaps the central tenet of German classicism, rest in motion (*Ruhe in Bewegung*). It is one of the most constantly evoked motifs associated with the Gradiva, beginning with Hanold's first contemplation of her peculiar stride:

> This movement produced a double impression of the extraordinary agility of the woman walking and at the same time of her sure composure. This flightlike poise combined with a firm step lent her a peculiar grace.

> Diese Bewegung rief ein Doppelgefühl überaus leichter Behendigkeit der Ausschreitenden wach und zugleich eines sicheren Ruhens auf sich. Das verlieh ihr, ein flugartiges Schweben mit festem Auftreten verbindend, die eigenartige Anmut. (24)[86]

Clearly, the double feeling of singular grace captures some of the play of stasis and motion so inseparable from Hanold's conflation of art and life: how the flow of life (history, desire, etc.) is arrested through its artifaction and, conversely, how the static work of art is mobilized, or put through its paces, by Hanold's present living needs, desires, and fancies.[87] But equally important, it shows all the more forcefully how the fascination evoked by the image is not a personal, individual one motivated by some hidden past "real" but rather a cultural, even national one, supported by a conspicuously present ideal, how the fascination is not directly with the Roman Bild itself (nor with the little girl next door) but rather with its corporeal reproduction (*körperhafte Wiedergabe*) of a retrojected German classical vision, something in no "low" sense contemporary ("etwas im nicht niedrigen Sinn 'Heutiges'").[88] Hanold's fantasy walks the Gradiva back into an ennobled past as his way of carrying it forward to incorporate and revive the contemporary adage (or banality).

Although her walking is obviously the Gradiva's most characterizing feature, and the one most invested with, or reflective of, Hanold's obsessive needs, desires, and fantasy, it is not her only such feature. There is also her countenance, or *Gesicht:* "her eye, which gazed calmly ahead, bespoke an entirely unimpaired, corporeal power of sight and thoughts quietly withdrawn" ("das ruhig vor sich hinsehende Auge sprach von voll unbeeinträchtigter leiblicher Sehkraft und still in sich zurückgezogenen Gedanken" [23]) and similarly, "After extensive observation he found [her Greek Bildung] confirmed by the expression of the face, for quite decidedly intelligence and a delicate spirituality lay hidden beneath its unassuming aspect" ("Bei eingehender Betrachtung fand dies [d.h., ihre griechische Bildung] in dem Ausdruck des Antlitzes Bestätigung, es lag entschieden unter seiner Anspruchlosigkeit Kluges und etwas fein Durchgeistigtes verborgen" [26]). Two intimately related points, or processes, seem to be at issue here. First, the attribution of the power of sight to the picture bespeaks a complex, but by now quite recognizable, mechanism of reversal or inversion on Hanold's part. His own contemplating vision is installed into the image as its own inherent quality; even the supposedly unimpaired and non-impairing (*unbeeinträchtigt*) quality of his archaeologist's gaze is reproduced as a feature of her gaze (even as her "gaze" is the indisputable evidence of impairment). What he sees in the "seeing" of the picture is in fact a reflective projection of his seeing of the picture. Second, by almost the same mechanism by which the *Reliefbild* is invested with the power of sight, it is also invested with indrawn thoughts (*in sich zurückgezogenen Gedanken*). That is, the attribution of a psychic, interior, thoughtful, even spiritual world—nourished by Greek Bildung, no less—is entirely accomplished through a moment of reversal or inversion on Hanold's part. His own contemplative, idealizing, and yet fantastic gaze directed *at* the picture becomes incorporated as an interior quality emanating from behind the picture itself. Its concealed psyche and withdrawn thoughts are a reflection, indeed a product, of his revealing science and projected ideals. Hanold acknowledges as much near the end of the novella when he states his exclusive claim over her figure: "for he had discovered the Gradiva, he had observed her daily, taken her into his life, to a certain extent he had imbued her with his life force, and it seemed to him as if he had given her back a life that she would not have possessed without him. And therefore he felt he had a right, to which he alone could make a claim" ("denn er hatte die Gradiva . . . entdeckt, sie täglich betrachtet, in sich aufgenommen, gewissermaßen mit seiner Lebenskraft durchdrungen, und ihm war's, als ob er ihr dadurch ein Leben wieder verliehen habe, das sie ohne ihn nicht besessen hätte. Daraus aber fiel seinem Gefühl ein Recht zu, auf das er allein Anspruch erheben durfte" [67]).[89]

We will want to return to this complex mechanism whereby the contemplating gaze installs itself as a psychic structure, or space, later when we address more concretely the question of how archaeology becomes introjected as subject psychology in the novella. For now, I want to secure the more immediate and simple point raised by the issue of the image's imputed power of sight, or *Sehkraft*. It underscores how the Bild is taken up into an egregiously narcissistic relation with Norbert Hanold, how in a significant fashion it functions as a mirror for Hanold, reflecting back his own (counterfeit) image, and how, *pace* Freud, the "original" hidden behind the Gradiva is not the past Zoë but the very present Hanold.[90] This narcissistic arrangement is an essential aspect of the image's simulacric identity, and it drives the story from start to finish. When Hanold attempts to ascertain the objective reality of the Gradiva's depicted stride, he begins by measuring his own. Later, when, having just woken up and still disheveled, he ventures out into the street in pursuit of a woman who might possess the walk, someone yells out to him, "Are you looking for your bed here in the street? You would do better to first go home and look at yourself in the mirror" ("Suchen Sie hier auf der Straße nach Ihrem Bett? Da tun Sie besser, erst mal nach Hause zu gehen und sich im Spiegel zu besehn" [30]). Once he arrives in Pompeii and encounters Gradiva-Zoë, he is the one who, when they meet, is consistently described as petrified, frozen, caught in his tracks (47, 57, 70). Similarly, despite all his speculations about her ability to speak (*Sprachfähigkeit*) and the insubstantiality of her person, he is the one caught in a language crisis (*Sprachkrise* [79]) and described as a shadow-figure (*Schattengestalt* [76]), and so on. That is, it is not so much the similarity, or *Ähnlichkeit,* between Zoë and the Gradiva that strikes us as it is the similarity between Hanold himself and his Bild; and it is not so much a matter of Zoë asserting her own reality, her voice and substance, against the imposed image of the ancient artwork as it is of Hanold achieving his own identity, his language and sense of substance, *through* the artwork—and that includes, of course, Zoë in her role as the embodiment of the artwork. This last point is secured in the figures whom Freud himself identifies as the decisive means for the resolution of Hanold's dilemma: the German couple (significantly the only other Germans present) who arrive near the end, whose couplehood and erotic dalliance Hanold approves and implicitly reads in terms of his own desired relation with Gradiva-Zoë. Significantly, however, what most attracts Hanold to them is that he believes they are siblings (*ein Geschwisterpaar*), an imagining that oversteps all the pronounced differences in their appearances to make them closely resemble each other. The more than gently suggested incest motif is merely a variant manifestation of the more broadly sustained motif of narcissism. Hanold's fixation on both the Gradiva and Zoë is, initially and ultimately, about himself, his identity, and his resemblances.[91]

The implication of Hanold's narcissism into the dynamics of the story, including the relation between Gradiva and Zoë, is also apparent in another dimension of the story, namely, the foregrounded play with names, itself part of the story's more general concern with issues of language, philology, and etymology. As mentioned, Hanold claims that "Bertgang" means the same as "Gradiva" ("Bertgang mit Gradiva gleichbedeutend ist" [82]).[92] But while the "GANG" (from *gehen,* "to go") of Zoë's patronym is evidently the same as "Gradiva," the "BERT" seems just as evidently to echo back "NorBERT." It is, as it were, the unacknowledged addition that Norbert makes to the Gradiva to make both it and Zoë *gleichbedeutend.*[93] Nor is this the end of it. In a story so alive to its philological aspect—with its protagonist well-versed (lit., "traveled") not only in the classical languages but also in the etymology of the Germanic ("nicht nur in den klassischen Sprachen, sondern auch in der Etymologie der germanischen bewandert" [82]) and constantly surrounded by English speakers—every element of Norbert Hanold's name resonates. "HAN" is Middle High German for *Haben,* itself embedded in the narrative by the inviting injunction "Have" the young archaeologist finds at his feet at the threshold to the Casa di Meleagro. To an ear saturated with the chatter of English-speaking tourists, "HANOLD" seems to suggest an appropriation of the ancient: *des Alten Besitzen,* as it were. "NOR" seems to resonate with the *nordlich,* or northern, that occurs throughout to designate Norbert's German origin (e.g., 39), so that, roughly translated, Norbert Hanold's name (chiastically) parses out as "appropriate the ancient and Germany shines." That is, hidden in the plain sight of our protagonist's name is the by now open secret: the narcissism at issue in his tale is not a personal but a national one. And philology is not only our means for revealing this hidden agenda; it is also, as we will see, one of the story's chief means for carrying it out.

WHITE ARCHAEOLOGY

Why is Hanold sitting in his study contemplating the Bild in the first place? Why the narcissistic need for a reflected splendor (*Glanz*) and self-image? And how does the trip to Italy further that cause? Again, the answer to these questions seems to depend less on Hanold's personal psychological identity and more on his more general German one. Hanold and his family belong to the rising elite of a professional academic class of nineteenth-century Prussia. Their social status is considerable, as we see not only in the substantial property ("beträchtlichen Vermögensbesitz") Hanold inherits from his father the *Universitätsprofessor* and archaeologist (*Altertumsforscher*) but also in the nuanced depiction of the class relations conveyed in Hanold's interactions with the servant girls and ladies of his city streets and then again in the portrayal of the social gatherings he is obliged to attend—in both cases, a social status that must be assiduously maintained. This is partly because Hanold's class identity and standing are somewhat peculiar and, more importantly, fragile, during a time when, we know, class identity—and hence self-identity—were unusually unsettled in Germany in general.[94] The social status of Hanold and his family is based neither on the inherited nobility of the aristocratic class, whose actual political credit had by this time been severely reduced but whose virtual ideal (of "nobility") still remained strong, nor on the capital gains of the newly arrived bourgeoisie, whose actual commercial strength had done so much to undermine the standing of the aristocracy without, however, having been rewarded with much cultural or political status of their own. The class standing of the Hanold clan is, then, based neither on concrete political power nor on crude material wealth but rather on the considerable cultural capital invested by nineteenth-century German society in classical studies, a direct inheritance of Humboldt's educational reforms at the beginning of the century that, in the wake of the defeats by Napolean's Romanic armies, sought to reconstruct a sense of German social identity on the basis of a *Bildungsprozeß* heavily weighted with classical, and especially Greek, learning. Hanold's class was both the administrator and representative of this process; as James Porter puts it, their German class *identity* was directly dependent on their (and not only their) *identification* with the classical past.[95] In other words, the splendor of Hanold's family name ("der Glanz des väterlichen Namens") is a more or less immediate reflection of the splendor Germany in general and this class in particular attributed to the classical world. So, sitting in his book-lined study, reflecting on and identifying with his antique *Reliefbild,* seemingly completely isolated from any meaningful activity in the social or political sphere, Hanold is actually engaged in precisely that cultural activity designed to fabricate and secure his privileged, socially important, but always tenuously grounded German identity. His fantastic efforts—unsupported by any base in reality—to fashion a noble identity for the Gradiva are merely projected symptoms of how the study of the

Gradiva is intended to forge an equally base-less "noble" identity for himself.[96] In a strange but highly significant fashion, Hanold's class identity, especially its *Glanz,* its nobility, is as groundless, as simulacric, as the Gradiva on his wall—and that is equally true of the broader German identity his class was charged with representing. As fragile, fantastic, and remote from reality as Hanold's fabrications may seem, they are nonetheless the very engine for the manufacture of a broadly real, idealized German self-image.

This is perhaps nowhere more apparent than in the example of Hanold's north German traveling companions to Italy, the many so-called Augusts and Gretes who seem always to swarm about him on the train, in the hotels, and in the museums. The trip to Italy is as required (*vorschriftsmäßig*) for these young couples as it is for the young archaeologist, and that should be as puzzling a coincidence for us as it is obvious to those in the tale (and for that matter, to Freud). It points to an overlap in their respective motives for the journey that has very little to do with repressed erotic aspirations on Hanold's part and almost everything to do with expressed class, or social, aspirations on everyone's part. August and Grete travel to Italy to properly train their desires, both public and private. At this moment of their assumption of publicly recognized social standing and identity, they are also culturally compelled to assume, to "take in," the classical world, which will in turn grant them its splendid, or *glänzend,* cultural base.[97] And while this socializing process all-too-evidently fails to transform the Augusts' and Gretes' all-too-earthly insipidity, that very failure illustrates and exposes all the more clearly both the means and the need for such a transformation. Hanold cannot help but overhear their conversation as they walk through a display of Pompeiian housewares:

"O look, that was practical of them; we will certainly have to get a food-warmer like that ourselves."

"Yes, but for the meals that my wife cooks it must be made of silver." . . .

"No—is that a thimble? Did people back then have sewing needles?"

"It almost seems so, but you couldn't have done anything with that, my sweet, it would be much too big even for your thumb."

"O sieh mal, das hatten sie praktisch, solchen Speisenwärmer wollen wir uns doch auch anschaffen."

"Ja, aber für die Gerichte, die meine Frau kocht, muß er aus Silber gemacht sein." . . .

"Nein, das ist ja ein Fingerhut! Haben die Leute damals schon Nähnadeln gehabt?"

"Das scheint beinah' so, aber du hättest nichts mit ihm anfangen können, mein Herz, dir würde er noch für den Daumen viel zu groß sein." (37)

As the first line so ironically attests, by walking through the classical past, these couples are virtually outfitting themselves for their future social establishment. Indeed, it is how they are to be established. But their crudely bourgeois character, their hopeless imperviousness to the uplifting effect of this past inheritance, reveals itself both in the "low" domestic level of their identification—only what corresponds with their own *bürgerlich* existence attracts their attention—and in the equally low and crude means by which they idealize themselves out of the identification: *their* food warmers will be of silver, *their* fingers are delicate, and so on. The mechanisms of identification and idealization, the very same mechanisms as those at work in Hanold's case, are in place, intact. It is just that here August and Grete prove incapable of identifying with what is noble in the classical world, and this in turn marks them as excluded from the noble class of cultivated, *gebildeten* Germans. As a result, these emphatically typical couples prove embarrassing, unsatisfactory examples of typical German identity. As Hanold is made to feel, "his racial identity with them awoke in him no feeling of pride, but rather an opposite one . . . for one could not compare the present day race with the sublime beauty of the ancient artworks" (seine Stammeszugehörigkeit zu ihnen [rief] durchaus kein Stolzgefühl in ihm wach, vielmehr nur das ziemlich entgegengesetzte . . . denn mit der erhabenen Schönheit der alten Kunstwerke durfte man das heutige . . . Geschlecht nicht in Vergleich bringen [33–34]). A German racial identity worth being proud of can only be accomplished through the detour of an identification with the elevated beauty of classical art, which will yield a similarly elevated social status at home, negating and rising above the banal base-ness of bourgeois sensibility. "Germany" itself depends on Hanold and his base-less ideals and actions, his base-less class and standing.

A point that is more difficult to formulate but equally important is that the classical ideal seems involved in fashioning not only a more or less public social self-image and set of values for these German travelers but also an apparently more private set of values, which is to say, desires. And through the complicated but all-too-familiar process that identifies desire per se with male desire and male desire with its female object, the search for a noble German identity fashioned through an identification with the classical world manifests itself also as the search for a beloved German woman fashioned through the same identificatory chiasmus. The "proper" erotic drive and object are determined not by inherent psychological instinct but by installed societal norms; nothing reveals one's social identity more clearly than the identity of what one desires, and the same issues of authenticity that assert themselves in respect to class or racial identity also emerge in relation to "true" love. So for instance, Hanold overhears the German couple in the hotel room next door:

> "My only August, you please me more than the Apollo Belvedere." "My sweet Grete, you are far more beautiful than the Capitoline Venus."

> "Mein einziger August, du gefällst mir besser als der Apoll von Belvedere." "[M]eine süße Grete, du bist viel schöner als die capitolinische Venus." (35; see also 33)

In this instance, we have a self-identification that forgoes the identification with classical models; the result is a crassness of desire and, by extension, of the couple that precludes any sense of nobility to their love.[98] We can compare this with Hanold's self-parodying but also revelatory dream in which he sees "the Apollo Belvedere suddenly lift up the Capitoline Venus, carry her away, and lay her safely down on some object in a dark shadow. . . . This mythological occurrence did not further surprise the young archaeologist, but it did strike him as remarkable that the two spoke not Greek but German to one another" ("auf einmal den Apoll von Belvedere, der die capitolinische Venus aufhob, forttrug und in einem dunklen Schatten gesichert auf einen Gegenstand hinlegte. . . . Dieser mythologische Vorgang verwunderte den jungen Archäologen nicht weiter, nur fiel ihm als merkwürdig auf, daß die beiden nicht Griechisch, sondern Deutsch miteinander redeten"

[36]).[99] As significantly close as this juxtaposition reveals Hanold and August and Grete to be, it also reveals a crucial difference that will distinguish Hanold's case from theirs. With his desires properly trained by his classical studies, his lovers become the classical works, which in turn come to speak German. The result is an admittedly parodied idealization of desire and the lovers that promises something truly classic about their love. In a difficult to define but crucial fashion, the search for a proper German identity plays itself out as the search for a proper love as well.

Given, then, that Hanold's fascination with the Gradiva, and especially his fantastic fabrication of a noble identity for her, are intimately involved in a fabrication of a noble class identity for himself in Germany, and that this identity is forged by means of a broadly sanctioned identificatory mechanism of the time and place; and given too that to a certain extent Hanold's pursuit of a noble and representatively German identity also expresses itself in the form of his erotic desires and the ideal of woman and of true love he pursues, where the truth or genuineness of the latter (of the woman and the love) becomes support for the genuineness of the former (noble German identity). We still need to recognize that it is not just a matter of how a proper German identity must be fashioned through the reflective detour of the classical world; it is also a matter of how the classical world must be properly fashioned to reflect, and embody, that German ideal and identity.

This preparatory fashioning of the classical as somehow "German" entails several steps. First and most important, it requires wresting the classical world away from the possession of Romanic culture, which means both from the ancient Romans *and* from the present-day Italians (not to mention the French—and Catholics).[100] In fact, even as the classical becomes the embodiment of the German desire for a noble identity, so too do present-day Italians become the invested repository for the plebian crudeness the Germans are trying to detach from themselves *and* from the classical past (i.e., from themselves through a classical past); the detachment of the Italians from the classical becomes a displaced reenactment of the detachment of philistine vulgarity from the Germans themselves (without negating how it is also and more directly an appropriation of the classical from Romanic culture). We might well read Hanold's fantastic removal of the Gradiva from the great, noisy metropolis of Rome ("der großen, lärmvollen Stadtwelt Roms") in his opening imaginings as symptomatic of this first step, including the extent to which the bustling city of Rome seems to reflect, or repeat, the noisy bustle ("das vielfältige Gelärm") of Hanold's own north German metropolis (*Großstadt* [29]).[101] Even more symptomatic are Hanold's thoughts as he takes the train away from Rome:

> To escape the inseparable "Augusts" and "Gretes," he made the trip in a third class coach, expecting at the same time to find there an interesting and scientifically useful company of Italian folk-types, the former models of ancient artworks. But he found nothing but the usual dirt—little warped fellows flailing about with their arms and legs, and representatives of the female sex, in contrast with whom his countrywomen seemed to his memory almost like Olympian goddesses.

> Dies tat er, um den Inseparables [d.h., den Augusts und Gretes] zu entgehen, in einem Wagen dritter Klasse, zugleich in diesem eine interessante und ihm wissenschaftlich förderliche Umgebung von italienischen Volkstypen, den ehemaligen Modellen der antiken Kunstwerke, erwartend. Doch er fand nichts als landesüblichen Schmutz—kleine, windschiefe, mit Armen und Beinen fuchtelnde Kerle und Vertreterinnen des weiblichen Geschlechtes, gegen die ihm seine zwiegepaarten Landsmänninnen in der Erinnerung fast noch als olympische Göttinnen erschienen. (36–37)

Here, in the service of the scientifically useful ("das wissenschaftliche Förderliche"), we see Hanold detaching the models for the ancient artworks from the Italian people, who are described as just so much dirt and debris (in *need* of removal)—crude, repulsive, physically warped, and hopelessly lower class. In the vacant space left by their disqualification, it is the Germans, the German women, who step forth as the imaginary models of ancient artworks ("Modelle der antiken Kunstwerke")—but only because the Italians have come to embody the vulgarity Hanold so abhors in the Germans themselves. We see this in the very shape of this passage, where Hanold begins by wishing to escape the oppressive ordinariness of his German traveling companions and does so by attributing it instead (and in spades) to the Italians, arriving at the end with a new version of Germans as well-nigh Olympian, and certainly *not* lower class. But we see its results too in the comparison of this passage with that quoted (and occurring) earlier, wherein Hanold rues his racial identity (*Stammeszugehörigkeit*) with the Germans and proves unable to compare them with the sublime beauty of ancient artworks ("mit der erhabenen Schönheit der alten Kunstwerke" [33–34]). It is precisely the Italians, degraded and rejected, who provide the solution that will make possible both identifications: Hanold with his race and the Germans with the classical.

As we have noted several times, once detached from the Romans and Italians, the Germans' classical world must then be Hellenized, led "back" to Greece. It is not, however, stepped back to a real Greece but rather to a Greece never actually seen or visited: not by Winckelmann or Goethe or Nietzsche or—until late, and then with shocked disappointment—Freud, and certainly not by Hanold.[102] Greece too is a decidedly base-less simulacrum, part of the same simulacric economy as the plaster cast *Reliefbild* and Hanold's social class. It is an essentially empty and aestheticized image of some pure unsullied origin before the contamination of the Roman and Italian, projected *out* of Italy as an imagined (purely imagined) anteriority. We know from Nietzsche the persistent desire "to establish a permanent alliance between Greek and German culture, without being attached to the lead-strings of Romanic culture";[103] we have seen how Freud fantasizes this alliance as biological in ways that bypass the Roman altogether; and we have seen how Hanold similarly imagines the Gradiva out of its Roman context and makes it Greek as a necessary step in making it reflectively his own (even himself).[104] In all of these cases, the classical becomes the German by first becoming Greek, and not least by thereby becoming, as it were, *blank,* a purely imaginary shine, or *Glanz:* hence the mirrorlike back and forth, the backward as forward. The emptiness of the Greek is modeled on the emptiness of Hanold's social identity, which is in turn to be given substance and confirmation by the mirroring reflection of the Greek—even as it also evacuates and disavows the Roman (*and* the vulgar German). Like the initiating plaster cast Gradiva itself, all are representations without real-world originals, representations that negate and replace originals. Again, we can think of the two hotels that perch like twin predators on the site of Pompeii, the Dioscuri pair of the Hotel Suisse and the Hotel Diomede, with their well-nigh incestuous, mirroring equivalence and identical store of counterfeit classica and invading, Baedeker-toting northerners, both (the Teutonic and the

Hellenic) somehow displacing the indigenous present Romanic with their appropriative simulations.

Nowhere is this process of making the classical past German by making it non-Italian and, instead, blankly Greek more conspicuous and disturbing than in the motif of whiteness that runs throughout Jensen's novella. It clearly helps sustain the related theme of *Glanz,* which conveys at once a sense of idealizing splendor, polish, and mirrorlike reflection, and it is also one of the assumed features of the *Reliefbild*—although it should be noted that, in fact, like all plaster casts, it actually looks rather dirty in the story's frontispiece so that the attribution of whiteness involves some willful imaginary effort. But even before its connection to the artwork, the motif of whiteness is intimately bound up with the novella's concern with German identity, and not in completely palatable ways. The association of the German and the white is part of the all too easy slide between concerns with a national social identity and (Aryan) racial doctrines that plagued Germany—and German archaeology—in the late nineteenth and early twentieth centuries, symptomatic of its anxious efforts, in the face of a weakly defined and fractured political unity, to assert an original and unified self-image. We see the slide into racial models for constructing the German even in Freud, in the archaeological *Phantasie* cited earlier. We see it too in Hanold's appeal to racial identity (*Stammeszugehörigkeit*) as his designation for overarching German identity.[105] The link between the German race and whiteness is also axiomatic in this time period. It was, of course, central to Nietzsche's notion of the blond beast, and we are in no way surprised to find that Norbert too is blond—"der blonde Norbert," as it were (81).

Throughout the novella, the north Germans are always identified—and usually exclusively identified—by the whiteness of their skin, which they are depicted as assiduously guarding against the danger of contamination by the darkening, or reddening, Italian sun.[106] A particularly egregious example of this comes up in the dialogue of August and Grete, as she asks, "Do we really have to go to Pompeii itself?" ("Müssen wir eigentlich auch noch nach Pompeji selbst?"), an idea he reassuringly rejects and adds:

> "I fear the sun would be too hot for your delicate complexion, and I could never forgive myself for that."
> "And if you should suddenly have a negress for a wife?"

"No, fortunately my fantasy does not reach that far, but even a freckle on your little nose would be a misfortune for me."

"Ich fürchte, die Sonne würde dort auch für deinen zarten Teint schon zu heiß sein, das könnte ich mir nie verzeihn."
"Wenn du auf einmal eine Negerin zur Frau hättest."
"Nein, so weit reicht glücklicherweise doch meine Phantasie nicht, aber eine Sommersprosse auf deinem Näschen würde mich schon unglücklich machen." (37–38)

The whiteness of the delicate complexion—later called the northener's complexion (43)—is simply assumed to be a mark of German racial identity and of superior good fortune (*Glück*), a mark of immaculate purity whose most minor violation, whether by the Italian sun or "Pompeii itself," is a threat to the "fantasy" and its ideal of racial identity. Grete seems to exaggerate the danger by associating the tainting of her pure white skin in Italy with becoming "a negress," with all its implicitly racist (and racistly erotic) shadings. But it should be noted that the story itself also maintains this link between the African and the Italian sun, with all the associated degradation of the nonwhite Italian this brings with it (see 43). For Grete to lose her whiteness would be to lose her German racial identity altogether and, with it, her source of superior fortune (and, implicitly, her sexual purity or chastity). Thus, whiteness is the mark of the German, of the pure, and of the superior—and also, of course, of the artificial, of a carefully guarded remove from the real ("Pompeii itself!").

Whiteness is, then, the mark of the northern German untainted by the Italian sun. But it is also the mark of the classical world untouched by Italian culture—or more specifically, untouched by "Pompeii itself." Christiane Zintzen has emphasized the central role played by Pompeii and nearby Herculanum in the nineteenth-century debates concerning the "coloring" of the ancient world, the question of whether classical statues were originally white marble or instead gaudily—and for the modern sensibility, degradingly—painted in bright, polychromatic tints. The preserved ruins of Pompeii provided archaeologists with some of the first hard evidence of such ancient painting. As a result, polychromy became associated with Pompeii, and the perceived bad taste (even lewdness) of these added layers of nonwhite color became part of the perceived late, hedonistic decadence of the city. In particular, Pompeii became associated in the nineteenth century with a specific shade of red, Pompeii red: sunburnt, sensuous, and suspiciously Oriental, almost African.[107] The impulse to detach the world of classical statuary from the taint of color was to detach it from the degrading sensuality and late, accrued decadence of specifically Italian/Romanic culture and to "restore" it, make it "once again" Greek, the underlying virginal Greek, as it were—and, by virtue of its recovered whiteness, to make it "German" as well.[108] And it is worth noting how the white world of ancient art comes to signify not only the Greek and the German but also the pure and original, the untainted and untouched. As we will see, Hanold imagines the Gradiva to be Greek, white, and a virgin, and all for the same reason: so that she can be imagined as German, and the German can be imagined as pure, original, and whole.

The impulse toward white detachment asserts itself already in Hanold's first imaginings of the Gradiva in Pompeii, with the assistance of his classical training ("unter Beihilfe seiner Altertumskenntnis" [25]). He initially conceives of the city as crowded with baseness and commerce—not unlike his own metropolis or that of the to-be-rejected Rome—and then expands (or abstracts) his vision:

> Wherever the eye turned, it fell upon lively colors, gaily painted wall surfaces, pillars with red and yellow capitals; everything reflected the glitter and glare of the dazzling noonday sun. Farther off, on a high base, a statue, gleaming white, rose up high.

> Wohin das Gesicht sich wendete, stieß es auf lebhafte Farben, bunt bemalte Mauerflächen, Säulen mit roten und gelben Kapitellen; alles funkelte und strahlte in mittägiger Sonne Blendung zurück. Weiter abwärts ragte auf hohem Sockel eine weißblitzende Statue empor. (25)

In the midst of this colorful, quotidian, commercial Pompeii and yet also somewhat detached, further back and higher up, stands the shimmering, all white statue: a kind of death in the midst of life but also clearly an intact, unaffected, morally and aesthetically distinct classical presence in the midst of the surrounding sensuality and bustling activity (*geschäftigem Treiben*). Hanold then depicts the Gradiva moving through this scene, as antiseptically detached from its squalor as he later imagines her from its common fountain.[109] In the almost immediately following dream of Pompeii's destruction, Hanold completes the identification, as he imagines the Gradiva basically becoming this statue. We are told, "At that moment, her face lost color and grew pale, as if changing to white marble" ("Dabei aber entfärbte ihr Gesicht sich blasser, wie wenn es sich zu weißem Marmor umwandle"); similarly, "From Vesuvius the red glow flared over her countenance, which, with closed eyes, was exactly like that of a beautiful statue" ("Vom Vesuv her überflackerte der rote Schein ihr Antlitz, das mit geschlossenen Lidern vollständig dem eines schönen Steinbildes glich" [28]). Even as he depicts her as shedding color (*sich entfärben*) and so becoming white marble or, alternatively, as a (white) statue only superficially colored by Pompeii's red, so between the first imagining and this dream has Hanold fantasized her as shedding her Romanic identity and becoming Greek. Becoming white (marble) and becoming Greek are presented as strictly analogous. Both involve the same removal; both are part of the same construction of the classical. But the final significance of both is fully revealed only in the closing image of Hanold's dream, when, we are told, the falling rain of ash "extinguished the last glimmer of her face and soon, like a Northern winter snowfall, buried the entire figure under a smooth, even cover" ("den letzten Schimmer ihres Gesichtes auslöschte und bald auch wie nordisch-winterliches Flockengestöber die ganze Gestalt unter einer gleichmäßigen Decke begrub" [28]). The final dominating whiteness that takes over and blankets the entire ancient picture with its uniforming cover is metaphorically northern. With all its acknowledgment of its fatal destructiveness and burial, the classical world is made white that it might, metaphorically, appear German—and not, let it be said, as dirty ash-gray and Italian ("Pompeii itself!").[110]

As we might expect, white is also a foregrounded feature of Gradiva-Zoë, and here especially we see how the detour through the imaginary classical produces an ennoblement of the German present. Like all the other German visitors, she too is conspicuous in her northern complexion (*nordländischen Teint*), but this is first perceived by Hanold as her alabaster countenance (*die Alabasterfarbe des Gesichtes*) and then again as her beautiful, alabaster brow (*die schöne alabasterfarbige Stirn* [47, 51]). Once she has spoken German, however, and with explicit reference back to Hanold's dream, the stakes are raised to "as calmly beautiful as marble" ("so ruhig-schön wie Marmor") and then again "as completely white as marble" ("ganz weiß wie Marmor" [52, 57]). Clearly the alabaster and marblelike whiteness of Zoë's skin is emphasized to facilitate her identificatory assimilation with the Bild of the Gradiva, to bring the living world into an equivalence with the world of art. In this respect, we should also note the pronounced whiteness of Zoë's sketchbook, which will appropriate to its pages all the artifacts and life of Pompeii, robbing them of color in the process—and which, significantly enough, Hanold explicitly associates with her speaking German (61). But something more than just an innocent identification of life and art is going on here. There is also a noticeable idealization at work that involves both Zoë and the plaster cast Gradiva. That is, Zoë's white German skin is not linked directly to the plaster of Hanold's copy cast, which, as mentioned, is rather dirty (and cheap) looking. Rather, both Zoë and the Gradiva are stepped from a somewhat mundane white (of skin and plaster) to an alabaster to a marble white that adds a splendor, a *Glanz,* not there at first: a marblelike shimmer not part of the original German objects nor, we note, part of the Pompeiian world into which the story is transported but rather of an imagined classical Greek world behind or beneath the polychromatic Italian, which then reflects back on the pale, delicate complexion of the German.[111] The original white of the Germans is transformed, ennobled, by the reflective splendor, the *Glanz,* of the Greeks, which is to say that German racial identity as superior and original and pure is dependent on the Greek, on a Greek that is, moreover, purely a construct of the Germans themselves.

Saxa Loquuntur

One final feature of the Gradiva Bild—more implicitly presented than those already discussed but no less consequential for Hanold's fantasy—is the fact of its silence. To some extent, the silence figures as part of the ongoing debate since the eighteenth century regarding the relation between the narrative and the visual arts, including especially sculpture: the relation between the silent plaster cast and its narrativization (i.e., its being brought to language) partakes of the interplay of stasis and movement mentioned before. To some extent too the silence of the Bild is part of its allegiance with death, with the underworld motif that so often accompanies this particular literary topos: for the Gradiva to be brought "back" into the realm of language is for it to be brought back to life.[112] But while both of these elements figure prominently in the presentation of the matter of the Gradiva's silence—and, by implication, of its relation to language—the story's central concern with archaeology adds a decisive, and somewhat different, dimension to the issue as well.

As we learn from the description of Hanold's background, archaeology was part of the field of classical studies in nineteenth-century Germany, a field that was dominated by philology and the study of (mostly) literary texts. We are told that Hanold takes his first compulsory trip to Italy "in connection with his brilliantly passed examination in philology" ("im Anschlusse an sein vorzüglich bestandenes philologisches Examen" [31]), and it is characteristic of this model of his profession that we are given abundant evidence of his training in both Greek and Latin philology and literature but none at all of any actual archaeological spade work. Again, Hanold practices a decidedly virtual archaeology, as seemingly divorced from the real (and dirty) world as literature (or his plaster cast). In any case, ancient texts and their professional study were privileged by classical studies precisely because they were felt to represent the foundation of the elevated cultural inheritance upon which Bildung was based and in whose image the contemporary German subject and society were to be formed. The role of archaeology was primarily a supportive or complementary one. It was meant to illustrate and buttress this written and largely aesthetic tradition. We see this repeatedly in the case of Hanold's most conscious understanding of his field. He sees it as devoted to the study of statues, primarily of divinities or otherwise ennobled figures, and primarily to material that seems to second what he already knows from literature, whether from Homer, Ovid, Aeschylus, or the Greek poet Meleager—much, we might say, like Schliemann and his referral of all his finds to Homer's texts.

But the relation between classical archaeology and classical philology—or as it was also called, between *Sachphilologie* and *Sprachphilologie*—was not only a corroborating one; it was also potentially a conflictual one. As mentioned, many of the objects that fell within the purview of archaeologists belonged to a fundamentally different, prehistorical and pretextual, world from that cherished by the philologists, which had the no doubt unintended effect of undermining the assumptions on which German Bildung was founded, namely, the idea of classical Greece as both origin and foundation of Western culture. As it turned out, classical Greece wasn't even an origin or foundation of itself. Admittedly, such objects and their concomitant challenge seem conspicuously absent from Jensen's novella, though their world does appear presumed in Zoë's reference to "some excavated antediluvian thing" ("etwas vorsintflutliches Ausgegrabenes" [81]) as well as in Freud's more or less contemporary reading of the tale. But some of the objects that are found in the story have a similar disruptive effect. That is, archaeology concentrated not only on prehistorical, pretextual—and so, in a sense, preverbal—and preclassical artifacts but also on *common* artifacts, on everyday and nonaesthetic objects, and this too contributed to the breakdown of a simple and complete identification of the ancient world—both Roman and "Greek"—with the textually based classical image. We see this, for instance, in the pots and pans, the food warmers and thimbles on display in the Museo Nazionale in Naples, in a room abutting its collection of sculptures and wall paintings, the latter, significantly enough, visited by Hanold, and the former by August and Grete. We see it too in the Gradiva Bild, which Hanold explicitly describes as possessing little or no aesthetic value, little or nothing classical and instead a good deal of the commonplace. From one perspective—that of a straight-up classicist—this leads Hanold to find nothing really noteworthy in it for his science ("eigentlich für seine Wissenschaft an dem Relief nichts sonderlich Beachtenswertes" [24]), but from another it is precisely the interest in what is not a product of the great art of the ancient world ("kein plastisches Erzeugnis alter großer Kunst") that comes to distinguish his archaeological "science" from that of classical studies in general. This emerging distinction is implicit in Hanold's scholarly specialty: "He possessed a decisive facility for deciphering puzzling graffiti and had already accomplished widely recognized work in this field" ("Er besaß eine entschiedene Fertigkeit in der Entzifferung schwer enträtselbarer graffiti, hatte schon rühmlich Anerkanntes darin geleistet" [45]). He applies his Greek and Latin philological training not to the noble cause of working with high-culture literary texts but rather to deciphering the rude scripts and sketches of anonymous street vandals, of graffiti that—to judge by the one example we are given—mocked the high-flown pretensions and deceitful praise (*Lobpreisung*) of official culture and texts as a rather questionable doctoring of a far more prosaic reality.[113] Two points: First, it is clear even if somewhat surprising that classical archaeology itself introduces into the picture of the ancient world much of the crudity and banality that classicism per se was meant to eliminate in the present-day self-image of the *gebildeten* Germans themselves.[114] Second, it is equally clear that the silent, nonverbal world of archaeology stands in considerable tension with the textual, lingual world of philology, a tension that threatens the very structure and function of the classical per se.[115]

Something of this tension, this threat to the language-based model of the classical world posed by the common objects of archaeology, can be seen behind the *Sprachkrise,* the language crisis experienced by Hanold just before the first appearance of the Gradiva *rediviva.* The crisis begins immediately upon Hanold's arrival in Pompeii:

> For his traveling companion, science, had decidedly much of an old Trappist about her, did not open her mouth when not spoken to, and it seemed to him that he was not far from forgetting in what language he had communed with her.

> Denn seine Reisebegleiterin, die Wissenschaft, hatte entschieden viel von einer alten Trappistin, tat den Mund nicht auf, wenn sie nicht angeredet wurde, und ihm kam's vor, er sei nicht viel weit davon, aus dem Gedächtnis zu verlieren, in welcher Sprache er überhaupt mit ihr verkehrt habe. (41)

And it reaches its flashpoint the next day, when he sits alone at noon among the empty ruins:

> He had a feeling that he did not understand Latin at all. . . . Not only had all his science deserted him but it had left him without the least desire to find it (or her) again. . . . What she uttered with puckered lips and learned mien and presented as wisdom was all vain, empty pompousness, and merely nibbled around at the dry rind of the fruit of knowledge, without revealing anything of its content, the essential core, or bringing it to the point of inner intellectual enjoyment. What she taught was a lifeless, archaeological view, and what came out of her mouth was a dead, philological language.

> [E]r trug ein Gefühl in sich, daß er überhaupt kein Latein
> verstehe. . . . Seine ganze Wissenschaft hatte ihn nicht allein
> verlassen, sondern ließ ihn auch ohne das geringste
> Begehren, sie wieder aufzufinden. . . . Was sie mit
> hochgelehrter Miene über die verrunzelten Lippen brachte
> und als Weisheit vortrug, war alles eitel leere Wichtigtuerei,
> klaubte nur an den dürren Schalen der Erkenntnisfrüchte
> herum, ohne von ihrem Inhalt, dem Wesenskerne etwas zu
> offenbaren und zu innerem Verständnisgenuß zu bringen.
> Was sie lehrte, war eine leblose archäologische Anschauung,
> und was ihr vom Mund kam, eine tote, philologische
> Sprache. (46)

Hanold's language crisis is, then, a professional crisis, a collapse of faith
in the philology-based classicism and its version of the classical world
and, by extension, of what matters most in the present, the essential
core (*der Wesenskern*) and its inner intellectual enjoyment (*innerer Verständnisgenuß*). The role of archaeology in this debacle seems necessarily double, a consequence of its own conflictual allegiances. On the one
hand, in its ancillary attachment to *Sprachphilologie,* the *Sachphilologie*
of archaeology shares in its fate, in no small part a victim of its own undermining influence. On the other, in its distinct devotion to the commonplace, to the scribblings of schoolboys on walls and to the businesses, bakeries, and barrooms of slaves and servants, archaeology has
lost touch with the classical ideal that was to animate and enliven its
view, to narrativize and motivate its subject matter, and thus to justify
and legitimate its enterprise. In both cases, archaeology fails to uphold
or support Hanold's sense of identity: the muteness to which he succumbs is the mark of this loss.

The crisis is resolved on two different fronts, both more or less at
the projected site of the Gradiva.[116] First, once the language of classical
philology has failed to sustain the classical imaginary (and hence too
Hanold's sense of self-identity) and the ancient objects fall silent and
dead, another language emerges, a language of those objects themselves. It is a language only audible to those, like Hanold, equipped
with a special sixth sense, a language apparently unheard by the English
or American tourists, by the native Italian guides, or by the obtuse Augusts and Gretes. For the trained German archaeologist, however,
Pompeii comes to assume

an entirely different appearance, but not a living one; it seemed rather now, for the first time, to be completely petrified into dead immobility. Yet out of this stirred a feeling that death was beginning to talk, although not in a way discernible to human ears. To be sure, here and there it sounded as if a whispering tone came out of the stone. . . . One had to stand alone and as the only one alive in the hot midday stillness here between the detritus of the past, in order not to see with the material eye and not to hear with the physical ear. Then it came forth everywhere and began to speak without sound.

ein ganz verändertes Gesicht . . . nicht etwa ein lebendiges, vielmehr schien's sich jetzt erst völlig zu toter Reglosigkeit zu versteinern. Doch aus dieser rührte ein Gefühl an, daß der Tod zu sprechen anfange, nur nicht in einer für Menschenohren vernehmbaren Weise. Allerdings klang es da und dort, als komme ein raunender Ton aus dem Gestein hervor. . . . [Man] mußte als einzig Lebendiger allein in der heißen Mittagsstille hier zwischen den Überresten der Vergangenheit stehen, um nicht mit den körperlichen Augen zu sehen und nicht mit den leiblichen Ohren zu hören. Dann kam's überall hervor, ohne sich zu regen, und begann zu reden ohne Laut. (43, 46; see also 44)

As Freud will famously declare, "saxa loquuntur."[117] The stones themselves come to speak a language uniquely their own—archaeology's own—entirely independent of the Greek and Latin of classical philology's texts. Crucially, this autonomous language is at once associated with the distinct objects of archaeology and with some special, privileged sense of spiritual or psychic interiority: as if one needed some unusual intuition to hear or decipher this archaeological language or record, something more than just philological training (which is to say that Hanold's "sixth sense," his animative fantasy, is not something other than or separate from his archaeological science and inner intellectual enjoyment but is in some ways its essential, distinguishing feature), *and* as if this special language spoke a truth about the human essence (*der Wesenskern*) not expressed by a dead, philological language.[118] Hanold's vision of the Gradiva captures the major features of this new language: not only does *saxum loquitur,* but the language it comes to speak is a *Geistersprache*—the language of spirits, evoking not only ghosts but also, crucially, *Geist.*[119]

Second, this new language, this *Geistersprache,* in which the archaeological past comes to speak, is not left so vaguely unidentified. Rather, as no doubt anticipated, this language is clearly identified as German—which becomes, as it were, the answer to Hanold's seemingly rhetorical question, in what language does he commune with his science (41). When Hanold first attempts to address the reputed *Reliefbild,* he does so in Greek and asks whether she corresponds to (or simply is) a figure out of classical literature. When she fails to respond, he shifts to Latin and inquires after her noble origin (*vornehmen Ursprung*). When again she fails to answer to his philologically based queries, he realizes, "she was obviously sitting there before him only as a mute image" ("offenbar saß sie nur als ein stummes Bild vor ihm"). This is the point at which she famously declares, "If you want to speak with me, you must do so in German" ("Wenn Sie mit mir sprechen wollen, müssen Sie's auf deutsch tun" [51]). Freud is surely wrong in his claim that the general fantasy of the Gradiva ends with this line. Quite to the contrary, this is where the fantasy begins in earnest, not only for Hanold but for the general (German) readers as well. It is indeed remarkable that it does not strike Hanold as in the least remarkable that she spoke German ("Ihm war's nicht im geringsten mehr auffällig, daß sie deutsch sprach"), that he "lost all feeling of strangeness beneath the two sensations that washed over him, the one, that the Gradiva possessed the capacity for language, and the second that was forced out from his inner being by her voice" ("verging jede Befremdlichkeit unter zwei über ihm zusammenschlagenden Empfindungswogen, der einen, daß die Gradiva Sprachfähigkeit besaß, und der anderen, die von ihrer Stimme aus seinem Innern aufgedrängt worden"), and that he asserts, "I knew that your voice sounded like that" ("Ich wußte es, so klänge deine Stimme" [52]). But we need not resort to repressed childhood memories and abandon our focus on the archaeological imaginary to explain this lack of strangeness and this knowledge: indeed, as I will argue, the idea of the explanation as residing in a "childhood memory" is part of the archaeological imaginary.

Rather, the shift away from Greek and Latin, and also from Italian, as the official authoritative language of archaeology and the emergence of German in their stead is one of the crucial transformations of the profession during the nineteenth century.[120] It reflected in part a weakening of the social and cultural capital invested in classicists by their philological training—a weakening occasioned in part by archaeology—and in part too a rise in the stock of German as a worthy national culture in its own right.[121] It came at a time when German "scientific" archaeology was beginning to assert its Europe-wide dominance over the entire field of classical studies and also—as Freud's archaeological *Phantasie* attests—at a time when racial theorists were proposing Aryan sources for the prehistorical world archaeologists were busily discovering behind the historical, text-based classical "inheritance." That the object of attention for the young archaeologist (*der junge Archäologe*)—and it seems significant that Hanold is identified by his professional identity at just this moment (52)—should fail to respond to the language of the classical philologist and instead insist on German is part and parcel of archaeology at this time. And the fact that the language of archaeology should also be associated with the language of inmost being adds to this ("the essential core," "the inner intellectual enjoyment," "out of his inner being," etc.). German is the language not only of science but also of interiority, of *Geist:* the *Geist* that is necessary to reveal the ancient world that is divorced from the textual record and the *Geist* that is felt to animate the world apart from its "philological" languages.[122] The shift to German as the language of both science and *Geist* is evident at the moment of revelation, when the young archaeologist proves himself well versed not only in the classical languages but also in the etymology of the Germanic (82). German replaces Greek and Latin as a professional language (and, moreover, as a language of origins, professionally secured), and the added *Glanz* the Gradiva acquires by being brought "back" to language ("zur Sprachfähigkeit zurückversetzt" [84]) as "Bertgang" is made to seem a decidedly interior quality.[123] The aestheticized splendor of the classical world is smuggled *into* the figure of Zoë: we are told, "the splendor in the eyes of the young daughter of the zoologist rivaled the pearls and diamonds of the beneficent rain" ("Mit [den 'Perlen und Diamanten' des wohltätigen Regens] wetteiferte auch ein Glanz in den Augen der jungen Zoologentochter" [85]). This is the fitting conclusion of the process that began back in Germany, with Hanold's fantastic incorporation of his own contemplative, idealizing, and cultured gaze into the plaster cast as a certain refined spirituality ("etwas fein Durchgeistigtes" [26]). The German imparts *Glanz* as *Geist,* a *Geist* that both reads itself into and out of the silent world, and archaeology and interiority come together in the emergent discourse of a highly questionable German ideal.

INTROJECTION

With this constellation of archaeology, German (language), and *Geist*, we have arrived at a point in our analysis of the novella where we can finally turn to the issue we deferred earlier: the issue of introjection, the mechanism by which the more or less impersonal conditions of social self-image related to archaeology become projected inward as a matter of individual psychological identity—in other words, the means by which socially contingent nationalism becomes reconstituted as an essential, inner psychology.[124] There are three particular examples of this introjection that I would like to touch on: the example of Vesuvius, the example of archaeology proper, and the example of the houseflies that pester Hanold from the moment he arrives in Italy until the very end.

Mount Vesuvius is a significant (counter)part to Pompeii proper, and while its looming presence is perhaps not as pronounced here as in other tales set in Pompeii, it still lurks suggestively at the margins of Jensen's novella. It sits smoldering on the horizon of both the ancient and the present-day city, a constant source of potentially eruptive elemental force—think of the red glow it casts in Hanold's dream—and, at the same time, of death and burial. Although not directly connected to issues of social self-image, two points to its use are important for our understanding of the story. First, Jensen draws a connection between the volcano and the wine, the *Vesuvwein* (55), that Hanold drinks in both the Hotel Diomed and the Hotel Suisse, the wine that seems to bring the ancient stories and modern ruins into motion, much as Hanold's imagination does the Gradiva. As the narrator explains, "Of course on the ground of this region—unsteady since ancient times— this could not be exactly surprising, for the subterranean fire lurked everywhere, awaiting eruption, and let a little of itself rise up into the vines and grapes from which the Vesuvian wine was pressed" ("Das konnte auf dem von altersher schwanken Boden der Gegend freilich nicht grade Wunder nehmen, denn die unterirdische Glut lauerte überall nach einem Aufbruch und ließ auch ein weniges von sich in die Rebstöcke und Trauben emporsteigen, aus denen der Vesuvio gekeltert wurde" [54]). It is not that an interior psyche animates and produces itself in the representations of the outside world but just the opposite: it is the outside world that produces itself in the representations of the interiorized psyche. Vesuvius and Pompeii are, as it were, introjected into Hanold every bit as much as they are (then) projected out of him. Second, Jensen also draws a connection between this wine and the motif of counterfeiting, sustained both by the venue of the two (simulacric) hotels and by the earlier presentation of ancient Pompeii's wine as suspect in its purity and authenticity: as questionable in its essence as the antique splendors (*antiken Herrlichkeiten*) set out for sale at the Dioscuri hotels.[125] That is, there is something as inauthentic and suspect about this method of introjection (the wine) and its concomitant interiorized condition (Hanold's psyche) as there is about just about everything else in the story. It too is part and parcel of the same simulacric economy as the Gradiva, Hanold's class, Greece, and so on.

Both the sense of from outside to inside and of fabrication are also evident in respect to the more dominant and, for us, more important instance of introjection in the story, that of archaeology proper. Freud, of course, calls attention to Jensen's use of archaeological metaphors for psychological conditions and operations and even more famously appropriates them for his own use. We would do well, however, to look more closely at Jensen's actual examples, which seem to point in a very different direction from that proposed by Freud. To do so, we need first to stress a point that Freud makes as well, namely, that Jensen's psychologized use of the archaeological metaphor involves an inversion, or reversal, of relations. The archaeologist, Hanold, becomes the archaeological site and the archaeological artifact, Zoë, becomes, as it were, the archaeologist. We have seen many such instances of inversion between Hanold and the Gradiva before, of reversals that seem to shuttle back and forth in unexpected but completely controlled ways, and archaeology, as at once the modern German science of inquiry and the ancient Romanic site of that inquiry, has been deeply implicated in the same transposing process. A similar play of inversion is also at work in the process of archaeology's introjection, similarly staged in the relations between Hanold and Zoë.

Let me begin with the most overt instance of these joined processes of inversion and introjection in the tale. Late in the story, on the day of his last meeting with Gradiva-Zoë, Hanold pauses beside a now dried up fountain on a street of Pompeii. He contemplates, from an archaeological perspective ("in archäologischer Hinsicht"), how two thousand years ago thirsty passersby must have casually stopped, stooped, and scooped water into their mouths from the fountain's faucet. He momentarily considers how the Gradiva might have done the same and then immediately rejects the idea with a shudder of anxiety (*Verdruß*). The Gradiva, from a well-educated family (*aus feingebildetem Haus*) and imbued with noble sensibility (*edlen Sinn*) is to have no connection with the activity and conduct of the "Plebs." For Hanold even to have thought it of her is degrading (*entwürdigend*):

> It frightened him that she might be able to see by looking at him that he had had this incredibly unreasonable idea, for her eyes possessed something penetrating. A couple of times when he had been with her, he had had the feeling that they were seeking for a way into the inside of his head and were searching around in it as if with a bright steel probe. For that reason he had to pay very careful attention that they not come upon anything foolish in his thought processes.

> [I]hn überkam's schreckhaft, sie könne ihm den unglaublich verstandwidrigen Einfall ansehen. Denn ihre Augen besaßen etwas Eindringliches; ihn hatte ein paarmal das Gefühl angerührt, während seines Zusammenseins mit ihr trachteten sie danach, einen Zugang ins Innere seines Kopfes auszufinden und darin wie mit einer stahlhellen Sonde herumzusuchen. Er mußte deshalb sehr behutsam achtgeben, daß sie nichts Törichtes in seinen Gedankenvorgängen antrafen. (68)

The steel probe and operation of *sondage* are the most conspicuous indices that we are moving within the field of nineteenth-century archaeology, but there are others. Two related themes that I previously discussed separately reassert themselves here in intimate connection. First is the matter of the Gradiva's *Sehkraft,* her power of sight. I mentioned how Hanold's opening attribution of sight or vision to the bas-relief bespoke a recognizable mechanism of reversal. His own contemplating gaze is installed into the image as its own inherent quality; what he sees as the "seeing" of the picture is a projected reflection of his seeing of the picture. Closely related to this installment of *Sehkraft* was Hanold's investment of it with "in sich zurückgezogenen Gedanken," with a psychic interior world—again, an inverted reflection of his own gazing contemplation, his own withdrawn, meditative regard. Here this fabricating inversion undergoes yet another reversal and another fabrication. Now the Gradiva is imagined as looking back at him and investing him with a psychic world that corresponds with her own, a psychic space as patently manufactured—*hin-eingebildet*—in Hanold as it was in the *Reliefbild* to begin with. Second, the theme of nobility weighs in. We have discussed how Hanold consistently invests a sense of nobility into the Gradiva in particular and the classical past in general as a means by which, through a reflective identificatory reversal, his own class identity will be secured and sustained. Here we see Hanold actively defending this image of the Gradiva, even against the challenge of a more vulgar, archaeological representation of the ancient world, and he does so in order that the nobilized, classical Gradiva might in turn invest or install such a noble, not vulgar, ideal in and as his own psyche.[126] That is, the classical world, a projection of the German need for a (virtual) noble identity, is introjected as a corresponding psychic world in Hanold. The classical "Bild" becomes German Bildung and imbues the subject with its legitimating ideal.[127]

There is a second effect of the metaphorical appropriation of archaeology and its application to the individual subject, an effect closely related to introjection and one of special significance for psychologists such as C. G. Jung and Ludwig Klages (to be discussed in chapter 3) but also, even if more modestly, for Freud. This is the effect of linking together the buried past of the ancient world and the buried past of the subject's childhood world, a linkage that also involves, for Freud, a connection between the so-called unconscious and both childhood and the ancient past.[128] Freud argues that Hanold selects the setting of Pompeii and its archaeological remains because he unconsciously draws an analogy between his repressed desires for the child Zoë and the buried remnants of the historical past. He cites the reference to Hanold as Zoë's "childhood friend who had, in a sense, also been excavated from the rubble" ("gewissermaßen gleichfalls aus der Verschüttung wieder ausgegrabenen Kindheitsfreundes" [85]) as a confirmation of this analogy.[129] As we have seen, this explanation is a woefully short-shrifted account for the formative role of Pompeii in Hanold's fantasy, but it is worth contemplating some of its far-reaching effects. The analogy draws on certain nineteenth-century anthropological ideas of so-called primitive societies as childlike and Western society as adult, with the implicit assumption that the childlike races would eventually develop into mature Europeanlike societies and that Europe had the grownup responsibility to regulate that development.[130] In other words, the analogy in its original context was to a great extent a legitimation of European colonialism and imperialism. In a step almost shocking in its overstepping of gaps, this model of primitive races was also applied to Europe's own alleged classical and prehistorical past, and the consequences for both archaeology and psychology were enormous. For one thing—and especially for the Germans, who had little actual colonial presence—archaeology became invested with the same legitimating rationale as imperialism and colonialism, that of adults dealing with children. For another, the classical past, situated far away in the remote reaches and foreign cultures of Mediterranean lands, became appropriated as part of northern Europe's own childhood, connected to their present as naturally—whether "racially" or "phylogenetically"—as an individual's infancy to his adult identity (a stolen childhood, as it were). And for psychoanalysis, the analogy not only led to the identificatory conflation of the individual and "collective" psyche, the idea that we somehow carry the whole of Western history inscribed in our psyche and that we can understand the ancient past in terms of childhood and childhood in terms of the ancient past.[131] Far more disturbing is how it led to a legitimizing of psychoanalysis as a kind of colonization of childhood, an attitude toward children, their inner worlds, and their relation to the adult world that has its roots in nineteenth-century imperialism and that persisted in psychology long after its place in anthropology—and archaeology—had been vacated. The analogy and its introjection of such anthropo-archaeological assumptions into our understanding of both the psyche and the child was not an innocent one, and it has left psychoanalysis open to some well-deserved critique.[132]

Jensen's novella relates a slightly different tale about the link between the archaeological metaphor and childhood from the one Freud's essay would suggest, a tale that exposes some of the questionable and insidious fabrication at stake in making the identification. Most importantly, rather than depicting a lost childhood memory of Zoë as the source for Hanold's subsequent obsessive fantasy with Pompeii and the Gradiva—a memory that is recovered at the end of the tale and that dispels the delusion of Hanold as he comes to embrace the original Zoë and to let go of the simulacric Gradiva—Jensen's novella seems to suggest just the opposite: that Hanold's obsessive fantasy with Pompeii and the Gradiva are the source for his subsequent attraction to his childhood acquaintance, a fantasy that imposes itself on Zoë at the end of the tale and fabricates itself as a memory of a revived childhood. When Zoë first—and finally—reveals her "true" identity, Hanold says, "Bertgang—then you are—Fräulein Zoë Bertgang? But she looked quite different" ("Bertgang—dann sind Sie—Fräulein Zoë Bertgang? Die sah aber doch ganz anders aus" [72]). No hint of some earlier attraction, no suggestion that some memory of her earlier appearance motivates the identification between her and the Gradiva.[133] Rather, it is only once Hanold is able to reassert his fantasy and observe that "it was indeed remarkable how exactly she then resembled the bas-relief of the Gradiva" ("merkwürdig in der Tat war's, wie genau sie dabei dem Reliefbildnis der Gradiva glich" [81]), not only in her present physical appearance, but also in her cream-colored drapes, dress, and scarf (none of which can relate to childhood, but all of which, we have seen, are inseparable from the fantasy), and only once he is able to manipulate by means of his philological training the name Bertgang to become the same in meaning (*gleichbedeutend*) with Gradiva—only then, with the fantasy once again triumphant, can Hanold say, "Yes. Now I recognize—no, you have not changed at all—you are it, Zoë" ("Ja nun erkenne ich—nein im Grunde hast du dich gar nicht verändert—du bist es Zoë" [82]).[134] That this fitting of Zoë to the cherished ideal of the classical past involves some fudging is openly acknowledged by Jensen. His narrator tells us, "If belief made for bliss, it assumed everywhere a considerable amount of incredibility in the bargain" ("wenn der Glaube selig machte, nahm er überall eine erhebliche Summe von Unbegreiflichkeiten in den Kauf" [81]), and in his own letter to Freud, Jensen insists, "[Hanold] himself produces the complete conformity of the two personages, because his wish inspires him to it" ("Die volle Übereinstimmung der beiden Persönlichkeiten aber erzeugt er sich selbst, weil sein Wunsch sie ihm eingibt").[135] It is this self-produced wish that is on display here and, with it, its manufactured memory of a childhood ground.[136] The question becomes not, How does the "recovered" memory dispel the fantasy and so fulfill the wish? but, rather, How does the simulacric memory *complete* the fantasy and so too the wish?

We know the wish: it is to make Hanold himself the rightful, legitimate embodiment of his classical ideal, both in his nobilized class standing and, as part of that, in his interior subjectivity. By making the Gradiva part of his (German) childhood, he discovers yet another means for appropriating the classical past as properly his own. His machinations are simply a privatization, a subjectification of the same strategy we saw deployed by Freud in his own archaeological fantasy, and that is part and parcel of the archaeological imaginary of the time: the imaginary tactic that makes the classical world the childhood background of the Germans (and not the Italians, or the present-day Greeks, not to mention the Turks, French, etc.), even, via racial theory, that makes the Greeks biologically an event in the prehistory of the Germanic tribes. Hanold realizes this program for national identity at the site of personal identity—and sadly, Freud's reading (Freud's psychology) gives a further legitimating seal to this questionable process. As I will discuss in chapter 3, Freud does self-consciously work to undo the linkage in his later writings, in ways others did not, as the political setting grew ever darker, but here, in this work, he abets this interiorization, this subjectification, of German/classical relations.

The last example of introjection in the novella is both the most comical and the most disquieting, presented with both the lightest and most crushing of touches. This is the theme of houseflies that seem to torture Hanold from the time of his arrival in Pompeii through to his final encounter with Gradiva-Zoë, when he complains about them to her and she wittily replies, "The flies? Do you have a fly in your head now?" ("Die Fliegen? Hast du jetzt eine Fliege im Kopf?" [73]), a remark that transports the topos from its place in the world into that of Hanold's psyche. Freud, of course, reads the movement the other way around, with the flies as a displaced embodiment of Hanold's erotic desires, also apparently torturing Hanold from the outset; and while I think Freud is right to link the flies to erotic desire, the way in which he is right is more circuitous than he allows. Certainly from the very first time they are mentioned the flies are linked in Hanold's mind with the honeymooning couples (*hochzeitsreisende Paare*), the Augusts and Gretes whom Hanold finds equally annoying. But what bothers him most about these flies, their defining attribute, is their *Gemeinheit*, their inescapable and completely unacceptable commonality (39, 73, etc.). This *Gemeinheit,* this plaguing vulgarity, is imagined as an ever-present threat to the classical ideal. Hanold imagines these same flies to have ruined the most sublime poetic thoughts (*Dichtungsgedanken*) in Aeschylus's head, to have caused an irremediable slip of Phidias's chisel, and to have crept over the bodies of the Olympic gods (and again, all this while both he and the flies buzz about Italy). We have followed this interplay of the common and the classical elsewhere in the novella, and how the "Greek" ideal is constructed specifically to negate the creeping threat of bourgeois baseness in Hanold's home world (and its projected equivalent in Italy). In this instance, the interplay is presented in a manner specifically designed to underscore its violence. It is not only that the flies themselves are conceived as embodied violence against the classical and *geistig* ideal. They also call forth an equal violence in Hanold to eliminate their violent, violating *Gemeinheit* in the service of that ideal—and that violence of his itself becomes idealized, becomes part and parcel of the classical ideal. The tortured Hanold longs for a *scacciamosche,* a flyswatter to annihilate this common pest, and feels "in his inmost being that the worth of a man was to be judged above all by the number of houseflies that he had killed, pierced, burnt or exterminated in daily hecatombs during his life, as an avenger of his entire race from the remotest antiquity" ("im Innersten, das Verdienst eines Menschen sei vor allem andern nach der Anzahl von Stubenfliegen zu bewerten, die er während seiner Lebzeit als ein Rächer seines ganzen Geschlechtes von Urzeit her erschlagen, aufgespießt, verbrannt, in täglichen Hekatomben ausgerottet habe" [40]). The hyperbole is clearly comic, but it also brings out much of what has implicitly lurked behind the theme of the banal and the classical throughout: that the shimmering calm of the classical world would distinguish itself from everything crude, vulgar, and violent, with the vulgar experienced *as* a kind of violence; that to achieve that radiant, *glänzend* distinction, it will exercise an equal, common violence against that which it deigns *gemein,* whether that be flies or the Italians on the train or even decadent and dark Pompeii as the site of the classical or the real Greece or even, especially, the German middle class; and that this latter violence will itself be idealized, become in fact the core impulse of *glänzend* classicism itself. As James Porter reminds us, it is almost impossible to discuss nineteenth-century German classicism without coming up against this complex interplay of reciprocating violences, and as Jensen's tourists, armed with their Baedekers and lusting after excavations remind us, this violence becomes all the more pronounced with archaeology and its sharpened shovels eager to toss aside so much mere debris.[137] Freud might well be right that Hanold's violent urges here can be read as counterformations to his own common erotic impulses, but I think we need also to face the fact (illustrated by those lusting tourists) that they can also be read *as* violence, as violence that itself becomes eroticized—and so idealized, *verklärt,* legitimated—and, of course, interiorized as a natural, essential, psychic core.

We see this play of violence and its increasing erotic interiorization at the end of the tale, and Jensen is careful to keep the archaeological very much at its center. After Gradiva-Zoë asks Hanold, "Do you have a fly in your head?" he suddenly sees, or imagines, such a fly on her and with an in-no-way gentle blow (*mit einem keineswegs gelinden Schlag*) he strikes the fly—and her (or, perhaps better, into her). This calls forth from her the reaction, "Then she pulled herself back with a start and said, 'You are quite obviously deranged, Norbert Hanold'" ("Dann zog sie sich mit einem Ruck fort, und sagte, 'Du bist doch offenbar verrückt, Norbert Hanold'" [73]). While Freud foregrounds the mention of Hanold's name, the diagnosis of *verrückt* (deranged) is equally important here: literally "dis-placed, shifted (back)," it connotes exactly the mechanism of Hanold's psyche, and not least the way his *Fliege im Kopf* becomes displaced, as a fly, onto the Gradiva, who becomes the very embodiment of this *Verrücktheit*—compare "zog sich mit einem *Ruck* fort," as earlier "in sich zu*rück*gezogenen Gedanken" ("withdrawn thoughts" [23]). We might say, on the one hand, that Hanold is exercising his violent impulse to eliminate everything base about Zoë by at once annihilating the common fly *and* fabricating her as the classical Gradiva and, on the other, that he is transferring, displacing, or investing his violent classicizing impulse—his *Fliege im Kopf*—into Zoë as an indispensible part of her classical Gradiva identity.

This latter point is especially evident in the aftermath of Hanold's in-no-way-gentle blow, when Zoë launches into her "unreserved, detailed, instructive, and punishing lecture" ("ihre rückhaltlose, ausführliche und lehrreiche Strafrede" [81]). Freud strangely (but revealingly) depicts Zoë as psychotherapist, curing Hanold of his delusion that she is the Gradiva. But the text evokes a somewhat different role for Zoë here: it describes her as a "young school mistress with a refined, intelligent face" ("die junge Lehrmeisterin mit dem feinen, klugen Gesicht" [80]), and stresses her pedagogical mission (*Lehrtätigkeit* [84]), itself an echo of her instructive, punishing lecture. Clearly, Zoë has here taken on the disciplinary role of academic institutional authority, the authority of the very institution of Bildung that has produced the fantasy of her as the Gradiva in Hanold's head in the first place. And in exercising and embodying that authority, or, more precisely, that disciplinary violence, far from dispelling the fantasy, she comes *all the more* to seem the realization of Hanold's classical ideal. We are told, "With that, Fräulein Zoë ended her punishing lecture, and it was indeed re-

markable how exactly she then resembled the bas-relief of the Gradiva"
("Damit beendete Fräulein Zoë . . . ihre . . . Strafrede, und merkwürdig
in der Tat war's, wie genau sie dabei dem Reliefbildnis der Gradiva
glich" [81]). The violence of Hanold slapping at the common fly on
the Gradiva returns as the violence of Zoë's pedagogical discipline (and
in the context of the story, pedagogy is always Bildung, classical Bildung)—both violences integral to the establishment of her desired
identity.

There is one more step to this incorporation of violence (as desire)
into the figure of the Gradiva, and it brings the implicit involvement of
classicism in Zoë's pedagogy to a far more explicit involvement of archaeology. Just at the moment where the likeness to the Gradiva is
completed ("das Ebenbild der Gradiva vollendet [war]"), Hanold
imagines he notices for the first time an entirely insignificant deviation
of the living Bild from the stone one ("zum erstenmal eine ganz ger-
ingfügige Abweichung der lebendigen von der steinernen"):

> The latter lacked something possessed by the former, which
> at that moment especially stood out clearly, a small dimple
> on the cheek, within which a tiny, indeterminable event was
> taking place. It was a bit puckered and wrinkled. . . . Nor-
> bert Hanold looked at it and his eyes had to submit once
> more to an optical illusion. For, in a tone triumphing pecu-
> liarly over his discovery, he cried out, "There is that fly
> again!"

> Dieser fehlte etwas, das jene besaß, und das augenblicklich
> besonders deutlich an ihr zutage trat, ein kleines Grübchen
> auf der Wange, darin sich ein winziger, nicht bestimmbarer
> Vorgang zutrug. Es hielt sich ein bißchen gekraust and
> gefältelt. . . . Darauf sah Norbert Hanold hin, und . . . seine
> Augen [mußten] doch nochmals einer optischen Täuschung
> unterliegen. Denn er stieß mit einem eigentümlich über
> seine Entdeckung triumphierende Ton aus: "Da sitzt die
> Fliege wieder!" (83)

He then snaps at the dimple/housefly (*Grübchen/Fliege*) with his lips,
then shifts both the "optical illusion" and his lips to her lips—and his
fantasy is sealed with the proverbial kiss. What interests me most is this

deviation (*Abweichung*) that is perhaps no deviation at all: the *Grübchen* that is also *die Fliege*. Freud does not mention it, but what with its puckering and wrinkling little folds, he would no doubt describe it as a sexual, indeed genital, image. The association with the housefly would follow from its (the fly's) embodiment of Hanold's repressed common sexual desires; his kissing it would bespeak the breakthrough acceptance or realization of those desires, of their true object in Zoë, and hence too of his own true inner self. There is certainly some truth to this: as Freud says, there is some truth to everything (150/80). But we need also, or instead, to note how that *Grübchen* (lit., "a trenchlet, a diminutive excavation") first of all evokes the images of digging and quarrying that have carried the archaeological metaphor from the beginning, and thus joins together Hanold's "discovery" of Zoë's sexuality with archaeology's mechanism of self-investment, of digging itself into (and out of) its chosen site, as well as with its fantasizing vision and its lusting, triumphant violence. Hanold implants his classical/archaeological impulses onto or, rather, *into* Zoë as a kind of eroticism but an eroticism as constructed, projected, and violent as the archaeological has proved throughout. The further association of the *Grübchen* with the housefly not only reinforces the image of violence attached to both motifs (of digging and hitting) and underscores how that violence is here transformed into eros; it also evokes the image of the ever-threatening banal, which is similarly transformed into the "happy" and idealized conclusion of Hanold's quest. From this perspective, the *Grübchen* proves no deviation, or *Abweichung,* at all. Zoë is all the more imagined as an archaeological site and stone (*steinerne*) object of desire. It is just that her quality as such an archaeological object of desire has been introjected—dug in, as it were (*begraben*)—as an imagined sexuality: even as Hanold's own archaeological interests, his own violent defense of a classical imaginary against the threat of a pestering *Gemeinheit,* has similarly been reconfigured as a kind of deranged (*verrückt*) but ultimately charming and "true" desire.

But two things have changed in the course of this displacement of the archaeological imaginary into a sexually based psychology that do present this *Grübchen* as in fact an *Abweichung,* as a deviation, deflection, or "softening" that should give us pause. Both are evident in Freud's reading, and both are implicit in what was just discussed. First, when Hanold attacks the *Grübchen* as earlier the housefly, Freud reads this as an expression of his willingness "to subdue Gradiva-Zoë and to bring into play the aggression which is, quite simply, a man's duty in the game of love" ("sich [Gradiva-Zoë] zu bemächtigen und die Aggression, die nun einmal Pflicht des Mannes im Liebesspiel ist, ins Werk zu setzen" [117/38]). Later, he calls this "the brutal, masculine impulse for possession" ("der brutale männliche Bemächtigungstrieb" [156]). By internalizing the violence and brutality that is everywhere apparent in the archaeological imaginary and *its* impulse for possession (*Bemächtigungstrieb*), and by making it something required, something manly, Freud—and Jensen—transform precisely what is most troubling into what is most valued, idealized, *glänzend;* (colonial) violence itself becomes the internalized, eroticized, noble ideal, the basis for an achieved and celebrated noble self-image.

Second, and I believe intimately related to this same moment, this same solution to the text's knotted thematics, many years after writing his essay, Freud referred to Jensen's *Gradiva* as "a minor and, in its own right, not especially distinguished novella that was not highly prized by the critics" ("[eine] kleine an sich nicht besonders wertvolle Novelle . . . die nicht von der Kritik am höchsten geschätzt [wurde]").[138] This sense of the novella as somehow not a little common (*gemein*) is not necessarily retrospective condescension on Freud's part, nor is it in contradiction with what is so immediately attractive, ideal, and highly accomplished about the tale. Rather, it is a recognition that the work as a whole is shot through with the very bourgeois banality its classicizing idealization is supposed to exclude, and this is nowhere more apparent than in the kiss and "happy ending" that serve to impart the closing *Glanz* on the tale—the same kiss that also makes bright the violence. We have seen how violence has been introjected as a sexuality—which is to say, subjectivized from an archaeological impulse to an erotic one—and so idealized, made manly, a noble duty, and so on. But in becoming the ideal, the erotic solution has also become almost unbearably banal: a happy ending.[139] The cost of rehabilitating the violence is that the ideal becomes (almost) identical with the very inanity it was meant to exclude. Nowhere is this unhappy fate more obvious than in Hanold's last words to Zoë: "We shall take our honeymoon in Italy and Pompeii!" ("unsere Hochzeitsreise machen wir nach Italien und Pompeii!" [85]). It is not just that, in the end, Zoë and Gradiva are one; Grete and Gradiva are one as well.

3

Bildung and the Archaeology of Images in Walter Benjamin's *Berlin Chronicle*

By the early 1930s, the world had changed. As Mann wrote in the foreword to *The Magic Mountain*, the world of Hans Castorp's *Bildungsgeschichte* "is already, so to speak, completely covered by the patina of history," situated "before a certain turning point, on the far side of a rift that cut deeply through life and consciousness . . . in the back then, the long ago, the old days of the world before the Great War, with whose beginning so many things began whose beginnings, it seems, have not yet ceased" ("ist sozusagen schon ganz mit historischem Edelrost überzogen . . . [Sie spielte] *vor* einer gewissen, Leben und Bewußtsein tief zerklüftenden Wende und Grenze . . . vormals, ehedem, in den alten Tagen, der Welt vor dem großen Kriege, mit dessen Beginn so vieles begann, was zu beginnen wohl kaum schon aufgehört hat" [9–10]). Of the many things that had so begun, the most consequential and clefting was, of course, the rise of German fascism, which effectively buried the suddenly obsolete, patinaed culture of German Bildung, both classical and Goethean—or rather, it did not so much bury and destroy as it refigured and revived Bildung in a fashion that its former champions and challengers could only wish themselves to bury and destroy, to disavow precisely what they had most prized and identified with: their sullied self-image.

Complicit in the crisis or turning point in *Bildungskultur* were the technologies of the aesthetic media, including photography; the prac-

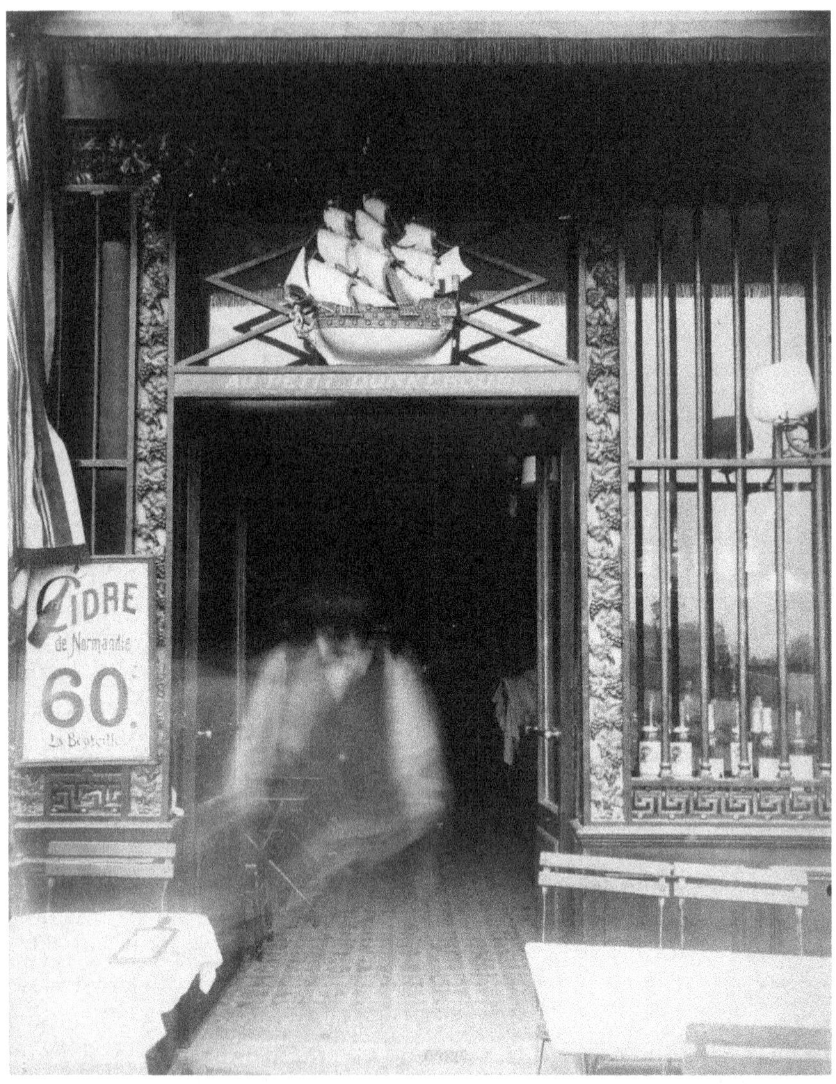

Eugène Atget (1857–1927), *Au Petit Dunkerque, 3 Quai Conti,* 1900. Abbot-Levy Collection. Partial gift of Shirley C. Burden (1.1969.1528). The Museum of Modern Art, New York. Digital image © The Museum of Modern Art. Licensed by SCAL/Art Resource, New York.

tices and discourses of classicism, including archaeology; and psychology, including Freud's. The question I wish to address is this: How did the constellation of photography, archaeology, and psychology in *Bildungskultur* change at this time, at this moment of its end and its new beginning? How did all three figure in the perversion of Bildung under German fascism and then again in the perversion of that Bildung by its would-be opponents? And how possible was it, really, to keep these two perversions apart? I wish to explore the topic first, and briefly, in terms of two of the authors that have concerned me in the previous chapters, namely Mann and Freud, then, and more exhaustively, in terms of Benjamin, with a special (though not exclusive) focus on his *Bildungsgeschichte* of 1932, *Berlin Chronicle* (*Berliner Chronik*).[1]

New Developments

Mann's belated disaffection with the Bildung tradition, including its grounding in classicism, a tradition he seemed still to support, however tenuously, in *The Magic Mountain,* is perhaps most famously registered in the figure of Serenus Zeitblom in *Doctor Faustus* (1947): the pedantic, slightly obtuse humanist classicist who is made to share responsibility for the cultural roots of National Socialism along with the well-nigh technological composer Adrian Leverkühn. But Mann's recognition of the dangerous complicity of the Bildung ideal in the modern project of national identity formation, and his literary response to it, are also evident earlier, in his work in the 1930s. We see it, for instance, in *Lotte in Weimar,* a novel written in response to the centennial celebration of Goethe's death (1932) and deliberately engaged in a kind of disenchantment, or sullying, of the numinous, *glänzend* image of Goethe that was being put to such objectionable political use at the time. But we see it even more in Mann's major undertaking of these years, the literary project that he would carry with him into exile in early 1933: *Joseph and His Brothers* (*Joseph und seine Brüder*).

It may seem difficult to imagine Mann's epic retelling of a biblical tale so remote in time and place from contemporary Weimar Germany as an active, tactical intervention into present-day cultural politics. And yet that is just what it was. The very choice of subject matter, along with the choice of narrative method, was designed to counter the prevailing mix of nationalism and mythology. The focus on a Jewish myth in the face of the fascist privileging of Hellenistic and Aryan models should certainly be seen in its antinationalist, anticlassical polemic.

In particular, we should consider the pressures of the changed cultural context that encouraged Mann to replace Hans Castorp's Arcadian vision, with all its conflation of the Goethean and Greek as the embedded, "inherited" cultural memory of the modern-day German subject of Bildung, with a vision of the Jewish past as the linked world to his contemporary audience. Fascism had transformed the former into the untenable and the latter into a topical affront.

If the subject matter of the Joseph novels seemed tactically deployed against the contemporary mix of nationalism and mythology, its manner of representation seemed even more so. Mann devised what, in all accuracy, we can describe as an archaeological mode of narration—specifically, an archaeology that, as we saw in *Gradiva,* has come to *oppose* a classicizing impulse, or what in this context amounts to much the same thing, a mythologizing impulse. Mann deploys archaeological realia and data—such as cuneiform tablets from Nineveh describing the Great Flood or the excavated statue of the Sphinx or even the great pyramid of Cholala in Mexico—and a (playfully) historicizing perspective in order to counter the kind of (solemn) mythical thinking that encourages nations to settle on some unique, privileged origin as the source of their race and people. And while the immediate target of this demythologizing strategy is the biblical tradition, it is equally—and more importantly—aimed at modern German culture as well, including its classical bent. Mann writes, "When we speak of 'antiquity,' we usually mean the Greco-Roman world" ("Sprechen wir von 'Altertum,' so meinen wir meistens die griechisch-römisch Lebenswelt" [25]), and he proceeds to engage in the archaeologically inspired argument that shows how the Greeks, far from being the origin and *Ur-Volk* of contemporary Western culture (i.e., of German *Bildungskultur*), were not even the origin of themselves, introducing ever-receding strata of earlier cultures that make such foundation myths more and more absurd. And he does the same thing with claims that the Indogermanic (*das Indogermanische*) is the oldest language, the original language (*die älteste Sprache, die Ursprache*), playfully, subversively suggesting that there must be an even earlier language level beneath that one, which included the roots of the Aryan as well as the Semitic and Hamitic tongues ("welche die Wurzeln der arischen sowohl wie auch der semitischen und chemitischen Mundarten in sich beschloß" [28])—destroying not only the Aryan claim to a foundational origin for all of Europe but also, in the process, conflating it with precisely that "Semitic" that its racial ideology would most abhor and which both the archaeological imaginary and fascist ideology worked so hard to distinguish from the "German"—effectively negating the defining difference between German and Jew.

Of course, it is never quite so simple. Mann had embarked on a rather precarious strategy, one that threatened to lend sustenance to the host ideology even as it sought its decomposition. Most obviously, in the context of the Babel-Bibel controversy that dominated archaeological discourse in the early decades of the twentieth century, Mann's archaeology-assisted dismantling of the uniqueness of Jewish history and myth, his integration of the biblical story into the broader and more quotidian cultural setting of the ancient Near East, contributed to a demotion, a destitution of Jewish culture and of the sanctity of the Old Testament that played into the hands of antisemitic German nationalists.[2] Mann's efforts to deflate the claims of Aryan nationalism, in part through the championing of a Jewish myth, also (albeit indirectly) contributed to the former by deflating the latter.

The problems are even more conspicuous in Mann's provocative but dangerous application of his archaeological perspective to matters not only of national history and racial identity but also of personal history and psychological identity. This is perhaps best seen in the example of the servant Eliezer, who identifies (or confuses) himself and his experience with the figures and memories of all the series of servant Eliezers who preceded him (4:419–24), a "foreshortening" and personalizing optic of appropriative identification that yields a notion of character as "in fact" constituted by successive strata of ever-earlier manifestations, in strict equivalence with the foreshortening optic of nations in constructing a unique origin for themselves—or rather, for constructing themselves as a unique origin—on top of the buried layers of their own (and other) earlier origins, and, of course, in strict equivalence with the model of an archaeological "tell."

It is worth noting how smooth the transition here seems to be between the psychological conception of character developed in *The Magic Mountain,* which was based on a photographic metaphor and yielded both the templated image of the grandfather in the individual image of Hans and the memory flash of the unconsciously stored image of ancient Greece, and the psycho-mythical conception of character in *Joseph and his Brothers,* based on an archaeological metaphor (the major difference being the additional factor of the parallels with conceptions of national character). As we will see, in Benjamin (and not only in Benjamin), the photographic and archaeological metaphors for memory come more and more to be consciously thought together and combined. But of immediate concern to us is how Mann's archaeological conception of subject identity, especially in its optically "foreshortened," dehistoricized, identificatory form, comes perilously close to mimicking the kind of racial mythical identifications that were so important to the fascists and that, we saw, were part and parcel of the increasingly suspect German classical humanist tradition of Bildung as well. A phantasmagoric sense of self, as it were. The latent dangers of Mann's literary strategy and conception of character, and especially the dangers of complicity in the very ideology he would oppose, became the explicit subject of critique by post–World War II German authors, especially in the case of *Doctor Faustus,* whose overt, intended attack on Hitler's mythologizing and demonizing Reich was felt to be covertly and unintentionally compromised by its own mythical demonizing of history, psychology, and so on.[3] But the danger, the problem, was already there in the Joseph novels of the 1930s—not in its demonized image, but in its brightened, celebratory image.[4]

Freud—also soon to be forced into exile from the Austro-German setting he most cherished—found himself engaged in much the same paradoxical problem as Mann in the 1930s, although perhaps in a more conscious, and certainly in a more troubled, manner. Directly inspired by his reading of Mann's Joseph novels, Freud too began writing about Old Testament narrative history in his work *Moses and Monotheism* (*Der Mann Moses und die monotheistische Religion* [1934–38]).[5] And like Mann, he was applying the most recent archaeological perspective to his quasimythical subject matter, integrating the biblical narrative into the broader context of primarily prehistoric Egyptian culture in such a way as to deprive it of its foundational function for Jewish identity—or, more fully, applying both an archaeological perspective *and* what he called a "Galtonischer Technik" of literary criticism to show that Moses was an Egyptian or, rather, a composite figure (much like Mann's Eliezer and Galton's *Mischphotographie*) of an Egyptian and a Jew.[6] That Freud should undertake, as he notes at the outset, "to deprive a people of the man whom they prize as the greatest of their sons" ("einem Volkstum den Mann abzusprechen, den es als den größten unter seinen Söhnen rühmt"), and so to counter "what are supposed to be national interests" ("vermeintlichen nationalen Interessen"), aligns his project, in both ends and means, with Mann's Joseph novels.[7] Like Mann's, the recursive target of Freud's study seems clearly to be the contemporary discourses of nationalism and race, which sought to identify both Germans and Jews in such terms. The impulse to disenchant this model and to replace it with a composite picture was all the more pressing for an Austrian Jew who so staunchly supported an assimilationist ideal.[8] But Freud was also acutely aware of how his work could be used to support the very powers he most vehemently opposed. In the prefatory note to the work's third essay, Freud acknowledges how his text—again, like Mann's—demotes and destitutes the sanctity of the religious tradition that currently offered the best tactical resistance to rising fascist nationalism in Austria, in this case Catholicism; the essay's equation of all religion with neurotic compulsion and psychic violence similarly threatened to erase differences between the positions of psychoanalysis and fascism and so too to provide justification for the almost prehistoric barbarism (*nahezu vorgeschichtliche Barbarei*) behind the new state ideology.[9] And so Freud resolved not to publish his work—not to bring it to light—so long as he was in the dark times of 1930s Austria. Like Mann's *Joseph*, and Benjamin's *Berlin Chronicle*, Freud's *Moses* accompanied its author into exile.

This is not to say that Freud any more than Mann was able to avoid the complicity of his cultural psychology in what now strikes us as some of the most worrisome tendencies of those dark times. Even in *Moses*, Freud continued to equate the history of nations and cultures with that of the individual subject—which is to say, he continued to map models of nineteenth-century anthropology onto individual psychologies (and not just the other way around), a tendency that we saw already in the *Gradiva* essay, and that acquired its most extensive formulation in *Totem and Taboo* (*Totem und Tabu* [1913]).[10] And in keeping with this, he continued to equate archaeology and psychoanalysis in ways that led to the construction of the psychological subject in terms of the archaeological imaginary of his time, a time when that imaginary had become more and more closely associated with the racial and national program of Nazism. No doubt the best known example of this equation—too well known to warrant citation or analysis—is Freud's tour de force description in *Civilization and Its Discontents* (*Das Unbehagen in der Kultur* [1930]) of the human mind in terms of the city of Rome, imagined as the simultaneous presence of all the successive strata of its various incarnations, from its earliest beginnings up to the present day. The model has much in common with the mythical, layered psychology Mann develops in the Joseph novels and attributes to the servant Eliezer, although it also, crucially, allows for a far greater heterogeneity of earlier identities; but even so, in its applied, foreshortening optic, it creates a model of the psyche that combines the most primitive origins of a people with the "most civilized" present day, and an emblem of the protonational (Rome) with the model of the individual subject, in potentially dangerously suggestive ways. A second, lesser known example comes in one of Freud's very last works, "Constructions in Psychoanalysis" ("Konstruktionen in der Analyse" [1937]). Written after *Moses,* and at a time when the complicity of German archaeology in Nazi ideology was undeniable, the essay still opens with Freud's most extensive comparison of the work of the psychoanalyst and the archaeologist, although, significantly enough, he also begins to argue for their differences as well as their similarities and perceives the latter to reside in their related projects of *construction*—of fabrication, as it were—a model of archaeology that is not only moving away from the discovery of pure origins but also moving toward an English model, away from Germany's Schliemann and toward his newly adopted homeland's Arthur Evans.[11]

The truly problematic complicity of psychoanalysis and archaeology with the ideology of National Socialism—problematic for Benjamin but not only for Benjamin—was not to be found in Freud but rather in two other major psychologists of the day: C. G. Jung and Ludwig Klages. Jung—another would-be archaeologist—pursued a psychology based on the introjection of the classical and Nordic past, and of mythical "types" as an unconscious substratum of the collective and individual psyche, "a deposit of world processes ('Weltgeschehens') embedded in the structure of the brain and the sympathetic nervous system [as] a sort of timeless and eternal 'Weltbild.'"[12] The individual German subject becomes imagined as a sort of archaeological site, with layers receding back into a quite specific archaic past, and the model is disturbing for a number of reasons: for its "mythical" conflation of the collective and the individual; for (à la Jensen) its imperialist appropriation of the cultural past as the "inherited" "basis" of contemporary German identity, with the implicit corollary that all these (present-day) cultures and societies properly and by rights already belong to the German people (much like American globalization today); and perhaps most for its naturalization, it biologization of its archaeologico-mythical model.[13] As we saw in the *Gradiva* essay and can see again in *Moses,* Freud too had leanings in this direction. But Jung more or less completely dispenses with the historicizing counterforce active in both Freud and Mann, the historicizing impulse that, we saw, classical archaeology itself came to exercise against the philology-based, aestheticizing classical ideal. It was this aspect of Jung's psychology that Benjamin saw as its most dangerous and most fascist: its rendering of the archaeological past and its archaic images as natural, as biologically, even racially inscribed in the psyche, and so as blinding (*blendend*), as nonhistorical, nonsocial, nonideological.[14]

Although hardly as well known today as either Freud or Jung, Ludwig Klages was also an important and influential figure in the elaboration of an archaeological psychology in this time period. A *Lebensphilosoph* associated with the Stefan George circle, heavily influenced by Nietzsche and of decidedly right-wing, antimodern leanings, he was read seriously by Benjamin and others, including Mann. Benjamin rather consistently pairs him with Jung—he intended to write a book on the image theme (*Bilderthema*) in both—and sees both as making common cause with fascism.[15] Klages's vitalistic psychology drew on the work of J. J. Bachofen, who posited a prehistorical, matriarchal culture that preceded the classical culture of the ancient Greeks (and others). Whereas this earlier culture was grounded in *ius naturale,* the material and corporeal, the mysterious and instinctive, and so on, the subsequent patriarchal culture was built on *ius civile,* rationality, intellectualism, and so on.[16] Klages introjected Bachofen's archaeologically layered mythical model into the individual psyche, and posited there a Pelasgian realm of "natural mythology" that had lain buried for thousands of years beneath the subsequent mechanized, rational world of human *Geist*. The "true" and the "real" were qualities that adhered only to this "deeper" prerational and pretechnological psychic realm of nature and myth. Later accretions of civilization were to be discarded as just so much debris—much like Schliemann's blasting through the layers of Roman and Hellenistic Ilios on his way to some "original" Troy. Like Jung (though perhaps more directly like Bergson), Klages described these true and effective elements that lay buried in this primitive substratum of the soul as images or Bilder. The prescribed task for the individual who would become liberated from the accrued dirt of present day civilization was to recover those latent memory images, a task which involved separating them (and oneself) out from the habit-formed context of everyday perceptions.[17] I mention this emphasis on retrieving stored images because, despite his explicit antitechnological bias, Klages's conception of the Bild brings his archaeological model of memory into close and consequential contact with the photographic model of his contemporaries, including (as we have seen) Bergson, and as we will see, Benjamin's concept of mnemonic Bilder floats easily between these two fields in ways clearly indebted to Klages.[18]

The changes taking place in psychology, especially in its archaeological dimension, and its troubling affinity with fascist ideology were also taking place more directly in classics and its archaeology. The "Führer" of the new movement in classical studies during the interwar years was Werner Jaeger, a former student of Wilamovitz-Moellendorff who had, tellingly enough, moved from occupying Nietzsche's chair in Basel during the prewar years to Wilamovitz-Moellendorff's in Berlin during the postwar period. Jaeger was largely responsible for a repoliticizing of classics and, especially, of Bildung during the 1930s. In his highly influential work of 1933, *Paideia,* he insisted on the state and the nation and the race as the bases and ideals of classical Greek culture, which mobilized *paideia,* or education—or, as Jaeger would have it, Bildung—to shape individual citizens to its current political needs. It was, he argued, the lack of a nation for themselves that misled Goethe and his generation into imagining an individual (and international) ideal of self-formation as characteristically Greek.[19] No less than Jung's, Jaeger's conceptual scheme worked to demote individualism and to promote collective consciousness; again like Jung's, it also worked to undermine the historicizing impulse that had characterized much of the more recent scholarship in his field and that had aimed at something of an anticlassical understanding of the ancient world—an understanding in which, we have seen, archaeology had played a major sullying role. Jaeger particularly deplored the equation of Greek *Kultur* with an anthropo-archaeological concept of culture that applied equally to Greece and to pre-Hellenic civilizations, to primitive societies and to Jewish, Egyptian, and Oriental traditions.[20] Instead, Jaeger wished to retain a notion of *Kultur* that was restricted to classical Greece as the beginning, the *arche,* of "our" history, which is to say to the vital relationship between ancient Greece and the modern European nations and races, the so-called Hellenocentric nations or, rather, since only the Germans, by the saving grace of Goethe, had privileged the Greeks over the Romans and so escaped the present pan-European malaise, Jaeger wished "Kultur" to refer almost exclusively to the privileged, vital, and "not merely racial" kinship between the ancient Greeks and modern-day Germans, a kinship stressed all the more by his questionable conflation of the concepts of *paideia* and Bildung and his claim that the one shaped the other, with both the German nation and individual subject directly connected to the Greek.[21]

Intentionally or not, Jaeger was making humanism more and more complicit with fascism, and as part of that, he was vehemently opposed to the corrosive effects of classical archaeology on the classical ideal and wished to exclude its focus on both material culture and pre-Hellenic Greece as not supporting the almost mystically conceived, vitalistic "organically unfolded 'Bildungswelt'" that spiritually joined the Greek and German peoples and nations.[22] The material and historical impulses that nineteenth-century archaeology had allegedly introduced into Hellenistic studies were to be opposed by two counterforces that might initially themselves seem opposed to each other but which came more and more to reveal their identity: a resurgence of an aestheticizing, classicizing impulse and the introduction of an antirational, myth-based, vitalist "appreciation" of Greek culture, an infusion of aestheticism and *Lebensphilosophie* that brought the mainstream Wilamovitz-Moellendorff defenders of classics into troubling proximity with their own seeming opponents, the adherents of the Stefan George circle. Archaeology, however, did not respond to this attempted exclusion by simply lying low and giving up. Rather, it refunctioned itself to conform to, even to further the newly dominant constellation of classicism, aestheticism, and vitalism. As Suzanne Marchand points out, it did so through a new emphasis on visuality and an aesthetic culture of beauty (*Schönheit*), and it accomplished this not least through a new alliance with photography.[23] As mentioned earlier, photography played a formative role in nineteenth-century archaeology, not least in Dörpfeld's and Schliemann's use of it in the field. But now photography was no longer employed for flat, scholarly documentation for specialists but rather for an aestheticized marketing of archaeology in ways meant to appeal to the collective masses and to inspire passion and an ideal of national unity. As Marchand also points out, Leni Riefenstahl's *Olympia* furthered this new direction cinematographically; photographically, the future Nazi Walter Hege's *Die Akropolis* of 1930 did much the same. Beautiful, artful black-and-white shots of ancient Greek buildings with all people and modern structures edited out, set against a seemingly timeless, almost mythical natural landscape whose ruggedness and winter setting seemed calculated to convey, as the introductory essay put it, a familiar (i.e., Nordic) ruggedness—all enlist archaeology and photography in the same problematic constellation that we also see in psychology, in Bildung, and in fascism.[24]

Such is the background matrix against which I want to consider Benjamin's *Berlin Chronicle,* a work begun in Berlin in 1932 and carried with him into exile that same year. Benjamin never published *Berlin Chronicle,* although substantial parts of it were reworked to form the core basis of his *Berlin Childhood around 1900 (Berliner Kindheit um neunzehnhundert* [1934/38]); the overlap is significant enough that the two works are often treated together. Still, there are unique features to *Berlin Chronicle* that warrant special focus. First, as many critics have pointed out, *Berlin Chronicle* contains a great deal of explicit self-reflection on the joint processes of remembering and writing, all of which gets edited out of the later work, and chief among these self-reflections are two extensive (and justly famous) passages that explore memory and its subject in terms of photography and archaeology, respectively, and that jointly lead us deeply into both the formal and thematic features of the work as a whole. And second, as Gershom Scholem points out, *Berlin Chronicle* covers a range of material that the later work does not, including, along with its description of childhood and family, Benjamin's student years (*Studentenzeit*), his friends and mentors, and his early erotic education; and it sets as its chronological endpoint the twinned terminus of the demise of his group and the beginning of the Great War, with a forward look to a complex double marriage that deliberately evokes both Goethe's *Wilhelm Meister* and *Elective Affinities (Die Wahlverwandtschaften* [1809])—which is to say that, unlike *Berlin Childhood, Berlin Chronicle* is recognizable as a *Bildungsgeschichte,* in both its more private and institutional strains.[25] Why it should be a *Bildungsgeschichte* and how both photography and archaeology make it the peculiar kind of *Bildungsgeschichte* that it is will be my major concern in what follows.

BERLIN CHRONICLE AS BILDUNGSGESCHICHTE

As far as I know, the idea of reading *Berlin Chronicle* as a *Bildungsgeschichte* and against the background of the Bildung tradition is a new one, and we certainly need to start with an informed recognition of how it both is a *Bildungsgeschichte* and is quite deliberately not one as well. To do this, we need to both identify the features, thematic and formal, that mark the work as about Bildung and explain the logic and technique of decomposition to which Benjamin subjects his material, including the very notions of the "I," of Bildung, and of *Geschichte* (meaning both "story" and "history"). I have already suggested some of the compromised positions, the sullied state to which both Bildung and its psychological construct of the subject had been brought by this time (this *Geschichte*). The task is to see how Benjamin responded, and to evaluate the features of that response against the background of what it intends to oppose.

As we have seen, Bildung, as it emerges out of the late nineteenth century, has two major strains. The first of these is the more or less private formation of the subject through the influences of the nuclear family, of an informal group of male mentors or guides, and of the subject's erotic adventures with women. All these influences are meant simultaneously to yield an individual (male) subject and his normative fit into the broader social regime; as I put it in chapter 1, they are meant to produce the "wondrous harmony between the individual's driving desires and society's normative expectations, the posited agreement between personal individuation and social assimilation." This predominantly private Bildung that yields the publicly fit man is usually identified with a Goethean ideal, as articulated in *Wilhelm Meister's Apprenticeship*, and as we saw, Bilder play a significant role in this *Bildungsprozeß*.

The second strain of Bildung is the far more public, institutional one. It is the official educative program of the German state in force throughout the nineteenth and into the early twentieth century, heavily weighted (since Humboldt) with classical learning and an ideal of national identity. As we saw in chapter 2, in the analysis of Jensen's *Gradiva,* this more institutional regimen does not therefore leave the private realm out of account. Rather, even as the former strain fashions the private psychological subject to develop toward the social norm, so does this official version of Bildung work to introject its cultural imaginary into the private subject's ideals and desires: to determine the kind of woman he wants, the domestic values he cherishes, the psychic forces he embodies. This strain of Bildung also has its claim to an inaugurating Goethean ideal in German classicism. And as we saw, it too deploys Bilder as part of its regulative program.

Of course, even more than Goethe, the common ground uniting these two strains is undoubtedly class. In either form, Bildung is always about the inculcation of specifically bourgeois values, usually "upper" bourgeois values, and part of that is almost always its own class construction of an aristocratic, noble ideal. We saw this class dimension to Bildung and classicism in *Gradiva;* we can see something similar in Hans Castorp's elevation into the aristocracy of the ill at Davos; and it is, of course, of central concern to Goethe's *Wilhelm Meister* (not to mention Keller's *Green Henry* or Stifter's *Indian Summer*).

The question of social class in Bildung figures prominently in *Berlin Chronicle* as well, where it is linked not only with classicism but also with school "class" (504/623). An early index can be seen in Benjamin's first philosophical essay, written near the end of his schooling, titled "Reflections on the Nobility" ("Gedanken über den Adel") and, we are told, jointly inspired by Pindar and Benjamin's aristocratic schoolmate (*Mitschulerin*) Luise von Landau (504/624, 465–66/595–96). I will have more to say about class as we go along. For now I want to stress how, from very early on, Benjamin's thinking and writing were preoccupied with both the private and public aspects of Bildung, in both their conflicts and collusions, and how this registers in the subject matter of *Berlin Chronicle*. It is worth noting how many of the anecdotes in the work address either Benjamin's school experiences—almost all of them negative—or his involvement in the so-called Youth Movement (*Jugendbewegung*) that aimed at educational reform during the prewar years. We know that Benjamin was personally very active in this movement, as was the group whose mutual relations, ideals, and activities are at the affective center of *Berlin Chronicle* (their own center a place called, appropriately enough, the Home [*das Heim*]: so great was the collusion between public and private in their efforts).[26] Benjamin gives a telling description of the ideals that preoccupied this group and himself during those years in an essay titled "The Life of Students" ("Das Leben der Studenten" [1914]).[27] In it, Benjamin argues vehemently against the assumption that the aim of study should be a socially conceived individuality and service to the state, against the perversion of the creative spirit into what he calls the vocational spirit, and against the lamentable loss of nobility that present day education entailed. Instead, he advocates the pursuit of an ideal of "totality," the achievement of a profoundly organic individual development (*Entwicklung*) that is also almost mystically linked with the spiritual rebirth of the nation. As part of this, he calls for joining the intellectual life and training of the student with the student's erotic experiences. He deplores how the erotic sphere had been as distorted for students by the institution of prostitution as the intellectual by that of learning, and he demands a unification of the spiritual life that overcomes the division of the intellectual and the erotic so as to restore what he calls an "eros of creativity."

For all its opposition to institutional education, this ideal of Bildung to which Benjamin and his friends devoted themselves, and to which they oriented their public political activity, proved a fairly traditional one, even a recognizably Goethean one: it simply pitted one major strain of Bildung against another.[28] And with the advent of the war and the almost simultaneous suicide of two key players of the group in the Home, Benjamin was forced to recognize their ideal as in some crucial way part of the problem, as sharing an identity with the very forces it would oppose. Benjamin stresses throughout *Berlin Chronicle* how the terminus of official Bildung had increasingly come to conflate the attainment of manhood (*Männlichkeit*) and the entrance into adulthood not only with a suitably productive bourgeois vocation but also with the injunction, "You must become a soldier" ("müsse Soldat werden" [509/627; see also 504–5/624, 510/628]). The complicity of *Bildungskultur* with militaristic nationalism—a complicity all the more evident in the 1930s—emerges in the work as one of the primary symptoms of its sullied degradation and one of the chief reasons for its needed demise. Benjamin repeatedly discovers in his memories his almost instinctive resistance to its imperatives, but he also, albeit more reluctantly, discovers in the Youth Movement itself certain questionable affinities with its ideals. He was, in part, forced to this discovery when his revered mentor, Gustav Wyneken, who first articulated the model of Bildung championed by Benjamin, joined in the enthusiastic advocacy for war in 1914.[29] But even Benjamin and his friends were, as he says, among the crush of bodies in front of the barrack gates on August 6, eager to enlist, moved not by enthusiasm for war (*Kriegsbegeisterung*) but by the ideal of companionship inseparable from their ideal of youth (481/607), and even they, in their movement, were engaged in "an extreme, heroic attempt to change the attitudes of people" ("ein äußerster, heroischer Versuch, die Haltung der Menschen zu verändern"), inspired by the same "heroic" idealism and push for spiritual rebirth that was now leading Germany to war—even as they also planned their revolt in the upscale homes of the same last true elite of bourgeois Berlin ("letzte wirkliche Elite des bürgerlichen Berlin" [478/605]) they were plotting to bring down. The situation was not unlike the moment Benjamin describes as "the truest expression of our impotence, that seemed the pinnacle of our strength," the night at *Die Aktion* when, at a moment of great contention, two speeches with the same title and almost identical texts were delivered ("zwei Reden gleichen Titels und von fast gleichem Wortlaut verlesen wurden" [479/606]), so slight were the differences in the opposing positions.[30]

This all came to an abrupt end on August 8, 1914, the date on which Benjamin's best friend, Fritz Heinle, and his girlfriend committed suicide, two days after the start of the war. This is the date from which Benjamin marks his disaffection with the Youth Movement and its Bildung ideal; it is also the date that marks, for all intents and purposes (save one), the chronological endpoint of *Berlin Chronicle*. In retrospect, Benjamin says "that the city of Berlin was never again to impinge so forcefully on my existence as it did in that epoch when we believed we could leave it untouched, only improving its schools, only breaking the inhumanity of the parents of its inmates, only making a place in it for the words of Hölderlin or George" ("daß zu keiner späteren Zeit die Stadt Berlin selbst in mein Dasein so mächtig eingegangen ist, wie in jener Epoche, da wir sie selber glaubten unberührt lassen zu können, um nur die Schulen in ihnen zu verbessern, nur die Unmenschlichkeiten der Eltern ihrer Zöglinge zu brechen, nur den Worten Hölderlins oder Georges in ihr ihren Platz zu geben"); much time would pass before the realization matured "that no one can improve his school or parental home without first smashing the state that needs bad ones" ("daß niemand Schule und Elternhaus verbessern [kann], der den Staat nicht zertrümmert, welcher die schlechten braucht" [478–79/605–6]). *Berlin Chronicle* is as much engaged in this project of destruction as in that of reconstruction of the hope-filled moment of Benjamin's involvement in his Youth Movement, and to this extent at least, it is equally poised as a *Bildungsgeschichte* and not one, but rather the *Geschichte* of how Benjamin comes to fight his way free from its ground.

Berlin Chronicle is equally concerned with the traditionally more private strain of Bildung (although again, the interpenetration of "school and parental home" makes any clean division between the two impossible). We see this in two ways: first in the sustained focus on the formative influence of family and early childhood experience—Benjamin concentrates especially on the relationship of the child with the mother and father, with a genre-typical exclusion of siblings (but inclusion of grandmothers and nursemaids), and, also typical of the genre, on the particular sphere of activity associated with the mother and father, respectively. The mother is linked with entertainment at home and on trips into the city: to visit the theater, to go shopping, to meet relatives, and so on (the maternal grandmother is an extension of this sphere, as are the nannies); the father is presented as the link between the family home and the world of business, as the medium through which the concerns of work, and technology, enter into the domestic sphere. Another key component of the private strain of Bildung, the concern with the protagonist's erotic education, is also well represented: Benjamin recalls his first love, the first stirrings of his sexual urge, the first object of his erotic fantasies, and the women who drew him into Berlin's café life every bit as much as the meetings with his group of Bildung-engaged male friends. As with the depictions of Benjamin's school experiences and involvements with the Youth Movement, these erotic experiences are dropped from the later *Berlin Childhood;* their inclusion here seems clear evidence of the Bildung allegiances of the earlier work.

But even as the accounts of his school experiences and involvement in the Youth Movement are almost unremittingly negative, so too are those of his erotic experiences and relationship with his family. The most obvious example of this is the reduction of erotic encounters to those with prostitutes, including the case of the woman in military dress at his father's place of business, who, we are told, determined Benjamin's most lasting early sexual fantasies: the complicity of the erotic in carrying on and instilling the values of the more public, patriarchal bourgeois sphere reaches almost grotesque proportions in this commodification and militarization of the sexual. But we see it too in the nursemaid's "cold shadow, driving away what I loved" ("kalte Schatten, der das Geliebte verschwinden ließ" [466/596]) and even more in the overwhelmingly antagonistic attitude adopted toward the figure of Benjamin's mother. Benjamin perceives his first act of resistance (*Resistenz*) in his refusal to walk next to her, a protest against her many "tests" that destroyed the child's faith in his fitness for practical life (466/596). He reports on the extreme unpleasantness of the shopping trips she led into the city (that betrayed her subjection to commercial forces), and he tells of his bitter indignation, his permanent feeling of misused and violated trust, at her crude and brutal coercion of his obedience on the occasion of an early visit to the theater—precisely an occasion, since *Wilhelm Meister,* traditionally marked as a warm and welcome initiation into the institutions of Bildung via the maternal realm. As Bernd Witte underscores, this negative relation to the mother is replaced by a positive and positively erotically tinged one in *Berlin Childhood,* which, by implication, underscores how the attitude depicted here, rather than being motivated by some extraliterary impulse, is tightly interwoven with this work's genre-specific attack on Bildung.[31]

The negative portrayal of the figure of the mother extends not only outward, into the figures of nannies, prostitutes, and cocottes, but also inward, into that of home life in general (and that includes the father and his telephone rantings and business conducted out of the house). This is perhaps most poignantly apparent in a section that seems almost the opposite: sentimentally nostalgic. Benjamin remembers the various songs his mother used to sing at home and his pleasure in hearing them. He associates their melodies with other sounds that belonged to the house (*zur Wohnung*), such as that of keys in his mother's basket, the lighting of the chandelier, the movement of the lift (*Aufzug*), or his father returning home at noon (511/629). But a closer look (or listen) reveals the destructive character lurking in each and every such memory. The jingling of the keys in the basket is a result of the mother's search for the purse or ledger that lay at the very bottom (*die zu unterst lagen*), that is, for those emblems of the economic base underlying the power and authority of the domestic sphere; and it is in good part just this more or less hidden base that warrants destruction of the whole. And so the songs Benjamin recalls stress the futility of the mother's labors ("Useless will your work be, so strain no more" ["Nutzlos wird die Arbeit sein Drum strenge dich nicht an"]), the fading and passing of this world ("Shadows are sinking" ["Schatten sinken nieder"]; "As the clouds go wandering" ["Wie die Wolken wandern"]), and the welcoming of its departure ("Farewell, loved ones, it is time to part" ["Adee nun Ihr Lieben Geschieden muß sein"]); the remembered sound of his father is that of his falling stock; the sound of the lift is its grating shriek; the pleasurable sound (of the chandelier) at the end of the day is the quiet explosion of gas set off by a burning match. That is, there is really no difference between Benjamin's joy in this seemingly secure domestic setting and the pride he feels when his parents' home is

burglarized, the house stripped of everything (*ausgeraubt*), all in fulfillment of his "prophetic" dream (512–14/630–31); the same wish to
destroy the domestic interior—"to smash the parental home"—as one
of the twin pillars of bourgeois Bildung lies behind both.

Admittedly, even as the depiction of the Youth Movement also
tries to recover a glimpse of forgotten promise, so too the depiction of
Benjamin's private Bildung includes its possibly redemptive moments:
in the erotic sphere, for example, in the memories of the market women
of Markthalle or of the awakening of his sex drive ("das Erwachen
meines Geschlechtstriebs") when he realized he would never make it to
the service required by his mother. I will have more to say about this
later. For now, I want to stress the dominant sense of *Berlin Chronicle*
that these relations, both familial and erotic, need to be attacked and
destroyed, and along with them the subject, the "I," to which they give
rise, and that one of the chief means of accomplishing this disaffection
is by exposing the class and economic structures they both obscure and
depend on. This is, perhaps, the truly crucial identity that Benjamin's
text shares with another of its *Vorbilder*, Proust's *In Search of Time Lost*,
which Benjamin spent years translating and to which *Berlin Chronicle*
is sometimes formally compared. The formal comparisons are, I believe, problematic, but as the essay "On the Image of Proust" ("Zum
Bilde Prousts" [1929/34]) makes clear, the significance of Proust's
work for Benjamin was not merely formal. Rather, Proust's project is
described as a merciless, deglamorizing smashing to bits of the unity of
family, of personality, of sexual morality, and of class honor
(2:316/2:241)—and if Benjamin differs from Proust in foregrounding
the economic and foregoing the tactic of self-absorption, he still very
much shares with him this fundamental project of disenchantment of
the private sphere and its subject.

The major conversation about the private sphere and its subject is
not, however, with Proust. Rather, Benjamin's engagement with the
more private strain of Bildung is to be seen in the second place—after
the engagement with his own family and the erotic—in relation to
Goethe. This is only indirectly, albeit still centrally, to be read out of
Berlin Chronicle itself. It is, however, directly central to Benjamin's
overall concern with Bildung up to the time of his writing this work.

Parallel with and inseparable from Benjamin's commitment to political activism and social change was his lifelong preoccupation with
Goethe. Indeed, his own increasingly nonaligned form of politics, his

complicated commitment to an individual and writerly mode of intervention that belied party allegiances, is well reflected in the place of Goethe in Benjamin's thought. Benjamin had his first major publication success with his now famous essay on *Elective Affinities*, an essay in which he read his own marriage and love affair into Goethe's plot and characters.[32] Then, in the late 1920s, he was engaged to write a major article on Goethe for a Soviet encyclopedia, which he wrote in good part for political reasons but which was rejected by the Soviet editors for the same reasons. As in the case of the earlier essay, Benjamin read himself into his subject, projecting his own political concerns into his depicted character. It is a particularly good index of his take on Goethe and on the kind of politics behind *Berlin Chronicle*.

In describing the type of writer that Goethe represents for him, Benjamin describes Goethe as someone who transforms "his inner life into a public matter from the very outset and makes the questions of the day into matters of immediate concern for his own personal thought and experience" ("seine Innenwelt von Anfang an zur öffentlichen Angelegenheit [und] die Zeitfragen restlos zu Fragen seiner persönlichen Erfahrung- und Denkwelt" [2:709/2:164]).[33] It is just this dialectic of inner and outer, personal and public, that allows the collective and political to be staged at the site of the individual and psychological. As a writer, Goethe is depicted as representing bourgeois culture and consciousness in a most fully realized way (including its aristocratic pretensions). But, Benjamin says, because "at that time the tendencies of the age found scarcely any means of expression other than the personal" ("damals die Tendenzen kaum einen anderen Ausdruck als den persönlichen fanden" [2:711/2:166]), this is where, and how, Goethe staged those tendencies. The individual subject was made to "express" the ideology of his time. The driving force to Goethe's "expressions"—that is, his personal embodiment of his class's ideals—was not conflict but unfolding ("nicht Auseinandersetzung sondern Entfaltung" [2:715/2:170]), or as Benjamin also puts it, his allegiance to one of the most despicable of principles, "Seek to give everything in your life a consequence" ("eine der abscheulichsten Maximen, 'Suche allem in Deinem Leben eine Folge zu geben'" [2:730/2:180; see also 6:205/2:686]). This is to say that the same bourgeois ideology that, on a larger scale, had eventually led to the naturalization and hence justification of fascist Germany (as both "natural" and inevitable in its unfolding) also expressed itself as the process of unfolding that gives coherent meaning to the individual subject's life: as Bildung, as *das Ich*. The Goethean subject of Bildung is recognized as the embodiment of a suspect, and now dangerous, imaginary: to destroy the bourgeois order means to attack not only its schools and parental homes but its "Ich" as well, whose model of coherent unfolding represents one of the legitimating institutions of the state's authority.[34] That is, Benjamin's reflections on Goethe give further indices for how, and why, *Berlin Chronicle* both is and is not a *Bildungsgeschichte*. The fact that public and political "questions of the day" can be staged at the site of the individual allows for issues of history (*Geschichte*) to be explored as *Bildungsgeschichte,* but the fact that *das bildende Ich* itself encompasses a contested mode of historical coherence means that it too must be demolished if the world that history supports is to be brought down as well.

Of course, and as we will see, this attack against the Goethean model of individual Bildung qua development (*Entwicklung*) or unfolding (*Entfaltung*) needs to be balanced against Benjamin's discovery and embrace of a different Goethean principle of unfolding, one associated with Goethe's *Urphänomen,* a mode of development that can emerge only once it has been salvaged from the ruins of the broader, more historical model of unfolding that Benjamin opposes.[35] As in the case of both the Youth Movement and the erotic, here too in the case of Goethe, Benjamin seeks to find a glimpse of something recoverable amid the piled up debris of his destructive project.

Perhaps the best indication of Benjamin's relation to Goethe—and the relation of that relation to the question of Bildung in *Berlin Chronicle*—comes in a short passage titled "Nr. 113" in *One Way Street* (*Einbahnstraße* [1928]), the published work of Benjamin's that most resembles *Berlin Chronicle* formally. It describes the metaphorical "house of our life" (*Haus unseres Lebens*), a house that is also somehow Goethe's house. The house is imagined as under assault ("enemy bombs are already striking" ["die feindlichen Bomben schlagen schon ein"]), and Benjamin rhetorically asks what displaced antiquities (*verschobene Altertümer*) are not laid bare in the foundations "there below, where the deepest shafts are reserved for the most commonplace" ("da unten, wo dem Alltäglichsten die tiefsten Schächte vorbehalten sind"). Among these are memories of his friendship and brotherhood with the best friend of his schooldays ("Freundschaft und Brüderschaft . . . mit dem ersten Kameraden meiner Schulzeit"). Then, in a dream, Benjamin finds himself "im Goethehaus," with whitewashed corridors like those in a school ("getünchte Korridore wie in einer Schule"). In the visitor's book, "I find as I turn the pages my name already entered in big, unruly, childish characters" ("finde ich beim Blättern meinen Namen schon mit großer ungefüger Kinderschrift verzeichnet"). At a desk in his study, in extreme old age, Goethe sits writing. He breaks off to give Benjamin a small vase, an urn from antiquity (*ein antikes Gefäß*), as a present. Then:

> Goethe rose to his feet and accompanied me to an adjoining chamber, where a table was set for my relatives. It seemed prepared, however, for many more than their number. Doubtless there were places for ancestors, too. At the end, on the right, I sat down beside Goethe. When the meal was over, he rose with difficulty, and by gesturing I sought leave to support him. Touching his elbow, I began to weep with emotion.

> Goethe erhob sich und trat mit mir in den Nebenraum, wo eine lange Tafel für meine Verwandtschaft gedeckt war. Sie schien aber für weit mehr Personen berechnet, als diese zählte. Es war wohl für die Ahnen mitgedeckt. Am rechten Ende nahm ich neben Goethe Platz. Als das Mahl vorüber war, erhob er sich mühsam und mit einer Geberde erbat ich Verlaub, ihn zu stützen. Als ich seinen Ellenbogen berührte, begann ich vor Ergriffenheit zu weinen. (4:87/1:446)

Here—and significantly here—we have our first example of the archaeological metaphor in Benjamin's work.[36] For now, I want to stress the constellation of elements in which it occurs: the association of Goethe with both school and family; the sense of Benjamin as somehow already inscribed, from childhood, in Goethe's book; Benjamin as the recipient of a transmitted gift, an artifact from both antiquity and the writing desk; the impulse to support Goethe but also the emphasis on his extreme old age, his fragility arousing tears; and the sense of attack that warns that the Bildung ideals of Benjamin's schooldays (*Schulzeit*), including those of camaraderie, friendship, and brotherhood, the very ideals on which the Goethehaus and "the house of our life" were founded, are no longer secure. This is the context that calls forth the project of archaeology, partly as recovery of fragments of a transmissible past, but partly too as the assault on the site itself.

TECHNIK: PHOTOGRAPHY, ARCHAEOLOGY

Such, then, are some of the most basic thematic affinities that align Benjamin's work with the tradition of Bildung: its concentration on a specific time span of autobiographical material; on the subject's experience of the official institutions of learning, including their gendering mechanisms; on his unofficial countereducation, including the influence of both friends and lovers; on his primary familial relations and entanglements with class ideology; and on an altercation, an *Auseinandersetzung,* with the Goethean inheritance. In each case, *Berlin Chronicle* engages these elements as much for purposes of disaffection as of evocation, as much for purposes of attack as of association.[37]

The engagement of *Berlin Chronicle* with the tradition of Bildung is not, however, staged only at the thematic level. Rather, as mentioned earlier, another feature of *Berlin Chronicle* that radically distinguishes it from the later *Berlin Childhood* is the highly self-conscious reflections on its formal tactics of composition and decomposition. Throughout his career, Benjamin was preoccupied with the formal modes of support and attack involved in writing, and he formulated the technical issues at stake in writing a *Bildungsgeschichte* most forcefully in an essay written some two years after *Berlin Chronicle,* "The Author as Producer: Address at the Institute for the Study of Fascism" ("Der Author als Produzent: Ansprache im Institut zum Studium des Faschismus" [1934]). Following up on an earlier observation, that "Whoever awakes as Heinrich von Ofterdingen today must have overslept" ("Wer heut als Heinrich von Ofterdingen erwacht, muß verschlafen haben" [2:620/2:3]), Benjamin declares here the impermissability of new literary masterpieces (*Meisterwerke*) and of the creative personalities who would produce them.[38] He specifically derides as a privilege of fascism (*Privileg des Faschismus*) the demand that "the *Wilhelm Meister,* the *Green Henry* of our generation" be written, countering, "Nothing will be further from the author who has reflected deeply on the conditions of present-day production than to expect, or desire, such works" ("Dem Author, der die Bedingungen heutiger Produktion durchdacht hat, wird nichts ferner liegen, also solche Werke zu erwarten oder auch nur zu wünschen" [2:696/2:777]). What Benjamin means here by the "conditions of production" is not, as the formula might imply, the labor relations of the proletariat but rather the bourgeois form or *Gestalt* of Bildung and its allied genre, the novel. The *Bildungsprivileg* is, he says, precisely what makes the writer a part of the bourgeoisie and, even more, makes it a part of him. Thus, when Benjamin asserts that the present-day author will neither expect nor desire a modern *Wilhelm Meister,* he is not suggesting that he abandon this means of production but rather that he stay within it, within his regimen of Bildung and *Geschichte,* and seek to transform or re-form (*umfunktionieren*) its conditions from within. As Benjamin describes it with the example of René Maublanc, the tactic of this *Umfunktionierung,* this refunctioning, is much like Brecht's technique of decomposition (*Zerlegung*), the interruption of the development of the given *Geschichte:*[39] the decomposition is at once of the subject and of its literary form of representation, and while Benjamin stresses how it might seem a purely destructive task, it is also, potentially, a constructive one, part of a mighty recasting of literary forms in the modern period (2:687/2:771). But the main point of the essay is that the refunctioning of Bildung, the decomposition of cultural ideology, is conceived by Benjamin as a *technical* problem, a matter of literary *Technik:* the political battle against the bourgeoisie and its manifold alliance with fascism is to be fought on the field of literary representation itself.

As Benjamin indicates in this same essay, one of the chief technologies by which literary composition can be refashioned and decomposed is to be borrowed from the field of photography, including (though not limited to) the techniques of photomontage. He says, "we—the writers—[must] take up photography; what is true of photographic form can also be applied to literary form" ("wir—die Schriftsteller—[müssen] ans Photographieren gehen; was von [der photographischen Form] gilt, ist auf die literarische zu übertragen" [2:691–92/2:774–75]), and *Berlin Chronicle* is heavily invested in just this project, especially in its appropriation of the *Technik* of montage. For Benjamin, this latter method has a special, revolutionary effect that derives from its ability to interrupt the illusion of a harmonious and continuous Bild, precisely the type of harmony and continuity on which Bildung, and the novel, traditionally depend; as Benjamin puts it, montage ruptures time ("sprengt die Zeit") and its totalizing, progressive ideal (2:692/2:774).[40] The importance of this for the writing of *Berlin Chronicle* can be glimpsed in Benjamin's programmatic assertion, "Reminiscences, even extensive ones, do not always represent an autobiography. And these quite certainly do not. . . . For autobiography has to do with time, with sequence, and what makes up the continuous flow of life. Here, however, I am speaking of . . . moments and discontinuities" ("Erinnerungen, selbst wenn sie ins Breite gehen, stellen nicht immer eine Autobiographie dar. Und dieses hier ist ganz gewiß keine . . . Denn die Autobiographie hat es mit der Zeit, dem Ablauf und mit dem zu tun, was den stetigen Fluß des Lebens ausmacht. Hier aber ist . . . von Augenblicken und vom Unstetigen die Rede" [488/612]). As we will see, this same irruptive function that Benjamin ascribes to the *Technik* of photomontage also proves true of the technology of photography in other ways as well, including its literary equivalents.

Photography (including montage) is not, however, the only *Technik* available for Benjamin to interrupt the narrativity and subjectivity of autobiographical *Bildungsgeschichten*. In fact, one of the most decisive features of *Berlin Chronicle* derives from a somewhat different technique, namely, its tactic of organizing its material spatially rather than temporally, according to the urban topography of the Berlin years (*berliner Jahre*).[41] The spatial plan allows Benjamin to abandon temporal sequence as an ordering biographical principle and to expand his focus from the narrowly individual to a more encompassing social field; it also aligns *Berlin Chronicle* with Benjamin's other experiments in city writing, including his accounts of Paris, Moscow, Naples, and Pompeii and, as part of that, with his experiments in the techniques, the arts of straying (*Irrkünste*) of the urban *flâneur*.[42] Benjamin explicitly compares these *Irrkünste* with the cutting techniques of photomontage (3:82/2:70), and we will want to explore how they too work to counter the course of Bildung proper. But first, we need to note how, almost imperceptibly, Benjamin's topographical schema introduces not only an added social dimension to the work but an added archaeological one as well. We see this not least through the repeated insistence that this all but empty city is somehow an underworld, underground, more a tunnel maze (*Irrstollen*) than a garden maze (*Irrgarten*), with hundreds of shafts (*mit hunderten von Schächten* [469/598])—a conceit that echoes Benjamin's accounts of both Paris and Pompeii, which also are approached as archaeological sites. This added archaeological dimension to Benjamin's scheme almost inevitably requires that his work intercede not only in the traditions of autobiographical and city writing but in that of archaeological writing as well. So before we consider the role of photography and its technology in Benjamin's text, let us first look at that of city writing and archaeology.

ARCHAEOLOGY OLD AND NEW

In "The Storyteller" ("Der Erzähler" [1936]), Benjamin claims there are two types of storytellers: those who have gone on a trip, have come from afar, and have "something to tell about" and those who stayed at home and know the local tales and traditions. To each of these types of storytellers there also corresponds a type of archaeology: the *Altertumswissenschaft* of institutional archaeology abroad and the more modestly conceived *Altertumskunde* of archaeology at home. We saw in chapter 2 how Jensen represents the former type of storytelling and archaeology and their concomitant mode of Bildung; in writing his account of Berlin, Benjamin is implicitly taking issue with this strain of writing and its problematic complicity in nationalistic identity formation, not least through its classicizing ideals.[43] This is not to say that the countertradition that Benjamin avails himself of to contest this "away" strain—namely, the tradition of those who stay at home—does not have its own problematic complicity in nationalist agenda, its own implications of an archaic past and classicizing idealization. It certainly does, and what we will want to trace is not only how Benjamin uses his Berlin to oppose the type of writing represented by Jensen's tale but also how he works to oppose the type traditionally represented by *Altertumskunde*.

As he tells us at the outset of *Berlin Chronicle*, Benjamin has a guide for negotiating this rather tricky passage: his friend and mentor Franz Hessel. Benjamin and Hessel had translated Proust's great memory work together; more important, Hessel had introduced Benjamin to the idea of *flânerie* and of a "modern" mythology and archaeology in Paris, and together they developed the "Tiergarten mythology" that plays such a central role in the representation of Berlin in both their works. Before writing his own book, Benjamin reviewed those of Hessel, namely, *Unknown Berlin* (*Heimliches Berlin* [1927]) and *On Foot in Berlin* (*Spazieren in Berlin* [1929]), and these reviews provide some of the best maps to the difficult territory of *Berlin Chronicle;* perhaps not surprisingly, much of the language and program ascribed by Benjamin to Hessel in these reviews reappears almost unaltered in his own writing later on.

Benjamin begins his review of Hessel's *On Foot in Berlin* with a distinction that adumbrates the one in "The Storyteller," dividing all existing descriptions of cities into two groups: those written by foreigners and those by natives. What the foreign tourist looks for and writes about in a given city is the superficial, or *oberflächlich,* which is to say the *Exotische* and *Pittoreske* (3:194/2:262). The sense of these terms is somewhat counterintuitive. What Benjamin means by the exotic is that the foreigner looks for (or at) the city's official culture, that image of the "other" that is securely located in the cultural imaginary of his world; by the picturesque, Benjamin means those prescribed, anticipated pictures or images (Bilder) that convey the intended splendor, or *Glanz,* of the other culture—in other words, the exotic and picturesque as represented by the foreigner's Baedeker guidebook, the simulacric image economy in which Jensen's tale is set or, more generally, in which the Grand Tour regimen of Bildung is traditionally grounded. Not incidentally, Benjamin associates this type of description with the city of Rome—not for nothing does he choose the Italianate word *Pittoreske*—whose streets, he says, are already too well paved (*schon allzu gebahnt*), so full of temples and national shrines (*nationale Heiligtümer*) that they can yield only "the great reminiscences, the historical *frissons*" ("die großen Reminiszenzen, die historischen Schauer" [3:195/2:263]). That is, such writing—whether its object be Rome or Berlin—can only support the phantasmagoric construction of national splendor qua history and memory. In fact, ultimately, it seems less decisive for Benjamin's distinction whether the writer is native or foreign, or even whether the description is of Berlin or Rome, than whether the writer focuses on the programmed imaginary, the "historical" reminiscences and national reliquaries that support both the classicizing and mythologizing impulses of the present, or does not.

Benjamin opposes to this first form that of the native writing about his homeland. Unlike the superficial pretext (*oberflächliche Anlaß*) of the person who travels to foreign parts, such a local draws on *tiefere Motive,* deeper motives, those of a person who journeys into the past. For him, we are told, each street leads downward, and "if not to the Mothers, then at least to a past that is all the more spellbinding for not being only the author's own, private past" ("wenn nicht zu den Müttern, so doch in eine Vergangenheit, die um so bannender sein kann, als sie nicht nur des Autors eigne, private ist" [3:194/2:262]). Benjamin stresses how this mode of writing seems always to straddle the line between personal memoir and an account of a broader, more collective experience or memory; he also underscores how, ideally, it seeks to subordinate the unique and nuanced, individual experience (*Erlebnis*) to the constant (*das Immergleiche*) of shared experience (*Erfahrung*). In exploring such a public imaginary at the site of the city and its buried nether realm, the writer of course runs the implicit risk of resembling precisely the type of authorship Benjamin would most oppose, by producing in turn "the great reminiscences," the collective history of the native city, and the risk is compounded when the city at issue is Berlin, the center of German nationalism and imperial pride, where the past into which the writer descends already threatens to become a journey to the Mothers, a journey into the nebulous, numinous realms of Goethean and Teutonic mythology.[44]

Benjamin was cognizant of these risks, just as he was of the rising importance of Berlin's ethnographical museums, whose archaeological artifacts were contributing just as much to the formation of German national identity as those of the "classical" museums harboring their appropriated foreign glory—especially with the support of the popular racial theories of such prehistorians (*Vorgeschichtler*) as Gustav Kossinna.[45] In his Hessel review, Benjamin sometimes seems to wish to avoid this risk by minimizing it and claiming that Berliners have changed ("daß die Berliner andre geworden sind"), that their problematic national pride (*problematischer Gründerstolz*) has given way to a sense of their city as at once more provincial and more European. But for the most part, both Hessel and Benjamin seem rather to work to bring this state about than to assume it as a starting point, and they deploy their considerable literary resources to do so—all the while aware that the very tactics by which they seek to dislodge the official culture can also be taken to support it.

For our purposes the most interesting and problematic of the literary strategies Benjamin's review highlights in Hessel's description of Berlin is the deliberate and sustained evocation of a classical background for the city (a strategy that finds its place in Benjamin's own *Berlin Chronicle*)—precisely the background that lies "deeper," "beneath" the city: in a word, its archaeology. When reviewing Hessel's earlier work, *Unknown Berlin* (1927), Benjamin introduces the premises of this strategy in terms of their common *Tiergartenmythologie:*

The pillared porticoes, the friezes and architraves of the villas in the Tiergarten have been taken at their face value in this book. The "old" West of Berlin has become the West of Antiquity—the source of the westerly winds that fill the sails of the boatmen whose vessels pass slowly up the Landwehr Canal, laden with the apples of the Hesperides, and tie up at the Bridge of Hercules. . . . What is unknown, "heimlich," about this Berlin is no windy whispering, no tiresome flirting, but simply this strict classical image-being of a city.

[D]ie säulengetragenen Vorhallen, die Friese und Architrave der Tiergartenvillen sind in diesem Buche beim Wort genommen. Der "alte" Westen wurde der antike, aus dem die westlichen Winde den Schiffern kommen, die ihren Kahn mit den Äpfeln der Hesperiden langsam den Landwehrkanal herauffflößen, um bei der Brücke des Herakles anzulegen . . . "Heimlich" an diesem Berlin ist kein windiges Wispern, kein leidiges Liebeln, einzig dies strenge und antike Bild-Sein einer Stadt. (3:82/2:69)[46]

Much the same strategy is described for *On Foot in Berlin,* wherein Hessel is said to introduce his readers to "the entire antiquity of the 'Old West' . . . the last monuments of an ancient culture of dwelling" ("die ganze Antike des "Alten Westens" . . . die letzten Denkmale einer alten Wohnkultur") including the *lares* beneath the threshold, the Muses of Magdeburgerstrasse, and so on (3:196–97/2:264–65). It is found too in Benjamin's *Berlin Childhood,* perhaps especially in the opening vignette, "Loggias" ("Loggien"), and his own "Tiergarten."[47] And it is found also in *Berlin Chronicle,* already on the opening page with the description of the child's first venture over the Bridge of Hercules, in such scattered instances as the description of the deserted resorts that seemed more ancient than Roman spas ("verödet[en] Kurorte, [die] altertümlicher als römische Thermen erscheinen" [484/610]), and throughout, in the sustained, dominant image of the city as a labyrinth, replete with both its Ariadne and its Minotaur—an image that recalls not only the theme of *flânerie* but also Benjamin's haunting description of the ruins of Pompeii as their own disorienting (*verirrend*) labyrinth.[48]

The literary strategy of classicizing Berlin in this way, the strategy underlying both Hessel's and Benjamin's depictions of Berlin, is a tricky one. On the one hand, it clearly plays into precisely the kind of monumental neoclassicism that Benjamin sees embedded in the "pillared porticoes, the friezes and architraves of the Tiergarten villas" and the museumlike buildings (*Musealen*) of the "Old West," that same neoclassicism that he found so thoroughly suspect for its phantasmagoric appropriation of the past as a prop for the present social-political order; for its splendid simulacral facade covering and legitimating the structures of power, whether economic or political, private or public; and perhaps especially for its erasure of history, its pretensions to a timeless enduring archetypal mythology that belied the particularities and contingencies of the present—those pillars that prop up and support at once the structures of the "great reminiscences" and of universal, *allgemeine Bildung*.[49] It is just such a neoclassical imaginary impulse—familiar to us from Mann's middle works, Freud's Oedipalizing, or Jensen's *Gradiva*—that seems almost dangerously to drive Benjamin's descriptions of the caryatids of Berlin's loggias, the Pompeiian red of its courtyards, its Hydras and Nemean lions, its almost unchanging, essential antiquity (*Altertümliches an sich*).[50] All these classical allusions, Benjamin tells us, leave the characters who move among them in danger of being transformed into heroes ("von der Gefahr betreten, in Helden verwandelt zu werden" [3:84/2:71]), the same kind of heroism into which Benjamin and his friends were misled by their Bildung ideals and German soldiers heading into the Great War by theirs—recalling Hanold, Jung, or Freud's "great men": "ein Privileg des Faschismus," as it were.[51]

On the other hand, such classicizing can also be seen to function as a counterforce to the intended monumentality of neoclassical mythology. That is, Benjamin seems not so much to evoke the classical in order to suggest a timeless, archetypal, mythological realm that absorbs and assimilates the historical particularities of the present—or conversely, in order to allow the hegemonic historical present to absorb and assimilate the particularities of the "classical past" as support for its own state and splendor—as he does in order to expose the phantasmagoric mythology of the *present* and to reveal both its contingency and its ephemerality. Far from emphasizing the abidingness of the past and present and the continuity between them, Benjamin's particular evocation of the classical works to bring to light the transitory nature of both. And he does so by radically refunctioning the discursive regime of archaeology for his project. Archaeology becomes an excavating of neither the foreign classical past nor the local tribal past but rather of the present, of the "new," or as he more precisely puts it, of what has only just become old ("das eben erst Alte" [3:197/2:264]). As he says of Hessel, "Those who know how to read his books can sense how they conjure up classical Antiquity between the walls of aging big cities and among the ruins of the past century" ("wer seine Bücher zu lesen versteht, fühlt, wie sie zwischen den Mauern alternder Großstädte, den Ruinen des vorigen Jahrhunderts, die Antike beschworen" [3:84/ 2:70]).[52] Benjamin and Hessel's "Tiergarten mythology" represents, as it were, an archaeology and mythology of modernity, a frank acknowledgment of Baudelaire's "cruel *aperçu* that the city changes faster than a human heart" ("grausame Wort von der Stadt, die schneller als ein Menschenherz sich wandle" [3:197/2:265]).

Benjamin suggests this functional shift in both the classical and the archaeological already in his review of Hessel's *Unknown Berlin*, where he insists that the "antiquity" of Hessel's "Old West" Berlin does not mean its inhabitants are "Greeks or Romans in modern costume, and even less are they our contemporaries in humanist carnival dress" ("Griechen oder Römer in modernen Kostümen, noch weniger Zeitgenossen in humanistischen Karnevalstrachten" [3:82/2:70]). Rather, these "fragile children of the world" ("gebrechliche Kinder der Welt") are seen through a distancing, alienating narrative perspective that renders them more or less instantly obsolete, old and "mythical" rather than natural or "real." It is a literary strategy that has obvious and important affinities with Brecht's epic theater—Benjamin refers to Hessel's *On Foot in Berlin* as "an epic book through and through" ("ein ganz und gar episches Buch" [3:194/2:262])—but that Benjamin more specifically identifies with the straying arts, the *Irrkünste,* of the French surrealists, that is, with their urban *flânerie* and interest in discarded debris, their special feel for ephemeral and outmoded things.[53] It is to evoke this tradition that Benjamin titles his review of Hessel's *On Foot in Berlin* "The Return of the Flâneur" ("Die Wiederkehr des Flaneurs") and, in *Berlin Chronicle,* explains how he learned the *flâneur*'s art from Hessel and in Paris. It is just this surrealist tradition of "archaeology" that both Hessel and Benjamin adapt in their work to refigure and challenge the classical tradition and its archaeology—not least through the pairing of Berlin with modern-day, European Paris and not with ancient, imperial Rome.

Let me expand a bit on this surrealist archaeology of what has only just become old: how it emerges, how it proceeds, and how it affects Benjamin's project. In "Surrealism" ("Der Sürrealismus" [1929]), Benjamin claims that André Breton was the first to perceive "the revolutionary energies that appear in the 'outmoded': in the first iron constructions, the first factory buildings, the earliest photos, objects that have begun to be extinct" ("die revolutionären Energien die im 'Veralteten' erscheinen, in den ersten Eisenkonstruktionen, den ersten Fabrikgebäuden, den frühesten Photos, den Gegenständen, die anfangen auszusterben" [2:299/2:210]). Clearly, technology played a crucial role in creating the conditions of accelerated obsolescence that yielded this "new" archaeology, with artifacts constructed and discarded and periods emerging and sedimenting at such a rapid rate that the nineteenth century alone seemed almost as layered with past cultural "eras" as were all the eras between it and the most remote, truly archaeological past. But as Benjamin insists, technology also played a role in changing the modes of perception that allowed for the recognition of this instant obsolescence to begin with. Due to changes in the medial technologies of perception—and chief among them that of photography—the contemporary observer *saw* differently from his predecessors, and this allowed him to turn an "early eye," an already distanced perspective on what had only just become old and archaic:[54] hence the essay's subtitle, "The Last Snapshot of the European Intelligentsia" ("Die letzte Momentaufnahme der europäischen Intelligenz"), hence too the insistence in *Berlin Chronicle* that his and Hessel's "Tiergarten mythology" only addressed that side of the city "truly receptive to photography" ("die wirklich der photographischen Aufnahme zugänglich ist" [470/599]). As Benjamin says of Hessel, "It should not be thought that a reverential glance latched onto museum-like buildings is enough to reveal the entire antiquity of the 'Old West' to which Hessel introduces his readers. Only a man in whom modernity has already announced its presence, however quietly, can cast such an original and 'early' glance at what has only just become old" ("Man meine aber nicht, ein pietätvoll, am Musealen haftender Blick sei genug, um die ganze Antike des 'alten Westens,' in den Hessel seine Leser führt, zu entdecken. Nur ein Mann, in dem das Neue sich, wenn auch still, so sehr deutlich ankündigt, kann einen so originalen, so frühen Blick auf dies eben erst Alte tun" [3:197/2:264]). In other words, this new archaeology was enabled, even occasioned, by changes in technology, including especially visual technology. To this extent, Benjamin's investment in archaeology and photography are inseparable.

This archaeology of the present entailed the discovery not only of new archaeological objects but also of a new mythology or, rather, of a new and specifically modern form of myth. This is meant in two different but related ways. First, under the distracted (*verirrende*) gaze of the surrealist observer—Benjamin refers to Hessel interchangeably as *flâneur* and dreamer (*Träumer*)—the material artifacts (the archaeological finds) of the preceding century's urban culture were regularly dissolved into a collection of dreamlike projections or phantasmagoria.[55] As Benjamin puts it in *Berlin Chronicle:*

> It had to be in Paris, where the walls and quays, the asphalt surfaces, the collections and the rubbish, the railings and the squares, the arcades and the kiosks teach a language so singular that our relations to people attain, in the solitude that surrounds us, in our immersion in that world of things, the depths of a sleep in which the dream image waits to shows them their true face.

> [E]s mußte in Paris sein, wo die Mauern und Quais, der Asphalt, die Sammlungen und der Schutt, die Gatter und Squares, die Passagen und die Kioske uns eine so einzigartige Sprache lehren, daß unsere Beziehungen zu den Menschen in der uns empfangenden Einsamkeit, unserm Versunkensein in jene Dingwelt, die Tiefe eines Schlafs erreichen, in welcher das Traumbild sie erwartet, das ihnen ihr wahres Gesicht offenbart. (490/614)

Once the found objects of this world of things (*Dingwelt*) were recognized as such *Traumbilder,* dream images, they could be read as the repository of the unconscious dreams, fears, and drives that determined that same culture's supposedly conscious, rational activity: as the manifest form of the unacknowledged and unrealized needs and wishes of its dominant bourgeois class—its cultural imaginary. The very fact that such dreams could be detected behind the ideals of the nineteenth century seemed to the surrealists to indicate a hidden underlayer of archaic forms of meaning deposited beneath the modern rational world, a layer that transformed its everyday material objects into distinctly mythical artifacts—or as Benjamin also calls them, into allegories and emblems. And so the examiner's task in handling such objects was actually twofold. First, he needed to expose their obsolescence, their place in a bygone, superseded era, however recently past—which is to say, their all but instantaneous archaeological status. And second, he needed to reveal the myth, the imaginary stamped onto their form, indeed giving them their form. In this respect, the archaeological and mythological prove as inseparable in the surrealist project as, from another perspective, do the archaeological and technological.

The surrealists' model of the mythological was not limited, however, to the specific imaginary of the nineteenth century. Rather, as John McCole points out, there was a persistent sense that the forces lurking just beneath the surface of the abandoned objects of the recent past derived from "a far more distant, literally primordial experience, at once historically specific and atavistic." Precisely because the dream forces of modern civilization had remained unmastered and unrecognized for so long, they had remained in what McCole calls "the realm of archaic compulsions."[56] The imaginary impulses shaping the present were as ancient and persistent as the social circumstances that engendered them. In other words, the archaeology of the specific, recent past was always also felt to be a reading of the remote past, of the *Urgeschichte* of Western culture; the mythology of the one was inextricably permeated with that of the other. In this sense, the surrealist archaeology of the recent past linked up firmly with a more traditional archaeology of the remote past; the one necessarily entailed the other, and so drew further resonance for its archaeological metaphor.

This dual character of the mythic clearly helps illuminate the central role of classical allusions and neoclassical artifacts in both Benjamin's and Hessel's projects. The classical was approached as both the dream-filled, outmoded kitsch of the bourgeois era—the material expression of its aging culture—and the repository of the actively archaic in the modern world. The neoclassical ornamental architecture of the Tiergarten villas, the Hercules Bridge, and the "Old West" was what needed to be brought to light, to the surface, to reveal the practically prehistorical, mythical consciousness still animating "noisy, matter-of-fact Berlin, the city of work and metropolis of business" ("das nüchterne und lärmende Berlin, die Stadt der Arbeit und die Metropole des Betriebs" [489/613]); by exposing it as the dusty and dirty, obsolete detritus of what had only just become old, they hoped to depose the rule of far more ancient forces over the city's life. At the same time, however, it must be admitted that their investment in exposing a mythic world behind the material objects of modern culture, and in privileging this world as somehow the more actual realm of modern experience, also ran a risk: the risk of resembling the vitalistic, *lebensphilosophische* phenomenology of Klages, Jung, and others—including the fascists— that Benjamin (and Hessel) so vehemently opposed. In fact, this seems to be just what Benjamin thought happened to the French surrealists themselves, the reason he came to consider them reactionary. They succumbed to a form of vitalistic affirmation of mythological forces much as had the George circle in Vienna (Klages included), who, in their opposition to institutional classicism, had nurtured an alternative that proved just as dangerous, just as reactionary, just as available to fascist ideals.[57] Clearly, even though Hessel and Benjamin embraced this new archaeology of the surrealists as a means for combating the traditional archaeology of the classicists, it also posed its own dangers—indeed, even some of the same dangers.

Benjamin's review of Hessel's *On Foot in Berlin* elucidates how his use of classical mythology is adapted to the program of unearthing what has only just become old, how it differs from, and works against, the "great reminiscences" and the reverent glance latched onto the museumlike ("den pietätvoll, am Musealen haftenden Blick"), and how it also works to avoid the reactionary trap of the surrealists. The vast majority of the classical references Benjamin ascribes to Hessel's works— the same ones that reappear in his own—refer to what I might call demoted deities: not the powerful, numinous gods who lend support to national ideologies, cultural imaginaries, or vitalistic psychologies, nor the more minor figures, such as the Gradiva, who lend themselves to a trajectory of regained (or added) splendor through a classicizing aestheticization, but rather resolutely minor deities whose power, authority, and stature, while perhaps once dominant, have declined, diminished, grown dirty and dusty over time. As Benjamin says,

> Among the *plebs deorum* of the caryatids and Atlases, Pomonas and putti, that Hessel reveals to the reader, his favorites are those once dominant figures that have now been reduced to *penates,* unassuming household gods on dusty

landings, in nameless hall niches, figures who have become guardians of the threshold. . . . He is unable to tear himself away from them, and their power wafts over him even when their images have long since vanished or become unrecognizable.

> Unter der plebs deorum der Kariatyden und Atlanten, der Pomonen und Putten, mit deren Entdeckung er [Hessel] den Leser hier aufnimmt, sind ihm die liebsten doch jene einst herrschenden, nun zu Penaten, unscheinbaren Schwellengöttern gewordenen Figuren, die angestaubt auf Treppenabsätzen, namenlos in Flurnischen einquartiert [sind] . . . Von ihnen kommt er nicht los und ihr Walten weht ihn noch an, wo ihre Abbilder längst nicht mehr oder unkenntlich stehen. (3:197/2:264–65)[58]

Similarly, Benjamin describes "how he sniffs out the *lares* beneath the threshold, how he celebrates the last monuments of an ancient culture of dwelling" ("wie er die Laren unter der Schwelle aufspürt, wie er die letzten Denkmale einer alten Wohnkultur feiert" [3:196/2:264]). It is just this sunken, dusty, ruined state that makes Hessel's search for these objects an archaeological one; and it is just this same "ruined" vanished state that is celebrated, spellbinding, and, in a peculiar way, powerful, not in its recovery (as we find in the surrealists), but in its loss. It is the testament to the *pastness* of their once dominant order that these objects are able to offer that Benjamin and Hessel find so powerful, the pastness of an order that otherwise would not be able to recognize that it is indeed past.[59] But what links the present world of Berlin to the ancient world of these classical references is not the promoting presence of the latter in the former but instead the demoted *Antike* of the former, every bit as bygone as the ancient world itself. The classical works to *de*mythify, to render what has only just become old truly old, as reduced in potency as Roman putti and as died out (*abgestorben*) as the Roman spas (484/610). This is why Benjamin also describes Hessel's work as a genuine manual of leave-taking ("ein wahrer Briefsteller des Scheidens"), an impulse not complementary to but identical with its classicizing impulse, as we see in Benjamin's example of Hessel's leave-taking (*Abschied*) from the Muses of Magdeburgerstrasse. Hessel writes, and Benjamin quotes, "They have long since vanished. Like broken stones they stood there, decorously holding their sphere or pen, those that still had hands" ("Sie sind inzwischen verschwunden. Bruchsteinern standen sie da und hielten artig, soweit sie noch Hände hatten, ihre Kugel oder ihren Stift" [3:197/2:265]). Even so has the German neoclassical impulse, far from reclaiming the glorious past for a glorious present, grown old, broken, without hands to hold or pass on; its Muses inspire the viewer not to sustain the classical tradition but to let it fall.

The focus on demoted deities—or deities of demotion—has further effects that further refunction the archaeological imaginary, both old and new. For instance, by focusing on the *lares* and *penates,* Benjamin shifts the arena of the archaeological past from the grandly national public (or alternatively, from the broadly cosmopolitan) to the more modestly and semi-privately conceived space of the household, especially the bourgeois household. While clearly this aids him in his critique of class and class(ic)ism, that is, of the bourgeois class in its complicity with the emerging fascist world order, and just as clearly, by moving the mythological into the private sphere, begins its journey inward to the psychological sphere of the bourgeois individual, the same move we see in Jensen, Jung, and Mann, it still does so in a manner that thoroughly deprives the mythological of its potential heroic dimension and its potential vitalistic dimension.[60] That is, whereas, say, Jensen's appropriation of the classical for the bourgeois realm seemed designed to invest a borrowed splendor and cultural authority in Hanold's class identity, and thus too in German national identity, and the surrealists' appropriation of the archaeological was meant to invest a well-nigh archaic mythical world in the modern bourgeois city, Benjamin's assignment of his mythical artifacts and references to the *bürgerlich* quarters is meant to strip them of all such numinous or ancient authority, all such *Glanz* that might induce the historical or mythological *frissons* by rendering them *gemütlich,* domestic, even kitschy, the very opposite of heroic, and in no case vehicles for some timeless, archaic truth, whether classical or surrealist—these objects remain far too banal, historical, and bourgeois for that, far too obviously the collected debris of the typical middle-class basement (*Abstellraum*) to inspire any kind of associative immersion or identification (see 480/606).

This changed status of the mythological modifies the nature of the archaeological metaphor still more, especially in regard to its classical strain. Whereas the dominant model of classical archaeology—the one we found metaphorically in Jensen, and can find "actually" in Schliemann—describes an excavatory search for those ancient artworks that recall the splendor of the classical world, buried beneath so much dirt and debris (much of it from later, more recent epochs), all of which is to be discarded that the past glory might once again be brought into the light and into the present—embodiments, as it were, of historical greatness and great history—Benjamin's archaeology focuses instead on the dirt and debris itself and regards the "major finds" and monuments of the ancient world as themselves junk or *Bettel* (3:195/2:263). Rather than privileging those artifacts that testify to Jaeger's organically unfolding *Bildungswelt,* Benjamin treasures what interrupts and refutes it. The corrosive effect of material archaeology, its simultaneous banalizing and fragmenting of the classical imaginary, that was so feared by Jaeger is precisely what Benjamin seems most to desire from it.

This is not to say that Benjamin, qua archaeologist, does not himself harbor hopes of some recovered splendor from his dig, that he differs from others—both classicizing nationalists and surrealizing artists—in not seeking an illuminating something that will connect his past artifact to his present moment and endow it with redeeming, even transformative, significance. He certainly, and certainly problematically, does. One of the most challenging aspects of *Berlin Chronicle* is how it seems both to oppose the mythic consciousness of the bourgeois order in its classicist, surrealist, and fascist manifestations and to promote an almost identical one that will somehow redeem us from within that order, how it seems both infinitely suspicious of the vitalists' affirmation of another, mythical meaning hidden beneath the rational, present-day world and endlessly tempted by it as well. In this respect at least, Benjamin's project seems no more immune from the dangers of inadvertent complicity in the kind of cultural imaginary he would oppose than were those of Mann and Freud at this same time; and while I will try to argue that he seems more self-consciously prepared to avoid this trap, I think we also need to prepare ourselves for the possibility that, just perhaps, he does not completely succeed.

The Archaeology of Bildung

Let me offer a few concrete examples of the kind of metaphorical archaeology Benjamin practices in *Berlin Chronicle* in more particular relation to the culture of Bildung. Perhaps the best place to start is with his analysis of the bourgeois dwelling and furniture of his maternal grandmother—quite literally a journey to the Mothers of the kind mentioned in the Hessel review, a journey that leads "downward" into a past that is at once the author's own private memory and an exercise in social cultural history (500–503/620–23). Benjamin initially introduces the grandmother (Hedwig Schoenflies) in her two different guises: as a great traveler to foreign lands whose picture postcards of distant parts (and monuments) provided the true adventure stories of Benjamin's boyhood years, and as the widowed old lady ensconced in her carpeted window alcove, ornamented with a little balustrade, and looking out over the dust-covered Blumeshof. In keeping with the basic distinction broached in the Hessel review, it is the latter guise that Benjamin takes for his subject, the grandmother and her house as monuments of an ancient culture of dwelling (*Wohnkultur*). The house is described as possessed by the *Signatur* of this ancient cult, the almost immemorial feeling of security ("das fast unvordenkliche Gefühl von Geborgenheit"); in memory it seems an almost mythological realm, "an Elysium, an uncertain realm of dead but undying grandmothers" ("ein Elysium, ein unbestimmtes Reich abgestorbener aber unsterblicher Großmütter"); it also seems already a depeopled, abandoned site, whose very emptiness conveys something of the archaeological to the setting, where the further back one goes in space, the further back one goes in time as well. The children who once occupied the apartment have long since moved out; the "back" rooms have become lost to the present in the rear of the house; the whole is covered by a silence that seems to have magically preserved it for a hundred years. It is neither accidental nor incidental that the extreme back recesses of this all but empty dwelling abut bare walls of Pompeiian red (in *Berlin Childhood*, this space is expanded to include caryatids, bronzes, vases and other exotic antiquities, all covered thickly with dust). Although unmistakably nineteenth-century Berlin, the dwelling, with the exaggerated size and number of its rooms, seems itself a minor ancient site, awaiting the spade—or as Benjamin also puts it, awaiting the "dusting off" if not with the pickaxe, then at least with a brush.[61]

In the absence of living inhabitants (he does mention a ghost), Benjamin focuses his attention on their material remains, the household objects that seemingly embody the desires and dreams of this ancient bourgeois *Wohnkultur*. What fascinates him most is the paradoxical relation to time represented by these artifacts; for all their show of security, solidity, durability, and permanence (*Sicherheit, Solidität,*

Haltbarkeit, Dauer), these forms proved so ephemeral that after the period of a single generation they were already superseded, already ready for the shabbiest of secondhand furniture shops (*der schäbigste Trödelladen*)—already archaeological debris that generated the very dust that covered them.[62] Benjamin perceives that what lent this manner of things its immemorial feeling of bourgeois security, its "idea of peculiar protectedness" ("Begriff jener besondern Geborgenheit")—the sense of trust, comfort, cosiness, and cheer ("das Vertraute, Beruhigende, Anheimelnde, und Tröstliche")—was precisely its nonchalant disavowal of history, or rather historicity, its comfortable conviction of its own permanence, precisely that history to which it so quickly succumbed, not least because it failed to entrust itself to history, to wear, inheritance, moves. As Benjamin says, it bespeaks a realm that denies death and so itself has suffered death, an Elysium of the died-off but undying. It is Benjamin's descriptive task to restore the sense of death. We might recall the connection he draws in *One Way Street* between such an apartment and the corpse in murder mysteries, and the remark "The soulless luxury of the furnishings becomes true comfort only in the presence of a dead body" ("Die seelenlose Üppigkeit des Mobiliars wird wahrhafter Komfort erst vor dem Leichnam" [4:89/1:447]). We might say that his archaeology of what has only just become old is always as much about burying bourgeois culture beneath the weight of its own dust and debris as it is about excavating it, as much about interring the dead city as conjuring or exhuming it.

If the maternal grandmother's apartment serves as an archaeological site of the bourgeois family interior, my second example serves as one of that other institution of bourgeois Bildung: the school. Again, the focus is on the material artifact, the building itself and its grounds, all but depopulated and abandoned by its former occupants. The so-called emblem of the school is itself a monument, albeit a notably diminished one: a plaster statue of Kaiser Friedrich, puny and pitiful (*klein und kümmerlich*), deposited in a remote corner of the playground, "never washed, and a considerable layer of dust and rust had settled over it during the course of years" ("nie gewaschen, und eine ansehnliche Schicht von Schmutz und von Ruß hat sich im Laufe der Jahre darüber gelegt" [473/601]). Like the dust in the Blumeshof, the rust that rains down and settles on the schoolyard seems "à l'instar de Pompeï," creating an almost instant internment. The fact that the layering, dirty rust is spewed out from the nearby railway station increases the sense of the archaic all the more, insofar as, for Benjamin, the railways are themselves something outdated that only encounters the ancient ("ein veraltetes, das nur auf das alte stößt" [470/599]). Benjamin later describes the experience of looking down into the playground from that railway station:

It now stands before me quite uselessly, like one of those temples that were excavated much too early and inexpertly, their frescoes having been long effaced by rain by the time the excavation of the ceremonial implements and papyri, which might have thrown some light on these instruments, could at last seriously begin. So I have to make do with what comes to the surface only today—isolated pieces of the interior that have broken away yet contain the whole within them, while the whole, standing there before me, has lost its details without trace.

Jetzt steht er, untauglich nutzlos vor mir, einem jener . . . Tempel ähnlich, die viel zu früh, unsachverständig ausgegraben wurden und deren Fresken unter Regengüssen längst bis zur Unkenntlichkeit verwaschen waren als endlich ernstlich die Ausgrabung der Kultgeräte und Papyri beginnen konnte, die etwas Licht auf diese Bilder hätten werfen können. So muß ich mich mit dem begnügen, was erst heute wieder auftaucht, vereinzelten herausgebrochnen Stücken des Interiors, die doch das Ganze in sich halten, während das Ganze, das dort draußen vor mir steht, sein Einzelnes so spurlos verloren hat. (509/628)[63]

Two finds (*Funde* [495/617]) emerge out of Benjamin's sifting through the material debris of the school: the crenellated crown molding that ran around the classrooms and the school bell. The first evokes quite definite militaristic ideals, the second a sense of unending captive time, both not so much in contrast to as in secret, uneasy agreement with the protectedness (*Geborgenheit*) and permanence (*Dauer*) of the bourgeois interior. The plaster cast of Kaiser Friedrich already points to the troubling martial ideals behind the official culture of Bildung; it watches over the hordes of schoolboys playing war much as the Bild of the sickly prince watched over the childhood games of Wilhelm

Meister or the Gradiva over Norbert Hanold's studies, and with the same intended inculcating effect. Inside—where the dirt and soot are washed away—the infamous carved wooden battlements over the doors were designed to achieve much the same effect, and in two ways. First, they formed an unbroken, continuous link joining together the entire school, even the entire society. Surrounding the pictures (Bilder) of the kaiser on the wall with a kind of ornamental corona, they then extended through the classrooms where the students had their lessons, into the faculty room, on to the arts-and-crafts rooms, where they became the emblem of a certain guildlike respectability ("Emblem einer gewissen zunftgerechten Biederkeit"), turning from the first, second, and third forms up to the upper classes, where they acquired an allusion to the *Abitur* that was soon to crown the labors of their members ("eine Anspielung auf das Abiturium welches bald die Mühe ihrer Angehörigen krönen sollte" [510/628])—which is to say, their indoctrination into a thoroughly militarized society. By linking all the various aspects of the educational institution, and by linking all its progressive stages, the molding secured the seemingly inevitable, inescapable issue of official Bildung and gave it its crowning credo: the need to become a soldier ("müsse Soldat werden" [509/627]). Second, the molding achieved much the same effect of inescapable continuity by forming a similarly unbroken chain linking together historical periods. The wooden crenellations were designed, Benjamin notes, to remind one of a Gothic castle (much like the building's brick exterior [507/626]). "Heraldic and chivalric obtuseness shone forth wherever possible" ("heraldischer und ritterlicher Stumpfsinn prunkte wo nur immer möglich" [474/602]). Although clearly not classical, the architectural reference still performed the same dehistoricizing, archaizing function of imbuing its present-day, martial *Bildungskultur* with mythical national depth and foundation. And this mythical effect was not lessened but increased by how the molding linked up with the Jugendstil ornaments in the great hall: the ornaments with their "unspeakable" gray-green and their "absurd" bosses and scrolls, and the great hall, where the students themselves, in their leave-taking ceremony (*Abschiedsfeier*), were to be linked up with the modern "real" world. If in the grandmother's house the advent of Jugendstil gave the lie to the timelessness and endurance of her bourgeois furniture, exposed it as a mere style in its own right, a superseded period, here in the school Jugendstil seemingly perpetuated the lie of the molding's timelessness, by carrying on, through different and changing strata of architectural styles, the one constant of its imaginary values.

The temporality/nontemporality of this setting is experienced in two different ways by Benjamin. On the one hand, in contrast with the comforting security of the bourgeois interior, the captive sense of time here becomes a kind of prison for the child (which is to say, a slightly different kind of security system), symbolized by the school clock and "the invisible bars of our timetable cage" ("unser unsichtbar gegitterter Stundenkäfig") or, alternatively, by the ring signal (*Klingelzeichen*) of the school bell, which shrilly dictated the start and end of school and classes, and woe to him who found himself still outside the door after this bell had rung. To be part of this official *Bildungskultur* was to be part of its temporal schema, which seemed inflexibly unchanging and rigidly progressive—from the opening of the school gates to the end of the last period, from the first form through to graduation, from the Gothic brick and battlements to the Jugendstil bosses and scrolls. On the other hand, however, and very much in keeping with the fate of the grandmother's furniture, there opens up a sense of obsolescence in the very midst of this apparent *durée*. For the schoolboy, this sense is perhaps most poignantly broached by a seemingly innocent query made by a seemingly hostile fellow student. The child Benjamin is asked, "whether my *Alter* [slang for "old man" but also meaning "age," "epoch"] was already gone" ("ob mein Alter schon weg sei" [475/602]) and the question—not understood in its surface sense—opens up an abyss before him, which he sought to bridge with a convincing protest ("mit einem bündigen Protest"). Fortunately, however, it is too late. The fissure once opened is not to be closed, and the continuum of the *Alter* is abruptly interrupted. It gives a new, liberating meaning to the image of the leave-taking ceremony, not as an indoctrination, a coming-of-age, but truly as a leave-taking, a letting-go-of-an-age; it gives new meaning to the sound of the last bell; and it gives a new, strangely exciting sense to the experience of "too late!" ("zu spät gekommen!") that used to terrorize the child when confronted by the closed classroom door, by the violation of the timetable, but that now fills him with an immense pleasure ("einem großen Lustgefühl") and blasphemous indifference ("blasphemischer Gleichgültigkeit" [512/630]), the same anarchistic protest exercised in walking a step behind his mother and now promising to let him fall out of step with his fellow students-to-be-soldiers, and so too to leave that particular door into adulthood forever closed ("noch immer verschlossen" [505/624; see 494/617]). The critical archaeological perspective that can see the seemingly present as already gone, already too late, already a past age, counters the idealist archaeological perspective that would see the distant past still very much active in the present day, imbuing it with its "timeless" splendor. It offers a different, competing sense of falling out of time—and out of Bildung.

My last example of Benjamin's "archaeology of the new" focuses on his discussion of Markthalle. It raises key issues of class and sexuality; it also raises issues of the potential problems of Benjamin's project once it turns affirmative. The connection with the archaeological metaphor is differently but just as insistently drawn. Shopping for Benjamin, whether at the Markthalle or elsewhere, is always a journey underground, to the depths (490/614, 499/620), primarily because it is a journey "down" through the various strata, or *Schichten,* of social class (see 483/608; "the under world of the maidservants" ["die untere Welt der Dienstmädchen" (503/623)]). As befits the archaeological metaphor, these class strata are often hidden (as in Benjamin's own house, with the hidden economic basis); in the case of Markthalle, this hiddenness is evident in the very name of the place. Benjamin insists, "First of all, let no one think that we are talking of a *Markt-Halle* [covered market]. No: one said '*Mark-Talle*'" ("Vor allem denke man nicht, daß da von einer Markt-halle die Rede war. Nein, man sprach 'Marktalle'" [475/603]). Like the ancient mosaic inscription on the innkeeper's stoop in Jensen's Pompeii, the original meaning of the word has been worn away (*verschlissen*), such that the memories, or Bilder, that the word evokes retain nothing of the original concept of buying and selling.[64] But he also insists that such words—there are others—often retain something unfathomable (*das Unergründliche*) and that "a number of indivisible finds of this kind have played a large part in my decision to write down these memories" ("einige unteilbare Funde, diesem gleichend, viel Anteil an meinem Entschlusse haben, diese Erinnerungen aufzuzeichnen" [495/617]).[65] Like the demoted deities that both Hessel and Benjamin discover discarded among the debris and dirt of the modern city, such worn but preserved words are the particular, all-but-material objects of Benjamin's attention: not only for what they can discover once recovered and restored, but for what their very sinking or burial reveals as well.

The excavatory discovery of the original concept of buying and selling buried in the word, and place, of *Markthalle* also brings into play the work's thematics of classical mythology, in ways that contrast dramatically with the buying and selling in Benjamin's own more circumscribed bourgeois field. Benjamin mentions that the economic basis on which the finances of his parents rested was surrounded by deepest secrecy—"thickly covered" ("dicht verhüllt" [496/617]). The sense of mystery, the apparent freedom of its values from a material base and from the work and labor (the hierarchical social system) that nonetheless supported it, contributed greatly to the legitimacy of those values, to their sense of being value-free values, universal, without interest (much like Jaeger's "organic Bildungswelt" for the ancients); and Benjamin's archaeology is aimed at revealing both the material basis and the sense of stratified society supporting that basis as part of his effort to dispel its mystery and undermine its legitimacy. He describes the shopping trips he would take with his mother into what might be called the first layer or stratum of economic relations, to buy shirts at Arnold Müllers, shoes at Schiller's, or suitcases at Mädler's (496/618; see also 499/620), places preordained by tradition, and visits that always occurred with a ceremoniousness befitting an initiation ("mit der Feierlichkeit, die einer Einweihung ansteht" [496/618]). While scratching the surface of the material base of the bourgeoisie, such ventures really only supported the *Glanz* and baselessness of this class, not least by their status as sources (*Quellen*); and the falseness of their status as such sources—after all, all their goods came from elsewhere, from the labor of a lower, hidden stratum of society—reappears in Benjamin in the falseness of the status of its quasi-religion. These trips are experienced as a form of humiliating idolatry (*Götzendienst*), a worshipping of *Idolen:* being fitted with one of their suits makes the child feel his hands stick out of the sleeves "like dirty price tags" ("wie schmutzige Preistafeln" [499/620]).

All this can be instructively contrasted with Benjamin's shopping trips to Markthalle, where the dirt is all the more conspicuous, but so too is a new, different kind of elegance and *Glanz*. Here Benjamin is about as close as he comes to the lowest stratum of society or, rather, of economic production, on which the upper edifice of the bourgeoisie rests—and as true as the source of goods seems here, so too the truth of its gods, its mythology. In a manner truly exceptional in *Berlin Chronicle,* Markthalle becomes the occasion for an undisguised celebration of myth—and not unincidentally of the erotic as well. The women at the market become "priestesses of the mercantile Ceres" ("Priesterinnen der käuflichen Ceres"), "sacrosanct, wool-clad Colossi" ("unantastbare, strickwollene Kolosse"), whom a god of the market himself ("ein Marktgott selber") has endowed with all their material goods, lovingly listed by Benjamin in all their concrete detail (489–90/613). These are, to be sure, all minor, demoted deities, but they are all invested with a mythical status seemingly as real as their work and their production. They bespeak a new kind of classicism, one inseparable from, even invested in, the dirt and debris of the setting.

Moreover, the same base of production that yields their "real," redeeming mythology yields a real eroticism as well. Benjamin calls the market women procuresses (*Kupplerinnen*) and rhetorically asks, "Didn't it bubble, seethe, and swell beneath the hem of their skirts, was this not truly fertile ground?" ("Brodelte, quoll und schwoll es nicht unterm Saum ihrer Röcke, war nicht dies der wahrhaft fruchtbare Boden?" [489–90/613]). This sexual energy, so inseparable from the sense of "true" economic production and of the "true" bottom layer, or *Boden* (from this, the "true" trip to the Mothers), is in such stark contrast to what I mentioned earlier, namely, the unrelentingly negative images of other women in *Berlin Chronicle:* of Benjamin's mother and nannies, those female figures who usually figure so prominently in the erotic Bildung of the bourgeois child; of the prostitutes that populate the Berlin streets, socially provided to students as a kind of unofficial bourgeois Bildung institution in its own right, whose own linkage of the erotic and economic rivals the mother's and demonstrates so well the perversity of the whole Bildung culture;[66] and perhaps especially of that sailor-suited prostitute whom Benjamin spies at his father's ice rink (bought, we are told, to bring even the family's amusements into harmony with his business practices ["um auch die Zerstreuungen der Familie in Harmonie zu seinen kommerziellen Unternehmungen zu bringen" (499/620)]), who seems to embody in her sexuality the business and military interests that underlie Bildung at home and at school, the somehow "proper" fantasy from which Benjamin is desperately trying to awake. The sexuality of the market women is something entirely different, comparable only with Benjamin's account of his first sexual urges when he realized he would never make it to the prescribed religious service on time—in both cases, an eroticism based on falling *out* of Bildung, its rituals, and its sexuality.

For all the positivity of this representation of the market women, however, it also poses a problem—precisely in its positivity, in its affirmation of an emphatically vital, mythological, and archaic realm that lies buried beneath the layers of rationalized, present-day bourgeois culture and Bildung, a realm invested with an energy and sense of the real and true that is studiously denied to the worn-out, false world of more "civilized" Berlin. In this respect at least, Susan Buck-Morss is surely right to point out Benjamin's investment of a utopian dimension in the mythical, whether conceived politically, as the vestiges of a dream of a classless/proletariat society, or theologically, as a "weak" possibility of messianic redemption: the example of the market women shows how that investment manifests itself in classical, mythological images saturated with vitalistic resonances (and just at that moment where class seems most dissolved, and religion most at issue).[67] The problem, of course, is the inescapable complicity with the vitalistic philosophies of Klages and Jung and the vitalistic ideology of the fascists and their affirmations of the archaic and mythological over and against the modern and rational.[68] Benjamin's assault on Bildung and its alliance with fascist ideals seems constantly threatened by its own such alliance, and although I will continue to argue for how Benjamin seeks to distinguish his archaeological project from such unwanted comparisons, the threat of similarity still, I believe, persists.

INTROJECTION: ARCHAEOLOGY

The manner in which the economic productive forces of the market women—and mother and prostitutes—become transformed, or reconfigured, as their sexuality gives us a way to understand one of the two most important features to Benjamin's application of the archaeological metaphor to the field of the individual subject, the feature most surely designed to distinguish his position from that of other psychologies in the internal field where their common concerns, and especially those associated with memory, are most to be contested. The feature (indirectly) foregrounded by the market women's sexuality is how, for Benjamin, this importation or introjection of the social realm, including its archaeology, into the psychological or subjective is not just a metaphor. Rather, it bespeaks the conviction that structures all the writing of *Berlin Chronicle:* that the individual subject is constructed by the specific socio-historical domain—and that includes its imaginary (its mythology); that, via what Benjamin calls the mimetic faculty ("das

213

mimetische Vermögen"), the outside becomes the inside, such that the self truly *is* a kind of city, its internal labyrinth an effect of the external one in which it finds itself (see 491/614).[69] The introjection of a social imaginary that we saw so surreptiously taking place in Freud and Jensen, a disavowed introjection as it were, is the foregrounded point in Benjamin. Rather than seeing the surrounding world shaped by the projected imaginings of the individual, Benjamin insists on depicting the individual as shaped by the introjected imaginings of the surrounding world. Rather than the myths of the (collective) unconscious that regulate the individual psyche arising out of some far distant, supposedly archaic psychic past, Benjamin sees them arising out of the material historical present, in all its kitschy banality and troubling reality.[70] This introjection is everywhere implicit in *Berlin Chronicle;* it is also explicit in one of the most haunting passages in the entire work, in which Benjamin recounts the experience of returning home in the evening by railway, and, in the backyards of tenements close by the tracks, seeing

> the dusky lamps that had shone in isolation from courtyard windows, often without curtains, from staircases encrusted with dirt, from cellar windows hung with rags. . . . These last five fearful minutes of the journey before everyone got out of the train have been transformed into the gaze of my eyes, and there are those perhaps who look into them as into courtyard windows in damaged walls, in which at early evening a lamp is set.

> die düstern Lampen, die vereinzelt in den Höfen geschienen hatten aus Fenstern, denen oft die Vorhänge fehlten, in schmutzstarrenden Treppenhäusern, aus Kellerfenstern, in denen Lappen hingen. . . . [D]iese letzten fünf Angstminuten der Einfahrt eh alles aussteigt, haben sich in Blicke aus meinen Augen verwandelt und es gibt vielleicht Menschen, die in sie sehen wie in Hoffenster, die in schadhaften Mauern stecken und in denen am frühen Abend die Lampe steht. (503/623)

The city, with its dirt, its debris, and its dusky lights, is "transformed" into the observing subject himself. As Benjamin asks, "But isn't this, too, the city?" ("Aber ist nicht auch das die Stadt?" [503/623]). And clearly it is. Benjamin does see his archaeological realm of the city, in both its glamour and its grime, as the origin of the psychological realm of the subject.

The first feature, then, of Benjamin's application of archaeology to the individual subject and his memory is its literalness, its implicit insistence on the subject as a historically specific, material artifact, or site—which is to say, its basic antipsychological, anti-*lebensphilosophische* stance. The second important feature, related to the first, is its polemical position, its deliberate opposition to and reconfiguration of the reigning archaeological imaginary as it applies to both archaeology proper and its psychoanalytical appropriation. Not surprisingly, much of this reconfiguration follows along the same lines as Benjamin's city description, including the basic distinction posed at the outset of the Hessel review but now more specifically staged in the interior realm. Benjamin's critique is necessarily an immanent one, a refunctioning of the common metaphorical field. I believe the best way to present it is to pair it with a representative counterpiece from Freud and to quote both pieces in detail. Let me begin with the Freud, citing an especially Schliemannesque passage from "The Aetiology of Hysteria" ("Zur Ätiologie der Hysterie" [1896]) to which I briefly alluded in the preceding chapter. Here it is in full:

Imagine that a traveling investigator arrives in a little known region where his interest is aroused by a field of ruins with the remains of walls, fragments of columns, and tablets with half-effaced and unreadable inscriptions. He can content himself with inspecting what lies exposed to view, then questioning the perhaps semi-barbaric inhabitants who live in the vicinity about what tradition tells them about the history and meaning of these monumental remains, then writing down what they tell him and then—proceed on his way. But he may act differently. He may have brought picks, shovels, and spades with him, and he may set the inhabitants to work with these implements. Together with them he may attack the field of ruins, clear away the rubbish, and, beginning with the visible remains, uncover what is buried. If his work is crowned with success, the discoveries are self-explanatory: the remains of the walls belong to the ramparts of a palace or treasure house, out of the fragments of columns emerges a complete temple, the numerous inscriptions which, by good luck, are bilingual, reveal an alphabet and a language, and, when they have been deciphered and translated they yield unsuspected explanations about the events of the remote past, to commemorate which the monuments were built. *Saxa loquuntur!*

Nehmen Sie an, ein reisender Forscher käme in eine wenig bekannte Gegend, in welcher ein Trümmerfeld mit Mauerresten, Bruchstücken von Säulen, von Tafeln mit verwischten und unlesbaren Schriftzeichen sein Interesse erweckte. Er kann sich damit begnügen zu beschauen, was frei zutage liegt, dann die in der Nähe hausenden, etwa halbbarbarischen Einwohner ausfragen, was ihnen die Tradition über die Geschichte und Bedeutung jener monumentalen Reste kundgegeben hat, ihre Auskünfte aufzeichnen und— weiterreisen. Er kann aber auch anders vorgehen; er kann Hacken, Schaufeln und Spaten mitgebracht haben, die Anwohner für die Arbeit mit diesen Werkzeugen bestimmen, mit ihnen das Trümmerfeld in Angriff nehmen, den Schutt wegschaffen und von den sichtbaren Resten aus das Vergrabene aufdecken. Lohnt der Erfolg seine Arbeit, so erläutern die Funde sich selbst; die Mauerreste gehören zur Umwallung eines Palastes oder Schatzhauses, aus den Säulentrümmern ergänzt sich ein Tempel, die zahlreich gefundenen, im glücklichen Falle bilinguen Inschriften enthüllen ein Alphabet und eine Sprache, und deren Entzifferung und Übersetzung ergibt ungeahnte Aufschlüsse über die Ereignisse der Vorzeit, zu deren Gedächtnis jene Monumente erbaut worden sind. *Saxa loquuntur!* (6:54/3:192)

Clearly, Freud's psychologist qua archaeologist operates in a manner more than roughly analogous to the tradition of the outsider's city descriptions described by Benjamin in his Hessel review. Moreover, he operates in a manner much like that we saw in Jensen, certainly no less disturbing in its casual, quasicolonialist violence. The analyst/archaeologist here arrives on the scene as a representative of a foreign colonial power; he comes from elsewhere—and the whole "little-known" region is conceived and "inspected" from the perspective of that elsewhere—invested with power in the form of knowledge or, rather, of a means of knowing, by which he comes to appropriate the site for his own distant, but dominant, culture. The inhabitants of the region are condescendingly depicted as *halbbarbarisch,* their own knowledge and experience of their place decidedly inferior and almost irrelevant, making the place "little known" and their tradition about its history and meaning only significant once written down by the visitor. The archaeologist's first project is, we are told, to clear away the rubbish: the soil, the living surface, the present-day culture and all the accumulated layers that directly connect the past to the modern inhabitants is wrested away and carted off as just so much debris—as indeed was already the case with their history, meaning, and tradition. What the analyst qua archaeologist seeks and finds instead is "self-explanatory": isolated fragments and ruins "complete" themselves as palaces, treasure houses, and temples; inscriptions yield "unsuspected" conclusions about the remote past, to whose memory these monumental buildings were constructed in the first place. That is, the archaeologist focuses exclusively on the monumental, the classical, the great public and official reminiscences. He works to complete them, to make them continuous and whole—in a manner that makes it seem as if the building is actually physically there, from the prehistoric past, when clearly it is instead a matter of imaginary construction, a "completion" by virtue of his present knowledge (his imaginary) that yields "complete" knowledge (that is completely imaginary)—and yet, remember, that is only achieved by first dismembering (forgetting) the continuous connection with the dirt, the debris, the present-day inhabitants: it becomes completely "classical" by first being taken from the (undeserving and unrelated) "barbaric" them. And significantly enough, when the stones do speak, they speak classical Latin; indeed, they quote classical Latin, fully assimilating the find to classical Bildung.

As we saw in Jensen, this particular conflated mix of national, imperialist identity and subject identity instituted by archaeology qua psychoanalysis is a most problematic one.[71] Many of its colonialist assumptions reassert themselves in its attitude toward the psychological "I," whether adult or child: for example, that the child/subject is in need of colonization; that the subject's "native" self-understanding is of negligible importance, especially compared with the foreign observer's imaginary constructions; that the present, the living surface, is just rubbish, *Schutt,* of little or no importance in determining meaning and identity, and only what lies deeply buried in the past (or, rather, only its imaginary reconstruction) has formative or revelatory significance; that the goal—the targeted subjectivity—is something complete, coherent, continuous, "explained" and narrativized; and that identity is to be identified with, or determined by, the most monumental, the most "public" or official of governing institutions and structures, and so on. Conversely, we see many of its colonialist/archaeological assumptions legitimized by their correspondence with the psychological; for example, the classical past becomes truly "ours" not only because we alone can know it but also because it is, as it were, merely the objective confirmation of our psychic reality, the material counterpart of *our* inner lives, and similarly, the classical ideal itself becomes somehow true, not only because of the apparently seamless suturing of our imaginary classical constructions onto the fragmented historical remains, but also because the classical becomes the hidden, buried reality or truth of our very selves, our "true" selves. National and individual identity, classical and psychological reality, all are disturbingly conjoined by the standard Freudian conflation of archaeology and psychoanalysis.

There are, of course, other aspects of Freudian psychology that run counter to this archaeological mode, aspects that Benjamin, for instance, but not Freud himself, will even successfully integrate into an archaeological mode. But the passage cited has the great advantage of providing a most useful, representative background against which to set Benjamin's archaeological metaphor for memory, which we have in two slightly different versions: one as a short, slightly earlier fragment or thought image (*Denkbild*) titled "Excavation and Memory" ("Ausgraben und Erinnern" [1932]) and the other as a part of *Berlin Chronicle*.[72] The latter reads as follows:

> Language has unmistakably made plain that memory is not an instrument for exploring the past but its theater. It is the medium of past experience, just as the earth is the medium in which dead cities are buried. He who seeks to approach his own buried past must conduct himself like a man digging. This determines the tone and bearing of genuine reminiscences. They must not be afraid to return again and again to the same matter; to scatter it as one scatters earth, to turn it over as one turns over soil. For the matter itself is a mere deposit, a stratum, which yields only to the most meticulous ex-

amination what constitutes the real treasure hidden within the earth: the images, broken loose from all earlier associations, that stand—like precious fragments or torsos in a collector's gallery—in the sober rooms of our later insight. True, for successful excavations, a plan is needed. Yet no less indispensable is the cautious probing of the spade in the dark earth, and it is to cheat oneself of the richest prize to preserve as a record merely the inventory of one's discoveries, and not this dark joy of the place of the finding as well. Fruitless searching is as much a part of this as succeeding, and consequently remembrance must not proceed in the manner of a narrative or still less that of a report, but must, in the strictest epic and rhapsodic manner, assay its spade in ever-new places, and in the old ones delve to ever-deeper layers.

Die Sprache hat es unmißverständlich bedeutet, daß das Gedächtnis nicht ein Instrument zur Erkundung der Vergangenheit ist sondern deren Schauplatz. Es ist das Medium des Erlebten wie das Erdreich das Medium ist, in dem die toten Städte verschüttet liegen. Wer sich der eigenen verschütteten Vergangenheit zu nähern trachtet, muß sich verhalten wie ein Mann, der gräbt. Das bestimmt den Ton, die Haltung echter Erinnerungen. Sie dürfen nicht scheuen, immer wieder auf einen und denselben Sachverhalt zurückzukommen; ihn auszustreuen wie man Erde ausstreut, ihn umzuwühlen wie man Erdreich umwühlt. Denn Sachverhalte sind nur Lagerungen, Schichten, die erst der sorgsamsten Durchforschung das ausliefern, was die wahren Werte, die im Erdinnern stecken, ausmacht: die Bilder, die aus allen früheren Zusammenhängen losgebrochen als Kostbarkeiten in den nüchternen Gemächern unserer späten Einsicht—wie Trümmer oder Torsi in der Galerie des Sammlers—stehen. Und gewiß bedarf es, Grabungen mit Erfolg zu unternehmen, eines Plans. Doch ebenso ist unerläßlich der behutsame, tastende Spatenstich ins dunkle Erdreich und der betrügt sich selber um das Beste, der nur das Inventar der Funde und nicht auch dies dunkle Glück von Ort und Stelle des Findens selbst in seiner Niederschrift bewahrt. Das vergebliche Suchen gehört dazu so gut wie das glückliche und

> daher muß die Erinnerung nicht erzählend, noch viel weniger berichtend vorgehn sondern im strengsten Sinne episch und rhapsodisch an immer andern Stellen ihren Spatenstich versuchen, in immer tieferen Schichten an den alten forschend. (486–87/611)

The passage is undeniably difficult, far less accessible than Freud's; any reading of it should both acknowledge and account for this. To begin, we can note how the obscurity that contrasts so starkly with Freud's rational and well-constructed narrative is at least partially a result of Benjamin's commitment to a certain dreaminess (*Träumerei* [510/628]) as central to the mnemonic project when carried out by the subject, the "native," at the site of his own buried past. I mentioned earlier how dreams function in the surrealist's archaeology of what has only just become old; they also form the key link joining Benjamin's social analysis to his psychoanalysis, and in two different ways. First, the concept of the dream identifies the objects of attention, whether for the internally remembering or for the externally observing subject, as banal, ephemeral fragments that somehow elude the realm of consciousness and practical purposive reason and that require a forgetting of their everyday waking connections in order to emerge—that *need* to be "broken loose from all earlier connections" before they can yield their meaning; that need to be dislodged from their place in the grand public structures (the monuments, temples, and treasure houses) before they can become the more modest object of contemplation for the private collector; that need to be denarrativized *before* they can speak.[73]

Second, "dream" characterizes not just the object but also the mode of investigation for both Benjamin's urban archaeologist and recollecting subject. Earlier, I spoke of the *Irrkünste,* the straying arts through which the surrealist flâneur approaches the found objects of his excavated world. The same schooling (*Schulung* [469/598]), the same deliberate abnegation of conscious attention becomes the *modus operandi* for the remembering, digging subject as well. That is, the *kind* of consciousness required to recover these buried dream objects is itself dreamy, a deliberate surrender of the reign of reason, of that form of knowing so central to Freud's analyst/archaeologist and the model of Western power, and Bildung, he represents. Thus, not only does Benjamin's archaeologist not seek out grand monuments, palaces, or treasure houses but only banal fragments broken loose from all earlier connections; he also deliberately makes no attempt to restore them to their "original" state of completion or connection—or what amounts to the same thing, he makes no attempt to come up with a present imaginary construction that will complete or connect them but then also pose as their original, complete whole, no attempt to narrativize, to order and explain them as a complete, coherent subject. Instead, Benjamin insists that the discovered fragments remain fragments ("Trümmer oder Torsi"), that the archaeologist resist the impulse to arrange and narrativize and proceed instead in the strictest epic and rhapsodic manner (i.e., discontinuously, scattering [*ausstreuend*] and turning over [*umwühlend*])—which to a very significant degree means never fully understanding or "completely" mastering what he finds. As Benjamin writes, "Fruitless searching is as much a part of this as succeeding," and his archaeologist must be prepared to dig again and again, both in different places and in the same places—very much in keeping with both Benjamin's prose, its sometime failure to fully reach the light of understandability, and his tendency to return again and again to the same motifs, both in *Berlin Chronicle* proper and between *Berlin Chronicle* and other works (the Hessel reviews, the "Denkbilder," *Berlin Childhood*, etc.). Revisiting, rewriting, redigging is part of the plan; a rational, coherent narrative of the kind that supports both rationalized power and institutional Bildung is not.

Of course, in working to avoid the pitfalls of Freud's Schliemannesque psychology, Benjamin's runs the risk of falling into a different trap, namely, back into complicity with the more vitalist psychologies of Klages and Jung and their availability to fascist ideals. Insofar as the mnemonic objects sought out by the digging subject are thought to have eluded the realm of consciousness and purposive reason, to have been deposited in some deeper layer of untouched, uncompromised experience, they come very much to resemble Klages's Bachofean-based archaic Bilder. Insofar as the kind of consciousness required to recover them is itself a kind of archaic or mythic one, a deliberate surrender of the reign of reason, it too retains potentially worrisome affinities with *Lebensphilosophie*. As in the case of its external application, Benjamin's archaeology proves tightly bound with mythology here as well; nor should we overlook how, even as Freud's passage wrests a classical realm from its "semi-barbaric" setting, so does Benjamin's import an equally classical world (torsos, epic, rhapsodic) into—or, rather, beneath—his supposedly German site and surrealist practice.

For all the potential affinities, however, Benjamin's model of memory qua archaeology can still be shown to include this vitalist tradition in its polemic, its *Umfunktionierung* of the archaeological field of psychology. Indeed, he seems to negotiate the passage between the Freudian and Klagesian models here as warily as he did that between the Symplegades of *Altertumswissenschaft* and *Altertumskunde* of city descriptions before (see 479/606). Benjamin's psycho-archaeology distinguishes itself from that of the vitalists in relation to both the mode and object of excavatory investigation. The manner in which it addresses the former of these two aspects displays particularly clearly how Benjamin can both identify with the Freudian model to distance himself from the vitalists (whom we already saw him use to distance himself from Freud) and identify the Freudian and vitalists with each other to distance himself from both. Let me explain.

For all Benjamin's apparent submission to a kind of dream consciousness when remembering his past or analyzing the most recent social past (which includes its surviving, atavistic primeval history, or *Urgeschichte*), he never abandons his commitment to awakening, and more particularly, to awakening to history; which is to say, he never abandons his stance in the *terra firma* of the present, his awareness of what his dream memories are *for*—namely, to help us awaken from the nightmare of the historical present.[74] This present focus, this refusal to sink into and fully immerse himself in the archaic dreamworld itself, makes its mark on Benjamin's archaeological metaphor, although perhaps more clearly in the earlier version than in the one cited here. In the former, Benjamin writes, "genuine memory must also provide an image of the one who remembers, even as a good archaeological report not only indicates the strata out of which its findings originate, but also all those others that had first to be broken through" ("wirkliche Erinnerung muß ein Bild zugleich von dem der sich erinnert geben, wie ein guter archäologischer Bericht nicht nur die Schichten angeben muß, aus denen seine Fundobjekte stammen, sondern jene andern vor allem, welche vorher zu durchstoßen waren" [4:401/2:576]). The rememberer qua archaeologist keeps himself coolly cognizant of the history and dirt of his present medium even as he searches randomly for his precious past findings (*Fundobjekte*), and the one is no less important to him than the other. He is not just after archaic finds, nor does he just proceed from an abandoned, unconscious vantage. Rather, he is always most concerned with bringing those objects out to the present, to the top layer of dirt, to the now of consciousness, "the sober rooms of our later insight." In this respect, Benjamin's archaeologist more clearly resembles Freud's rational observer than the surrealists' oneiric artist or Klages's ecstatic subject; "sober" balances out "rhapsodic," draining it of its rapture while retaining its "strictest" historical sense (of stitching together random miscellaneous pieces from the past).

Although not as clearly expressed in *Berlin Chronicle,* the same point is made by the equal attention paid by Benjamin to the finds (*die Funde*) and the earth (*die Erde*) of the archaeological site, and in focusing as much on the dirt as on the dead city, his metaphor declares most forcefully its difference from both the vitalists and Freud. For Klages (and Jung, etc.), the dirt is nothing but the accumulated layers of rationalized culture that need to be cleared away to get to the real treasures (*die wahren Werte*) of prerational experience. For Freud too the dirt is just so much debris to be carted off and dismissed, along with the history, meaning, and traditions of the current semibarbaric inhabitants. But for Benjamin, the dirt is perhaps the most crucial object of his archaeological attention, precisely because it is the native "medium," the connecting element joining the past to the living historical present. The dark joy (*das dunkle Glück*) of the excavator derives as much from his cautious probing of the dark earth (*das dunkle Erdreich*), from the place itself, as from any particular object or artifact found therein.[75] Even as Benjamin's depiction of the market women bespoke a new kind of classical mythology, one inseparable from the dirt and debris of the city setting, so too does his depiction of memory here bespeak a new kind of archaeology, one equally invested in the dirt and debris of *its* setting.

IMAGES (BILDER)

The second means by which Benjamin would distinguish his mnemonic project from that of the vitalists concerns the intended objects of excavation, the real treasure (*die wahren Werte*) that he is digging for: Bilder. This concern with Bilder represents one of the most intriguing aspects of Benjamin's archaeology, and the one that most closely joins his overall project with our overall interest in the connections between Bilder and Bildung. When Benjamin first brings up Markthalle, he describes how all images of the place have been worn away by time ("alle Bilder verschlissen" [475/603]); similarly, when describing the Kaiser Friedrich school as like an excavated temple, he imagines all the long-preserved Bilder washed away by rain once the building is exposed again to light (509/628). Still, it is just such evanescent Bilder that, in his archaeological metaphor, Benjamin says he is seeking; as he explained already in the Hessel review, "Now, if we recollect that not only people and animals but also spirits and above all images can inhabit a place, then we have a tangible idea of what concerns the *flâneur* and of what he looks for. Namely, images, wherever they lodge" ("Will man sich nun erinnern, daß nicht nur Menschen und Tiere, sondern auch Geister, und vor allem Bilder wohnen, so liegt greifbar vor Augen, was den Flaneur bechäftigt und was er sucht. Nämlich die Bilder wo immer sie hausen" [3:196/2:264]). Insofar as Hessel's *flâneur* is always going down, underground, in search of his found objects, his Bilder, it is clear what is at stake for both Hessel and Benjamin: an archaeology of images, both outside and in.[76]

As Rolf Tiedemann and others have argued, the concept of Bild is central to all of Benjamin's writing, *Berlin Chronicle* included.[77] But trying to determine exactly what Bild means here is complicated by the need to consider it against the background not only of Benjamin's own usages of the term but also against those of others from whom he would distance himself. In regard to Benjamin's own notions of Bild, we have already mentioned two. The first is connected to his key concepts of allegory and emblem. In *Berlin Childhood*, Benjamin speaks of "die Bilder und Allegorien" that comprise the *Tiergartenmythologie*, and, in *Berlin Chronicle,* the image of the crown molding that Benjamin recovers from the "excavated" Kaiser Friedrich school is twice referred to as an "Emblem" (474/601, 510/628)—a Bild from his postcard collection is also referred to in this way. As I said in respect to Benjamin's surrealist archaeology, such allegories or emblems represent a way of reading found objects for their imaginary qualities, their cultural meaning. The second notion is that of the thought image, or *Denkbild,* a genre developed by Benjamin, Adorno, and others as a vehicle for staging philosophical meditations at the site of concrete particulars. It was under this rubric that Benjamin published the first version of his memory-as-archaeology metaphor. Clearly Bild in *Berlin Chronicle* in general, and in the archaeology metaphor in particular, resonates with both of these related concepts.

But the Benjaminian category most important for understanding the archaeological Bild in *Berlin Chronicle,* and especially for understanding what distinguishes his Bilder from those of the vitalists, is no doubt that of *das dialektische Bild,* the dialectical image. The concept is notoriously overdetermined. It is, however, central to Benjamin's quarrel with the archaic or mythical images, the *Urbilder,* of his opponents; as he says, "Only dialectical images are genuine (i.e., not archaic) images" ("Nur dialektische Bilder sind echte [d.h. nicht archaische] Bilder").[78] The essential difference between the two lies in how the archaic image is considered to have its full and complete meaning in itself: one has only to cast off the layers of accumulated time and its accompanying historical (rational, cultured) consciousness to be in possession of its promise, its truth. As Benjamin writes of Klages in particular,

> In the first rank of the realities of "natural mythology," which Klages in his studies attempts to retrieve for human memory from an oblivion that has lasted thousands of years, he posits the real and effective existence of certain elements he calls "images." It is only with the aid of these that a deeper world can be revealed to mankind in a state of ecstasy and can impinge through human agency on the mechanical world of the senses.

> Unter den Wirklichkeiten der "natürlichen Mythologie," die Klages in seiner Forschung aus jahrtausendlanger Vergessenheit dem menschlichen Gedächtnis zu erneuern sucht, stehen in erster Reihe die sogenannten "Bilder" als wirkliche und wirkende Bestandteile, kraft deren eine tiefe, in der Ekstase einzig sich erschließende Welt in die Welt der mechanischen Sinne durch das Medium des Menschen hineinwirkt. (3:44/1:427)[79]

Clearly, one of the things Benjamin most opposes in Klages's Bilder is the biologism implicit in "natural mythology," a biologism that we find again in Jung's *Urbilder* but that contrasts so sharply with Benjamin's insistence on the historical quality of his "Tiergarten mythology" and his Bilder. But *dialektische Bilder* are also historical in a slightly different, albeit equally decisive sense, in that they are historically *unfolding* images. Unlike the archaic images of Klages and Jung, the dialectical images of Benjamin do not have their full and complete meaning in themselves, completely detached from (even hidden by) the later layers of accumulated time. Instead, that meaning is a property only recognized in the present ("in the rooms of our later insight"), because it has only been realized through the course of its historical unfolding (*Entfaltung*), which alone has revealed what that meaning originally was.[80] The present observer must deliberately detach the past image, or experience, from its original context and read it—recognize it—as an omen of what is to come, of what is now.[81] As Benjamin puts it in the "Antiques" ("Antiquitäten") section of *One Way Street*, "what one has lived is at best comparable to a beautiful statue that has had all its limbs broken off in transit, and that now yields nothing but the precious block out of which the image of one's future must be hewn" ("was einer lebte, ist bestenfalls der schönen Figur vergleichbar, der auf Transporten alle Glieder abgeschlagen wurden, und die nun nichts als den kostbaren Block abgibt, aus dem er das Bild seiner Zukunft zu hauen hat" [4:118/1:467]). These are the Bilder, the "precious fragments" and "torsi" of which Benjamin speaks in the archaeology passage in *Berlin Chronicle* and with which he reconfigures the vitalists' *Urbilder* as *dialektische Bilder*, replacing archaic images with images that are relentlessly historical: in their origin, their unfolding, and their requirement of the present optic for purchase on their meaning.

What is particularly important for us about this refunctioning, or *Umfunktionierung*, of the Bild is how it rescues the image from vitalist archaism (and that includes its counterpart in classicism) by investing it with properties of image development, or *Entwicklung*. Susan Buck-Morss has suggested the dependence of Benjamin's concept of Bild on Simmel's discussion of the so-called *Urphänomen*, which, as we noted earlier, ultimately derives from Goethe; it is the principle of development that Benjamin clings to even as he rejects the broader program of Bildung per se.[82] Like dialectical images, "Ur-phenomena become such only insofar as in their own individual development—'unfolding' might be a better term—they give rise to the whole series of . . . concrete historical forms, just as the leaf unfolds from itself all the riches of the empirical world of plants" ("Urphänomene werden [solche] erst, indem sie in ihrer selbsteignen Entwicklung—Auswicklung wäre besser gesagt—die Reihe der konkreten historischen Formen . . . aus sich hervorgehen lassen, wie das Blatt den ganzen Reichtum der empirischen Pflanzenwelt aus sich herausfaltet").[83] This is, of course, classical Bildung or, rather, *Entwicklung*, with a vengeance. Even as Benjamin resolutely works to destroy all faith in the continuity and progressive trajectory of historical time on which the traditional program of Goethean Bildung depends, he still embraces a belief in the development—even the historical development—of his isolated moments or Bilder. It is not, then, that *Entwicklung* is rejected in Benjamin's scheme; indeed, it is absolutely central to his concept of Bild in its difference from that of vitalist psychology.

As important as these German contexts are for understanding Benjamin's Bilder, we cannot fully appreciate their force without also placing them against their French contexts, which in their own way work to oppose the positions of Klages and Jung, not least simply by interrupting the exclusive equation of mythical consciousness with German nationalism. David Darby has suggested the influence of Baudelaire's *tableaux* on Benjamin's *Tableaux berlinois*.[84] Others have noted the importance of the work of Bergson, whose conception of the spontaneous images of memory that remain stored more or less independently of consciousness exerted an enormous influence on modernist thought in general and on Benjamin in particular; in "On Some Motifs in Baudelaire" ("Über einige Motive bei Baudelaire" [1939]), Benjamin explicitly privileges the work of Bergson over the "fascist" philosophies of Klages and Jung and pairs it with his analysis of traumatic shock memories in Freud and Baudelaire.[85] I will want to return to this particular Baudelaire/Bergson/Freud constellation later on, but I need first to add one more point to the figure: Proust.

Benjamin himself links the Bergsonian concept of the memory image to Proust's work, that is, to the *mémoire involuntaire* of *In Search of Time Lost,* and Carol Jacobs has argued persuasively for the need to see this enormous memory project lurking in the background of *Berlin Chronicle* and providing a definitive context for understanding Benjamin's own memory image (*Erinnerungsbild*).[86] As mentioned, besides his many years spent translating Proust's novel, while writing *Berlin Chronicle* Benjamin was also working on the essay "On the Image of Proust" ("Zum Bilde Prousts" [1929/34]), an essay that, inter alia, focuses specifically on the Proustian "reality" of the Bild, which, we are told, resides in a special, bottommost stratum of memory (2:314/2:240, 323/246–47). Benjamin explicitly evokes the Proustian "Form" at the beginning of *Berlin Chronicle,* as one of the only two "in which remembering can legitimately—that is, with a guarantee of permanence—be done" ("in denen das [Erinnern] auf legitime Art, das heißt mit der Gewähr der Dauer geschehen kann" [467/597]). He evokes it, however, only to renounce it, and it is worth pointing out why he does so. Benjamin writes, "He who has once begun to open the fan of memory finds ever new sections, new spokes, no image contents him, for he has seen that it can be unfolded, and only in the folds does the truth reside—that image . . . for whose sake all this has been split open and unfolded; and now remembrance progresses from small to smallest details, from the smallest to the infinitesimal, while that which it encounters in these microcosms grows ever mightier" ("Wer einmal den Fächer der Erinnerung aufzuklappen begonnen hat, der findet immer neuer Glieder, neue Stäbe, kein Bild genügt ihm, denn er hat erkannt: es ließe sich entfalten, in den Falten erst sitzt das Eigentliche: jenes Bild . . . um dessentwillen wir dies alles aufgespalten, entfaltet haben; und nun geht die Erinnerung vom Kleinen ins Kleinste, vom Kleinsten ins Winzigste und immer gewaltiger wird, was ihr in diesen Mikrokosmen entgegentritt" [467–68/597]).[87] Benjamin rejects this deadly play and, with it, its principle of nearly endless, vertiginous unfolding of the given Bild, primarily because its principle of *Entfaltung* differs from his own in one crucial aspect. For all its endless unfolding, Proust's image remains firmly situated in the past, finds its purpose in the past, every bit as much as the archaic image of Klages or Jung, and every bit as much as theirs it desires a forgetting of the present; whereas, again, Benjamin's dialectical image is to unfold forward, toward the place of the present subject.[88] Both the absence of a present focus and the insatiable appetite for the endless interpolations of imagination into the past lead Benjamin to distance himself from the Proustian form of unfolded images; here too Goethe seems to play the more important part.

In any case, Benjamin proposes a second form, different from Proust's, the one he says he firmly hopes to realize in writing *Berlin Chronicle*. He does not, however, specifiy what that form is nor with whom it is associated, except to say that it too is strictly associated with Paris. We could, of course, join Darby in identifying it with Baudelaire. But the very lack of specification to this specified second form presents, I believe, a rather open invitation to speculation. As a thought experiment I would like to suggest that this second form be associated with photography, and perhaps especially with the photography of Eugène Atget. For as we will see, the photographic Bild displays just those qualities that distinguish Benjamin's *dialektische Bilder* most radically from the *archaische Bilder* of Klages and Jung (and, to a lesser extent, from those of Proust as well), and so most distinguish his archaeology of images from theirs, not only because the photographic Bild is decidedly modern, a kind of Bild that can only belong to the imaginary of a present observer, nor only because it is decidedly technological, not biological, and so confounds the distinction between the "real" and "mechanical" that we see in Klages and others, nor even only because it is (f)actual and not simply phantasmatic or mythical. Rather, the dialectical Bild is also photographic and so decidedly not archiac because it is only developed (*entwickelt*) later, in the darkroom of our later life, where for the first time the Bild appears, and because its *Entwicklung* differs so radically from the genetic model of sequential unfolding through historical time by being temporally staggered, delayed, first "snapping" an isolated image from the sequence in which it occurred and then experiencing its consequence—its development—at a quite different, present moment, in a manner that might well "snap" that now moment as well. For memory and its Bilder, the evocation of photography dispels both mythic consciousness and its archaic images and classical Bildung and its progressive subject. Photography not only creates the conditions that allow Benjamin's archaeology in the first place; it also creates those that allow that same archaeology to fulfill its self-assigned task.

I am, however, getting ahead of myself. Unlike Mann (or Proust), Benjamin was keenly interested not only in the metaphorical regime of photography but in its actual history and practice as well; and he was interested not only in the metaphorical intersections of photography and archaeology as models for the psyche but in their quite concrete intersections in the work of Atget too, work that provides a significant model for his own literary undertaking. So before jumping too much into the abstract thick of metaphorical things, let us pause and develop photography's more solid ground in Benjamin's thought.

Photography Old and New

The time of Benjamin's writing of *Berlin Chronicle* is also that of his most intense preoccupation with photography, not only directly, as in his seminal essay "Little History of Photography" ("Kleine Geschichte der Photographie" [1931]), but also, as he declares in "The Author as Producer," in his attempts to think together the practices of photography and writing, not least, as we mentioned, in opposition to writing *Bildungsgeschichten* (2:696/2:777). As in the case of his interest in an archaeology of what has only just become old, Benjamin's interest in writing as a form of photography was clearly influenced by the French surrealists ("The Last Snapshot . . .") and their theories of language and the image, about which he says, "language seemed itself only where sound and image, image and sound interpenetrated with automatic precision and such felicity that no chink was left for that penny-in-the-slot called 'meaning.' Language and image take precedence . . . Not only before meaning. Also before the self" ("die Sprache [schien ihnen] nur sie selbst, wo Laut und Bild und Bild und Laut mit automatischer Exaktheit derart glücklich ineinandergriffen, daß für den Groschen 'Sinn' kein Spalt mehr übrig blieb. Bild und Sprache haben den Vortritt . . . Nicht nur vor dem Sinn. Auch vor dem Ich" [2:296–97/2:208]). This connection with the "new" archaeology is not incidental to Benjamin's engagement with photography in *Berlin Chronicle,* and in a rather surprising way. That is, the form of photography is not only useful in providing Benjamin as writer with the revolutionary, avant-garde technique of photomontage; it is also useful for just the opposite reason: not because it is cutting-edge and modernist, but because it itself is already outdated, archaic, no longer a part of present-day, fluid existence ("das heutige fließende Dasein" [470/599]). Benjamin emphasizes this at the outset of *Berlin Chronicle,* where he first introduces photography in the context of his and Hessel's development of their "Tiergarten mythology" and remarks on the affinity between their sought-after Bilder and those produced by photography, and develops an intricate comparison between, on the one hand, the "old city" of their mythology, the images of photography, and railways and, on the other, "the new City" of modern Berlin, the images of cinematography, and automobiles.[89] Photography, like the railway, has already begun to grow old (*zu veralten*); it can only mobilize an outdated *Technik* to grant access to the city and so can only confront us with the archaic in the city and its world. In a paradox characteristic of Benjamin in general and *Berlin Chronicle* in particular, photography is at its most revolutionary, its most disruptive, precisely when it is almost outmoded, almost discarded, precisely because it thereby reveals the outmoded and discarded.

The same "outdated" role of photography introduced at the outset of *Berlin Chronicle* is also central to Benjamin's discussion in "Little History of Photography." Though one of the earliest important theoretical essays on photography that we have, it is primarily concerned with its subject from an "archaeological" perspective—as something that is almost already outmoded and past and as something that can make things past. That is, the function of photography is closely linked by Benjamin with its historical rise and fall, and the rise and fall of photography is closely linked by him with the rise and fall of what he famously calls "aura." Like his concept of the dialectical Bild, his notion of aura is, or rather becomes, hopelessly overdetermined over the course of Benjamin's writings. However, it appears here for just about the first time, with a meaning tightly connected with the specific medium of photography or, rather, with a specific, past moment in the history of the medium of photography. As we will see, like the myths or dreams behind Benjamin's archaeological objects, aura in photography proves to be closely connected with bourgeois culture and so, like those myths and that culture, needs to be approached first and foremost in relation to history.

Benjamin claims that early photographs—those from the mid-nineteenth century—were invested with aura, and he attributes this to two reciprocal phenomena, both of which are about time, and more specifically, about *durée*. The first such phenomenon was occasioned by the technical limits of the medium itself. Benjamin stresses the considerable period of exposure required by early photography, a period (and procedure) that "itself caused the subject to focus his life in the moment rather than hurrying on past it" ("selbst die Modelle veranlaßte, nicht aus dem Augenblick heraus, sondern in ihn hinein zu leben") such that the subjects "grew in to the picture, so to speak" ("wuchsen gleichsam in das Bild hinein" [2:373/2:514]); or, as Brecht says, during the long exposure time, multiple expressions would appear on the plate, such that on the final Bild there would be composed a more universal and livelier expression ("ein universalerer und lebendigerer Ausdruck . . . zusammengefaßt").[90] The very sense of long time required by the medium—and its visual equivalent, long light, as it were, compressed illumination—imposed itself as a sense of fullness and security onto the subject photographed. The technical effect of the recording medium became an almost spiritual quality of the object recorded, a spiritual quality practically defined by its exemption from the ephemerality of the passing moment. As Benjamin says, in such early photographs, "the very creases of clothing in these pictures have an air of permanence" ("selbst die Falten, die ein Gewand auf diesen Bildern wirft, halten länger" [2:373/2:514]). It is just this imparted "air of permanence" that constitutes the aura of these images: a medium effect introjected as a psychological or even material quality—or should I say in part a medium effect. For as Benjamin insists, the phenomenon of the long exposure time of the early cameras was matched by the air of permanence that these same subjects brought with them into the studio, where every subject was a member of the rising class of the imperialist bourgeoisie ("der Angehörige einer im Aufstieg befindlichen Klasse . . . des imperialistischen Bürgertums"), whose confident, increasingly hegemonic ideals invested their material possessions with an aura of stability and endurance "that had seeped into the very folds of their frockcoat or floppy cravat" ("die bis in die Falten des Bürgerrocks oder der Lavallière sich eingenistet hatte" [2:376/2:517]) every bit as much as it did in our earlier example of the grandmother's furniture. Aura is a product of this particular confluence of technology and ideology. Benjamin cites as its objective accessory the classical pillars that frequently appeared in such early photos, set among the other typical accoutrements of a bourgeois apartment. Practically, these marble or stone columns were there as substitutes for (or remnants of) the head clamps and knee braces required in the period when, because of the long exposure time, subjects had to be given supports so they would not move (2:375/2:515). But ideologically, they bespoke the culture of universal, or *allgemeine,* Bildung on which these same bourgeois subjects based their sense of legitimacy and duration—the irony of which was captured by the placement of such a pillar on a foundation of easily worn-out carpet.[91] In any case, in the "Little History" essay, Benjamin's sense of photographic aura is decidedly not vitalistic but rather represents an historically specific amalgam of media technology and class ideology; and if he seems prepared at times to celebrate the early *Technik,* its implication with the imperialist bourgeoisie—with all its own complicity in dehistoricizing by insisting on its own *durée*—is always there to hold that impulse in check.

If Benjamin seems discreet in his judgment of this first appearance of the photographic aura, leaving us noncommittedly poised between its laudable and questionable features, he is far more vehemently forthcoming in his response to what occurs in the next phase, when both photography and the bourgeoisie changed, especially when both changed their relation to time: after 1880, when photography lost its need for long exposures and developed the snapshot (*Momentaufnahme*), and the imperialist bourgeoisie began its period of decline, the increasing degeneration (*zunehmende Entartung*) that signaled, or betrayed, its own momentary quality. For all intents and purposes, aura was effectively banished from the Bild both technologically and socially or ideologically, and this called forth two different responses in the field of photography itself. The first is exemplarily represented for Benjamin by the work of Renger-Patzsch, *The World Is Beautiful* (*Die Welt ist schön*)—the same work lauded and defended by Mann, albeit for reasons very different from those for which Benjamin condemns it.[92] In Benjamin's account, Renger-Patzsch's work aimed to restore the aura by simulating it through the arts of retouching, by engaging in a kind of *embellissement stratégique* of its subject matter through "creative" (*schöpferisch*) intervention.[93] As Benjamin says, "The creative in photography is its capitulation to fashion. 'The world is beautiful'—that is its watchword" ("Das schöpferische am Photographieren ist dessen Überantwortung an die Mode. 'Die Welt ist schön'—genau das ist ihre Devise" [2:383/2:526]); or similarly, "It can no longer photograph a tenement block or a refuse heap without transfiguring it. . . . For it has succeeded in transforming even abject poverty—by apprehending it in a fashionably perfected manner—into an object of enjoyment" ("sie [kann] keine Mietskaserne, keinen Müllhaufen mehr photographieren, ohne ihn zu verklären. . . . Es ist ihr nämlich gelungen, auch noch das Elend, indem sie es auf modisch-perfektionierte Weise auffaßte, zum Gegenstand des Genusses zu machen" [2:693/2:775]). Clearly, Benjamin's primary objection to this mode of simulacral aestheticization is political: photography's technical means of production are put in the service of maintaining or even producing the imaginary splendor, or *Glanz,* of bourgeois capitalist culture when it has been lost in reality. Although the original aura of early photography was also a result of a combined imposition of technical means and cultural ideology, this simulated aura is more clearly manufactured in bad faith, in an attempt to disavow its inevitable loss: to disavow its passing, its historicity, its moment. As Benjamin underscores in "The Author as Producer," such a form of photography has much in common with the long-since counterfeit wealth ("längst verfälschten Reichtum") of "creative" writing that would produce a modern *Wilhelm Meister* or *Green Henry* (2:695/2:777), which would likewise perpetuate the ideal of historical—and personal—continuity and endurance; it also has much in common with that form of city description that concentrates on "the great reminiscences, the historical *frissons*," with that form of archaeology that serves nationalism and monumentality, and with that form of psychology that promotes vitalistic *Urbilder*. All similarly mythify and in so doing seek to secure an imaginary continuity with the past as a prop (a pillar) for the present (cf. our earlier example of Walter Hege and his photos of the Acropolis).[94]

There was another, contrary response to this double loss of aura after 1880, one opposing the example of Renger-Patzsch, that was best represented for Benjamin by the work of Eugène Atget; and if the former is associated with the kind of Bilder and *Bildungsgeschichte* Benjamin is evidently avoiding, even attacking, in *Berlin Chronicle,* the latter is clearly associated with the alternative sort of Bilder and photo-writing he was seeking to develop.[95] Benjamin credits Atget with initiating the emancipation of the object from aura ("die Befreiung des Objekts von der Aura" [2:378/2:518]), the project that was to become central to the Bilder of the surrealists so admired by Benjamin as part of their archaeology of what has only just become old. Atget took as his subject the "native" city of Paris; and like Benjamin's (and Hessel's) native Berlin, Atget's Paris was primarily approached in terms of its topography, architecture, and incidental material artifacts. The vast majority of his images were intended for the photographic archives of various museums and historical societies and so from the start were invested with a quasidocumentary function, that is, with an historicizing gaze focused on the present world. Atget took quick, un-retouched snapshots of those aspects of "old Paris" that were already in the process of disappearing, including its whores, its tradespeople, and its buildings and streets, with their ornaments and doorways—and its late-eighteenth- and early-nineteenth-century neoclassicism, with its slightly dirty, slightly decayed statues, vases, and facades. What people he did include were not individual portraits but studiously generic types; for the most part, and most remarkably, almost all these pictures are empty ("sind aber fast alle diese Bilder leer"), cleared out (*ausgeräumt*) of people, including friends and associates.[96] At most, his city shots are haunted by the occasional "ghost" of a blurred, transient figure passing fleetingly before the camera's lens.

Although Atget's pictures were often solicited by and sold to museums and other official preservation societies, Benjamin insists that they were decidedly not intended to preserve their subject matter, and especially not for the reigning institutional order. Instead, motivated by a vehemently unaffiliated and yet still politically committed aesthetic much like Benjamin's own, Atget produced his images in order to detach their objects from the present and from their institutional function of imaginary support: to deprive them, and their present, of aura. Benjamin notes how Atget almost always passed by the great sights and so-called landmarks ("die großen Sichten und die sogenannten Wahrzeichen"), refusing, like Hessel in Berlin, to contribute to official culture and its nationalist agenda.[97] Instead, and again like Hessel (and the surrealists), he sought out what was forgotten and cast aside (*das Verschollene und Verschlagene*), debris whose "images work against the exotic, romantically sonorous names of the cities: they suck the aura out of reality like water from a sinking ship" ("Bilder sich gegen den exotischen, prunkenden, romantischen Klang der Stadtnamen [wenden]; sie saugen die Aura aus der Wirklichkeit wie Wasser aus einem sinkenden Schiff" [2:378/2:518]). As many critics have noted, Atget's pictures are neither beautiful (*schön*) nor deliberately artistic. Rather, they present their subjects—often in multiple, revisited takes that Maria Morris Hambourg has called "discontinuously accumulative"[98]—detached from established aesthetic norms as well as from the prescribed perspectives of traditional archival photography *and* detached from the human nexus of social relations that would keep them alive, as it were.[99] Instead, these photographs deploy the post-1880 speed or momentariness (*Flüchtigkeit*) of their image-making *Technik* to capture, render, and expose the precisely equivalent momentariness of their objects and of the culture that produced them: to rob them of their *durée,* of the "air of permanence" that invests them with aura, with *Glanz.* Benjamin offers as an example Atget's pictures of "the tables after people have finished eating and left, the dishes not yet cleared away, as they exist by the hundreds of thousands at the same hour" ("den abgegessenen Tischen und den unaufgeräumten Waschgeschirren, wie sie zu gleicher Zeit zu Hunderttausenden da sind" [2:379/2:519]). He could just as well have referred to the pictures of deserted streets with horse dung left in the middle, of worn-out doors left half ajar, or of the twilit, neoclassical stairways at St. Cloud, whose chipped and discolored stone steps lead off precisely nowhere. All such hauntingly empty images—dirty pictures all—depict an abandoned world, a dirty world bereft of its inhabitants, a world already long gone. The sense of greatly accelerated, even immediate obsolescence, the sense of almost instant death that, as we saw earlier in *The Magic Mountain,* adhered to the photographic Bild, is itself invested into the photograph's subject matter to amplify *its* obsolescence, its nonendurance, its death. As with Hessel's classical images of Berlin, Atget's photographs of Paris are first and foremost a form of leave-taking; and as one can see, the photographic in Atget shares many, many important features with the archaeological in Benjamin and Hessel, not least in their common rendering past of the present, their common depeopling of their native sites, and their common *Umfunktionierung* of the ever-present Bildung function of such Bilder, away from their traditional function of preserving the public imaginary and toward an awareness of its end (2:379/2:519; see also 2:696/2:777).

One of the chief devices deployed by Atget to disrupt the aura—which is to say, the nexus, or *Gespinst,* of associations (or relations) that lodge the given subject in its accustomed time and place and impart that air of fixedness to the subject itself—is what Atget himself came to call the *détail,* a tactic of special importance to Benjamin's appreciation of photography in general.[100] As Hambourg notes, Atget's practice was to move his camera ever closer into the visual field in order to withdraw the given subject—or partial subject—from its surrounding context, "not as a detail subsidiary to a larger whole, as was usually the case with painting. . . . [Rather,] Atget learned to do without a broad clarifying context and to concentrate wholly on the immediate issue."[101] Benjamin sees this as the basis for the later surrealist practice of publishing pictures that "are captioned 'Westminster,' 'Lille,' 'Antwerp,' or 'Breslau' but that show only details, here a piece of balustrade, there a treetop whose branches crisscross a gas lamp, or a seawall, or lamppost with a lifesaver on it with the town's name" ("unter der Beschriftung 'Westminster,' 'Lille,' 'Antwerpen' oder 'Breslau' nur Details [zu]bringen, einmal ein Stück von einer Balustrade, dann einen kahlen Wipfel, dessen Äste vielfältig eine Gaslaterne überschneiden, ein andermal eine Brandmauer oder einen Kandelaber mit einem Rettungsring, auf dem der Name der Stadt steht" [2:378/2:518]), details that work against the romantically official representation of the given town.[102] In the process, these detail photographs reveal something else, a different Bild, as it were, and it is crucial to Benjamin's estimation of photography's effect that it serves not only a negative, debunking function, in the disruption of aura, but also a positive, revelatory one, in the irruptive disclosure of something that, in his later writings, Benjamin came to think of as an aura in its own right—a gleam of other meaning behind the *Glanz* of its normally intended, historical meaning.[103]

Benjamin first describes this other, positive function of photographic details—this other source of other (but still, perhaps, auratic) significance—in an earlier essay, his 1928 review, "News about Flowers" ("Neues von Blumen"), wherein he dwells on the new image worlds (*neue Bilderwelten* [3:152/2:516]) that are opened up by photographic enlargements of plant parts and forms.[104] Such details obviously have much in common with the archaeological fragments, the "images broken loose from all earlier connections" that Benjamin evokes in *Berlin Chronicle*, and so get us closer to grasping some of the most essential connections between his archaeological and photographic models, closer to comprehending precisely how the Bilder he is digging for are "broken fragments or torsi" and how their (interrupted) embeddedness in historical context is related to that of archaeological details (such as the crown molding, which was, of course, an aura too). Significantly, however, Benjamin himself stresses what they have in common with Goethe's *Urphänomene*. He sees such isolated detail images as charged with inner image imperatives (*Bildnotwendigkeiten*) that harbor a principle of unfolding, an *Entfaltungsprinzip* (see 3:153/2:156), which is to say, an/other *Bildungsprinzip* behind or apart from the nexus of Bildung proper—even as they harbor an/other aura behind or apart from the nexus of aura proper. It is, that is, in the Bild as *détail* that Benjamin's models of photography, archaeology, and Bildung come into that particular convergence that, we saw, come to comprise the dialectical Bild and, apparently, the auratic Bild as well.

It is important to note that, for Benjamin, the detail detached from its given, composed context and offering a different Bild or meaning (or aura) apart from the contextually (i.e., historically) constructed one is not only to be found in the isolated, or cropped, close-up; it can also repose in a rather traditional photograph—especially an old photograph, one where the original intentionality of the photographer's art has begun to wear (but are not all photographs instantly old?)—as an unintended, unexpected trifle almost, whose obscure significance pulls the viewer in a decidedly different direction from that of the picture as a whole. Much like Barthes's notion of the *punctum* that interrupts the cultured *studium* of the photograph, this embedded-but-separate detail of Benjamin's—or rather, its meaning, its truth—turns out to be as much a matter of the present viewer as of the original image itself, as indeed was the case with the dialectical Bilder qua archaeological fragments as well. Benjamin describes the unruly desire (*ungebärdiges Verlangen*) aroused in the viewer by the indolent, downcast eyes of a fishwife in a photograph by David Octavius Hill, a desire to discover a "reality" in or to her that exceeds or goes beyond the photographer's original intentions, his art (*Kunst*), or a similar desire aroused in the viewer by the photograph of Karl Dauthendey with his fiancée, wherein "he seems to be holding her, but her gaze passes him by, absorbed in an ominous distance" ("er scheint sie zu halten; ihr Blick aber geht an ihm vorüber, saugend an eine unheilvolle Ferne geheftet"). He says,

> No matter how artful the photographer, no matter how carefully planned the pose of his subject, the beholder feels an irresistible urge to search such a picture for the tiny spark of contingency, of the here and now, with which reality has, so to speak, seared the subject, to find the inconspicuous spot where in the immediacy of that long-forgotten moment the future nests so eloquently that we, looking back, may discover it.

> Aller Kunstfertigkeit des Photographen und aller Planmäßigkeit in der Haltung seines Modells zum Trotz fühlt der Beschauer unwiderstehlich den Zwang, in solchem Bild das winzige Fünkchen Zufall, Hier und Jetzt, zu suchen, mit dem die Wirklichkeit den Bildcharakter gleichsam durchgesengt hat, die unscheinbare Stelle zu finden, in welcher, im Sosein jener längstvergangenen Minute das Zukünftige noch heut und so beredt nistet, daß wir, rückblickend, es entdecken können. (2:371/2:510)

It is the ability of the photograph to capture, preserve, and represent this inadvertent "tiny spark of contingency" that, Benjamin says, most radically distinguishes it from painting, a distinction that emerges most clearly after a lapse of time. Whereas old paintings are scrutinized for evidence of the painter's art, his subject all but ignored, old photographs come more and more to detach themselves from the photographer's studied art and come to be regarded for an other meaning nestled in their subject matter. It is here in this other meaning, this other regard, that Benjamin situates the critical convergence of photography and psychoanalysis, of photographic *Bilder* and psychoanalytical *Tech-*

nik. He claims, "It is through photography that we first discover the existence of this optical unconscious, just as we discover the instinctual unconscious through psychoanalysis" ("Von diesem Optisch-Unbewußten erfährt [man] erst durch [die Photographie], wie von dem Triebhaft-Unbewußten durch die Psychoanalyse" [2:371/2:512]).[105] Benjamin clearly has Freud foremost in mind here, although his twofold schema of meaning—the manifest composed one and the imbedded, unintended one—also suggests the Bergsonian/Proustian schema of voluntary and involuntary memory and the Jungian/Klagesian one of rational consciousness and archaic *Urbilder.*[106] Benjamin does, of course, differ from these others, and especially from Klages and his vehement disavowal of modern technology, in his insistence that this other, hidden meaning, these other Bilder, are actually products of the new *Technik,* that they are "actual" images, not archaic, revealed for the first time by the modern devices of photography (moreover, with a future rather than prehistoric orientation). This does not, however, completely secure his investment in such an other meaning, an other aura, from suspicions of a sustained identity with precisely the kind of quasimystical forces Benjamin himself finds to make common cause with fascism.

The Photography of Bildung

Let me offer an example of how, in *Berlin Chronicle,* Benjamin's ideas about photographic aura come to be applied to memory images (*Erinnerungsbilder*) and Bildung—in other words, how his text actually achieves the photo effect that the "Little History" essay describes.[107] The example I choose is the account of Benjamin's earliest impressions of the theater (*Theatereindrücke*), although I could just as easily have selected his recollections of his first books. Both rather self-consciously engage central motifs of the Bildungsroman tradition (i.e., set encounters with the traditional media of traditional Bildung) and work both to emancipate them from aura and to disclose an/other kind of aura nestled therein. I focus on Benjamin's theatrical impressions because their interactions with the Bildung tradition—and especially with *Wilhelm Meister* and *Green Henry*—are the more conspicuous: their engagement, that is, with the motif of what Friedrich Kittler calls "Theaterspiel als Sozialization" that I briefly described in chapter 1.[108]

The memories of Benjamin's earliest visits to the theater are rather emphatically presented under the sign of aura. He begins the section by announcing, "Just as lights on a foggy night are surrounded by gigantic rings, my earliest theatrical impressions emerge from the mist of my childhood with great aureoles" ("Wie Lichter in der Nebelnacht mit riesenhaften Kreisen sich umgeben so tauchen aus den Nebel meiner Kindheit mit großen Höfen die frühesten Theatereindrücke" [505/624]).[109] And the source of this aura is not hard to find: it emanates out of the web, the *Gespinst,* of social relations and ideals that have been invested in these experiences, these rites of cultural initiation, by the culture of bourgeois Bildung. Benjamin artfully sketches in this accustomed context. The first visits are heavily supervised by his family members, with his mother (and grandmother) playing the foregrounded role, as in *Wilhelm Meister;*[110] the sense of social "improvement" to the occasion is captured by not only the *glänzend* program but also the eminent dress-circle seats ("nicht nur das glänzende Program, sondern auch die ansehnlichen Rangplätze"). The collusion and competition with the official institution of Bildung—namely, school—is also prominently presented. Such a context imbues the entire remembered event with a misty splendor (*Nebelglanz*), with a rosy-gray cloud of seats, lights, and faces ("ein rosa-graues Gewölk von Sesseln, Lichtern und Gesichtern"); but this "Glanz" does more to obscure than to reveal the actual experience, and Benjamin proceeds rather systematically to "suck the aura" out of the remembered picture. The actual source of light (*Lichtkern*) of the moment, the happening on stage that lies buried beneath the surrounding glow, is not, as in *Wilhelm Meister,* a production of the biblical David and Goliath, nor even, as in *Green Henry,* of Goethe's *Faust* or Schiller's *Wilhelm Tell,* but rather the pranks of poor little monkeys in an *Affentheater:* the human animal and his mimetic learning abilities are reduced to their most basic and unflattering form.[111] The sense of underlying social discipline that accompanies all such customary initiations (*übliche Einweihungen*) erupts into the foreground as a moment of "brutal" coercion on the part of Benjamin's mother, who would make his pleasure in the proferred performance, his deep and lasting gratitude (*dauernde und tiefe Dankbarkeit*) for that evening, conditional upon his submission to her authoritarian will—as in fact such pleasure always is, insofar as submitting to this pleasure, internalizing its structure, proves one of the "deepest" and "most lasting" forms of coopting socialization Bildung is capable of.[112] And the dazzling, *glänzend* program and imposing dress-circle seats (*Rangplätze*) that are to convey an almost aristocratic ideal of wealth and richness onto the participant bourgeois audience, to invest them with their own aura of cultural nobility and power, are deflatingly countered by Benjamin's separate memory image of himself, long frustrated, standing in line at the box office, barely adequate pocket money in hand, trying to gain entrance—but then never actually purchasing the entrance ticket: this far and no further ("Hierher und nicht weiter").

Having detached these memories from the surrounding aura of the *Bildungbürgertum*'s ideals, Benjamin notes "in the end I can no longer even distinguish dream and reality" ("am Ende kann ich selbst Traum und Wirklichkeit nicht mehr scheiden" [507/626]). The misty *Glanz* that veils the experience and conceals its reality in the dreamy, auratic haze of the social imaginary is also—precisely also—the web of consciousness, of significance, that fixes and orders the experience into a coherent whole or sequence (rather like the crown molding that joined together the school). To lose the aura, the social imaginary, is to lose the nexus of cohesive, completing memory.[113] And so, rather than a well-ordered, comprehensive account of these early experiences, Benjamin can only bring forth scattered, nonsequential, and inconsequential fragments, mostly on the edges of the theatrical impressions proper—a fragmentary, *détail*-oriented form of memory dictated by the process of deauratization, the functional equivalent of the fading of the grip of the photographer's intentional, compositional art over the reception of his Bild. However, once freed from this original web of meaning, some tiny (*winzig*) fragment can emerge as the vehicle of a different meaning, a different *Glanz,* as what Benjamin calls "the source of light that made the city suddenly gleam so differently" ("jene Lichtquelle vor welcher die Stadt mit einem Mal so verändert strahlte")—which is to say, as the source of a different aura.

The source of this other aura, this other *Glanz,* is, indirectly, the memory of one of the picture postcards (*Ansichtskarten*) that Benjamin collected and that are primarily associated with his maternal grandmother's travels to distant, exotic locales.[114] Benjamin's recollection of his trip with his mother to see an opera at the local *Volkstheater* reminds him of one such Bild in particular, "the most jealously guarded item in my postcard collection, the depiction of the Halle Gate in pale blue on a darker blue background: the Belle-Allianceplatz was to be seen, with the houses that frame it; the full moon was in the sky" ("jene innigst behütete Stück meiner Postkartensammlung: die Darstellung des

Halleschen Tors in halben Blau auf dunkler blauem Grunde: der Belle-allianceplatz war darauf mit den Häusern zu sehen, welche ihn einrahmen; der volle Mond stand am Himmel" [507/626]). For all its potential significance, Benjamin forgoes any description of the *Volkstheater* itself—in its own way perhaps too much in a major key, too much part of "the great reminiscences"—and concentrates instead on an incidental detail, the silent and solitary journey there, "through a snow-covered, unknown Berlin spread out in the gaslight around me" ("durch ein verschneites, unbekanntes Berlin, das sich im Gaslicht um mich ausbreitete" [507/626]). It is this moment that reminds Benjamin of his postcard Bild, which in every way but one resembles "one of those picture postcards which, around 1900, showed such pretty town views, bathed in blue night, with a touched-up moon" ("eine [jener] Ansichtskarten, wie sie um 1900 herum die Städtebilder so schön zeigten, in blaue Nacht getaucht, mit retuschiertem Mond" [2:378/2:518]), that is, one of those banal photographs that Benjamin contrasts with Atget's and condemns for serving the nationalist program of "exotic" and "picturesque" cultural identity formation that, throughout *Berlin Chronicle,* Benjamin himself works to avoid.[115] Whereas in the "common" case mentioned in the photography essay, the moon is touched-up, here, we are told,

> The moon and the windows in the façades, however, had been freed from the top layer of card; their contrasting white disrupted the picture, and one had to hold it against a lamp or a candle to see, by the light of windows and a lunar surface parading in exactly the same illumination, the whole scene regain its composure.

> Der Mond aber und die Fenster in den Fassaden waren von der obersten Kartenschicht befreit; sie stachen weiß aus dem Bild heraus und man mußte es gegen die Lampe oder die Kerze halten, um beim Scheine der in genau gleichem Licht paradierenden Fenster und Mondflächen alles sich beruhigen zu sehen. (507/626)

In the "Little History" essay, the arts of touching-up (*die Künste der Retusche*) were specifically associated with the simulation of aura in the time of its decline (2:377/2:517), that is, with the deceitful mask of creative photography (2:383/2:520). Atget's achievement was, by contrast, to have removed the makeup from reality (*die Wirklichkeit abzuschminken* [2:379/2:518]). Clearly, this particular postcard Bild participates in such a demasking (*Abschminkung*), such a peeling away (*Entschälung*) of the image, and hence too in the destruction—the ruin-ation—of its aura. But it just as clearly does more: it introduces a new sense or source of aura, of *Glanz,* into the Bild, and it does so by rendering the picture somehow archaeological—layered. The top, covering stratum, or *Schicht,* of the image needs to be removed, and then another light emerges from behind or beneath it to illuminate the whole picture, to bring it to a renewed state of composure.

How are we to read this illuminated Bild and its light? Coming at the end of the section, it seems deliberately to recall the line with which it began ("Like lights on a foggy night surrounded by gigantic aureoles"), and Benjamin describes the same, or a similar, confusion of dream and reality attached to this memory image as he does to those of his other theatrical impressions, with the dreamlikeness that invades the reality emanating from the source of light (*Lichtquelle*) of the one and the hazy *Glanz* of the other. He says, "Perhaps that evening the opera we were approaching was the source of light that made the city suddenly gleam so differently, but perhaps it was only a dream that I had later of this walk, the memory of which has displaced what previously stood in for reality" ("Vielleicht war an jenem Abend die Oper, auf die wir uns hinbewegten, jene Lichtquelle vor welcher die Stadt mit einem Mal so verändert strahlte, vielleicht aber ist es auch nur ein Traum, den ich später von diesem Wege gehabt habe und von dem die Erinnerung sich an die Stelle derer gesetzt hat, die vordem Platzhalterin der Wirklichkeit war" [507/626]). Certainly Benjamin offers many indications that this second illumination, this other *Schein* is of the same order, and hence of the same questionability, as the *Glanz* permeating the earlier memories: from the banally exotic and romantic scenario of the postcard to the equally romantic epexegesis of "a lamp" with the quaint, antiquarian "or a candle" as the source of this *Schein* to the speculation that perhaps the source of light that particular night was the expected opera itself, with all the invested expectations that, we have seen, such theater visits traditionally entail. Benjamin offers all these qualifications, and we need to consider why, since they make the light, and its city, seem much like the elsewhere evoked "strip of light beneath the bedroom door on evenings when there was 'company' [lit., society]" ("abendliche Lichtstreif unter der Schlafzimmertür wenn drinnen 'Gesellschaft' war" [503/623]), a moment that Benjamin explicitly links with the expectations of theater visits and that seems but a privatizaton of the bourgeois social *Glanz* writ small—whereas in other ways it seems much more like the quite different, far more haunting light of the dusky lamps that had shone in isolation from courtyard windows ("die düsteren Lampen, die vereinzelt in dem Höfen geschienen hatten aus Fenstern"), whose profound, disruptive mimetic effect on Benjamin's consciousness I briefly mentioned earlier.[116] That is, this light, this illuminating *Schein* that implicates itself into the Bild, seems to emanate from a different source and to be differently evaluated. Unlike the other, whose hazy *Glanz* settles over the memory and, over time, conceals it, this one emerges suddenly (*mit einem Mal*) from beneath it and reveals it; unlike the other, whose dream obscures the more essential reality, this *Schein* seems itself the essence, one itself previously obscured by mere reality. There is something mysteriously meaningful in this latter light, something profoundly, if partially, redemptive in this spark, this Bild, and as the archaeological dimension hints at, this bid for a deeper truth beneath or behind the banal surface, for all its undeniable appeal, puts Benjamin in some questionable company. Is it to guard against or to acknowledge his potential fellow travelers, his fellow purveyors of alternative redemptive Bilder, that Benjamin so qualifies his light, his Bild, as if to insist on its sameness with the *Glanz* he would destroy? And is it for the same reason that, despite the archaeological structure to the Bild, Benjamin reverses the expected timeline, suggesting that the "source of light" and "dream" come later, more the retrojected effect of the present-day rememberer than anything truly "behind" the memory proper? Non liquet; non liquet.

INTROJECTION: PHOTOGRAPHY

The transformed "unknown" Berlin that Benjamin remembers in terms of his picture postcard is a solitary, deserted one; the fact that it is so empty is one of its chief affinities with the Bilder of Atget, as is indeed the relative absence of people from the memory images of *Berlin Chronicle* as a whole, an absence that, as mentioned, aligns both Atget's and Benjamin's works with the world of archaeology. But unlike for archaeology, the absence of people poses a most special case for photography, and for the kind of first-person *Bildungsgeschichte* Benjamin is writing. Benjamin notes, "to do without people is for photography the most impossible of renunciations" ("der Verzicht auf den Menschen [ist] für die Photographie der unvollziehbarste unter allen"); similarly, "In our age there is no work of art that is looked at so closely as a photograph of oneself, one's closest relatives and friends, [and] one's beloved" ("Es gibt in unserem Zeitalter kein Kunstwerk das so aufmerksam betrachtet würde, wie die Bildnisphotographie des eigenen Selbst, der nächsten Verwandten und Freunde, [und] der Geliebten" [2:379/2:519]), which is to say that photography is intimately related not just to the representation of our "primal acquaintances" (*Urbekanntschaften* [491/614]) but also to the representation of ourselves, to the formation of—and scrutiny of—self-identity.[117] This is, of course, also true of the genre of *Berlin Chronicle*. However much Benjamin, like Atget, seems to attempt a renunciation of the representation of others and, even more, of a conventional—even conventionally psychological— "Ich," people do play a central role in the work, as does self-scrutiny, which is to say, self-formation: psychology.[118] The question, then, becomes how does photography figure in the representation of people in *Berlin Chronicle,* and especially in that of the self, while at the same time sustaining its project of decomposing the traditional *Bildungsgeschichte*?

As for the representation of others, Benjamin engages in two basic practices, both again reminiscent of Atget's. First, he tends to depict the kind of deindividualized character types or physiognomies—the prostitutes and market women, the shopkeepers and teachers, and so on—that recall Atget's "Petit Metiers" series and that Benjamin also associates with the photography of August Sander and that Thomas Mann associated with the photographs of Renger-Patzsch. This identification of photography with a deindividualizing typology is, we have seen, rather widespread. We have seen it not only in Mann, Freud, and Barthes but also in Darwin and Galton, and photography was, we saw, instrumental in the development of typology as a dominant principle in archaeology, one that eventually led to certain rather distasteful theories of racial types and, in the case of Jung, of psychological archetypes.[119] Benjamin's typology differs from most of these others, and affirms its affinities with Atget and Sander, by disavowing biological, archaic, mythical, or racial explanations for its typing and insisting on present social ones: objective social forces shape the very features of individual subjects, and photography, in its own privileged objectivity and authenticity and its own inherent, deindividualizing reproducibility, is uniquely able to capture that.[120] Second, when Benjamin does focus on the individual "people who were closest to me in Berlin" ("Menschen, die in Berlin mir die nächsten waren"), he presents them in a manner—it may be called fleeting or eternal ("man mag sie flüchtig oder ewig nennen")—that recalls those fleeting, ghosted figures caught as a blur across Atget's city settings. As Benjamin says, "The atmosphere of the city that is here evoked allots them only a brief, shadowy existence. They steal along its walls like beggars, appear wraithlike at windows, only to vanish again" ("Die Luft der Stadt, die hier beschworen wird, gönnt ihnen nur ein kurzes, schattenhaftes Dasein. Sie stehlen sich an ihren Mauern hin wie Bettler, tauchen in ihren Fenstern geisterhaft empor, um zu verschwinden" [488–89/612–13]). Such spirits, or *Geister,* have little in common with the vitalistic images of contemporary occultism (or with the ghosts of archaeology and psychology). Rather, they are "medium effects" of memory as for photography. Just as the fleetingness of (Atget's) photographic images uniquely convey something of the elegiac transience of historical human life, so do Benjamin's memory images: memory not as a medium for preservation, for investing permanence, but for acknowledging, even promoting loss and passing.

As for the representation of the self or, rather, the scrutiny of the self, photography figures in two different ways in *Berlin Chronicle,* both related to memory and both with important affinities with archaeology. First, and as mentioned, Benjamin associates photography's discovery of the optical unconscious with psychoanalysis's discovery of an instinctual unconscious. This leads him to practice a peculiarly photo-psychological mode of reminiscence, of viewing his memories: scanning over his various general topics, or Bilder—first books, theater visits, school experiences, home life, and so on—with studied disregard for grasping the whole in a retroactively composed order and sequence and searching instead for the *punctum,* the unexpected detail, the symptomatic little spark, or *Fünkchen,* of fleeting and secret images that speak otherwise to the present. It is a mode, in both its quarry and its method, that has obvious (and important) parallels with Benjamin's concept of memory qua archaeology: the dreamlike focus on dreamlike fragments, on scattering and cautious probing quite apart from some plan, and the insistent avoidance of narrative continuity. But second, and again like archaeology, Benjamin also introjects photography as a metaphor for memory itself.[121] In making this in-corporating turn, Benjamin is, of course, participating in a broadly modernist movement, as we saw in chapter 1. Beginning with Ernest Hello, the conception of the remembering subject as a kind of negative plate awaiting exposure and development came more and more to dominate the various schemata of identity and its formation found in the works of Bergson, Proust, Freud, Mann, and others. But again, as was the case with his use of archaeology, Benjamin's use of this common photo-memory discourse is more remarkable for its reworking, its refunctioning of the topic, than for its reproduction, which in many ways it refuses to give.

There are two, related passages in Benjamin that draw out the metaphor of memory as photography: a short, somewhat obscure text on Proust and the more fully developed fragment in *Berlin Chronicle*.[122] The first is especially useful for illustrating how Benjamin's photographic *Erinnerungsbilder* distinguish themselves from the vitalists' *Urbilder* and from the traditional schema of Bildung. Speaking of Proust's notion of *mémoire involuntaire*, Benjamin writes

> Not only do its images come uncalled-for; even more, these are images that we never saw before we remembered them. This is mostly clearly so in the case of those images in which—exactly as in many dreams—we see ourselves. We stand before ourselves, as we might well have stood once, somewhere, in a prehistoric past, but certainly never before our own eyes. And these images, developed in the darkroom of the lived moment, are certainly the most important we ever get to see. One could say that our deepest, most profound moments have been endowed with a little image, a photograph of ourselves.

> Ihre Bilder kommen nicht allein ungerufen, es handelt sich vielmehr in ihr um Bilder, die wir nie sahen, ehe wir uns ihrer erinnerten. Am deutlichsten ist das bei jenen Bildern, auf welchen wir—genau wie in manchen Träumen—selber zu sehen sind. Wir stehen vor uns, wie wir wohl in Urvergangenheit einst irgendwo, doch nie vor unserm Blick, gestanden haben. Und gerade die wichtigsten—die in der Dunkelkammer des gelebten Augenblicks entwickelten— Bilder sind es, welche wir zu sehen bekommen. Man könnte sagen, daß unsern tiefsten Augenblicken . . . ein kleines Bild-

chen, ein Photo unsrer selbst, ist mitgegeben worden" (2:1064/my translation).

What makes the memory Bild photographic, and so decidedly *not* archaic, is the fact that, despite the reference to its origin in a prehistoric past, it is only developed later, in the darkroom of the lived moment. It is this process of development, this *Entwicklungsprozeß,* that transforms the past image into a dialectical one. Moreover, as in the case of other modernist examples of the photo/memory metaphor—including Proust's own—what makes this *Entwicklung* so different from the genetic model of sequential unfolding through historical time on which traditional Bildung depends is the fact that its development is temporally staggered, delayed, first "snapping" a single image from the time sequence in which it occurred and then experiencing its consequence—its *Entwicklung*—at a quite different, present moment, in a manner that might well "snap" that now moment as well.[123] As I said before, the point is that for memory and its Bilder, photography, as the new mode of data processing (*Datenverarbeitung*) for the modern subject, dispels at once both mythic consciousness and its archaic images and classical Bildung and its progressive subject, even as, more generally, its sheer *Technik* opposes the organicist assumptions and antimodernist leanings of both *Lebensphilosophie* and traditional Bildung.

The *Berlin Chronicle* passage on memory as photography further develops these same basic points, but it also evokes additional motifs that are, however, still recognizably Proustian. It opens as follows:

> Anyone can observe that the length of time during which we are exposed to impressions has no bearing on their fate in memory. Nothing prevents our keeping rooms in which we have spent twenty-four hours more or less clearly in our memory, and forgetting others in which we have passed months. It is not, therefore, due to insufficient exposure time if no image appears on the plate of remembrance. More frequent, perhaps, are cases when the half-light of habit denies the plate the necessary light for years, until one day from an alien source it flashes as if from burning magnesium powder, and now, in a snapshot image, transfixes the room on the plate.

> Jeder kann sich Rechenschaft davon ablegen, daß die Dauer, in der wir Eindrücken ausgesetzt sind, ohne Bedeutung für deren Schicksal in der Erinnerung ist. Nichts hindert, daß wir Räume, wo wir vierundzwanzig Stunden waren, mehr oder weniger deutlich im Gedächtnis halten, und andere, wo wir Monate verbrachten, ganz vergessen. Es ist also durchaus nicht immer Schuld einer allzukurzen Belichtungsdauer, wenn auf der Platte des Erinnerns kein Bild erscheint. Häufiger sind vielleicht die Fälle, wo die Dämmerung der Gewohnheit der Platte jahrelang das nötige Licht versagt, bis dieses eines Tages aus fremden Quellen wie aus entzündetem Magnesiumpulver aufschießt und nun im Bilde einer Momentaufnahme den Raum auf die Platte bannt. (516/632)

As with Hans Castorp's flashlike vision of Pribislav Hippe, the type of memory Bild at issue here is what Bergson calls *spontané* and Proust *involuntaire*. The contrast is made with the type of conscious memory nurtured by "the half-light of habit," which is to say, that particular web of space and time (*sonderbares Gespinst von Raum und Zeit*) that lends its common glow—its misty *Glanz*—to the remembered experience by fixing it firmly in the surrounding context of time and place— in other words, the type of memory that is crucial to the assimilative, cumulative project of Bildung and its corresponding concept of self-identity.[124] There are, however, experiences that escape this nexus, that slip through consciousness and fix themselves on the plate of remembrance but without appearing there as Bild.[125] Such experiences might well have escaped the conscious mind not because they were too powerful, too traumatic to be successfully contained, but because they were too banal, too insignificant to warrant notice; their very triviality allows them to preserve their potential future charge intact. In any case, such experiences acquire the quality of latency, or *Nachträglichkeit,* that we saw in chapter 1, which is surely *the* principal new feature of the psychic apparatus in the age of the photographic apparatus and the one most immediately disruptive of the traditional project of Bildung. As Benjamin says, the necessary light for development of the image flashes (*aufschießt*) one day from an alien (*fremd*) source, at which point the Bild appears.[126] Crucially, the light that develops the image comes from a *different* time and place, providing a different context for the experience from that in which it originally occurred (but managed not to register).[127] This sudden, belated light seems a very different one from the extended light of exposure time (*Belichtungsdauer*) associated with the original Bild, and if the latter, the *Belichtungsdauer,* seems to resonate with Benjamin's original notion of aura, the former, the light from an alien source, seems to echo his other, later notion of aura as well: aura as a product not of *durée* and a controlling consciousness but of consciousness brought up short (*zum Stehen gebracht* [2:385/2:527]).

As with the excerpt on Proust cited first, the present passage thus far rather neatly conforms to the modernist schema of Mann, Freud, and others of memory as a photographic plate and shares in their common challenge to traditional Bildung and its subject. And the passage also rather neatly conforms to the model for social or cultural history that Benjamin himself is most famous for, the past that can be seized "only as an image that flashes up at the moment of its recognizability, and is never seen again" ("nur als Bild, das auf Nimmerwiedersehen im Augenblick seiner Erkennbarkeit eben aufblitzt" [1:695/4:390]), thus securing a significant parallel between his social project and his personal one, between his tactic at the levels of history and of psychology for opposing the reigning bourgeois(/fascist) ideology, a tactic in both cases indebted to photography. But Benjamin's passage does not end there, and what follows manages to unsettle our own quasicomfortable nexus of associations and to propel us into territory far less familiar. Benjamin himself inserts this disjointing "but" into the center of his passage:

> But it is we ourselves who are always standing at the center of these rare images. Nor is this so enigmatic, since such moments of sudden illumination are at the same time moments when we are outside of ourselves, and while our waking, habitual, everyday self is involved actively or passively in what is happening, our deeper self rests in another place and is touched by the shock, as is the little heap of magnesium powder by the flame of the match. It is to this sacrifice of our deepest self in shock that our memory owes its most indestructible images.

> Im Mittelpunkt dieser seltnen Bilder aber stehen stets wir selbst. Und es ist nicht so rätselhaft, weil solche Augenblicke plötzlicher Belichtung gleichzeitig Augenblicke des Außer-

> Uns-Seins sind und während unser waches, gewohntes, tag-
> gerechtes Ich sich handelnd oder leidend ins Geschehen
> mischt, ruht unser tieferes an anderer Stelle und wird vom
> Chock betroffen wie das Häufchen Magnesiumpulver von
> der Streichholzflamme. Dies Opfer unseres tiefsten Ichs im
> Chock ist es, dem unsere Erinnerung ihre unzerstörbarsten
> Bilder zu danken hat. (516/633)

Despite Benjamin's disclaimer, almost every element of this is indeed
"enigmatic," beginning with the phrase "at the center." Drawing on
the passage cited first, we can, perhaps, imagine "we ourselves" quite
literally to stand, pictured, in the center of such a shot—albeit only as
a self, a Bild, that never existed (at least not to us). But then Benjamin
no sooner claims we stand at the center than he takes away the notion
that we have a center at which we can stand. The self is divided into two
differently located selves: our waking, habitual, everyday self and our
"deeper," or even "deepest," self that rests in another place—a place,
moreover, that is simultaneously posited as outside of ourselves and
deep within us. Even this decentering division is further divided, not
spatially, but temporally, between the experiencing and remembering
self, and although one might want to graft the one division onto the
other and imagine "our everyday self actively or passively involved in
what is happening" as the pictured, remembered self and "our deeper
self in another place" as the picturing, remembering self, this is difficult
to do.[128] First, the everyday self is also the habitual self, and Benjamin
has just described the half-light of habit as what keeps the plate of remembrance from developing its stored Bild, from which perspective
this self is not the past self pictured and remembered but the very present self, fully immersed in what *is* happening and so unable to either
picture or remember the past anything. Second, the deeper self is not
identified by Benjamin with the photographer/recorder and still less
with the plate of remembrance but rather with the little heap of magnesium powder that needs to be consumed, burned up, or sacrificed for
the Bild to be taken in the first place (and not just belatedly developed,
having been previously deposited on the negative plate; photo-memory
is not, as in Freud, Mann, and others, about storage, retrieval, and subsequent development but rather about an initial exposure and its instantaneous, simultaneous storage and development, about a snapshot,
a *Momentaufnahme*). In any case, this deeper self cannot be present to

observe the image but must be destroyed so that the undestroyable image can be made. From this perspective, neither of these two selves is, so to speak, in the picture (*im Bilde*): the one incapable of remembering, its associative mechanisms (*Assoziationsmechanismus*) needing to be shut down and cast aside, the other consumed for the memory to come into being to begin with and nothing but a pile of dirty ashes afterward.

Benjamin associates neither of his two selves with the plate of remembrance proper, which is to say that, strange as it may seem, the self does not seem for him to be part of memory proper.[129] Rather, the self figures only as a source of light, either the half-light of habit of the one or the sudden illumination of the other. But while the latter provides the necessary light for the fixing of the image on memory's plate, it cannot even be said that it is the deeper self, "the little heap of magnesium powder," that is the source of that required light and still less that it is the agent of the photograph. Rather, the light source, the necessary light, comes from the shock, "as from the flame of a match." The source of this source (*Quelle*) is left notably undetermined. About all we can say is that the term "shock," redolent with Benjamin's reading of Freud on trauma and of Baudelaire on the modern city, seems even further to vitiate or negate the role of the self in the photography of memory.[130] The (alien) source of illuminating light is not the "deeper" self but something brought from its own elsewhere to this other, deeper place, something completely outside the self, from the external world—even if the adjective "alien" ("fremd") discourages us from simply equating that source with the habitual, everyday, familiar world.[131]

The added twists of this passage are not, I believe, merely products of a more close-paced reading than such a slim (and never published) passage can bear. Rather, they are integral to the passage itself and to the notion of the subject Benjamin's photographic metaphor implies. Far more than in Mann or Proust, who use the caustic analytical chemicals of photographic development to somewhat similar effect, memory qua photography in Benjamin is not about the formation of the subject but about his dissolution. The everyday, continuously unfolding self is dismissed as inimical to development (something like the bright overhead light in *The Magic Mountain*); the deeper self is consumed and sacrificed so that the Bild might come to be. We are left with an image, a *Momentaufnahme*, but no self as part of the picture—except, again, the picture of a self "at the center" that never actually was. The sense of the vanishing subject is further exacerbated by the far more complicated role of time in Benjamin's model. Whereas for Mann, Freud, and others, memory as photography disrupts the sequential unfolding of the traditional nineteenth-century subject by introducing the principle of belatedness, Benjamin's model takes away even the residues of temporal directionality or progress still implicit in the sequence of exposure and subsequent development. Here the relations between past, present, and future and the place of the self in those relations have become far more unstable, as evidenced by the inextricable intertwinings in this passage of the processes of exposure and development, of the initial fixing of the image and its appearance on the plate, all of which are reduced to, or concentrated into, one "moment" impossible to fix temporally. No doubt this can be explained in part by Benjamin's relegating the model of latent-image photography drawn on by Mann and Freud to the same technological pastness as the even earlier, and also outdated, long exposure times of the mid-nineteenth century and grappling instead with the immediacy of the new snapshot photography. But this shift also corresponds to Benjamin's more radical rejection of the significance to be invested—by either the individual or his culture—in the forward development of time or in the archaic images of the past, and his famously weak hope in the sudden moment ("whether fleeting or eternal") that disrupts, indeed explodes, both time and the subject grounded in time.

An additional point at which Benjamin's model of memory as photography works to dismantle the notion of the psychological subject, and for all intents and purposes to undo the very introjection he seems to be practicing, comes in his insistence on the externality of both the igniting impulses behind the fixed images of memory and the Bilder themselves. Here the polemic with other models of the psychic apparatus is perhaps best seen not in relation to other photographic models but in relation to other archaeological models. Whereas Jensen and Freud both implicitly—and crucially implicitly—participate in an introjection of culturally and socially contingent impulses into the psychological subject, where those impulses become naturalized and legitimized as "personal" biological drives completely divorced from historical social context, Benjamin reverses this process and insists that it is the external, "shocking" world that impinges on the individual and shapes his image repertoire, which itself derives from the store of his everyday surroundings. Despite the references to our "deeper" and "deepest" self, Benjamin's memory qua photography dispenses at once with a psychology of interior drives and one of mythically/inherently deposited Urbilder, the latter something neither Mann nor Freud quite manages to do, indeed something their photographic memories tend to foster. The point is crucial. At a moment in cultural history where the individual subject and his individual memories are increasingly and dangerously being sacrificed to a more "typical" subject identity and set of phylogenetic memories, Benjamin will not allow his sacrifice of the individual subject to yield to the same type of conclusion. Hence it is, finally, not his everyday self that yields but his deepest self that is destroyed—and *not* that somehow emerges. Conversely his "indestructible images" are *not* deep, not mythical or archaic but instead photographic, quotidian, and external.[132]

LITHOPHANIC ENDINGS

I would like to close this discussion with a reading of a section that interweaves many of the most central themes we have followed throughout this chapter: Bildung and Bilder, Goethe and classicism, archaeology and photography, myth and aura, Benjamin and fascism. It is the section in which Benjamin describes the graphic schema of his life ("das graphische Schema [s]eines Lebens") and the profound, or deep, symbolic Bild of the four rings ("das tiefe Sinnbild der vier Ringe" [490–94/614–16]). The latter represents the chronological endpoint of *Berlin Chronicle*. It depicts an event at the very beginning of the war, shortly after the suicide of Fritz Heinle and his girlfriend and Benjamin's own disaffection with both the Youth Movement and the German nation, and so in many ways it also represents a conclusion (or a second conclusion) to Benjamin's *Bildungsgeschichte* and a fitting place for us to conclude as well.

I want to make three general points about the section as a whole. First, although Benjamin begins by emphasizing again how small a role people play in the memories of his text, this section is very much about the people closest to him and his relations to them. It addresses what he calls his primal acquaintances (*Urbekanntschaften*)—"my biographical relationships to people, my friendships and comradeships, my passions and love affairs in their most vivid and hidden intertwinings" ("meine biographischen Beziehungen zu Menschen, meine Freundschaften und Kameradschaften, meine Leidenschaften und Liebschaften in ihren lebendigsten, verborgensten Verflechtungen" [490/

614])—in other words, the traditional domain of Bildung, perhaps more emphatically so than any other section. However, in keeping with the strategy found throughout, Bildung is approached not directly, through an exploration of such human relations, but indirectly, through an exploration of the world of things (*die Dingwelt*), which is to say, of Bilder, in this case the leaf of paper (*Blatt*) of Benjamin's biographic schema and the deep symbolic image (*tiefe Sinnbild*) of the four rings. Bildung and Bilder are tightly intertwined.

Second, and in keeping with the pronounced focus on Bildung, this section is also the most overtly Goethean in *Berlin Chronicle*. This is true in relation to both its parts. The discussion of Benjamin's *Blatt* is a sustained meditation not only on primal acquaintances but also on principles of Bildung (*Bildungsgesetze*) and the complex interweavings of self and fate that, we saw, were so central to Benjamin's essay on Goethe; nor does it seem accidental that this first part ends with the suggestive phrase "zum Meister führen" ("leading to *Meister*" [the master] [492/615]). The discussion of the four rings offers in turn a sustained evocation of *Elective Affinities* (and by extension, of Benjamin's essay on that work) through its depiction of the shifting erotic allegiances of the principal characters (all reduced to initials) and, through its concluding gesture toward an involved double marriage that depends centrally on a brother/sister pair, of the closing scene of *Wilhelm Meister* as well. I might add that, in keeping with the focus on both Bildung and Goethe, this section is also the most overtly classical in *Berlin Chronicle,* and again in relation to both its parts. This will become clearer in what follows.

Third, the segment as a whole is closely associated with the photographic effects that we saw Benjamin describe in his photography essays and work to achieve in the literary technique of *Berlin Chronicle* itself, most especially in the section on his first impressions of the theater—but with a twist. In the case of his theater impressions, Benjamin's strategy was to proceed from the accumulated, auratic, misty *Glanz* encompassing this traditional Bildung experience toward the sudden, flashlike illumination of his memory of his picture postcard; this follows the same basic direction of lighting effects as that outlined in the "Little History" for photography itself. Here, however, the trajectory of illumination seems just the opposite. The passage opens with a reference to "insights that came in a flash, with the force of an illumination" ("Einsichten, die blitzartig, mit der Gewalt der Erleuchtung mich überfielen"), moves through a discussion of a much more sustained, cumulative light effect of one of the four rings, and ends with a different kind of recognition (*Erkenntnis*), one that only emerges (indeed unfolds) over extended time. The opening, flashlike illumination seems to identify Benjamin's *Blatt* as one of those snapshots, those rare and indestructable Bilder discussed in the previous section, but the closing one seems to embrace an ideal of *durée* that is elsewhere associated with a quite different kind of Bild, and usually a disparaged one. The different trajectory of this passage seems to present something of a reversal in Benjamin's thought or, more precisely, to present that principle of reversal that, we have seen, is so characteristic of Benjamin's thought, that always dangerous tactic of identifying with what he also seems to oppose—his own version, as it were, of the photographic principle of inversion that we saw first in Mann.

Benjamin first describes the piece of paper that suddenly and with compulsive force ("mit einem Mal und mit zwingender Gewalt") revealed to him the primal acquaintances that, he says, result only from neighborhood, family relationships, school comradeship, and companionship on travels ("Nachbarverhältnisse, Verwandtschaft, Schulkameradschaft [und] Reisegenossenschaft") and that have most shaped his life course;[133] in its way, much like the certificate of apprenticeship (*Lehrbrief*) that Wilhelm Meister receives at the end of his *Bildungsgeschichte,* the narrative that reveals the figures and forces that were secretly shaping and scripting his Bildung all along. But unlike Wilhelm's scroll, Benjamin's original *Blatt* is also depicted as lost, and as Carol Jacobs observes, necessarily lost. The schema that Benjamin reconstructs in its place is no orderly narrative of a classically complete, whole, and realized self, such as we find at the end of *Wilhelm Meister* but rather a figure that seems a labyrinth—a classical self, to be sure, but one that disappoints the usual associations of the classical every bit as much as it does the Goethean and instead simply expands the sense of being lost first introduced by the missing *Blatt* itself.[134]

This sense of loss is further emphasized by what Benjamin says will not concern him in his present contemplation of the labyrinth, namely, what is installed in the chamber of its enigmatic center, self or fate ("was in der Kammer seiner rätselhaften Mitte haust, Ich oder Schicksal"). This is, of course, a central concern of the Bildung tradition, one normally closely allied with the role of the primal acquaintances. It is the question that Wilhelm Meister discusses in his encounter with the stranger at the very beginning of his story, that Mann poses for Hans Castorp at the beginning of his, that Benjamin himself discusses at length in his essay "Fate and Character" ("Schicksal und Charakter" [1921]), and that, as mentioned, he makes central to his analysis of Goethe and his interweaving of personal experience and tendencies of the age. Benjamin says he will not be concerned with addressing the matter of the center but only with the many entranceways ("die vielen Eingänge"), which accords well with the missing center we have noted before, but he also goes on to ask, "And above all: are there something like hidden laws of Bildung in an individual's existence for those many individual ways?" ("Und vor allem: gibt es im Einzeldasein etwas wie verborgene Bildungsgesetze jener vielen Einzelgänge?").[135] Here, in the context of the self and its schema, Benjamin explicitly avoids answering his query, but by the end of the section, in the discussion of his primal acquaintances and the last of the four rings, he seems to insist on just such a center (*Mittelpunkt*) and fate (*Schicksal*) in the figure of that final ring's recipient. The center, then, has not so much been lost as displaced—the *Blatt* returns as the figure of the rings.

The point is crucial to an understanding of both how *Berlin Chronicle* is and is not a *Bildungsgeschichte* and, more particularly, how the deep symbolic Bild of the four rings is to be read in terms of Bildung. The self that is the traditional center of Bildung is not available for scrutiny, at least not directly, and that includes the crucial interplay between that self and those outside forces that, qua Bildung, traditionally come to shape it. The interplay itself, however, does not disappear; it is merely displaced onto the site of the primal acquaintances or, rather, onto the symbolic image (*Sinnbild*) that represents those primary relations—onto the four rings. As Jacobs stresses, in contemplating these rings Benjamin is engaged in *self* contemplation (*sich betrachten*) or, more fully, in contemplation of the relations between his self and his shaping, surrounding world: of Bildung and its issue.[136]

Benjamin's encounter with the four rings is framed by a setting that deliberately evokes the archaeological metaphor that has run throughout the work, in both its traditionally classical and its more surrealist, "only just old" forms. The encounter takes place in one of the houses of "old" Berlin that, we are told, "with their smooth, aristocratic façades may have stemmed from the Schinkel period" ("mit ihren schlichten vornehmen Fassaden . . . aus de[n] Schinkelschen Jahren stammen [mögen]" [492/615]) The allusion to the nineteenth-century architect Karl Schinkel subtly engages the neoclassical impulse that would link the classical past to the German bourgeois era, especially the intended ennobling function of its classical facades for the German present; that is, it engages just that juncture of classicism, classism, and nationalism that is typical of Bildung.[137] Benjamin goes to one of these houses to meet a "significant" antiquities dealer (*einen bedeutenden Antiquitätenhändler*). He stresses how the dealer had no exterior display and that one had to enter inside the *Etagenwohnung* ("flat," lit. "tiered dwelling") to view his artifacts. This turn inward suggests, I think, how the significance of the classical encountered on the outside in the neoclassical architecture is to be explored instead in the more limited compass of the interior—a suggestion very much in keeping with the central role of Benjamin's self here as the object of attention, especially that self as the interiorized version of the same shaping (Bildung) forces at work in the more public, outside realm.[138] The centrality of Bildung to the encounter is further emphasized by Benjamin identifying his companion on the trip, A.C., as "my schoolfriend" and calling specific attention to the reading material that conditions his response to the artifacts he finds there inside, Alois Riegl's work on late Roman art—reading material, moreover, that counsels a turn away from the macroscopic and, instead, a focus on the individual, the world-in-small (*die kleine Welt*).[139]

The archaeological artifacts that Benjamin and his companions find inside include a selection of prehistoric brooches and clasps, Lombard earrings, late Roman neck chains, medieval coins, and many similar valuables ("eine Auswahl vorgeschichtlichler Spangen und Fibeln, langobardischer Ohrgehänge, spätrömischer Halsketten, mittelalterlicher Münzen und vieler ähnlicher Kostbarkeiten"); the jewels they come especially to see are Greeks gems, Renaissance cameos, and rings from the imperial period, mostly work carved in semiprecious stone ("griechische Gemmen, Kameen der Renaissance, Ringe der Kaiserzeit, meistens in Halbedelsteine geschnittene Arbeit").[140] All these artifacts pick up and carry on the classical thematics suggested by the houses' smooth aristocratic facades but with some significant differences. First, and most obviously, the authenticity of these antiquities contrasts sharply with the exterior, neoclassical facades—although we should also note the literally "half-noble" (*halbedel*) quality of the ring stones that, along with their modest and quotidian craftmanship, contrasts with the monumental nobility (*Vornehmheit*) of the facades, equally, if differently, calling attention to the false pretenses of the one and the more genuine quality of the other.[141] Second, but still related, the intentionally vague, universalist notion of the classical that is implicitly deployed by the neoclassical architecture, in support of its legitimating function for both the bourgeois class and the German nation, is countered here by a classicism carefully nuanced by historical specification and stratification, imbuing a sense of both layers (*Schichten*) and history (*Geschichte*) to the ancient world; that is, it foregrounds that aspect of the archaeological whose historical and material focus works against the (timelessly) classical.[142] And third, along with the intrusion of the historical into the classical comes that of the political. With mention of the Lombards, the Renaissance, and especially the imperial period (*Kaiserzeit*), the issues of public political power that seem always to lurk within the classical, no matter how "smooth" its appearance, are subtly brought back into the picture. To contemplate the classical, no matter how authentic, how self-regarding and inwardly turned, is always also to contemplate the workings of cultural political power.

Four rings are selected by Benjamin and his companions, each linked with one of his primal acquaintances and each making its unforgettable (*unvergeßlich*) impression on him, each an artifact (an emblem) to be contemplated for what it reveals about both Benjamin's own identity and his connections with those outside shaping figures and forces. The first two rings are both, albeit for different reasons, quietly downplayed, even dismissed. The first is a bright yellow smoky topaz: "the workmanship was Grecian and it depicted in a tiny space Leda receiving the swan between her parted thighs" ("Die Arbeit in ihm war griechisch und stellte auf winzigem Raum die Leda dar, wie sie zwischen ihren geöffneten Schenkel den Schwan empfängt" [492/615]). Although he admits it was most graceful ("Er war sehr anmutig"), Benjamin also says this is the one ring he has lost sight of ("aus den Augen verloren"), the one that has most fallen out of consideration, the entranceway that is no more. A number of its attributes combine to identify this ring with the idea of origins, of "first things": that it is the first ring; that it seems to come from Greece, the reputed foundation of classical, which is to say Western (read: German) culture; that it depicts a scene of conception, a conception, moreover, often marked as the beginning of history (the Trojan War) emerging out of myth; and that it is lost. That is, as with the *Blatt* with which this section begins, the quality of being lost is inseparable from the status of being original: Benjamin will not be drawn into the foundational myths that have proved so dangerously attractive for both German nationalism and psychology and have proved such a key part of classicism's appeal but will instead, and again, let go.

The allure of the second ring seems more easily resisted, even if its troubling presence in Benjamin's life proves far more lasting: an amethyst in which "a fifteenth or sixteenth century Italian had carved a profile which Lederer claimed was that of Pompeii" ("ein Italiener des 15ten oder 16ten Jahrhunderts ein Profil—Lederer behauptete das des Pompejus—eingeschnitten hatte").[143] If the first ring suggests the idea of mythical origins and foundations, this ring evokes that of political ends and reenactments. The figure of Pompeii, one of the great heroic wielders of imperial power in ancient Rome, and his resurrection in the culture and imagination of Renaissance Italy, all this reeks too much of the ideals of fascism and its own resurrection of the imperial past to hold much continued attraction for Benjamin, who gave up his faith in direct (heroic) political activity with the demise of the Youth Movement. For all its unforgettable impression on him, Benjamin is able to bring little admiration (*Bewunderung*) to his contemplation of this ring. Moreover, the pairing of these first two rings, or emblems, proves even less to be admired than either on its own. The pairing of foundation myths and ideals of (renewed) imperial power can only appear too disastrous in its contemporary cultural form for Benjamin to wish to do anything but distance himself from them in their more private form.

The third ring presents more of a challenge to Benjamin. It was, he says, "the most fascinating ring I have ever seen" ("der faszinierendste Ring, den ich je gesehen habe"):

> Cut in a dark, massive garnet, it depicted a Medusa head. It was a work from the Roman imperial period. The open [lit. "light"] setting was no longer the old one. When worn on the finger, it was merely the most perfect of signet rings. Only he who took it off and, holding the head against the light, contemplated himself entered into its secret. As the different strata of the garnet were differently translucent, and the thinnest so transparent that it glowed as if rose colored, so one thought to see the dusky bodies of the snakes on the head surge up over the brow, beneath which two deep glow-

ing eyes looked out of a face that, with the purple-black planes of the cheeks, receded once more into the night.

In einen dunklen massigen Granat geschnitten, stellte er ein Medusenhaupt dar. Es war ein Arbeit der römischen Kaiserzeit. Die lichte Fassung war nicht mehr die alte. Trug man den Ring am Finger, so war er nur der vollkommenste von allen Siegelringen. In sein Geheimnis trat erst ein, wer ihn abzog und nun das Haupt gegen das Licht gehalten sich betrachtete. Da die verschiednen Schichten des Granats verschieden lichtdurchlässig waren, die dünnste aber so transparent, das sie wie rosenfarben glühte, so glaubte man die düstern Schlangenleiber des Hauptes über eine Stirne wellen zu sehen, unter der zwei tiefe glühende Augen aus einem Antlitz sahen, das mit den purpurschwarzen Flächen der Wangen wieder in die Nacht zurücktrat. (493/616)

The description itself is so fascinating that some critics, most recently Carol Jacobs, have identified it with Benjamin's own ideal, indeed even as a *mise en abîme* for the intended effect of *Berlin Chronicle* itself.[144] There is evidence to support this. Benjamin introduces the description by declaring how this particular ring was intended for him ("war mir zugedacht") and closes by saying, "Later I tried more than once to stamp a seal with this stone" ("Später habe ich einigemale versucht, mit diesem Stein zu siegeln" [493/616]); it seems, that is, his signet, his emblem, the signature of those many mesmerizing moments that emerge obliquely out of *Berlin Chronicle,* out of Benjamin's contemplated past, and fix the present writer (and reader). At the same time, however, Benjamin also works to distance himself from this emblem.[145] He qualifies the statement that the ring was intended for him by adding "but only as a very temporary owner; it was really meant to go through me, as a gift, to my then fiancée" ("doch nur als ganz interimistischen Besitzer; im Grunde war er bestimmt durch mich als mein Geschenk an meine damalige Verlobte . . . zu kommen"), and he qualifies the claim that he had tried to seal with its stone by adding "but it showed itself inclined to fissure" ("es zeigte sich aber, daß er zu Rissen neigte") and "shortly after giving it away, I dissolved my relationship with its new owner" ("kurze Zeit nachdem ich ihn verschenkt hatte, löste ich meine Beziehungen zu seiner neuen Besitzerin" [493/616]). As important as it is to recognize the allure of this ring for Benjamin and to see its close identity with his own practice, it is even more important to discover the reasons for this needed distance, this needed *Lösung*—this needed loss.

Perhaps the most pressing point is how much the quality and effect of this *faszinierend* ring resembles not only Benjamin's ideals but those he associates with fascism. The inclusion of the latter in Benjamin's description is subtle but insistent, not only in the word "faszinierend," but also in the added details—that it was a work from the Roman imperial period, which links the emblem (much like that of Pompeii) with the realm of ancient imperial power, and that the setting was no longer the old one, which signals its resetting in a contemporary frame. The word *massig* might also be taken to contain a hint of the need to consider the effect of this ring not only at the level of the individual and his experience but on a far more massive scale as well.[146] Further, indirect evidence of this aspect of the Medusa ring can be seen in the last paragraph of the essay "Theories of German Fascism" ("Theorien des deutschen Faschismus" [1930]), where the Medusa head also appears. Benjamin writes, "Not before Germany has exploded the Medusa-like tangle of traits that here confront it can it hope for a future" ("Nicht ehe Deutschland das medusische Gefüge der Züge, die ihm hier entgegentreten, gesprengt hat, kann es eine Zukunft erhoffen" [3:249/2:320]). He further characterizes this enemy as "the habitués of the chthonic forces of terror, who carry their Klages in their knapsacks" ("die Habitués chthonischer Schreckenmächte, die ihren Klages im Tornister führen"), honing in on just that convergence in myth of the political and psychological that the ring itself seems to embody and that now seems so difficult to affirm, no matter how close to one's own ideal. Inclined to fissure, indeed.

The recognition of the negative political and psychological dimensions to this ring allows us to approach more clearly, and cautiously, the dimensions that most fascinate us, namely, the archaeological and photographic dimensions of the ring, expecially in their linkage with classicism and myth. The archaeological and photographic are almost impossible to separate here. The ring is not only itself at once an archaeological artifact and a Bild for Benjamin; it is also in itself an archaeological site, composed of different strata through which the light pours to produce its own otherwise hidden Bild. In ways that clearly recall our earlier example of Benjamin's postcard of the Halle Gate, the ring depends upon a combination of strata and light for its almost magically emergent effect. There was, we saw, an ambivalence to that illuminating photo-effect in the former case; that ambivalence is multiplied here along with the number of translucent strata through which the effect is achieved. Rather than the result of light passing through a single layer, here the mesmerizing effect is cumulative, a concentration of discrete moments, layers, or images into a single powerful Bild that would fix the present viewer with its gaze. It is, as it were, the functional equivalent of the aura-producing, moment-eliding mechanism of early-nineteenth-century photography, which found its own functional equivalent in the bourgeoisie's eliding of history, its collapse of discrete epochs into its own imperialist present—itself a particular manifestation of the more general tendency to view history in its cumulative continuum, and so to invest it with almost mythic power, the power of fixation—the same power, the same teleology, as Bildung exhibits in a more personal dimension. Aura and myth, *Bürgertum* and Bildung, all look out with the same deep glowing eyes of the compounded Bild.

The problem with this is, of course, that the *light* setting was no longer the old one ("die *lichte* Fassung nicht mehr die alte [war]" [493/616]). Even as, after 1880, aura could only be simulated in photography, so now, in the postwar era, the lighting conditions—the conditions of illumination—have changed, rendering the past myth, the past ideal, unviable. And in keeping with this, Benjamin's own lighting conditions have changed as well. In the case of his treasured postcard, Benjamin imagined his light held behind the Bild, investing it with all the power and mystery of a dream, a revelation that infused the night with transforming luminescence. Here, however, the light with which he contemplates the Bild is not behind but before it, and the Bild, rather than yielding an irruptive brightness, recedes once more into night. It is, I would say, much the same light with which Benjamin says the Medusalike tangle of German fascism must be exploded or, perhaps better, loosened ("gesprengt—besser vielleicht gelockert"):

This is not to say it should be done with kindly encouragement or with love, both of which are out of place here; nor should the way be prepared for argumentation, for the wantonly persuasive rhetoric of debate. Instead, all the light that language and reason still afford should be focused on that "primal experience" from whose mute darkness this mysticism . . . crawls forth on its thousand unsightly conceptual feet.

> Das soll nicht heißen, mit gütigem Zuspruch oder mit Liebe, die hier nicht am Ort sind; es soll auch nicht der Argumentation, dem überredungsgeilen Debattieren den Weg bereiten. Wohl aber hat man alles Licht, das Sprache und Vernunft noch immer geben, auf jenes "Urerlebnis" zu richten, aus dessen tauber Finsternis diese Mystik . . . mit ihren tausend unansehnlichen Begriffsfüßchen hervorkrabbelt. (3:249/2:320)

Even as in his earlier archaeological metaphor Benjamin stressed the need to bring the dreamlike Bilder up out of their depths into "the sober rooms of our later insight," to contemplate these archaic images in the clear light of the present day, and in so doing distinguished himself from both the surrealists' and Klages's ill-conceived immersion in mythical "primal experiences," so here in his well-nigh Settembrinian, enlightened view of the Medusa Bild. Here in the essay on fascism, with its thousand unsightly feet crawling forth, the Bild is an undeniably ugly one, a deliberately dirty picture of a dirtied reality, deprived of any stylized beautification, its aura all sucked out. By contrast, the Bild in *Berlin Chronicle*, seems, as it were, its inverse, the positive to its negative; it retains its auratic and archaic power, its mythical and aesthetic force. But I believe we nonetheless misread the Bild if we do not see how it is still the *same* image and, along with Benjamin, work to loosen our engagement with its present possessor.

It has long been a convention of the Bildungsroman tradition that the protagonist's life choices in the spheres of character formation and socio-cultural ideals can be signalled by the choices he makes in the erotic sphere, by the kind of woman he rejects as well as the one he selects, which indirectly but decisively determines the kind of man he has become, the ideal of manliness (*Männlichkeit*) he has attained and so too the Bildung he has achieved. We see it in *Wilhelm Meister* as well as in each of the works we have explored in preceding chapters. And we see it here in Benjamin's turn from the recipient of the third ring to that of the fourth, an erotic turn that seems also to signal a turn of ideals, a most decisive and in some sense conclusive turn.[147] Not surprisingly, this is also the most heavily Goethean moment in the work, where the references to the erotic forms of *Elective Affinities* and *Wilhelm Meister* seem most layered and developed—and where, in the figure of a woman, Goethean ideals seem most clearly to provide a final figuration to the volatile elements of Bildung, classicism, and photography that we have followed throughout.

This final ring is described as a lapis lazuli with a lute wreathed in foliage engraved on it ("der Lapislazuli mit der von Laub umrankten Laute, die in ihn geritzt war" [494/616]); Benjamin himself sends it to A.C.'s sister together with a sonnet he wrote, now as lost to us as the biographic schema and first ring were to him. The ring, with both its lute and wreath, emphatically evokes the image of the classical poet, and Benjamin just as emphatically identifies himself here with that poet; he does not, however, directly discuss the ring, nor himself (his *Ich*) but rather the ring's recipient and her role as the center, the *Mittelpunkt*, of fate for himself and his circle. That is, it is her attributes that become the *Mittelpunkt* for the emblem of the closing ring, the chosen center of Benjamin's self and art, the decisive center of his social group (and by extension, of his society). Benjamin had already announced in the opening pages of *Berlin Chronicle* the figure of Ariadne, and defined the only thread that leads through the labyrinth, the word love (*Liebe*). Here, in the recipient of the fourth ring, we find her and her thread.[148]

Benjamin first mentions but declines to dwell on her beauty, which was itself not *glänzend* but rather inconspicuous and without luster ("ihre Schönheit, die selbst nicht glänzend sondern unscheinbar und stumpf war"). It is, that is, a beauty explicitly opposed to the ideal of *Glanz* that dominated the Bildung deployment of classicism (and art and culture) in Jensen's *Gradiva*, that Benjamin has set himself against in the traditions of both "archaeological" city writing and photography, and that, in its matte quality, seems the very opposite of the Medusa's "glowing" fascination.[149] What Benjamin does dwell on is her plantlike passivity and indolence ("ihre pflanzenhafte Passivität und Trägheit"). It is a notably feminine ideal, what Benjamin elsewhere calls the feminine and vegetable principle of life ("das weibliche und vegetabilische Lebensprinzip" [3:153/2:157]), and it is a notably natural ideal, one that Benjamin expands upon by repeating the adjective "plantlike" once more in the same sentence and then adding the image of a seed (*Keim*) in the one after that. In both these ways, it is also a notably Goethean ideal, an ideal closely tied up with his (Goethe's) model of unfolding, of *Entfaltung*. Benjamin explains, "Many years were needed before what was then in part beginning to unfold in its seed, and in part still dormant, emerged in its ramifications to the light of day" ("Vieler Jahre bedurfte [es], ehe in seinem Zusammenhange an den Tag trat, was damals teils im Keim zu entfalten anfing, teils noch schlummerte" [493/616]), namely, the fate (*Schicksal*) of erotic affinities embodied in this fourth ring's recipient.

How are we to evaluate this ideal, this turn of affection? So much seems suspect, even wrong here: the embrace of a gender distinction that has its complement in a masculine ideal of engaged and progressive activism that, in its militarized form, Benjamin seems to have abandoned, and certainly to have questioned throughout his *Bildungsgeschichte;* the use of a natural, biological metaphor that resonates with vitalism and seems to play into the mythologization of social and psychological drives Benjamin seems elsewhere vehemently to oppose; the promotion of a Goethean model of continuous, slow-paced, and inevitable development, of a process of realization that seems so opposed to the type of snapshot illumination privileged elsewhere in the work, that modernist photo-effect devised especially to interrupt the normal, unbroken unfolding of time, of history, of Bildung; and the ring signature of the classical artist, the Olympian creator of masterpieces, the producer of traditional literary forms. It seems, that is, willfully old-fashioned, naïve, a retreat from the present, a risky turn back to the past: to the lost, to the sullied.

I am not sure we can dismiss this as just "seeming": we have had too many instances of this identity with ideals he also opposes to justify speaking Benjamin clear here. But I would suggest that what Benjamin is imagining here is a model of the feminine separated from the masculine, of nature separated from myth, and of unfolding separated from Bildung—and in all cases, a separation that is only possible, only *perceptible,* in the present and only realizable in a form of art radically different from classicism and the "masterpieces" of the literary tradition, Bildungsromane included.[150] Let me explain what I mean by referring again to Benjamin's review essay "News about Flowers." The subject of the essay is the new vision of the plantlike, *das Pflanzenhafte,* that is opened up by modern photography and its techniques of stop-time and enlargement—which is to say, of interrupting the continuum, the whole, and seizing upon the unsuspected detail. As Benjamin says, only photography can do this ("nur die Photographie vermag das" [3:153/2:156]). What these photographic enlargements reveal are what Benjamin calls vegetal "Forms of Style" (*vegetabilische "Stilformen"*)—the reference is to the work of Alois Riegl, the same historian of classical and late Roman art mentioned in connection with the four rings. The "Forms of Style" of classical art are seen to be repeated in the enlarged forms of plants, even as the oldest forms of columns (*älteste Säulenformen*) emerge in horsetails or "the shoots of a monk's hood unfold like the body of a gifted dancer . . . Leaping towards us from every calyx and every leaf are inner image-imperatives, which have the last word in all phases and stages of generated things" ("der Sproß eines Eisenhufes enfaltet sich wie der Körper einer begnadeten Tänzerin . . . Aus jedem Kelche und jedem Blatte springen uns innere Bildnotwendigkeiten entgegen, die in allen Phasen und Stadien des Gezeugten . . . das letzte Wort behalten"). This image-imperative (*Bildnotwendigkeit*) resonates with Goethean notions of *das Urphänomen,* and Benjamin closes his review by celebrating Goethe as the genius who followed this "feminine principle of life." But the key point for us remains this: it is detail, stop-time photography that first reveals this new "plant" world of the natural, the classical, and the Goethean, together with their common "feminine" principle of unfolding; for all its antiquarian and vaguely vitalistic quality, it is a decidedly modern and photographically uncovered realm.[151]

The second key point can also be derived from the combination of photographic enlargement, Riegl's classicism, and Goethe's principle of unfolding. Benjamin says, "We observers, however, wander under these giant plants like Lilliputians" ("Wir Betrachtenden aber wandeln unter diesen Riesenpflanzen wie Liliputaner" [3:153/2:157]). Only for giant spirits (*Riesengeistern*) such as Goethe is it left to suck all the sweetness from these calyxes ("ist es noch vorbehalten, alle Süße aus diesen Kelchen zu saugen"). The present "observer," it seems, must be content with something far more modest: with a different kind of art, one willing to stage its allegiance to the natural and classical on a far more limited and diminutive scale.[152] It is, I would suggest, an artist less like the grand, classical poet most often associated with the ring's lute and wreath and far more like the miniaturist, anonymous craftsman who cut the stone and made the ring in the first place. Such a craftsman—as important for his typicality as for his individual touch—holds a special place in the ancient world that Benjamin evokes by way of Riegl: not a participant in the fine arts tradition, of the monumental classicism that has over and again proved such a firm support for nationalist (and classist) designs and myths of historical development, but rather a shaper of more ephemeral, banal, little things that nonetheless keep faith with tradition and, in a way, with nature (and dirt) as well ("wreathed with foliage").

It is, of course, just this image of the artist as craftsman that Benjamin celebrates in "The Storyteller," an image, he says, that has only recently (from the present distance) come into view, and it is telling how he several times links his image of the storyteller with that of a gemcutter who is also a ringmaker.[153] Like Riegl's ancient craftsman, Benjamin's storyteller keeps faith with nature but in a way that opposes myth; he keeps faith with the age of naïve poetry (*die Zeit der naiven Dichtung*) of the Greeks and Goethe but in a way that resolutely opposes their classical culture, and he embraces a principle of unfolding but one that opposes the project of Bildung and its corollary in history.[154] Indeed, even as Riegl's craftsman stands opposed to the fine arts culture of monumental classicism, so does Benjamin's stand opposed to the "high" culture of the bourgeois novel, including the Bildungsroman. He aims at the unfolding of a single image or event (its germinative power, or *Keimkraft*) outside the categories of historical, progressive time, not in the service of an individual, bourgeois psychological identity, but of a common, shared social identity, and he entrusts his work to a present conceived as no better than his own but nonetheless better for the small gems he passes on.[155]

This is, I suggest, the conclusion to *Berlin Chronicle* or, rather, its second conclusion: one that works at once to destroy the ideals of the Bildungsroman tradition and to recover almost all its most important elements—including its pedagogic ones—for its own continuing project. We see this second conclusion in the reformation that *Berlin Chronicle* takes in becoming *Berlin Childhood*: in the formal changes that have led critics to see its units, its Bilder, as fashioned at once like photographic snapshots and like ancient handcrafted artifacts and in the thematic changes that have dropped the material more traditionally identifiable with the individual's Bildung and concentrated on more typical social experiences—and on unfolding moments of childhood divorced from, liberated from, the genetic fabric of time and biography.[156] It is, I am told, Benjamin's most beloved book and by his own admission the one most shaped by love; it is also the one most informed by a sense of the irretrievability of the past and of letting go. It is, that is, an embrace not of the past but of its loss, its necessary loss; it offers its

Bilder to a fate, a future, in the hope that they might, seedlike, contain the capacity, at their core, to preform later historical experience ("in ihrem Innern spätere geschichtliche Erfahrung zu präformieren" [7:385/3:344]), Bilder left for our dirt, our light, and our unfolding.

Epilogue (Nachbildung)

Bildung, Archaeology, and Photography in W. G. Sebald

Home is the land of one's childhood and youth. Whoever has lost it remains lost himself.

Die Heimat ist das Kindheits- und Jugendland. Wer sie verloren hat, bleibt ein Verlorener.

Jean Améry, Jenseits von Schuld und Sühne

In the summer of 2000, in the early research stages of this project, I traveled to London with my wife and my then ten-year-old daughter. Together we visited the British Museum and, once we got past the construction site at the entrance, visited its displays of Greek artifacts and household objects and, beyond them, the rooms devoted to Egyptian art and mummies. Everywhere there were groups of schoolchildren quietly gathered around some teacher and selected artwork, dutifully adding its outline to their sketchbooks. My daughter, who had already used up her camera taking pictures of pigeons and squirrels in the park ("to show the dogs at home"), showed no discernible interest in the activity of her peers other than to ask why English children went to school in summer. The next day we visited the Victoria and Albert Museum, where I had a particular interest in exploring its vast archives of nineteenth-century photographs, its extensive collection of slightly browned and always fragile plaster casts of classical statues that, while now banished from the classical art collections themselves, had become museum pieces in their own right, and the many exhibits of nineteenth-century crafts, fashions, and technology, the very embodiment of the kind of instant archaeology that had so fascinated Benjamin and the surrealists. My daughter, however, was bored; the signs insisting that the plaster

271

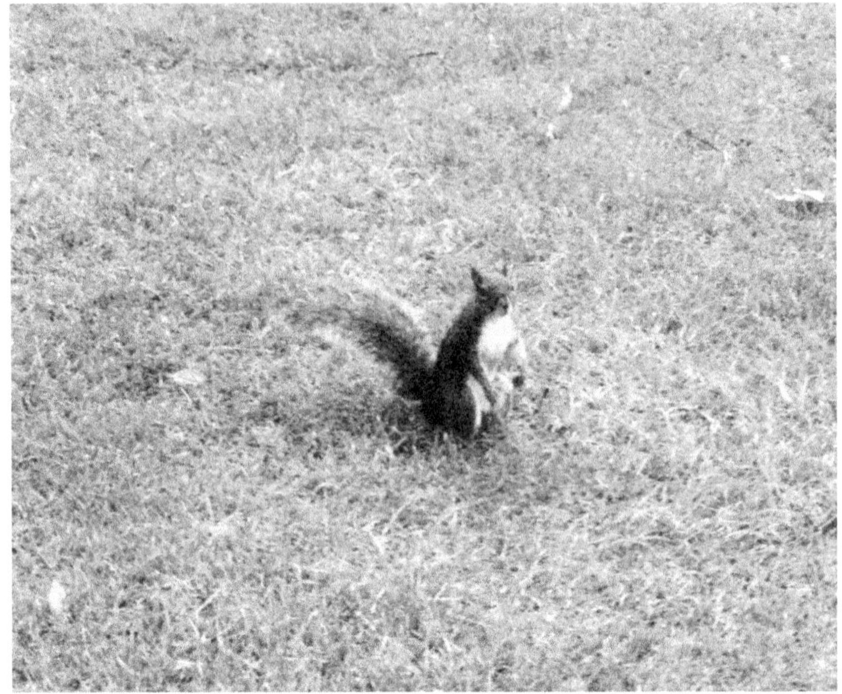

Andy Downing, *London Squirrel,* 2000.

casts not be touched worked like magnets, drawing her fingers to feel the material, and she kept wondering out loud why the British would put their department store displays in a museum—couldn't we just go and buy souvenirs on the street outside?

The next day it was clearly time to split up. My wife decided to take our child to Brighton, where they spent much of the afternoon trying to relocate a New Age gift shop in which my daughter had seen a crystal ball; when they did find it, the shop was closed. I headed off to visit the Freud house, where, behind velvet ropes, I got to see Freud's study with its myriad archaeological artifacts (including his Gradiva); its many photographs (including one of the Sphinx emerging out of the sand over his patient couch); and its bookcases, on which I could just make out the titles of Schliemann's *Ilios* and Mann's Joseph tetralogy. On the landing of the staircase was an ashtray with a half-smoked cigar but no ashes. The upstairs rooms had been occupied by Anna, the dutiful daughter. In contrast to the softness and clutter of the downstairs rooms, these were starkly bare, almost empty. One was under construction and closed; another had been emptied out and fitted with folding chairs and a movie projector but no movie; a third held only Anna's strangely oversized loom but no weaving. Downstairs, in the gift shop on the way out, I bought my daughter one of those three-inch-high statuettes of a black, obedient Egyptian cat that have become almost as much of an icon of psychoanalysis as the Gradiva itself.

I recalled this trip as I was working on *Berlin Chronicle,* and especially on the formal changes the work had undergone in becoming *Berlin Childhood* and their implications for Benjamin's altercation, or *Auseinandersetzung,* with Bildung and subject formation in the modern period. The more I thought about Benjamin's decision to concentrate solely on childhood experiences and to detach them from any teleological or genetic relation to the adult world—even to the adolescent world—the more impressed I became with his well-nigh utopic but still practical investment in a vision of children freed from the constructs of Bildung and psychoanalysis. And the more impressed I became with the significance of that vision, the more self-conscious I became of myself on that trip, and the more grateful for my daughter's unstudied resistance to my direction.

Benjamin's preoccupation with childhood as a fundamentally distinct realm of experience that adults were constantly attempting to develop in their own adult image—and so of childhood as a site of conflict less of the child with the adult than of the adult with the child ("und zwar weniger des Kindes mit den Erwachsenen, als der Erwachsenen mit ihm" [3:128/2:118])—was lifelong.[1] One of his earliest essays, "A Child's View of Color" ("Die Farbe vom Kinde aus betrachtet" [1914/15]), defends the child's perception of color as primary and the borders it marks in the spectrum as real against the adult view that color reality is illusory, its distinctions mere gradations in a single continuous order. As Benjamin says, "Productive adults find no purchase in color; for them it can only subsist within law-given circumstances. Their task is to provide a world order, not to grasp innermost reasons and essences but to develop them" ("Erwachsene, produktive Menschen finden an der Farbe keinen Halt, für sie ist sie nur in gesetzlichen Beziehungen möglich, denn sie haben eine Weltordnung zu geben, aber nicht die innersten Gründe und Wesenarten aufzufassen, sondern eben sie zu entwickeln" [6:111/1:51]). This implicit allegory of childhood itself, and of the attitude toward it of pedagogical adults, is carried over into Benjamin's several essays on children's books, of which he was an avid collector. It is entirely characteristic that he was far less interested in the beautiful copy (*das schöne Exemplar*) than in the patina deposited by unwashed children's hands that kept the "book snob" at a distance ("die Patina, wie ungewaschene Kinderhände sie über die Blätter legen, [und die] den Büchersnob fernhält" [3:14/1:407]). Benjamin notes that children's literature first arose in Germany during the Enlightenment, as part of its emphasis on the *Bildungsprozeß*. But he also notes that the pedagogical intent of these texts was often circumvented by their illustrative Bilder, in which artists and children swiftly came to an understanding over the heads of the pedagogues ("über die Köpfe der Pädagogen hinweg Künstler und Kinder sich verständigt haben" [3:17/1:409]). The resplendent, self-sufficient world of colors (*selbstgenügsam prangende Farbenwelt*) of these pictures drew the child into a very different world from that of so-called life (*das sogenannte Leben*) and rather into the dreamy life that objects lead in the minds of children ("das träumerische Leben, das die Dinge im Geist der Kinder führen"). If the Bilder happened to be black-and-white, the child, inhibited by no *noli me tangere,* would color them in, without regard for prescribed borders or forms.[2] And the same concern for the child's independent refunctioning of Bildung material is evident in Benjamin's writings on children's toys. Benjamin frequented the exhibits of historical toys at several different museums and declared, "The time had to come when someone would . . . write the archaeology of toyshops and dolls' parlors" ("Es mußte endlich . . . die Archäologie der Kaufmannsläden und Puppenstuben geschrieben werden" [3:127/2:117]). His interest was again in how toys, in devolving upon the child's world from the adult's, were fundamentally transformed into something else, something discrete, and as such presented a way out of the "schematic individualism of the arts-and-crafts movement and the picture of the child given by individual psychology" ("schematische Individualismus des Kunstgewerbes und das individualpsychologische Bild vom Kinde" [3:128])—which is to say, a way out of Bildung in both its aesthetic and psychological forms.

Perhaps the most concise formulation of Benjamin's views on

childhood comes in the section titled "Construction Site" ("Baustelle") in *One Way Street:*[3]

> It is folly to brood pedantically over the production of objects—visual aids, toys, or books—that are supposed to be suitable for children. Since the Enlightenment, this has been one of the mustiest speculations of the pedagogues. Their infatuation with psychology keeps them from perceiving that the world is full of the most unrivalled objects for children's attention and use. And the most specific. For children are particularly fond of haunting any site where things are being visibly worked on. They feel themselves irresistibly drawn by detritus. . . . In waste products they recognize the face that the world of things turns directly and solely on them. In [using] these things, they do not so much imitate ("nachbilden") the work of adults as bring together, in the artifact produced in play, materials of widely differing kinds in a new, disconnected way. Children thus produce ("bilden") their own small world of things within the greater one.

> Pedantisch über Herstellung von Gegenständen—Anschauungsmitteln, Spielzeug oder Büchern—die sich für Kinder eignen sollen, zu grübeln, ist töricht. Seit der Aufklärung ist das eine der muffigsten Spekulationen der Pädagogen. Ihre Vergaffung in Psychologie hindert sie zu erkennen, daß die Erde voll von den unvergleichlichsten Gegenständen kindlicher Aufmerksamkeit und Übung ist. Von den bestimmtesten. Kinder nämlich sind auf besondere Weise geneigt, jedwede Arbeitsstätte aufzusuchen, wo sichtbar die Betätigung von Dingen vor sich geht. Sie fühlen sich unwiderstehlich vom Abfall angezogen. . . . In Abfallprodukten erkennen sie das Gesicht, das die Dingwelt gerade ihnen, ihnen allein, zukehrt. In ihnen bilden sie die Werke der Erwachsenen weniger nach, als daß sie Stoffe sehr verschiedener Art durch das, was sie im Spiel daraus verfertigen, in eine neue, sprunghafte Beziehung zueinander setzen. Kinder bilden sich damit ihre Dingwelt, eine kleinere in der großen, selbst. (4:93–94/1:449–50)

The rejection of pedagogy, enlightenment, and psychology, the building blocks of Bildung, and the fixation on detritus (*Abfall*) and the *Umfunktionierung* of the waste products of the grown-up world into new, disconnected relations that construct (*bilden*) out of these building blocks the child's own new world—such is the construction site in which Benjamin seems most to invest his hopes for the future, not just of children, but of adults as well.

The future, however, turned out differently than Benjamin had hoped. His construction site was replaced by an entire landscape of destruction. This is perhaps nowhere more poignantly presented than in the work of W. G. Sebald, the contemporary author most closely aligned with the tradition we have followed from Mann and Freud through to Benjamin in the 1930s. But whereas Benjamin presents us with the dream of a childhood severed from all teleological attachments to adulthood, Sebald presents us with the opposite: with the nightmare of an adulthood severed from all its original attachments to childhood. The difference lies, of course, in the experience of an exile such as Mann, Freud, and Benjamin only began to know, with Benjamin in particular committing suicide before (even rather than) enduring the radical break, and in the experience of a world war that turned Benjamin's angelic vision of the destruction of history into a hellish reality for everyone to see (or, perhaps, to refuse to see). I would like to conclude this study with a brief look at the fate of its constellated themes in the contemporary postmodern world in the work of Sebald, and especially in his Bildungsroman *Austerlitz*.[4]

That Sebald is self-consciously writing in the tradition of Benjamin is clear. In "Paul Bereyter," one of the four life stories in *The Emigrants* (*Die Ausgewanderten* [1993]), the protagonist comes to read Benjamin's works on his way toward realizing his own exile status and his own planned suicide. In "Air War and Literature" ("Luftkrieg und Literatur" [1999]), Sebald's essay on the function of literature in postwar Germany, he closes by quoting Benjamin's famous description of the Angel of History. And in *Austerlitz*, the narrator loses sight of the protagonist as he (Austerlitz) leaves Paris to follow the track of his father, who is imagined to have fled the Nazis by going south, on foot, across the Pyrenees and to have perished somewhere along the way—a journey that links the imaginary father's fate with Benjamin's own. But the connection with Benjamin is also more extensive than this and more tightly joined to the topic of this study. For the particular strains of Benjamin's work that we find most persistently reproduced in Sebald's own are those that revolve around the themes of Bildung, archaeology, and photography, with a special emphasis on the double investment of all three in matters of memory and subject identity. Sebald's work moves safely, almost obsessively, within these familiar tracks. But as his more or less direct references to Benjamin already suggest, Sebald is also up against the end of those tracks, the point where their continuance becomes more and more difficult to maintain.

The concern with Bildung in both its more public and private strains is perhaps the least noticeable of these themes in Sebald's work but only because it is so pervasive as to seem almost inconspicuous. His stories are densely populated by both teachers and students whose experiences of education are overwhelmingly negative and usually aborted. Most emphatically, there is the story of Paul Bereyter, the elementary school teacher firmly devoted to the ideals of the *Wandelvögler*, whose notions of Bildung resonate with those of the Youth Movement of Benjamin's time, not least in their opposition to the strict, factorylike regimen of institutional education. Paul loses his teaching position with the rise of the Nazis, and although he returns to continue after the war, the breach proves unbridgeable, the *Nach-Bildung* ("after-Bildung" but also "imitation") a counterfeit sham in which Paul comes thoroughly to detest his students, Germany, and himself as both a teacher and a German. In the story that follows, "Ambros Adelwarth," the narrator's Aunt Fini is similarly trained as a teacher and then denied a position and forced to emigrate; in the last, "Max Aurach,"[5] the protagonist's Uncle Leo, a teacher of Greek and Latin, is dismissed from his position and emigrates to England, soon to be joined by his nephew; and the first-person narrator of this book even describes his own attempt to return to the German-speaking world as a schoolteacher, only to give up in disgust and return to his exile in England.[6] All are faced with the brutal repercussions of the Nazis' appropriation of the culture of Bildung, an appropriation most poignantly caught in the distance between two images: that in *The Emigrants* of the cockchafer case on the wall of Paul Bereyter's classroom, where the students could follow the mysterious processes of metamorphosis that so closely paralleled their own, and that of the silkworms at the end of Sebald's next novel, *The Rings of Saturn* (*Die Ringe des Saturn* [1995]), whose cultivated metamorphosis the Nazis tried to regulate and impose as an industry on the whole nation, beginning with the children in the schools. And the situation does not improve for the characters in Sebald's last novel, *Austerlitz* (2001). Three of its major figures—the narrator, protagonist, and Věra—are all teachers by training, but Věra never finds a position, Austerlitz eventually abandons his, and the narrator seems destined to follow his protagonist's lead. As Věra says, "she had indeed gone into the teaching profession and done what was necessary to maintain herself, but almost all her feelings had been extinguished, and she had not truly breathed since that time" ("Zwar habe sie ihren Schuldienst geleistet und sich um die zur Selbsterhaltung notwendigen Dinge gekümmert, aber gefühlt und geatmet habe sie seit jener Zeit nicht" [296/205]). The master narrative of Bildung has been lost, its guiding thread cut off; all attempts to carry it on into the present fail.

Official Bildung fares no better when viewed from the students' perspective. This is true even when the schooling takes place in England, as it does for both Dr. Henry Selwyn and Max Aurach in *The Emigrants* and for Jacques Austerlitz in his novel; even when the complaint addresses more the lack of discipline than the excess of order; and even when the student's course is in fact a very successful one, nurtured by at least one caring and effective mentor.[7] Indeed, the negativity to the experience is especially acute for those exiled children educated in England, mastering their lessons exceedingly well amid the general disorder. Both Dr. Henry Selwyn and Jacques Austerlitz come increasingly to realize that their investment in Bildung served as a mechanism for disavowing, or substituting for, a knowledge of themselves. Rather than developing the self, Bildung became a way of extinguishing, or at least ignoring, the self.[8] As Austerlitz puts it, "I had constantly been preoccupied by that accumulation of knowledge which I had pursued for decades, and which served as a substitute or compensatory memory" ("[Ich] war ja auch andauernd beschäftigt mit der von mir Jahrzehnte hindurch fortgesetzten Wissensanhäufung, die mir als ein ersatzweises, kompensatorisches Gedächtnis diente" [206/140]). As with Paul Bereyter's return to teaching, *Nach-Bildung* emerges more and more as a counterfeiting sham, a transmission of cultural heritage that pretends to a continuity with the past but manages only, and unsuccessfully, to deny the depth of the breach—a breach, in other words, that transforms all Bildung into *Nachbildung,* an inauthentic imitation of a merely imaginary imaginary. And we should note that, along with the educational institution, two other pillars of official Bildung seem to have fallen: classicism and psychology. Although several of the characters in *The Emigrants* travel to Greece, usually in an attempt to recapture a sense of youthfulness and wholeness that has otherwise vanished from their lives, and although the narrator of *The Rings of Saturn* reports on his own journey to the Greek Isles, the desired effect is no longer forthcoming. Dr. Henry Selwyn and his friend sit looking so long in silence at a Bild of their trip together to Crete "that the glass in the slide shattered and a dark crack fissured across the screen" ("daß zuletzt das Glas in dem Rähmchen zersprang und ein dunkler Riß über die Leinwand lief" [AU 28–29/17]); the narrator of *The Rings of Saturn* recalls only the Greek island burning, exploding, and collapsing in a consuming conflagration. As a rule—with perhaps the sole exception of the rather Benjaminian vision in "Max Aurach" of Manchester as an Elysian field haunted by children—the classical world has vanished from Sebald's landscape.[9] So too psychoanalysis, whose passing is perhaps most indelibly presented in the image of the abandoned mental hospital the narrator of *The Emigrants* visits in upstate New York, where the former head has lost faith in his discipline, particularly in the shock treatments that inevitably again recall Benjamin, but almost completely changed in the materialization of his metaphor. The shocks and hidden memories they release quite literally destroy the subject and his person without the slightest sense of redemption or cure. Many of Sebald's characters find themselves in such mental institutions, including the narrator of *The Rings of Saturn* and the protagonist of *Austerlitz*. None, however, is helped or formed by them. As with both Bildung and classics, the institutions and master narratives of psychology have also come to signify only a condition of disconnection or breakdown.[10]

For our purposes, one of the most significant effects of this breakdown that has transformed Bildung into mere Nachbildung, the German imaginary into an imaginary imaginary, is on the tradition of the Bildungsroman itself. Sebald addresses this effect directly in "Air War and Literature," in which he deplores the tendency of postwar authors to mythologize the "real horrors of the time . . . by invoking pseudohumanist philosophical notions" ("realen Schrecken der Zeit . . . mit pseudohumanistischen Philosophismen" [LL 56/50])—in other words, to assimilate the "just past" experience to the discredited representational regimes of the prewar period. The particular objects of his critique are two novels, Hermann Kasack's *The City beyond the River* (*Die Stadt hinter dem Strom* [1946]) and Hans Erich Nossack's *Nekyia*

(1947). He writes, "*Nekyia*, like *Die Stadt hinter dem Strom*, is the account of a journey to the kingdom of the dead, and like Kasack's novel the book contains teachers, mentors, masters, ancestors both male and female, much patriarchalist discipline and much prenatal obscurity. We are in the midst of that pedagogical province which, in the German tradition, extends from Goethe's idealistic vision in Wilhelm Meister of a community devoted to self-improvement through to [the Nazis themselves and their] idea of an elite operating outside and above the state as the guardian of secret knowledge" ("*Nekyia* ist, genau wie *Die Stadt hinter dem Strom*, der Bericht von einer Reise ins Totenreich, und wie bei Kasack, so gibt es auch hier Lehrer, Mentoren, Meister, Urahnen und Urmütter, sehr viel patriarchalische Disziplin und sehr viel pränatales Dunkel. Wir sind also mitten in der pädagogischen deutschen Provinz, die von Goethes idealischer Vision [bis zu den Nazis reicht und zu ihrem] Modell einer vor und über dem Staat wirksamen, ein geheimes Wissen hütenden Elite" [LL 56–57/50]). The novelistic assimilation of experience to the "so utterly discredited" representative regime of the traditional Bildungsroman is, Sebald believes, no longer permissible; the profound metaphysical fraudulence (*metaphysische Schwindel*) of the German imagination that it betrays can only be countered by a steadfast gaze bent on reality ("einen unverwandten Blick auf die Wirklichkeit" [LL 57/51]), which is to say, by an eschewal of traditional fictional forms. It is just such a gaze and such an eschewal that Sebald prizes in the work of Jean Améry and his accounts of his origins, childhood, and youth, his *Unmeisterliche Wanderjahre* ("Angaben über Herkunft, Kindheit und Jugend, über seine unmeisterlichen Wanderjahre");[11] and it is to the model of Améry that Sebald turns to write his own anti-Bildungsroman, *Austerlitz*—which, for that very reason, is also, formally, Sebald's most traditional novel.[12]

It is also, apparently, in the service of such a "steadfast gaze bent on reality" that both archaeology and photography come to play such a key role in Sebald's work, including *Austerlitz*. As so often in Benjamin, these regimes are valued for the quotidian, even banal materialist and documentary purchase they can bring to bear on idealist, classico-humanist (and, inevitably, fascist) representational strategies. But what gives Sebald's use of these two regimes—of archaeology and, especially, of photography—their particular postwar value and postmodern form is not, I would suggest, their ability to break through the artifice of abstraction (*Abstraktionskunst*) of the inherited representational regimes and ideologies of Bildung and its genre, the novel. This ability, this function, this dream of interruption and destruction, was lost along with Benjamin himself with the destruction of the war: Sebald can no more continue Benjamin's deconstructive project than he can the Bildung project. Both have equally become counterfeit shams, Nachbildung, and archaeology and photography are caught up in the same fate. Rather than mechanisms for countering "metaphysical fraudulence" with the hard facts of raw reality and immediate truth, both instead reveal an inability to escape either metaphysics or fictions, the inability to achieve the very project they set out to accomplish. Instead, and as we will see, both expose the mire of the simulacral world and self.

It is no doubt in the archaeological dimension of Sebald's works that one most readily recognizes Benjamin's landscape—one might even say Benjamin's world. But for that very reason, it is also here that one can most assuredly mark the changes in that world. As in Benjamin, the archaeological terrain through which Sebald and his companion figures wander is a decidedly modern one, a realm of instantly archaic objects and debris in the midst of the present-day world, a world already somehow empty and abandoned.[13] This is true whether the site is German, as in the ruined buildings and heaps of rubble that Sebald remembers from the Munich of his childhood; English, as with the city of Manchester described as long since deserted, now a necropolis or mausoleum, the windmills of Reedham as like relics of an extinct civilization ("wie Mahnmale einer zugrundegegangenen Zivilisation" [RS 42/30]), and the ruins of a weapons factory at Oxfordness as like the tumuli in which the mighty and powerful were buried in ancient times ("wie Hügelgräber, in denen in vorgeschichtlichler Zeit große Machthaber beigesetzt worden waren" [RS 281/236]); or American, where the empty and all but abandoned town of Tom's River is slowly being buried by encroaching sand dunes and upstate New York is covered with the ruins of another world long since forsaken ("[die] Ruinen einer anderen, längstaufgegebenen Welt" [AU 153/105]). But regardless of where such ruins are located—and more problematically, regardless of whether the artifacts and their burial are imagined to have been caused by human or natural forces[14]—the specter of the destruction of World War II seems to permeate everything, to provide the base condition for the ruined status of the modern world—even the industrial ruins of Manchester, the abandoned and obsolete realm of nineteenth-century technology, emerge as a displaced replica of the Germany destroyed by the fascists and the war. This gives a new, completely changing twist to the otherwise quite Benjaminian (or Baudelarian) sentiment, "It takes just one awful second, and an entire epoch passes" ("Eine Schrecksekunde, und ein ganzes Zeitalter ist vorbei" [RS 44/31]); it also provides the defining difference between Sebald's often Atgetlike black-and-white photos and those of Atget himself.[15] For while Benjamin seeks the archaeological in the classical facades of new Berlin or in the outmoded furniture of its bourgeois homes, and Atget seeks it in the isolated details or overlooked buildings of Old Paris, for Sebald the ruins—the archaeological—are far less figural than actual. Sebald's figures wander past buildings reduced by bombs to facades with no interior behind them at all and through old cities still in rubble amid the rising structures of the new.[16]

The overshadowing role of World War II in the history of destruction that has turned the twentieth century itself into archaeological territory has also, inevitably, changed the nature of the archaeologist's excavations within these dead cities and their ruins. To begin with, it has radically altered the alliance of archaeology and national identity from that of the prewar period. Archaeology is still a collective project, one deeply invested in matters of national identity. But now that project has become a more or less compulsory and unpleasant one, something the Germans—and the English and the French—must do to come to terms with their past, their common guilt and common loss; which is to say that archaeology is no longer oriented toward the glorified justification of the nation but toward acknowledging its dirt or, as Sebald puts it, the slagheaps of our collective existence ("die Abraumhalden unserer kollektiven Existenz" [LL 67/60]). For this very reason, however, because of the sense of historical burden, the archaeological project has also become a more or less avoided one, a project that, when realized, is accomplished almost inadvertently, as an almost accidental byproduct of its intended avoidance. And crucially, this is true not only of European (and especially German) society as a whole but also of those individual figures who seem charged with confronting that avoidance, that disavowal—such as those solitary, narrating Sebaldian *flâneurs,* whose archaeological investigations are peculiarly and inescapably weighted with this particular national-historical task. For one of the ruling ironies and tragedies of Sebald's postwar world is that the individual has come to introject and reproduce precisely the condition of disconnection from the past that society as a whole has so culpably come to embrace, and all his efforts to overcome the one are thwarted by his own unintended repetition.

We can see this changed condition for the archaeological project most clearly in two examples from *Austerlitz:* the account of the history of Broad Street Station in London and that of the new Bibliothèque Nationale in Paris, both of which, for all their different national settings, necessarily resonate with the German history of postwar reconstruction that Sebald makes the particular subject of "Air War and Literature." In the case of the Broad Street Station, the renovation work that was begun in 1984 in an effort to modernize the setting, and so in a sense to replace the past, began with the demolition work that brought to light over four hundred skeletons beneath a taxi stand ("unter einem Taxistand über vierhundert Skelette zutage [brachte]" [192/130]) and so immediately transformed the intended construction site into an archaeological one (Austerlitz comes to talk with the archaeologists), the intended foundation of the transporting new into an excavation of the mournful, enmiring past. As so often in Sebald's world, the slightest scratch of the surface suffices to unearth the buried past, including the scratch that would somehow scratch it out; indeed, the very violence of the demolition with which every reconstruction project begins reproduces the violent history it would demolish and deny. In the case of the Bibliothèque Nationale, the "Babylonian" monument intended to celebrate the new France of Mitterrand, an official manifestation of the increasingly important urge to break with everything that still has some living connection to the past ("offizielle Manifestation des immer dringender sich anmeldenden Bedürfnisses, mit all dem ein Ende zu machen, was noch ein Leben habe an der Vergangenheit" [404/286]), was built, so Austerlitz tells us, on the site of the extensive warehousing complex to which the Germans brought all the loot they had taken from the homes of the Jews of Paris ("große Lager, in dem die Deutschen das gesamte von ihnen aus den Wohnungen der Pariser Juden geholte Beutegut zusammenbrachten" [407/288]). "The whole affair," we are told, "was buried in the most literal sense beneath the foundations of our pharaonic President's Grand Bibliothèque" ("[D]ie ganze Geschichte [ist] im wahrsten Wortsinn begraben unter den Fundamenten der Grand Bibliothèque unseres pharaonischen Presidenten" [409/289]). But while the building itself is ostensibly designed to break with this past, to cover up the hidden historical strata on which it is founded, it nonetheless, even if inadvertently, also reproduces its archaeological foundations in its very structure: not only in its architectural design—which, for all its upward (and onward) sweep, still enforces on the observer from the heights of the so-called belvedere a downward look at "the entire urban agglomeration which has risen over the millenia from the land beneath its foundations, now completely hollowed out" ("die gesamte im Laufe der Jahrtausende aus dem jetzt völlig ausgehöhlten Untergrund herausgewachsene Stadtagglomeration" [405/288]) and so too enforces an awareness "of the various layers that have been superimposed on each other to form the carapace of the city" ("von den verschiedenen Schichten, die dort drunten auf dem Grund der Stadt übereinandergewachsen sind" [407/288])—but also in its very function and organization, its complex system of storage for cultural artifacts inevitably recalling and reproducing the Nazi warehouses they were meant to efface and replace, as Sebald further underscores by juxtaposing his description of this library with that of the one where the Nazi records of Theresienstadt are currently stored.[17] Not for nothing does he refer to the building as pharaonic and Babylonian. The library reproduces the very imperial past it would break with, becomes the instantiation of the very archaeology it would deny—even as, for Austerlitz, the newly built train station in England necessarily recalls the death trains and diasporic deportations of wartime Europe. And again, as Sebald emphasizes in "Air War and Literature," this rebuilding in both England and France is always reflective of the far more massive campaign of rebuilding in Germany after the war, which for all its attempted disavowal of the wartime destruction merely continues it. As he says, "every reconstruction is a second liquidation," every new building a reenactment of the ruin it would replace.[18]

The inevitable reappearance of the disavowed past in every disavowing present structure, which is to say, the archaeological dimension to every (post)modern moment, is only half the melancholy equation of Sebald's world. For while the past seems impossible to escape and to represent itself in every present moment, it also proves impossible to reproduce, to make present in its representation, and it is this circumstance that lends the true sense of postmodern paradox to Sebald's claim that every reconstruction is tantamount to a second liquidation. The example of the Broad Street Station illustrates this particularly well and underscores how the archaeological dimension to Sebald's world does not so much secure the presence of the past as it dissolves it into the purely imaginary (or, if you will, the epiphenomenal). The demolition work of 1984 brings to light the four hundred skeletons that bring in the archaeologists. But the skeletons are all jumbled together. We are told, "more and more keep coming, a never-ending succession of them . . . graves are dug through existing graves to accommodate them, until all the bones in the cemetery lie jumbled together . . . [so] that on average the skeletons of eight people had been found in every cubic meter of earth removed from the [archaeologists'] trench" ("es kommen ja immer neue nach, in unendlicher Folge, zu deren Unterbringung zuletzt . . . Gräber durch Gräber gegraben werden, bis auf dem ganzen Acker die Gebeine kreuz und quer durcheinander liegen . . . [so] daß in jedem Kubikmeter Abraum, den man aus dieser Grube [der Archäologen] entfernte, die Gerippe von durchschnittlich acht Menschen gefunden worden sind" [192/130]). As a result, the specific history of the destructive social practices of nineteenth-century industrial culture—or even more specifically, the history of the destruction of World War II— that Sebald wants to uncover and to see reembodied (or reconstructed) in the new train station itself—this specific history is lost in its archaeological extension, its generalization, even as it is also, from a slightly different perspective, lost in its specificity in the representation of the present train station. "Hard facts" are precisely what we do not get—only abstractions, generalizations, and simulacra. The same is true in the case of Sebald's archaeological landscape in general, which while necessarily recalling in its every ruin the specter and traces of World War II, also insures that the destruction of World War II has no specificity, no singular reality, only an endlessly reproducible, and reproduced, metaphysical presence. And from a slightly different perspective, it is also true of the Bibliothèque Nationale, which for all its spectral reproduction of the Nazis' warehouses nonetheless reduces that previous "raw reality" to nothing but a representation in its representation. Very much like the images of Pompeii that are described by both Freud and Benjamin, the images of the immediate past in Sebald seem to disappear as soon as they surface into the present, lost on the one hand in the jumble of the more general past and on the other in the reconstructions of the representing present.

We can see the same set of paradoxes—that the reconstruction that would deny the past destruction ends up reproducing it and that the reconstruction of that same past ends up effacing it—in Sebald's depiction of old houses such as Somerleyton Hall in *The Rings of Saturn* or Iver Grove in *Austerlitz,* old houses that form something of a counterpoint to the new buildings just discussed. Sebald specifically says of Somerleyton Hall, "many ages are superimposed here and co-exist" ("viele Zeiten haben sich hier überlagert und bestehen nebeneinander fort" [RS 49/36]), and he says something very similar of Iver Grove, that all moments of time have coexisted simultaneously ("daß sämtliche Zeitmomente gleichzeitig nebeneinander existierten" [152/101]). Such houses in Sebald's landscape highlight the archaeological past permeating the present and so give the lie to a present that would disavow it, but they do so in a way that itself proves something of a lie and a fiction. The attempt to use such houses, qua archaeological sites, to represent the presence of the past ends up amounting to its own denial, to an unwillingness to accept the irretrievable pastness of the past, and so too the necessary lie or fiction to its present representation. Such, for instance, is the case of the billiard room and nurseries of Iver Grove, closed off in 1941 and then reopened decades later, where, we are told, nothing had changed in any way ("nichts war . . . in irgendeiner Weise verändert"), sealed away from the flow of the hours and days and the succession of generations ("vom Fluß der Stunden und Tage und vom Wechsel der Generationen" [157–58/107–8]). Such timeless spaces are common in Sebald. In *Austerlitz,* we see them again in the protagonist's ragings against the reality of time and history in the Greenwich Tower, ironically undercut by the narrator's comment, "It was around three-thirty as I left the Observatory with Austerlitz" ("Es war gegen halb vier Uhr nachmittags . . . als ich die Sternwarte mit Austerlitz verließ" [152/101]); in the basement of the Liverpool Station, where Austerlitz has his hallucinatory fantasy that leads to his "remembering" his childhood past; and, most problematically, in Věra's apartment in Prague, where nothing, apparently, has changed in the last sixty years, Věra included. But rather than being spaces for the emergence of a revelatory, past-restoring truth, they always prove instead (or also) the sites for a self-deceiving, past and present denying fiction.[19] The sight of the time-exempted rooms in Iver Grove inspires its proprietor to run outside and fire his rifle several times at the little clock tower on the coach house, a gesture clearly reminiscent of Benjamin's similar image in the "Concept of History" essay. But the gesture no longer has any redemptive or revolutionary value; it only underscores its own futility and the sad facticity of the present it would deny ("the marks he made are visible to this day" ["man (könnte) die Einschläge heute noch sehen" (161/108)]).

Perhaps the most fascinating and pervasive topos for the problem of archaeological time in Sebald's work, and the one most clearly evocative of Benjamin, is the matter of dust. Dust is everywhere in Sebald's world: it hovers in the projector's light beam during Dr. Henry Selwyn's slide show of his trip to Crete; it gently covers the abandoned apartment of Paul Bereyter in Switzerland and the Solomons' house on Long Island; and in upstate New York, the entire psychiatric sanatorium of Dr. Abramsky is turning to dust before his eyes. In *The Rings of Saturn,* all the furnishings of the Chinese emperor's palace were thick with dust, as if the house had long since been deserted; the house in Ireland where the narrator once stayed is coated with a velvety layer of dust; near the end of his journey, the same narrator is suddenly overtaken, almost suffocated, by a storm of dust. In *Austerlitz,* dust covers the secluded rooms of Iver Grove, the deathbed of Austerlitz's foster mother, and perhaps most poignantly, the writing desk in Marienbad, where Austerlitz is seized by the sudden desire to have the surrounding, now extinct Bohemian volcanoes erupt and cover everything with their black dust. The motif ramifies outward in Sebald's work, intersecting and interweaving with his equally frequent images of burying sand, ash, and snow, but it always retains its Benjaminian roots, its recollections of the dust covering the trees of Berlin, the furniture of its bourgeois apartments, raining down from its train stations over schoolyards, or settling inexorably over the streets, buildings, and people of Paris, "just as at Pompeii." As in Benjamin's, the accumulated layers of dust in Sebald's world lend an almost instant archaeological dimension to the most recent past, bespeaking a lost, abandoned, peopleless world. As one of his characters says of Flaubert, "For him, every speck of dust weighed as heavy as the Atlas mountains" ("jedes Stäubchen wog für ihn soviel wie das Atlasgebirge" [RS 17/8]), and for Sebald too the thinnest layer of dust covers as completely as the ash of Vesuvius.

Susan Buck-Morss says that in Benjamin dust "provides material evidence that history has not budged. Indeed, history stands so still, it gathers dust."[20] But dust signals more than this in Benjamin, and more in Sebald as well. History not only gathers dust; it generates it. It continually returns to dust and produces the very dust that covers the past over. At one point in *Austerlitz,* Sebald mentions Maxime du Camp—the same du Camp who traveled as a photographer to Africa with Flaubert—and his claim that the deserts of the Orient are formed from the dust of the dead ("aus dem Staub der Toten" [406/287]). And there is certainly a sense in Sebald that dust not only inters the landscape, and so buries the dead, but also is itself a form of death and as such a form of violence too. Indeed, the violence of dust (or sand or ash) proves as palpable in Sebald as the violence of the past it covers over, as we see, for example, in Abramsky's fantasy of his collapsing sanatorium or in Austerlitz's fantasy of the erupting volcanoes or in the dust storm at the end of *The Rings of Saturn*. For our purposes, this violence is nowhere more apparent than in the role of dust in the thematics of forgetting and oblivion, a special instance of both its deathfulness and its destruction. Dust is not only the emblem, the index of all that has been forgotten and left untouched and unexplored in the past, willfully consigned to neglect and oblivion, to the earth and archaeology. It is also the very agent of obliteration, and as a result, the past not only stands still, unchanged, but it is also continually, actively, turning to dust and disappearing. This leads to something of a paradox in Sebald's work, where there is both an undeniably utopic dimension to dust, most poignantly captured in the repeated, wishful images of the desert that seem to promise precisely that timeless realm so often sought out by his characters, and a distinctly dystopic dimension, where it serves as the preserving evidence of our neglect of the past, indeed too as the destroyer of all evidence of our destructive past.

In all these various turns of death, violence, and forgetfulness, dust in Sebald seems merely to amplify and extend the dust in Benjamin; in fact, in both it lends something more than vaguely Baroque to the narrated landscape. But there are at least two further turns to the motif that seem peculiarly Sebaldian and peculiarly postmodern. The first is most readily illustrated by an example from *Austerlitz* that involves not dust per se but a closely related motif, namely, snow, but the point holds good for dust as well, indeed, for all instances of archaeological burial and retrieval in Sebald's work. As a child, when faced with the image of how "snow fell through the branches of trees, soon to enshroud the entire forest floor" ("der Schnee durch das Gezweig der Bäume herabrieselt und bald den ganzen Waldboden bedeckt"), Austerlitz would worry, so Věra tells him, "But if it's all white, how do the squirrels know where they've buried their hoard? Those were your very words, said Věra, the question that constantly troubled you. Indeed how do the squirrels know, what do we know ourselves, how do we remember, and what is it we find in the end?" ("Aber wenn alles weiß sein wird, wie wissen dann die Eichhörnchen, wo sie ihren Vorrat verborgen haben? Genau so, sagte Věra, habe die von mir immer wieder wiederholte, stets von neuem mich beunruhigende Frage gelautet. Ja, wie wissen die Eichhörnchen das, und was wissen wir überhaupt, und wie erinnern wir uns, und was entdecken wir nicht am Ende?" [295/204]). The answer, of course, is that the squirrels do *not* know; much of their buried stores they never find, and those they do dig up are as likely to have been buried, and so to belong, to some other squirrels as to themselves, a jumbling of "finds" much like the skeletons at Broad Street Station, where it takes a willful act of imagination to assign a personal, determinative specificity to the uncovered hoard. For all the apparent similarities, this is a far cry from Benjamin's model of more or less random searching with the spade, sometimes succeeding in finding something but often not, for in Benjamin the site itself was always assumed to be securely one's own and so the recovered past identifiably one's own as well. But in Sebald, it is just this personal connection to the site that has been lost beneath the snow—and dust— and as a result, one never knows to whom the uncovered past belongs and what possibly flawed, imaginary constructions one is engaged in by trying to identify with what one finds.[21] This leads to a far different and more anxious equation of the individual and collectively typical than anything we find in Benjamin (or Mann or Freud), for it is always haunted by the spectral possibility that the equation, the identification—and hence too the identity—might be a false one, a purely imaginary linkage to a general, but not personal, past.

The second turn is more specific to the motif of dust but also ramifies outward into Sebald's archaeological landscape in general, and in specifically postmodern ways. The turn is this: whereas dust or, rather, the accumulation of dust is a sure sign of forgetfulness, of a kind of willed and culpable obliviousness, and as such a form of violence toward the past, so too is dusting. People, and especially Germans, are continually dusting in Sebald's works, trying to brush away the layered dust and dirt to present a clean, pure, and vehemently present world to themselves; dusting and cleaning are as much acts of denying history and of willful obliteration as is the allowing of dust to cover and conceal what came before.[22] And whether it will or no, the excavations and "dusting off" of archaeology fall prey to the same paradox. There has always been a sense of violence to archaeological excavations, a kind of second destruction of what was already destroyed; one need only think of Schliemann's famous trench and wagonloads of carted-off debris to realize this. But in Sebald's post–World War II world, the stakes are even higher, the dusting off more insidious, not only because the dusting off reproduces the same compulsion for purity and order that produced the past horrors it is meant to efface, much as does the building of the Bibliothèque Nationale or of Germany's own "modern" cities at the site of their shameful ruins, but also because every time an object is dusted off and returned to the present—to Benjamin's "sober rooms of later insight"—it becomes something else: something *present,* an object of display, an emblem of the past, a representation of itself in a way that denies both itself and the past. It becomes present, and then there is only a present; it becomes a token, and then there are only tokens. There is, for example, something vaguely obscene in the image of the polished knickknacks in the antique store in Theresienstadt, already part of a present economy different from the past Nazi one that provided them, or in the vast transformation of Nazi horrors into a museal and archival business, carefully preserving and presenting its artifacts to the visiting public: everything already no longer itself but its own simulacrum.

Significantly, though hardly surprisingly, the archaeological metaphor, with all its paradoxes, is also carried over by Sebald into the spheres of both aesthetic representation and individual psychology. And as in Benjamin—and Mann and Freud—this carryover cannot merely be understood as metaphorical trope. Rather, the cultural conditions that regulate or determine the broader external social context are shown necessarily to reproduce themselves and to determine the more narrow internal personal sphere as well, in the realms of both art and subjectivity. The most elaborated example of the former comes in Sebald's description of the painting practices of Max Aurach in *The Emigrants.*[23] The archaeological appears in two, apparently opposite forms in Aurach's work. First, we are told, "Since he applied the paint thickly, and then repeatedly scraped it off the canvas as his work proceeded, the floor was covered with a largely hardened and encrusted deposit of droppings, mixed with coal dust . . . in places resembling the flow of lava" ("Da er die Farben in großen Mengen aufträgt und sie im Fortgang der Arbeit immer wieder von der Leinwand herunterkratzt, ist der Bodenbelag bedeckt von einer . . . mit Kohlestaub untermischten, weitgehend bereits verhärteten und verkrusteten Masse, die stellenweise einem Lavaausfluß gleicht" [237/161]).[24] Aurach claims that this tell, and not the paintings themselves, was the true product of his continual endeavors ("das wahre Ergebnis darstelle seiner fortwährenden Be-mühung"), and the narrator adds, "I often thought his prime concern was to increase the dust" ("In der Tat dachte mir oft, es ginge ihm vorab um die Vermehrung des Staubs" [238/161]). This production—or as it is also called, this exercise in destruction (*Zerstörungsstudie* [269/180])—is variously evaluated, in keeping with the ambiguity of archaeology elsewhere in Sebald. On the one hand, Aurach tells us that he loved dust and debris more than anything in the world, that he found nothing more unbearable than a well-dusted house, and that it was extremely important to him that nothing should change at his place of work, that everything should remain as it was ("daß nichts an seinem Arbeitsplatz sich verändere, daß alles so bleibe, wie es vordem war"), with nothing added but the debris of his painting and the dust that continually fell, as a kind of testimony to the twinned truth that nothing ever changes and everything dissolves, little by little, into noth-ingness ("Hauch um Hauch, sich auflöst in nichts" [238/161]). His studio becomes an archaeological site, recording both the processes of preservation and destruction; it is, as it were, the pile of debris thrown up before Benjamin's Angel by the storm of progress, here thrown up before the artist by the progress of his work. In other words, it is an oc-casion of truth, of testimony. On the other hand, however, Aurach also calls his tell the most palpable proof of his failure. It records the failure inherent in his desire for places where things remain undisturbed ("wo die Dinge ungestört daliegen dürfen"), the introjected failure to con-front, to dig up the past, to disturb things beneath their built-up pro-tective layers, the failure inherent in the desire (evident in his painting) *not* to represent but to efface, to bury. The accumulated dust and de-bris are the proof of the destructive act Aurach engages in to avoid the destructive acts to his own past; his archaeological site is the image not of truth but of denial, not of testimony but of silence, not of represen-tation but of obliteration.[25]

The second form in which the archaeological appears in Aurach's work comes in the paintings themselves. They too represent an inter-woven process of creation and destruction, representation and obliter-ation. Sebald describes a process almost equally devoted to applying layers of charcoal dust and then erasing them, a process in which Au-rach both continually destroys the Bild he has drawn (badly damaging the surface as he does so) and seeks to excavate (*herauszugraben*) the image from the accumulated strata left behind. The result, we are told, is that a given portrait might have up to forty variants smudged one after another back into the paper, with every new attempt overdrawn upon them, so that an onlooker might well feel that the finished Bild had evolved "from a long lineage of grey ancestral faces, rendered unto ash but still there, as ghostly presences, on the harried paper" ("aus einer langen Ahnenreihe grauer, eingeäschterter, in dem zerschundenen Papier nach wie vor herumgeisternder Gesichter" [239–40/162]). This seems, as it were, the postmodern, painterly equivalent to the kind of typologizing or templating composite photography we encountered in Mann, Galton, and Freud and as such gives some indication of the affinities between the archaeological and photographic dimensions found in Sebald's work. But it also seems the painterly equivalent of the archaeology at the Broad Street Station in *Austerlitz*, with its jumble of excavated skulls and with the same disconcerting associations: the foregrounded sense of destruction and effacement to the project, so different from anything in Mann or Freud and, along with that, the sense that the final portrait is not a record of the uncovered identity of the artist's model but only of what remained ultimately unknowable for him, the artist ("für ihn [d.h., den Künstler] letztlich unbegreiflich" [239/162]). The singularity of the subject gives way to the archaeological record, which is itself only the accumulated debris of traces that never succeeded and did not survive.

Archaeology also functions as a figure for the processes of memory for the individual subject and so too for the construction—or deconstruction—of individual identity. Here especially we can see how the individual has introjected the condition of disconnection from the past that modern European, and especially German, society has suffered as a whole. The archaeological metaphor for individual memory, including its relation to the broader and more concrete archaeology of postwar society in general, is implicit in the crucial fantasy scene experienced by Austerlitz in the abandoned, deserted underground rooms of the Liverpool Station, when he first feels he has reconnected with his earlier and then forgotten—deliberately forgotten—life. But it is also and more explicitly present in the encounter with Michael Hamburger in *The Rings of Saturn*, in ways that adumbrate the case of the later work. Like so many of Sebald's characters, including Austerlitz, Hamburger left Germany as a child during the 1930s and found himself transported to a foreign country, his memories of his boyhood and native country gradually buried, "little by little," beneath the new identity he came to assume in his new setting. Like Austerlitz, he seems to conspire in the obliteration, the forgetting of his past, willingly allowing it to disappear beneath the accumulated sediment of his new self and surroundings, not least through Bildung. But also like Austerlitz, this condition comes slowly to oppress him, to undermine his ability to sustain a sense of self-identity of the kind posited by Bildung, and the intolerability of this condition drives him into an effort to excavate his lost boyhood, his "Berlin Childhood" ("Berliner Kindheit" [RS 210/177]). All he can recover from his buried past are broken, isolated fragments: the mane of a Prussian lion, a Prussian nanny, caryatids bearing the globe on their shoulders, and a series of well-nigh Proustian smells and shapes. But unlike in Proust—or for that matter, in Benjamin—these isolated images and sensations yield neither memory nor recovered identity. As Hamburger puts it, "Whenever a shift in our spiritual life occurs and fragments such as these surface, we believe we can remember. But in reality, of course, memory fails us. Too many buildings have fallen down, too much rubble has been heaped up, the moraines and deposits are insuperable" ("Immer wenn aufgrund irgendeiner im Seelenleben vor sich gegangenen Verschiebung ein solches Bruchstück in einem auftaucht, dann glaubt man, man könne sich erinnern. Aber in Wirklichkeit erinnert man sich natürlich nicht. Zu viele Bauwerke sind eingestürzt, zuviel Schutt ist aufgehäuft, unüberwindlich sind die Ablagerungen und Moränen" [RS 211/177]).[26]

As Hamburger says, much of this rubble is real, and the lost memory of his youth is a "vestigial image" of the ruins of Berlin itself. But by the same token, much of the recovered past identity he might seek to reconstruct at the site of those ruins, those surviving fragments, proves as simulacric and fundamentally false as we find in the German cities themselves.[27] For the insuperability of the deposits, the irrecoverability of what has been buried, does not arrest the project of memory and identity building. Indeed, as Sebald observes, it engines it, fostering an almost pathological hypermnesia in a past otherwise emptied of content ("in einer ansonsten ausgeleerten Vergangenheit eine ans Pathologische grenzende Hypermnesie"),[28] what he elsewhere calls Korsakov's syndrome, an illness which causes lost memories to be replaced by fantastic inventions ("[ein] Syndrom, bei dem der Erinnerungsverlust durch phantastische Erfindungen ausgeglichen wird" [AU 149/102]). What this irrecoverability entails, then, is a change to the conditions and results of subject formation, increasing the dependence on abstraction and imagination in the absence of actuality, Nachbildung in the place of Bildung. In many ways (and in keeping with the connections between buildings and selves already noted), the project of subject formation becomes indistinguishable from the project of building a model of the Temple of Jerusalem that Sebald describes immediately after his meeting with Michael Hamburger. The model is fashioned on the basis of archaeological data, but the interpretation of the supposed significance of that data is constantly shifting. "In the end," says the model maker, "our entire work is based on nothing but ideas, ideas that change over the years and that time and again cause one to tear down what one had thought to be finished, and begin again from scratch" ("Unsere ganze Arbeit beruht doch letzten Endes auf nichts als auf Ideen, Ideen, die sich im Verlauf der Zeit andauernd verändern und die einem darum nicht selten veranlassen, das, was man für bereits vollendet gehalten hat, wieder einzureißen und von neuem anzufangen" [RS 291/245]). The dependence of the reconstruction work on an abstract discursive framework, its only tenuous, indeed imaginary, connection to the past it would reconstruct, results in an unstable self as well, a tentative past whose only imaginary basis leaves it always open to error, falsehood, and misidentification, to an ever-readiness to begin again from scratch, based on the ever-present possibility that one has only inaccurate ideas for one's model, one's past, one's self.

> One photographs things in order to drive them out of the mind. My stories are a kind of closing of the eyes.
>
> Man photographiert Dinge, um sie aus dem Sinn zu verscheuchen. Meine Geschichten sind eine Art von Augenschließen.
>
> Kafka[29]

Much the same conditions that determine and reconfigure the field of archaeology in Sebald's work also shape and refashion the field of photography therein, and for the same reason, photography in Sebald proves just as distanced from its role in such modernist figures as Mann, Freud, and Benjamin and just as condemned to a postmodern condition of simulation, of *Nachbildung*. This is particularly revealing because, at first blush, Sebald seems rather self-consciously to be participating with Mann, Freud, and their contemporaries in associating photography with memory, or rather, with the remembering subject (i.e., with the subject who, in remembering, develops his self-identity). After all, Sebald's stories, almost all retrospective and obsessed with self-identity, are filled with photographs and with characters pouring over photographs, scrutinizing them for clues about the past, even with characters such as Austerlitz obsessively taking photographs as part of their project of self-construction.[30] Moreover, in *The Emigrants,* Max Aurach relates the startling anecdote of how "the British Medical Association archives contained the description of an extreme case of silver poisoning: in the 1930s there was a photographic lab assistant in Manchester whose body had absorbed so much silver in the course of a lengthy professional life that he had become a kind of photographic plate, which was apparent in the fact . . . that the man's face and hands turned blue in strong light, or, as one might say, developed" ("Im Archiv der Britischen Medizinischen Gesellschaft werde . . . die Beschreibung eines extremen Falls einer Vergiftung aufbewahrt, derzufolge es in den dreißiger Jahren in Manchester einen Fotolaboranten gegeben haben soll, dessen Körper im Verlauf seiner langjährigen Berufspraxis derart viel Silber assimiliert hatte, daß er zu einer Art fotografischer Platte geworden war, was sich . . . daran zeigte, daß das Gesicht und die Hände dieses Laboranten bei starkem Lichteinfall blau einliefen, sich also sozusagen entwickelten" [AU 244/164]), an image that manages to join Sebald's fascination with dust with a seeming literalization of the modernists' photo-metaphor for self-development. And we might pair this with the passage in *Austerlitz* in which the protagonist explains his own early fascination with photographic processes: "In my photographic work I was always especially entranced, said Austerlitz, by the moment when the shadows of reality, so to speak, emerge out of nothing on the exposed paper, as memories do in the middle of the night, darkening again if you try to cling to them, just like a photographic print left in the developing bath too long" ("Besonders in den Bann gezogen hat mich bei der photographischen Arbeit stets der Augenblick, in dem man auf dem belichteten Papier die Schatten der Wirklichkeit sozusagen aus dem Nichts hervorkommen sieht, genau wie Erinnerungen, die ja auch inmitten der Nacht in uns auftauchen und die sich dem, der sie festhalten will, so schnell wieder verdunkeln, nichts anders als ein photographischer Druck, den man zu lang im Entwicklungsbad liegenläßt" [117/77]), a passage that clearly echoes the evanescent, self-consuming quality of photographic memories we observed particularly in Mann.

But despite these parallels, and rather in keeping with the actual inclusion of photographs in the narratives—something not even found in Benjamin despite his interest in photography per se[31]—photography in Sebald in fact proves not a model for memory but rather, I would suggest, a destructive counter to it, something like we find prophesied by Plato for the catastrophic effect on memory of writing, with his apparently exaggerated fears of a narcotized subject completely dependent on external tokens or souvenirs and incapable of remembering himself and his living cultural inheritance, or like what we find proposed by Kracauer, who, as mentioned, was almost alone among the modernists in opposing the processes of memory and photography and who claimed, "A shudder runs through the viewer of old photographs. For they make visible not the knowledge of the original but the spatial configuration of a moment: what appears in the photograph is not the person but the sum of what can be subtracted from him. The photograph annihilates the person by portraying him, and were person and portrayal to converge, the person would cease to exist" ("Es fröstelt den Betrachter alter Photographien. Denn sie veranschaulichen nicht die Erkenntnis des Originals, sondern die räumliche Konfiguration eines Augenblickes; nicht der Mensch tritt in seiner Photographie heraus, sondern die Summe dessen, was von ihm abzuziehen ist. Sie vernichten ihn, indem sie ihn abbildet, und fiele er mit ihr zusammen, so wäre er nicht vorhanden").[32] Something like this seems to be happening with the medium of photography in Sebald's work as well, especially in *Austerlitz*. Authentic memory is being erased, replaced by inauthentic simulacra, and no longer securely fixed in the subject's own psyche, and along with memory is going all secure sense of the self and of a narrative that might fix that self.[33]

The opposition between photography—or, more generally, mimetic representation—and the authentic recording of "reality" is to be found everywhere in Sebald's work. It permeates his understanding of art, of history, and of individual identity from his first fictional work to his last. Perhaps the best illustration of this first point (the understanding of art) comes in a passage from *The Rings of Saturn* describing not a photograph but a painting, Rembrandt's *Anatomy Lesson*, but, as we will see, the basic claim made applies equally to photography, and writing as well. Sebald is concerned to foreground the far-from-simple inaccuracy of this famous painting, and he begins by noticing how, in it, none of the observers is looking at the actual body being dissected but instead all are directing their gaze "just past it to focus on the open anatomical atlas in which the appalling physical facts are reduced to a diagram, a schematic plan of the human body" ("[die Blicke] gehen, freilich haarscharf, an ihm vorbei auf den aufgeklappten anatomischen Atlas, in dem die entsetzliche Körperlichkeit reduziert ist auf ein Diagramm, auf ein Schema des Menschen" [RS 23/13]). The real is, as it were, being overlooked, unseen or disregarded, and replaced by a representation, a generalized and schematized simulacrum that substitutes for the particular real. And as Sebald notes, this process of substitution perpetrated by the observers' gaze finds its way into the very subject matter of the painting in such a way that "this otherwise true-to-life painting turns into a crass misrepresentation at the exact center point of its meaning" ("das sonst, wenn man so sagen kann, nach dem Leben gemalte Bild genau in seinem Bedeutungszentrum . . . in die krasseste Fehlkonstruktion umkippt" [RS 27/16]). The left hand of the criminal body being dissected in the painting is not (and cannot be) the actual hand of that body but is instead a mirror image, an upside down right hand, seemingly out of proportion to the rest of the body. It is, Sebald says, a transposition of the image being looked at in the anatomical atlas onto the site of the body being represented. A process of substitution is at stake in which the individual real is being violently replaced by the schematized simulacrum, is actually being eliminated or destroyed by the competing copy in the copy (i.e., the painting), and this, as Sebald stresses, in a painting whose verisimilitude has always been much admired (*vielgerühmt*) and taken for granted.

The same basic process of the annihilating replacement of the real by its representing copy that Sebald describes for Rembrandt's painting he also describes for the written histories of the Germans recollecting World War II. In "Air War and Literature," Sebald addresses the Germans' lost power of accurate memory occasioned by their traumatic war experiences, wherein the survivors' impressions seem to have been erased by the very violence of their impact and, at the same time, to have given rise to an almost pathological hypermnesia in a past otherwise empty of content.[34] To fill this void, the Germans have recourse to a language, a mode of writing, remembering, and representing that is heavily laden with inherited clichés, and as Sebald tells it, these clichés are deployed not so much to serve memory as to banish it, not so much to render as to cover up and neutralize experiences beyond our ability to comprehend ("die über das Fassungsvermögen gehenden Erlebnisse zu verdecken und zu neutralisieren" [LL 32/25]). Such clichés, which work to "mythologize" experience, do not arise out of an extraordinary use of language but rather precisely out of the most ordinary. The very process of verbal representation destroys the reality of what it intends to depict or, as Sebald puts it, "the apparently unimpaired ability of everyday language to go on functioning as usual raises doubts about the authenticity of the experiences they record" ("das anscheinend unbeschadte Weiterfunktionieren der Normalsprache . . . ruft Zweifel herauf an der Authentizität der in ihr aufgehobenen Erfahrung" [LL 32/25]). Crucially, this is true not only of the eyewitness accounts of such events—Sebald's own descriptions of the air-raids are notably as saturated with clichés (even the same clichés) as those he holds up for our viewing—nor is it true only of our experience of our own history, the history we know firsthand. As Austerlitz's history teacher tells him,

> All of us, even when we think we have noted every detail, resort to set pieces which have already been staged often enough by others. We try to reproduce the reality, but the harder we try, the more we find the pictures that make up the stock-in-trade of the spectacle of history forcing themselves upon us. . . . Our concern with history is a concern with the preformed images already imprinted on our brain, images at which we keep staring while the truth lies elsewhere, away from it all.

> Wir alle, auch diejenigen, die meinen, selbst auf das Geringfügigste geachtet zu haben, behelfen uns mit Versatzstücken, die von anderen schon oft genug auf der Bühne herumgeschoben worden sind. Wir versuchen, die Wirklichkeit wiederzugeben, aber je angestrengter wir es versuchen, desto mehr drängt sich uns das auf, was auf dem historischen Theater von jeher zu sehen war. . . . Unsere Beschäftigung mit der Geschichte [ist] eine Beschäftigung mit immer schon vorgefertigten, in das innere unserer Köpfe gravierten Bildern, auf die wir andauernd starrten, während die Wahrheit irgendwoanders . . . liegt. (109/71–72)

These clichés of everyday language and preformed, stock-in-trade images of history are, as it were, the functional equivalents of the master templating quality of photographic *clichés* we explored in the modernists; they are also, clearly, aligned with the schematized arm in Rembrandt's painting and the jumble of skeletons Sebald describes at contemporary archaeological digs. But whereas such templating for the modernists was felt to bring forth an essential truth about the individual subject and event—a truth, moreover, crucial to Bildung—for Sebald it seems instead to signify the essential falseness of recorded experience, the fundamental loss of the authentic and the singular in the annihilating mix of simulacric Bilder.[35]

What holds true of the representation of history writ large holds true for the representation of history writ small; the individual too, in recalling his own past, is at the mercy of those preformed images that negate authentic memory. This is the subject of the first section of Sebald's first novel, *Vertigo* (*Schwindel. Gefühle* [1990]), centered on the figure of Henri Beyle (aka Stendhal), whose notes, we are told, provide eloquent proof of the various difficulties entailed in the act of recollection ("demonstrieren eindringlich verschiedene Schwierigkeiten der Erinnerung" [V 8/5]). Significantly, these difficulties pertain not only to the gray patches (*grauen Felder*) of his past but also to images of such extraordinary clarity that he can scarce credit them ("Bilder von solcher ungewöhnlicher Deutlichkeit, daß er ihnen nicht glaubt trauen zu dürfen") because, he explains, even when images of memory are true to life one can place little confidence in them ("es sei selbst da, wo man über lebensnahere Erinnerungsbilder verfüge, auf diese nur wenig Verlaß" [V 10/7]). The chief example adduced to illustrate this concerns Beyle's vivid, cherished, and detailed memory of an evening ride he once took through the town of Ivrea in Italy. Many years later, when looking through old papers, "he came across an engraving titled *Prospetto d'Ivrea* and he was obliged to concede that his recollected picture of the town was nothing but a copy of that very engraving" ("[ist er] auf eine *Prospetto d'Ivrea* untertitelte Gravure gestoßen und [hatte] sich eingestehen müssen, daß sein Erinnerungsbild von der . . . Stadt nichts anders vorstellte als eine Kopie von ebendieser Gravure":

> This being so, Beyle's advice is not to purchase engravings
> of fine views and prospects seen on one's travels, since be-
> fore long they will displace our memories completely, indeed

one might say they destroy them. For instance, he could no longer recall the wonderful Sistine Madonna he had seen in Dresden, try as he might, because Müller's engraving after it had become superimposed in his mind; the wretched pastels by Meng in the same gallery, on the other hand, of which he had never set eyes on a copy, remained before him as clear as when he first saw them.

Man sollte darum, so rät Beyle, keine Gravuren von schönen Aus- und Ansichten kaufen, die man auf Reisen sehe. Denn eine Gravure besetze bald schon den ganzen Platz der Erinnerung, die wir von etwas hätten, ja, man könne sogar sagen, sie zerstöre diese. An die wundervolle Madonna von San Sisto beispielsweise, die er in Dresden gesehen habe, könne er sich bei aller Anstrengung nicht mehr erinnern, weil sie von der Gravure, die Müller von ihr gemacht habe, überdeckt worden sei, wohingegen er nach wie vor die miserablen Pastelle von Mengs aus derselben Galerie, von denen ihm nie und nirgends eine Nachzeichnung untergekommen sei, auf das deutlichste vor Augen habe. (V 12/8)

It is precisely the experience of recognizing the difference between the real and these simulacric memory images that gives the novel its title— a word, *Schwindel,* that in German implies not only a vertiginous experience but also a bit of a swindle. But it should also be noted that, in Sebald, the experience, the difference, is not always recognized as such by its principal, even when it is nonetheless in force. In *De L'Amour,* Beyle describes a journey he claims to have made from Bologna in the company of one Mme Gherardi. But "Mme Gherardi never really existed, despite all the documentary evidence, and was merely a phantom, albeit one to whom Beyle remained true for decades" ("Mme Gherardi . . . allen dokumentarischen Angaben zum Trotz in Wirklichkeit hat gar nicht existiert und ist nur eine Art Phantomfigur gewesen, der Beyle dann jahrzehntelang die Treue gehalten hat" [V 27/22]). It is possible, Sebald says, to remain true to a phantom, an imaginary construct, a figure fashioned completely out of documentary evidence and all the more unreal for that, and, as we will see, the possibility broached here in his first novel comes true with a vengeance in his last, in the figure of Austerlitz's mother, Agáta.

The same conditions of the replacement of the real by the representation that Sebald describes for Rembrandt's painting, for the Germans' written accounts of their war experiences, and for Henri Beyle's memories hold true for the art, history, and memory based on photographs as well. Indeed, the situation is greatly exacerbated in the age of photography, especially in its post–World War II phase. The vast expanses of the photographic realm, the nearly limitless proliferation of photographic images, ensure that there are almost no instances left such as Beyle's "wretched pastels by Mengs" where one has not seen a copy, and this at a time where our immediate contact with the past has often been interrupted by both amnesia-inducing trauma and displacement. Moreover, the increased accuracy of photography, its privileged documentary actuality, increases rather than lessens the problem of falseness and inauthenticity, because it eases the possibility of identifying the real and the representation, an identification that all too unobtrusively slides into an appropriative substitution of the former by the latter—even when the original was unproblematically experienced and recorded, and far more when conditions conspired to thwart that. And as I said, this falsification takes place even in the case of the most true and accurate photographs. In *The Emigrants,* Max Aurach's Uncle Leo rages against a doctored photograph of a Nazi book-burning rally and concludes, "so everything has been a fake, from the very start" ("so war alles eine Fälschung von Anfang an" [AU 274/183]).[36] But the fakery takes place even when the photographs are not doctored. Immediately after his account of the Nazis' falsified Würzburg photograph, Aurach recounts his visit to the same city with the same uncle, where they see Tiepelo's glorious ceiling fresco above the stairwell in the local palace, a fresco "which at that time meant nothing to me" ("die für mich zu jener Zeit bedeutungslos [war]" [AU 276/183]). Aurach "recalls" that visit years later when he comes across a book of photographic reproductions of the fresco, and "For a whole evening, said Aurach, I sat looking at those pictures with a magnifying glass, trying to see further and further into them" ("Einen ganzen Abend bin ich, sagte Aurach, über diesen Bildern gesessen und habe versucht, mit einen Vergrößerungsglas tiefer und tiefer in sie hineinzusehen"). But as the juxtaposition with the Nazi photo underscores, the whole point is that these "reproductions" produce a false record, a fantastic invention of a forgotten past; the effort to see further and further into them is only a way of erasing more and more the actual flawed *Gedächtnisbild* (memory image), which, as Kracauer reminds us, is organized according to very different principles from those of a photographic Bild.[37] Photographs are destructive, and in much the same way as new buildings are for Sebald: they not only work to bury and obliterate the past but also set themselves up, simulacrally, in their place.[38]

One of the most disconcerting consequences of the destructive effect of photographs on memory in Sebald is the always open possibility that the photograph that is mistaken for a genuine memory, and on whose basis a given character proceeds analeptically to construct his identity, to trace his development, as it were—which is to say, the Bild on which he bases his Bildung—that this photograph might not actually belong to *his* past at all, rendering the identity derived or developed (or simply pictured) from it false and baseless from the ground up. For once photographs have destroyed the singular authenticity of genuine memories and the binding link between the two has been dissolved, there is no longer any guarantee that a given photograph corresponds to any actual personal experience nor that the self thereon "recalled" corresponds to any actual personal identity. This is no doubt part of what Sebald means by the "nomadic" quality of photographs: they wander from one person's image repertoire into another's and bring their inherent errancy with them into that other person's life.[39] This is hinted at, for instance, in *The Emigrants,* in the story of Uncle Ambros's youth, where Aunt Fini tells the narrator that Ambros worked at the Grand Hôtel Eden in Montreux and then adds, "At least I think it was the Eden, because, in one of the postcard albums that Uncle Adelwarth left, the world-famous hotel is on one of the opening pages" ("Ich glaube jedenfalls, daß es das *Eden* war, denn in einem vom Adelwarth-Onkel hinterlassenen Ansichtskartenalbum ist dieses weltberühmte Hotel . . . gleich auf einer der ersten Seiten zu sehen" [AU 113/78]). The inference, however, is just as possibly mistaken and so too the specific *Bildungsgeschichte* of Ambros she recounts; while no doubt generically true, it might well be singularly false, in a manner that threatens to unsettle the identity of the protagonist—whether the Bild is true or false, one simply cannot know. And it is just such cases of ever possible misidentification opened up by photographs that provide the base conditions for Austerlitz's nagging suspicion, "At some point in the past I must have made a mistake, and now I am living the wrong life" ("Irgendwann in der Vergangenheit habe ich einen Fehler gemacht und bin jetzt in einem falschen Leben" [306/212]).

The same impulse that has Aunt Fini identify Ambros with this mass-produced picture postcard is also at work in various characters identifying themselves with others' photographs, and to the same effect. As a child, Austerlitz leafs through the photo albums of his foster father's childhood in a village now underwater, "until the people looking out of them became as familiar to me as if I were living with them down at the bottom of the lake. Sometimes I even imagined I had seen one or the other of them walking down the road in Bala [his own childhood village]" ("bis die Personen, die mir aus ihnen entgegensahen . . . so vertraut wurden, als lebte ich bei ihnen auf dem Grund des Sees . . . Bisweilen bildete ich mir sogar ein, die eine oder andere der Photofiguren aus dem Album gesehen zu haben auf der Straße in Bala" [81–82/71]). This is the background experience out of which come his later experiences in the Underground (again, like the lake, combining archaeological metaphors with photographic ones), where he says, "I thought I saw among the passengers a face known to me from some much earlier part of my life, but I could never say whose it was. These familiar faces always had something different from the rest about them, something indistinct. . . . It was at moments of particular weakness that my senses played these tricks on me" ("Dabei ist es mir in den Bahnhöfen wiederholt passiert, daß ich unter denen, die mir entgegenkamen . . . ein mir von viel früher her vertrautes Gesicht zu erkennen vermeinte. Immer hatten diese bekannten Gesichter etwas von allen anderen Verschiedenes, etwas Verwischtes. . . . Es war in Momenten besonderer Schwäche . . . daß mir dergleichen Sinnestäuschungen widerfuhren" [187–88/127]). And we might see similar "tricks" being played in the case of Sebald himself when, in "Air War and Literature," he tells us, "At the end of the war I was just one year old, so I can hardly have any impression of that period of destruction based on personal experience. Yet to this day, when I see photographs or documentary films dating from the war I feel as if I were its child" ("Bei Kriegsende war ich gerade ein Jahr alt und kann also schwerlich auf realen Ereignissen beruhende Eindrücke aus jener Zeit der Zerstörung bewahrt haben. Dennoch ist es mir bis heute, wenn ich Photographien oder dokumentarische Filme aus dem Kriege sehe, als stamme ich, sozusagen, von ihm ab" [LL 77/71]). In each case, the absence of firm impressions based on personal experience creates a void that invites filling with an imaginative identification. But as possibly admirable as this empathy might seem, it is, of course, clearly a symptom of an inability to identify actually with oneself, and of a substitution of someone else's past for one's own.[40] These photographs of the foster father that reappear in the displaced child's own life, the unknown but familiar images that superimpose themselves like apparitions on the faces of the crowd in the metro, or the photographs that Sebald himself adopts as foster images, as it were, these are all, again, the functional equivalents of those jumbled skeletons beneath the Broad Street Station, of the buried nuts dug up by squirrels beneath the snow of Prague, or of the schematized hand superimposed on the body in Rembrandt's painting. It is the plangently postmodern condition that dictates how Austerlitz can never have an identity of his own as long as, to reconstruct it, he depends on photographs—whether those he takes himself that then destroy and substitute for actual memory or those that wander into his possession from others—and that dictates how all of Sebald's works, all of his attempts to wield "a steadfast gaze bent on reality" and come to terms with the horrors of war, are necessarily, melancholically inauthentic, based on experiences not his own and a gaze bent not on reality but on photos, even as these same photos void the possibility of his having any experiences that are authentically his own. And finally, and certainly no less troubling, it is the condition for our own, often anxious reading of the photographs in Sebald's works, whether doctored or not. We seek to imagine the connections between image and text, between photograph and memoir, and to imagine that connection as real, true, and mutually confirming, but all the while we are cognizant of our construction, of our own elaborate mechanism for manufacturing a suitably supportive, individual past out of possibly—and often clearly—diverse, borrowed and falsified photos, all for a fictional character who, like Rembrandt's dissected subject, is himself invested with this remorselessly fictional, composite identity.

> The trails of light which [moths] seemed to leave behind them in all kinds of curlicues and streamers and spirals, did not really exist, but were merely phantom traces created by the sluggish reaction of the human eye, appearing to see a certain afterglow in the place from which the insect itself was already long gone. It was such unreal phenomena, the sudden incursion of unreality into the real world, that kindled our deepest feelings, or least what we took for them.

> Die Leuchtstreifen, die [die Falter] in verschiedenen
> Kringeln, Fahrern und Spiralen hinter sich
> herzuziehen schienen, existierten in Wirklichkeit gar
> nicht, sondern waren nur Phantomspuren, die verur-
> sacht wurden von der Trägheit unseres Auges, die
> einen gewissen Nachglanz an der Stelle noch zu sehen
> glaubt, von welcher das Insekt selber schon ver-
> schwunden war. Es war an solchen unwirklichen Er-
> scheinungen, am Aufblitzen des Irrealen in der realen
> Welt, daß unsere tiefsten Gefühle sich entzündeten
> oder jedenfalls das, was wir dafür hielten.
>
> *Austerlitz*

(139/92–93)

I would like to end this epilogue with a brief consideration of Austerlitz's encounter with two photographs at the end of his novel, photographs that illustrate in a particularly poignant manner the fate of
personal identity in the postwar, postmodern world: the photograph of
Austerlitz himself as a small boy dressed up as a page that Věra gives
him in Prague and that serves as the novel's front cover, and the photographic still, supposedly of his mother, Agáta, excerpted from a Nazi
propaganda film of Theresienstadt. Věra hands over the first picture
with the rather Benjaminian remark that it seems as if such photographs
that surface out of the past "had a memory of their own and remembered us" "als hätten [solche aus der Vergangenheit aufgetauchten
Photographien] selbst ein Gedächtnis und erinnerten sich an uns"
[266/182]). But as Austerlitz soon discovers, the problem is that their
memory is not our memory. He studies the photograph of the cos-
tumed child over and over: "Hard as I tried, I could not remember myself in the part" ("An mich selber in dieser Rolle aber erinnerte ich
mich nicht" [267/184]). Instead, he is compelled to dwell on the
merely contiguous details, on things that, as Kracauer stresses, only
shared space with the subject but no longer contain him: the bare level
field where the child is standing, the cape over his arm, the six buttons
on his jacket, even the folds of the child's stockings, "but otherwise all
memory was extinguished in me . . . I examined every detail under a
magnifying glass without once finding the slightest clue" ("doch sonst
war alles in mir ausgelöscht . . . jede Einzelheit habe ich mit einem Vergrößerungsglas untersucht, ohne je den geringsten Anhalt zu
finden").[41] The photograph, with its familiar but uncanny composite of

clichéd generic elements and endless concrete details, captured and connected only by the camera's all-inclusive spatial focus (and not by memory's selective, distilling grasp), seems to extinguish Austerlitz's own already tenuous, concrete connection to its subject. Moreover, Austerlitz feels himself "pierced by the inquiring gaze of the page boy who had come to demand his due" ("durchdrungen von dem forschenden Blick des Pagen, der gekommen war, sein Teil zurückzufordern"). The photograph demands its due from him and so displaces, even negates, the demand (the memory) he was due from the photograph. The result is that, again as Kracauer says, when the person and the photograph come together, the person disappears: "The photograph annihilates the person by portraying him, and were person and portrayal to converge, the person would cease to exist" ("Sie vernichtet ihn, indem sie ihn abbildet, und fiele er mit ihr zusammen, so wäre er nicht vorhanden"). So Austerlitz: "As far back as I can remember, I have always felt as if I had no place in reality, as if I were not there at all, and I have never had this impression more strongly than on that evening when the eyes of the page boy looked through me" ("Soweit ich zurückblicken kann . . . habe ich mich immer gefühlt, als hätte ich keinen Platz in der Wirklichkeit, als sei ich gar nicht vorhanden, und nie ist dieses Gefühl stärker in mir gewesen als an jenem Abend, als mich der Blick des Pagen durchdrang" [269/185]). This is the infinitely disconcerting consequence of Věra's seemingly simple claim "that is you" ("das bist du," [266/183]). The self is replaced by its photographic Bild and ceases to have a hold on its own identity.

The second photograph, that of Austerlitz's mother, Agáta, achieves the same countermnemonic effect but even more catastrophically. For we are not even sure that it is actually a Bild of her. It too has its Benjaminian aspect: Austerlitz takes the archived Nazi propaganda film and produces a new, slow-motion version that extends to four times its original length and reveals previously hidden objects and people, creating, by default as it were, a different sort of film altogether. Out of this he extracts a still-shot of only a few hundredths of a second, with a young woman barely emerging from the black shadows in the background, with a three-stringed necklace around her neck and a white flower in her hair. Austerlitz imagines this must be Agáta, although when he shows it to Věra, she does not concur, but Austerlitz still persists in trying to attach his memories of her—and his story of himself—to this photographic Bild: "She looks, so I tell myself, just as

I imagined Agáta from my faint memories and the few other clues I now have, and I gaze and gaze again at that face, which seems to me both strange and familiar" ("Gerade so wie ich nach meinen schwachen Erinnerungen und den wenigen Anhaltspunkten, die ich heute habe, die Agáta vorstellte, gerade so, denke ich, sieht sie aus, und ich schaue wieder und wieder in dieses mir gleichermaßen fremde und vertraute Gesicht" [354/251]). Sebald, however, has given us every reason to suspect the veracity of this image, indeed of the entire image of Agáta Austerlitz wishes to recall, beginning with the depiction of his trip to Prague on a much too bright, almost overexposed day ("an einem viel zu hellen, gewissermaßen überbelichteten Tag" [211/143]).

Austerlitz's pursuit of the "truth" about his childhood past—that past wanted to ground, even grant, his present sense of self—begins with a trip to Věra. Despite the ironic promise of her name, Věra is almost immediately revealed as a figure associated not with the true but with the fictional, and especially the fictional that arises out of the flawed constructions of broken memory. Her apartment (and she with it) is one of the chief examples in Sebald's work of those time-and-history-denying spaces, in which the world photographically stands still and images emerge with unimpinged clarity—much like Max Aurach says to the narrator when they meet again after many years, both much aged and changed, and gesturing toward a copy of a Rembrandt portrait on his studio wall remarks, "Only he doesn't seem to get any older" (AU 269/180). This is the realm of Věra; although almost sixty years have passed, Austerlitz tells us that she seemed quite unchanged ("daß sie ganz unverändert schien") and "everything was just as it had been . . . Images buried and locked away within me now came luminously back to mind as I looked out the window [in which I saw] a white blouse, just as it had always hung there in the past ("alles [war] geradeso wie vor . . . Bilder . . . so tief versunken und verschlossen sie in mir gewesen sind, so leuchtend kamen sie mir während des Hinausschauens aus dem Fenster nun wider in den Sinn . . . eine weiße Bluse hing [wie auch vordem oft] an der Klinke des Fensters" [223/230, 152/156]). Even as the image of the room and its contents seem uncannily—indeed, photographically—exempt from wear, change, and transience, so too do Austerlitz's memory images, whose very luminosity, like Henri Beyle's, call into question their credibility. Věra herself is a figure of this still, unreal, and unreliable world, and Agáta is even more so.[42] When Austerlitz pays a brief visit to a theater where Věra tells him Agáta once performed, he suddenly has a flashlike vision of a sky-blue shoe embroidered with silver sequins between the wooden floorboards and the curtain on stage, and although Věra encourages him in his belief that this image is of Agáta, it is clearly not derived from Austerlitz's "real-life" memory but from Hugo von Hofmannsthal's Entwicklungsroman *Andreas*. Later, when Věra recounts the memory of the men who came to take Agáta away to be deported, she more or less explicitly cites the opening scene of Kafka's *The Trial* (*Der Prozeß*). Both of these instances help motivate the persistent identification of Agáta with the figure of Olimpia from E. T. A. Hoffmann's famous story and Jaques Offenbach's opera (after whom Jacques Austerlitz himself is named) and explain the importance of Austerlitz's statement, "I was afraid Agáta had genuinely changed into someone else, who, though she might now be a magical figure, was also a complete stranger to me" ("ich fürchtete, Agáta hätte sich wahrhaftig verwandelt in eine zwar zauberhafte, aber mir doch vollkommen fremde Gestalt" [236/ 161]). Even as, in Hoffmann's tale, Olimpia is an unreal, fabricated figure who only seems real in the eyes of the desirous but deluded Nathanael, so too in Sebald's novel is Agáta a fictional construct who only seems real to the desperate, fantasizing Austerlitz. And this is nowhere more poignantly the case than with the quite possibly false or mistaken photographic Bild Austerlitz extracts from the Nazi film, and on which he pins not only Agáta's identity but his own as well. John Banville has written, "The moment, toward the close of the work, when we are finally shown a photograph of a woman who is almost surely Agáta, is one of the most moving moments that a reader is likely to encounter in modern literature."[43] But it is also, and even more, one of the saddest, because it is almost surely just as likely *not* Agáta, and the destituting effect of its assumption is, finally, as devastating and destructive for our reading as for Austerlitz's *Geschichte*.

What then has become of the subject in the age of *Nachbildung*, when the attempt to continue the project of Bildung at both the cultural and the personal level emerges as a counterfeit sham, a willful disavowal of the unbridgeable breach with a lost past, rendering notions of both national culture and personal identity inauthentic simulacra? What happens to the individual and his culture when the archaeological excavations of both personal and collective existence, the digging seemingly demanded by Sebald for the overcoming of our buried, forgotten past, of our willful presentism, prove, for all their unavoidability, impossible to accomplish, insofar as they yield not singular history but, in its archaeological extension, generalized and schematized clichés and, in its "dusting off," but another round of destructive denial and questionable presentism? And what happens to the subject's sense of memory and truth in the age of photography, where the very apparatus wielded to preserve the past destroys it, the means used to document its actuality transform it instead into inauthentic images, and the very ground on which individuals try to build their individual stories subjects them to borrowed, nomadic clichés and stolen—no, stealing—Bilder that rob them of any surety, any self, any memory, any story? And even more, what has become of literature in this age? Contrary to a too-quick reading of Sebald's claim that "the ideal of truth inherent in its entirely unpretentious objectivity . . . proves the only legitimate reason for continuing to produce literature in the face of total destruction" and "conversely, the construction of aesthetic or pseudo-aesthetic effects from the ruins of an annihilated world is a process depriving literature of its right to exist" ("das Ideal des Wahren, das in [ihrer] gänzlich unprätentiösen Sachlichkeit beschlossen ist, erweist sich angesichts der totalen Zerstörung als der einzige legitime Grund für die Fortsetzung der literarischen Arbeit . . . Umgekehrt ist die Herstellung von ästhetischen oder pseudoästhetischen Effekten aus den Trümmern einer vernichteten Welt ein Verfahren, mit dem die Literatur sich ihrer Berechtigung entzieht" [LL 59/53]), I would suggest that Sebald's own works suggest that the task assigned literature consists in addressing the paradoxical identity of these two statements: the truth that, in a world of ruins, the ideal of objectivity is inseparable from the construction of aesthetic effects, whether we are speaking of history or memory, nations or individual subjects, archaeology or photography. Literature is the privileged site not for the overcoming but for the staging of this destitution of truth, of reality, and of the subject. That is its truth, its reality, and its subject.

Notes

Introduction

1. Armstrong, *Fiction in the Age of Photography*.
2. The lines between archaeology and ethnology are very porous in the nineteenth century: whereas in a later period of more stringent discourse differentiation, typology might well be more exclusively associated with ethnology, this was not true during the period behind this study. See Daniel, *A Hundred and Fifty Years;* Trigger, *History of Archaeological Thought*.
3. This is not to say that the Bildungsroman was not involved in the inculcation of bourgeois ideology. But *Altertumswissenschaft* brought with it the added burden of its institutional instrumentality, a burden archaeology carried with it into the psychological realm.
4. See Traill, "Priam's Treasure" and *Schliemann of Troy*.
5. Greenblatt, *Shakespearean Negotiations*, 7.
6. Indeed, it strikes me as an abiding irony that Foucault and, in his wake, so many cultural theorists have adopted the "metaphor" of archaeology for their own work in such an uncritical fashion, not only because, for all its disavowal of Freud's psychoanalysis, Foucault's method nonetheless sites itself on precisely the same discursive basis, but also because, for all its insistence on historical contextualization, it remains so ahistorically formalist about its own image system.

Chapter 1

1. Mann, *Gesammelte Werke,* 10:291. All page references to Mann's pub-

lished work in both the text and notes are taken from this edition; those without a specified volume number refer to volume 3, *Der Zauberberg*.

2. All page references to the English translations from *The Magic Mountain* are taken from Woods's translation.

3. Kracauer, "Die Photographie," 32.

4. Mann, "Einführung in den *Zauberberg*," 11:602–17; see also Mann, "[Der autobiographische Roman,]" 11:700–704.

5. For Stifter, see Mann's letters to Philipp Witkop of October 4, 1917, and to Heinrich Mann of January 3, 1919, in Mann, *Briefe 1889–1936*, 139–40, 154–56; for Keller, see Mann, "Ein Wort über Gottfried Keller," 10:848–50.

6. Kaiser and Kittler, *Dichtung als Sozialisationsspiel*; Hörisch, *Gott, Geld, und Glück*; see also Smith, "Cultivating Gender," 296–325.

7. A bit further afield, Charles Dickens's *Oliver Twist; or, The Parish Boy's Progress* (1837–39) uses a portrait in a similar way to mark the protagonist's growing into his destined identity. The text makes a point of distinguishing the portrait from the images of the protophotographic "machine for taking likenesses" of its time. See Dickens, *Oliver Twist*, 128.

8. See Hörisch, *Gott, Geld, und Glück*, 206–39.

9. See, e.g., Mann, "Mein Verhältnis zur Psychoanalyse," 11:748–49.

10. Winthrop-Young, "Magic Media Mountain," 49.

11. An exception is the 1974 essay by Winfried Kudszus "Understanding media: Zur Kritik dualistischer Humanität im *Zauberberg*." More recent studies include Hörisch, "Die deutsche Seele"; Winthrop-Young, "Magic Media Mountain"; and Schultz, "Technology as Desire."

12. Kittler, "The Mechanized Philosopher"; also Kittler, *Grammophon, Film, Typewriter*. See also Wellbery, foreword.

13. Crary, *Techniques of the Observer*, 1–24.

14. For Mann on the technologization of music, see, for example, "Über das Theater" (10:290–91) and "Vorwort zur Schallplattenausgabe *Buddenbrooks*" (11:549–52).

15. For Mann on film, see, for example, "Über den Film" (10:898–901) and "[Unterhaltungsmacht Film]" (10:932–34).

16. Barthes, *Camera Lucida*, 88.

17. Mann, "Die Welt ist schön," 10:901–4. For more on Renger-Patzsch's book, see Newhall, *History of Photography*, 193–94; see also my discussion of Benjamin's critique of Renger-Patzsch in chapter 3.

18. Crary, *Techniques of the Observer*, 116–34.

19. Baudelaire, *Painter of Modern Life*, 9; Marx and Engels, *The German Ideology*, 109–11; see also Crary, *Techniques of the Observer*, 113–14.

20. Bergson, "Le mécanisme cinématographie" 298–307.

21. Benjamin, "Das Kunstwerk im Zeitalter seiner technischen Reproduzierbarkeit," *Gesammelte Schriften,* 1:471–508; Sontag, *On Photography.*

22. Benjamin, "Kleine Geschichte der Photographie," *Gesammelte Schriften,* 2:368–85. For an account of Charcot and Freud, see Kittler, *Discourse Networks,* 277.

23. Kracauer, "Die Photographie," 24–28.

24. Huysmans, *A Rebours,* 276.

25. Hello, *L'Homme,* 172–74. Oliver Wendell Holmes was already referring to photography as a "mirror with a memory" in 1859; see Newhall, *Photography,* 53–61; Draaisma, *Metaphors of Memory,* 120. But Hello seems to have been the first to turn the trope around and elaborate a model for memory as a form of photography.

26. McLuhan, *Understanding Media,* 177.

27. Foucault designates the principle of latency as the most central, constitutive factor in the new construction of subjectivity promulgated by the nineteenth century in general and psychoanalysis in particular (see *History of Sexuality,* esp. 66).

28. Freud, *Studienausgabe,* 9:571/*Standard Edition,* 23:126. Sarah Kofman, in *Camera Obscura of Ideology,* analyzes this and the following two passages from Freud from a very different starting point and to very different ends (21–28).

29. Miller, *The Novel and the Police,* 26.

30. Freud, *Studienausgabe,* 3:34/*Standard Edition,* 12:264.

31. Admittedly, there is also an important difference, in that in the new schema the installed exists in a negative or reversed state that needs to be reversed again by Entwicklung.

32. Freud, *Studienausgabe,* 1:292–93/*Standard Edition,* 16:295.

33. Foucault posits this policing, regulatory intervention, viz. inscription, as the necessary complement to the principle of latency (*History of Sexuality,* 66–67).

34. Faulkner, *Absalom, Absalom!,* 87–88.

35. Consider Hello's insistence on the role of an analytic solvent (*l'acide*) in the development of any stored memory (see note 25).

36. Settembrini's self-assigned role as Hans's chief "developer" is not necessarily exhausted by his enlightening function but could also be seen to include the photographic metaphor's chemical component, as represented by his role as a *Merkur* who guides Hans's steps. As the famous anecdote of how Daguerre first discovered the means for developing the latent image on a photo plate reminds us—he had placed previously exposed negatives inside a cabinet just happening also to contain a (broken) thermometer, and the mercury vapors from the thermometer developed the invisible images—mercury was the first photographic devel-

oper, which is to say, the first agent for *accelerating* development (see Gernsheim, *Origins of Photography*, 42). Mann draws connections between mercury and Hans's accelerated development throughout the novel.

37. Proust, *A la Recherche du temps perdu*, 3:896. English based on *Remembrance of Things Past*, trans. C. K. Scott Moncrieff and Frederick A. Blossom (New York: Random House, 1932), 2:1014.

38. Cohn, *Transparent Minds*, 146.

39. Hanney, "Proust and Negative Plates," 345.

40. Barthes, *Camera Lucida*, 103.

41. Mann, "Die Welt ist schön," 10:902.

42. Darwin, *On the Expression of the Emotions*. Charlotte Brontë's *Jane Eyre* (1847) might serve as an example of the earlier regime opposed by Darwin, which linked together painting, physiognomy, and mid-nineteenth-century psychology.

43. Galton, *Inquiries into Human Faculty;* see also Armstrong, *Fiction in the Age of Photography*, 16–22; Draaisma, *Metaphors of Memory*, 125–29; Sekula, "The Body and the Archive." For Freud's references to Galton, see Freud, *Studienausgabe*, 1:179, 2:155, 2:294–95, 2:475, 9:462, and especially Freud, *Gesammelte Werke*, 2/3:662–63. The technique of *Mischphotographie* was quite controversial, not least in its overt challenge to the realist aesthetics usually associated with photography; see Newhall, *History of Photography*, 76. It had its clear counterpart in the literary poetics of modernism, such as we see in Mann's chapter "Walpurgisnacht," where the scene is shadowed by a *Mischbild* constructed out of *Vorbilder* taken from Goethe's *Faust*, Shakespeare's *Midsummer Night's Dream*, Wagner's *Tristan and Isolde*, and Homer's *Odyssey*, or in the figure of Peeperkorn, whose master template combines, as it were, features of Dionysus and Christ. James Joyce and others deployed a similar composite template mode of representation, with a similar challenge to realist principles: Freud explicitly associates this form of literary typology with a *Galtonscher Technik* in "Der Mann Moses und die monotheistische Religion" (9:462).

44. Benjamin, "Kleine Geschichte der Photographie," *Gesammelte Schriften*, 2:368–85.

45. Bergson, *Matière et Mémoire*, 93–94. Bergson's work has long been recognized as an important source for Mann's model of memory in this novel; I believe it can also be recognized as the source for this rather Proustian passage from Benjamin (further discussed in chapter 3), wherein he elaborates on Bergson's photographic metaphor: "Nichts hindert, daß wir Räume, wo wir vierundzwanzig Stunden waren, mehr oder weniger deutlich im Gedächtnis halten, und andere, wo wir Monate

verbrachten, ganz vergessen. Es ist also durchaus nicht immer Schuld einer allzukurzen Belichtungsdauer, wenn auf der Platte des Erinnerns kein Bild erscheint. Häufiger sind vielleicht die Fälle, wo die Dämmerung der Gewohnheit der Platte jahrelang das nötige Licht versagt, bis dieses eines Tages aus fremden Quellen wie aus entzündetem Magnesium-pulver aufschießt und nun im Bilde einer Momentaufnahme den Raum auf die Platte bannt" (*Berliner Chronik, Gesammelte Schriften,* 6:516). Here in miniature, in the confines of a discussion of individual memory, we have the metaphorical basis for Benjamin's entire philosophy of history, with its complex apparatus of instant flashes, temporal continuities, and dialectical correspondences. See Cadava, "Words of Light." Benjamin discusses at some length Bergson's work in his essay "Über einige Motive bei Baudelaire" (1:605–55), where he also compares Bergson with Freud. By comparison, Mann's elaboration of Bergson's model seems more modest but still equally indicative of peculiarly modernist notions, equally disruptive of traditional schemas of historical development, and equally embedded in the photographic field.

Many critics assume an opposition between the modernist poetics or sensibilities of Mann and Benjamin, but *Der Zauberberg* proves a particularly well-suited ground for bringing these two key figures together. Benjamin claims to have felt an almost uncanny affinity for the novel, and the elements of attraction are well represented by the novel's use of photography. See the letters to Scholem of February 19, 1925, and April 6, 1925, in Benjamin, *Gesammelte Briefe,* 3:13–18, 3:25–29.

46. Benjamin, "Kleine Geschichte der Photographie," *Gesammelte Schriften,* 2:368.

47. Gabo and Pevsner, "Realist Manifesto"; see also Kevles, *Naked to the Bone,* 124–38.

48. See Nehamas, "Getting Used to Not," 74–75.

49. Barthes, *Camera Lucida,* 81.

50. The affinities between the models of photography and disease in Mann's novel are important and extensive, and it is worth remembering how the discursive field of tuberculosis surveyed by Sontag in *Illness as Metaphor* emerges out of basically the same nineteenth-century historical moment as both photography and psychoanalysis. Sontag describes much the same role for repression in the play of tuberculosis as Freud does for the photo-psyche in "Widerstand und Verdrängung." But the common mechanics of the two discursive regimes is far more extensive than the single instance of repression might suggest. After all, tuberculosis follows the same two-step process as that of the photograph: one is first "exposed," or infected, and then "develops"—perhaps after a long time and certainly not in every case (indeed, only given the proper repres-

sive/expressive conditions). Because of both the delay and the supplemental requirements of selection, the sense of an initial external exposure often fades into one of inherent potentiality: long after tuberculosis was known to be caused by an outside invasive agent, it was still considered somehow latent in the individual's self, an attitude easily confirmed by Mann's novel. And in its developing stage, tuberculosis is doubly figured as a set of released chemical solvents that work on the prepared but still hidden or latent material of the self, inducing its decipherment, bringing it out and making it transparent; and as a kind of enlightening "illuminieren," thus partaking of the same peculiar photochemical quality as photography itself. Although I will not be elaborating on them, Mann often makes the affinities between the thematics of photography and disease explicit in his novel.

51. Nehamas, "Getting Used to Not," 75.

52. Ibid., 83–84.

53. Adorno, *Minima Moralia,* 4:105.

54. See Winthrop-Young, "Magic Media Mountain."

55. Hörisch, *Gott, Geld, und Glück,* 209.

56. Hanney, "Proust and Negative Plates," 346.

57. Mann, "Über die Ehe," 10:196, 10:198.

58. Barthes, *Roland Barthes,* 132. For more on Barthes's concept of the neutral and the peculiar nature of photographic desire, see Mavor, *Pleasures Taken.* Oscillation, or *Schwanken*—closely related to Barthes's "neutral"—is a key quality of the erotic throughout Mann's novel: see the famous description of Clawdia's kiss (831–32).

59. Freud, "Die sexuellen Abirrungen," *Studienausgabe,* 5:56. It is worth pointing out that the same oscillating, "neutral" sense of the erotic is also at work in scenes that might seem predominantly homoerotic in the narrower sense, such as in "Humaniora." Kenneth Weisinger, in "Distant Oil Rigs and Other Erections," wonderfully analyzes the over-the-top same-sex play of this chapter; but we cannot discount the part played by the heterosexual in the form of Clawdia's portrait in generating the scene's operant homoeroticism. I should add that Hans Blüher's homosexual model for Bildung, mentioned by Mann in "Über die Ehe" (10:196), similarly suffers a breakdown in the face of Mann's quite differently conceived homoerotic model for Entwicklung. Not only does Blüher's model depend on the same sharp division between the homo and the hetero (and the public and private) as traditional Bildung, it also ultimately aims at the same masculine ideal. See Blüher, *Die Rolle der Erotik.*

60. It is the double androgyny to the female figure *and* the male protagonist that distinguishes it most radically from the androgyny also at issue in ear-

lier Bildungsromanen, including *Wilhelm Meister.* Catriona MacLeod, in *Embodying Ambiguity,* has definitively explored this trope in the Bildungsroman from Goethe through Keller; to some extent, the photographic androgyny of Mann's novel is yet another case of Entwicklung not so much opposing as incorporating and refiguring a facet of Bild-ung that was always there, even if not fully supported by the pictorial parallel.

61. Mann, "Über die Ehe," 10:194–95.

62. Benjamin, "Der Erzähler," *Gesammelte Schriften,* 2:438–64.

63. Barthes, *Camera Lucida,* 92–93.

64. Goethe, *Wilhelm Meisters Lehrjahre,* 7:505. The sentence continues: "man bekannt sich zwar nicht zu allen Zügen, aber man freut sich, daß ein denkender Geist uns so fassen, ein großes Talent uns so hat darstellen wollen, daß ein Bild von dem, was wir waren, noch besteht, und daß es länger als wir selbst dauern kann."

65. Barthes, *Camera Lucida,* 93–94.

66. Henry Peach Robinson, *Fading Away* (1858), combination albumen print (George Eastman House, Rochester, NY); rpt. in Newhall, *History of Photography,* 76.

67. Hörisch, *Gott, Geld, und Glück,* 216–25.

68. Koc, "Magical Reenactments," 113.

69. Admittedly, in the case of Behrens's diverting experiment here, the bacteria are cocci rather than tubercular bacilli, but the point still holds.

70. "Der grosse Stumpfsinn" is also, perhaps incidentally, the chapter in which Hans abortively experiments with the latest technology of color photography.

71. See Hörisch, "Die deutsche Seele"; Kittler, *Grammophon, Film, Typewriter.*

72. For a similar designation of Bildung, see Mann, *Gesammelte Werke,* 11:703.

73. Goethe, *Wilhelm Meisters Lehrjahre,* book 7, chapter 9.

74. Ibid., book 8, chapter 1.

75. See Keller, *Der Grüne Heinrich,* with its functionally equivalent recovery and restoration of Heinrich Lee's paintings and narrative at the conclusion of his Bildung in the castle of the Count.

76. These same conditions are also presented together in the accompanying motif of the similarly recovered painting of the sickly prince. And in Keller's novel, although the outcome of the ascension to the position of father is more problematic (because it is compromised and declined), it too is paired with the motif of the recovered paintings and narrative at the functionally equivalent moment in Heinrich's Bildung.

77. Von Schrenck-Notzing, *Materialisationsphänomene.* Mann insightfully notes the quite different reception of the first and second editions of the

book in Germany, the one appearing before and the other after World War I. See Mann, "Okkulte Erlebnisse," 10:140–41. For Conan Doyle's and Houdini's experiences with von Schrenck-Notzing, see Ernst and Carington, *Houdini and Conan Doyle.*

78. One might recall the so-called Hope Case and the activities of the Crewe Circle in England, both discussed in Ernst and Carington, *Houdini and Conan Doyle.* See also Sir Arthur Conan Doyle's books *The Case for Spirit Photography* and *The Coming of the Fairies,* the latter devoted to the famous Wright photographs. Two movies have been made on the topic: *Fairy Tale* (1997) and *Photographing Fairies* (1998). See also Gunning, "Phantom Images."

79. Von Schrenck-Notzing, *Materialisationsphänomene,* 29, 16.

80. Ibid., 15.

81. Von Schrenck-Notzing also mentions the not infrequent failures of the cameras and/or lights, failures that also seem to parallel those of the medium in producing his or her images.

82. Von Schrenck-Notzing, *Materialisationsphänomene,* 33.

83. Kittler, *Discourse Networks,* 229.

84. For a further association of black curtains and cameras, see Mann, *Der Tod in Venedig,* 8:523.

85. Von Schrenck-Notzing, *Materialisationsphänomene,* 28. Von Schrenck-Notzing's reconfiguration of the human subject as techno-instrument links his practice with that heavily thematized in Weimar film, from *Metropolis* through *Mabuse* and *Caligari.* See Huyssen, "Vamp and the Machine."

86. Von Schrenck-Notzing, *Materialisationsphänomene,* 29.

87. Ibid. We might note that this is the dialectical visual complement to the musical image in "Fülle des Wohllauts," where the mechanical reproductive apparatus seems to become the person singing. Here the person becomes the reproductive apparatus.

88. Ibid., 15.

89. Ibid., 42; see also ibid., 8.

90. Ibid., 42.

91. See, for example, Tatar, *Spellbound.*

92. Freud cites von Schrenck-Notzing as an expert in his essay "Die sexuellen Abirrungen," *Studienausgabe,* 5:47.

93. Von Schrenck-Notzing, *Materialisationsphänomene,* 9.

94. Ibid., 20. For childbirth as falling within the sexual/erotic domain, see Mann, *Gesammelte Werke,* 13:36.

95. See Huyssen, "Vamp and the Machine."

96. Mann, *Gesammelte Werke,* 10:146.

97. See Mann, *Gesammelte Werke,* 13:33–48.

98. Mann, *Gesammelte Werke,* 10:153.

99. Mann's parallel between occult phenomena and the X-ray is by no means merely capricious. After all, Sir William Crookes, the inventor of the so-called Crookes tube central to early X-ray technology, was also a major figure in occult studies due to his reconceptualizing the medium in scientific mechanical terms. See Ernst and Carrington, 92–93; von-Schrenck-Notzing, *Materialisationsphänomene,* 3.

100. For possible further resonances of the reference to St. Paul, see Weisinger, "Distant Oil Rigs," 189–91.

101. This is not to imply that things really go right in the earlier instance of Wilhelm's completed Bildung, just that they go differently wrong here.

102. I would suggest that the contrast in dress is not so much between the "black" and "white" color of the outfits as it is between the clothed and naked medium. In Mann's essay, Willi S. also puts on a white bathrobe over his black stocking suit because he is cold; Elly Brand is naked beneath hers, a condition meant to emphasize her *gläsern* constitution, another way of signaling the medium as photographic plate (see 925, "das gläserne Diapositiv").

103. See Koc, "Magical Reenactments," 113.

104. Hans specifically requests "eine Nummer aus 'Margarethe' von Gounod" (944). Perhaps significantly but certainly also missing the intended significance, "Margarethe" becomes "Faust" in the English translations of both Lowe-Porter and Woods.

105. See Kittler's citation of Ernst von Wildenbruch's "The phonograph is the soul's own true photograph," in *Discourse Networks,* 236.

106. See Benjamin, "Der Erzähler," *Gesammelte Schriften,* 2:438–64, on the social effects of mechanized warfare and the implicit link with the Bildungsroman later on in the same essay.

107. For more on the connections between modernism's aesthetics of fragmentation, especially in regard to subject identity and the scattered body fragments of young soldiers in World War I, see Maria Tatar's chapter on Otto Dix in *Lustmord* (68–97).

Chapter 2

1. For comparison sake, the British Archaeological Society was founded in 1843; see Daniel, *A Hundred and Fifty Years,* 114. For the institutional history of the DAI, see Wickert, *Das Deutsche Archäologische Institut* and the seminal work of Suzanne Marchand, *Down from Olympus.*

2. Bernal, *Black Athena,* 308–16. The actual (as opposed to literal) title for the translation of Müller's work in English is *Ancient Art and Its Remains.*

3. Newhall, *History of Photography,* 50.

4. Newhall, *History of Photography,* 105; Szegedy-Maszak, "An Eye for Antiquity," 56; Szegedy-Maszak, "Sun and Stone." Photographs of Athens were also included in Frith's collection; see Szegedy-Maszak, "True Illusions."

5. Newhall, *History of Photography,* 103; Szegedy-Maszak, "True Illusions." As Szegedy-Maszak points out, one of the key conventions of this particular photographic tradition was the exclusion of both modern structures and people from the given photograph: this will be important to my discussion in chapter 3.

6. It is worth pointing out that Germans were *only* allowed to take back photographs from Olympia: the imperialist project of appropriation was always rather virtual for the Germans. See Marchand, *Down from Olympus,* 84.

7. For one of the best readings of the mutual impact of photography and archaeology on visual culture, see Shanks, "Photography and Archaeology." For a study focused more specifically on the nineteenth century, see Hamilakis, "Monumental Visions."

8. Galton's cousin, Charles Darwin, whose work was published around this same time, was, of course, also key to the development of nineteenth-century typology. For the influence of both Darwin and photography on the typological schemata of Adolf Furtwängler and Giovanni Morelli, see Marchand, *Down from Olympus,* 106–8; see also Trigger, *History of Archaeological Thought,* 160.

9. See Adam, "Heinrich Schliemann."

10. With the advent of flight, aerial photography also became a part of archaeology, already by German military planes in the Ottoman Empire during World War I and then, at Olympia, by the Luftwaffe during the German occupation of Greece in the 1940s: more evidence of the suspect pairing of archaeology and imperialist, aggressive nationalism. See Marchand, *Down from Olympus,* 254, 353. For more on archaeology and the Nazi regime, see Arnold and Hassmann, "Archaeology in Nazi Germany."

11. See Daniel, *A Hundred and Fifty Years,* 116.

12. See Stray, *Classics Transformed;* also Turner, "Historicism."

13. See Marchand, *Down from Olympus,* 43.

14. The word "prehistory" first comes into currency at this time, circa 1851; see Daniel, *A Hundred and Fifty Years,* 86–87.

15. Much the same occurred in biblical lands, where the archaeological finds in Mesopotamia were diluting the authority of sacred Hebrew texts for modeling the ancient Middle East. This did not, however, have as direct an effect on the program of Bildung as what was occurring in the Hel-

lenic sphere. But see my discussion of Mann's Joseph novels in chapter 3.

16. This all-too-evident fissure between the textual/historical and the material/archaeological caused endless complications in the various efforts at ignoring it, from Schliemann's insistence on the conflation of his finds at Hisarlik with the Troy of Homer to Arthur Evans's insistence on designating the pre-Mycenean civilization of Crete as Minoan, and through to Werner Jaeger's belated attempt to restrict the ancient world relevant to Bildung to that consistent with the literary tradition alone. See Traill, *Schliemann of Troy;* also Daniel, *A Hundred and Fifty Years,* and Marchand, *Down from Olympus.*

    In a sense, the almost definitional importance of this problem remained a major cause for the continued isolation of classical archaeology from the rest of archaeology: the pitting of the advanced, civilized tradition of articulated Greek consciousness against the newly emergent but far older and also "base" realm of Greek nonverbal remains created a unique split context for fixing the place of archaeology in the cultural imaginary.

17. See Marchand, *Down from Olympus,* 176–77.

18. See Morris, *Classical Greece,* 20–21; Said, *Orientalism,* 86; Daniel, *A Hundred and Fifty Years,* 68–69.

19. See Daniel, *A Hundred and Fifty Years,* 22. We might see something of a parallel here in the tendency to divide up and separate the ancient Mediterranean world itself into discrete discursive territories such as classical studies, biblical studies, Egyptology, and Assyriology, with significantly different cultural value given to each "common" past. Even as differences were being reinforced in the modern European world, so too were they in the ancient Mediterranean world for the modern European.

20. Marchand, *Down from Olympus,* 64, 68, 346; Daniel, *A Hundred and Fifty Years,* 68.

21. Berman, *Enlightenment or Empire;* see also Zantop, *Colonial Fantasies.*

22. Marchand, *Down from Olympus,* 58–62.

23. For the most part, Nietzsche was magnificently uninterested in archaeology: there are few references to the field in his work and none that really support the valorization of its practices or metaphorical regimes. On the other hand, his association of the Greeks with music at the expense of language clearly complemented the archaeologists' challenge to the philologists' association of the Greeks with texts. By the end of the century, the Dionysian and prehistorical would at times become conflated in the elaborated psychologies of *Lebensphilosophen* such as Ludwig Klages; see chapter 3.

24. Daniel, *A Hundred and Fifty Years,* 166; Marchand, *Down from Olym-*

pus, 101.

25. See Bernal, *Black Athena,* 289.

26. The German Ludwig Ross was the first professor of archaeology in the new Greek nation-state; see Hamilakis, "Monumental Visions," 8.

27. For an account of how this tendency was particularly realized on the Acropolis, see ibid., 7.

28. This separation of the Greeks from the Ottomans was also promulgated visually in the pictorial and photo travel albums of the time, which would depict Turks in Orientalized costumes but not Greeks; see Szegedy-Maszak, "True Illusions," 126–27.

29. Szegedy-Maszak, "True Illusions."

30. For Freud's attitude toward Turks, see Tögel, *Berggasse-Pompeji und zurück,* 114.

31. See Daniel, *A Hundred and Fifty Years,* 199; Marchand, *Down from Olympus,* 196–97.

32. Bernal, in *Black Athena,* argues that there was an even earlier, eighteenth-century model of Egyptian/Greek that was also displaced during the nineteenth century: the current layout of the British Museum could be seen to support this.

33. The new archaeological interest in Ottoman territory also included an interest in Mesopotamia, which rapidly came to succeed Egypt and Greece as the reputed origin of civilization; see Daniel, *A Hundred and Fifty Years,* 132–36. One result was that the Ottoman Empire came to serve as the new "other," not only to Greece in classical studies and its imaginary, but also to Israel in biblical studies and its imaginary. This double duty no doubt influenced the image of the Ottoman in its relation to the Greek world but perhaps less than might be expected, for it also ran up against a powerful need to maintain the imaginary separation of the biblical and Greek worlds—which is to say, the Semitic and Hellenic worlds—from intermingling in the German mind. Of all the boundaries that classical archaeology had to police between itself and other archaeologies, this was perhaps the most important for sustaining the project of German subject and national formation in the image of the ancient Greeks.

34. See Daniel, *A Hundred and Fifty Years,* 22, 52.

35. Suzanne Marchand points out the seeming paradox of the excessive nationalism of archaeology at home for the Germans as opposed to their proudly "disinterested" archaeological ventures abroad, especially compared with their counterparts (in both fields) in France or England. As she shows, the seeming paradox is to a great extent just that: seeming (Marchand, *Down from Olympus,* 153–54).

36. For the nominal distinction, see Marchand, *Down from Olympus,* 161; for

the museology, see McIsaac, "Divide between Nature and Civilization"; Marchand, *Down from Olympus*, 288–94; Traill, *Schliemann of Troy*, 206, 211.

37. Marchand, *Down from Olympus*, 152–87. All this is ruthlessly parodied by Wilhelm Raabe in his short story "Keltische Knochen" (1864–65) and his novel *Das Odfeld* (1888).

38. For the rumor of spies, see Marchand, *Down from Olympus*, 174.

39. Quoted in ibid., 185; see also Bernal, *Black Athena*, 28; Trigger, *History of Archaeological Thought*, 163–64.

40. See Trigger, *History of Archaeological Thought*, 160, 166.

41. See Daniel, *A Hundred and Fifty Years*, 180, 183–84. It should be said that the Germans were not alone in recasting Greek prehistory in their own self-image. At the same time the Germans were claiming Mycenean civilization originated from Aryan tribes come down from the north, the British were claiming it originated and radiated out from the island nation of Crete.

42. Trigger, *History of Archaeological Thought*, 19.

43. Ibid.

44. It seems somehow appropriate that the term "archaeologist" was originally used to denote a category of actors who recreated ancient legends on stage through dramatic mime; see Bahn, *Cambridge Illustrated History*, viii.

45. See Morris, *Archaeology as Cultural History*, on the depeopled field of archaeology; also Kuspit, "Mighty Metaphor," 146.

46. The issue of the gender of the archaeological subject will be addressed in my discussion of Jensen's *Gradiva*.

47. This was especially the case after the discovery of prehistory: one might speculate how just at the time that the future lifespan of the European subject was being most radically curtailed through a declining belief in the Christian afterlife, the *past* lifespan of the species—and, via introjection, of the individual as well (ontology recapitulating phylogeny)—was being radically increased. Glyn Daniel quotes J. Y. Akerman as declaring in 1847 that "to the reflecting mind, the fact that Providence has veiled from us the future, and given us the past for retrospect and experience, is alone sufficient to justify the occupation of a portion of our leisure in the examination and elucidation of the remains of Antiquity" (*A Hundred and Fifty Years*, 115), which seems symptomatic of the new state of affairs. One can see how the dominant discourses of the time—including archaeology, Darwinism, and psychoanalysis—managed the replacement of the immortal soul with a mortal, but no less temporally extended, one.

48. Daniel points to the Romantic penchant for tomb-digging that yielded some quite practical results in late-eighteenth- and early-nineteenth-cen-

tury England; see Daniel, *A Hundred and Fifty Years*, 22–25. As one might expect, Foucault's use of the archaeological metaphor has little in common with the earlier tradition, partly, no doubt, because archaeology itself has changed so much in the post–World War II era. Still, his rather unquestioning valorization of this metaphorical field to characterize his own critical practice suggests an interesting blind spot in his thinking—all the more interesting in his privileging the same metaphor preferred by psychoanalysis, one of his favorite targets. (As Hubert L. Dreyfus and Paul Rabinow argue, Foucault eventually abandoned the archaeological metaphor in favor of the more Nietzschean notion of genealogy [see "Methodological Failure of Archaeology"].) For another, contemporary usage of the archaeological subject, see Sante, *Factory of Facts*, wherein he writes, "Every human being is an archaeological site. What passes for roots is actually a matter of sediment, of accretion, of chance and juxtaposition" (33).

49. Derrida, *Dissemination*, 78.

50. Mann, "Freud und die Zukunft," 9:501.

51. Storm, *Viola tricolor*, 3:273, 3:284 (my translation).

52. Marchand, *Down from Olympus*.

53. For photography and realism, see Armstrong, *Fiction in the Age of Photography*; for photography and archaeology, see Szegedy-Maszak "Eye for Antiquity," "Sun and Stone," and "True Illusions," and Hamilakis, "Monumental Visions"; for realism and Bismarckian nationalism, see Berman, *Rise of the Modern German Novel*, and Holub, *Reflections of Realism*; for archaeology and German nationalism, see Marchand, *Down from Olympus*.

54. See chapter 7 of Downing, *Double Exposures*.

55. Benjamin, "The Storyteller," in *Selected Writings*, 3:144.

56. For my own reading of Raabe, see Downing, *Double Exposures*, 216–59.

57. All references to both Jensen's text and Freud's essay will be to Urban and Cremarius's edition of Freud, *Der Wahn und die Träume*, which remains the most readily available edition of Jensen's novella. English translations of Freud's essay are my own, though I have consulted the *Standard Edition* and provide page references to that version of the essay in volume 9. English translations of Jensen's novella are my own, though I have consulted the translation by Helen M. Downey in Freud, *Delusion and Dream*.

58. Goethe, *Italian Journey*, 199. The reference is taken from a letter dated March 11, 1787. The common interest in the mountain's rock formations and its living fauna and flora is one of the more suggestive connections between Goethe and the figure of Professor Bertgang in Jensen's tale, a professor of zoology whom the protagonist meets just once, out-

side the town and on the mountain, chasing lizards.

59. For the vulgarity of Pompeii, see aphorism 77 of Nietzsche, *Die Fröhliche Wissenschaft;* for the identification with Vesuvius ("wir sind alle wachsende Vulkane, die ihre Stunde der Eruption haben werden—wie nah aber oder wie fern diese ist, das freilich weiß niemand"), see aphorism 9; for the identification with the local inhabitants (*"gefährlich leben!* Baut eure Städte an den Vesuv!"), see aphorism 283.

60. Benjamin, "Untergang von Herculanum und Pompeji" in *Gesammelte Schriften,* 7:214–20; Benjamin, "Neapel," in *Gesammelte Schriften,* 4:307–16. It is worth adding that while Benjamin underscores the incommensurable differences between Naples and any north German city, he compares Pompeii to the city of Karlsruhe; Nietzsche's discussion of Pompeii also has a comparison of Italian and German *Gemeinheit* (see previous note)—which is to say, both authors use the classical setting as a means to reflect on the contemporary German.

61. See Tögel, *Berggasse-Pompeji und zurück.*

62. The two fantastic projects are, of course, inextricably linked: to become an aesthetic artifact is to leave the realm of life altogether, and to become the first, dead woman is to become a representation, a *Nachbildung,* in one's own right. See the chapter "Second Wives, Second Lives: The 'Ligeia Impulse' in Th. Storm's *Viola tricolor*" in Downing, *Double Exposures,* 129–69; see also Bronfen, *Over Her Dead Body.*

63. Christiane Zintzen, in "Wilhelm Jensen's *Gradiva* im Kontext," suggests several other texts that similarly involve this narrative strain and archaeology: perhaps "uniquely" is overstated.

64. Subsequent sections that reproduce in detail Hanold's dreams and other particular passages actually increase the degree to which Freud's essay seeks to reproduce the original fiction. See Rohrwasser, "Wilhelm Jensens 'pompeijanisches Phantasiestück,'" 31. One might well detect a correlation between the fact that Freud's summary is a third as long as Jensen's story and the fact that Hanold's plaster cast reproduces the original Gradiva statue in *Drittel-Lebensgröße* (23).

65. The extent to which Freud seems to have succeeded may be judged by the title of Urban and Cremerius's edition of the two works: although Jensen's text is printed first, the volume is titled after Freud's.

66. Urban and Cremerius, *Der Wahn und die Träume,* 93; Jensen's letter to Freud, May 13, 1907, is reprinted in Urban and Cremerius, 12.

67. Freud himself seems to compound the identification of his reading practice with the rhetorical tactics of the innkeeper when, in his description of the brooch, he substitutes the Latin term "Fibula" for Jensen's more contemporary and prosaic German "Spange," thus imparting to it a dignity and past dimension to which it pointedly has no real claim.

68. For more on the peculiarly Pompeiian quality of the psyche qua archaeological site, see the famous passage in Freud's "Ratman" study, *Standard Edition*, 10:16–7; also 2:139.

69. Freud further argues that the metaphorical regime of archaeology provides the material to represent not only the repressed erotic memory but also the act of repression itself—and not only the act of repression but also its professional removal, its bringing forth of what had been buried. Freud writes, "Hat [Hanold] einmal die eigene Kindheit mit der klassischen Vergangenheit zur Deckung gebracht, so ergibt die Verschüttung Pompejis, das Verschwinden mit Erhaltung des Vergangenen, eine treffliche *Ähnlichkeit* mit der Verdrängung" (127–28), i.e., a repression that not only covers but preserves. And as Hanold uses archaeology to "cover" repression, so, Freud argues, does Zoë—his chosen double in the tale—use archaeology to represent her own activity in therapeutically uncovering the repressed memory from beneath Hanold's archaeological fantasy. These dimensions of the archaeological metaphor will be discussed later.

70. The same assumption also underlies Freud's analysis of E. T. A. Hoffmann's *Der Sandmann* in his essay "Das Unheimliche" in *Studienausgabe*, 4:214–74/*Standard Edition*, 17:217–56.

71. Rohrwasser, *Freuds pompejanische Muse*, 28.

72. Reprinted in Urban and Cremerius, *Der Wahn und die Träume*, 13.

73. For Freud's engagement with the mythological premises of J. J. Bachofen, see Freud, *Totem und Tabu*, in *Studienausgabe*, 9:428, 9:432/*Standard Edition*, 13:144, 13:149; see also *Der Mann Moses und die monotheistische Religion*, in *Studienausgabe*, 9:531/*Standard Edition*, 23:83.

74. For Schuchhardt's and others' racial theories, see Marchand, *Down from Olympus*, 348–49.

75. See 114, 127, 133; also 116, "dieser Name [Gradiva] erweist sich nun als Abkomme."

76. This claim too has affinities with an admittedly more elaborate realist aesthetic, such as we encounter in Gottfried Keller's *Romeo und Julia auf dem Dorfe,* wherein the narrator posits a recurrent *Urfabel* that repeatedly asserts itself—reproduces itself—both in actual events in the real world and in fiction, including both Shakespeare's Renaissance drama and his own modern novella. But Freud's claim is also different from Keller's in a number of important ways. First, rather than to *Urfabeln,* Freud refers to "die antiken Typen," to specifically classical types that are brought back to the surface (*auftauchen*) in "our" midst, i.e., in the modern Germanic world. The shift from "Ur" to "antik" places a far different emphasis on the nature of the reproduction, stressing the cultural

specificity of both the model and the copy in ways that raise new issues of effaced otherness and appropriative identities. Second, rather than an underlying *Urfabel* that can produce itself either in reality or in art, Freud describes antique types from art ("Typen, die wir in den Sammlungen antreffen") that produce themselves as the contemporary real. In other words, Freud posits classical art that returns as modern German life, a rather different, more narrow, and more troubling claim than what we find in Keller. For more on Keller, see Holub, *Reflections of Realism,* 101–31.

77. Letter of May 25, 1907; reprinted in Urban and Cremerius, *Der Wahn und die Träume,* 13.

78. Freud also triumphantly proclaims, "Das von Jensen für römisch ausgegebene Relief des so schreitenden Mädchens, das er 'Gradiva' benennen läßt, gehört in Wirklichkeit der Blüte der griechischen Kunst an." See Urban and Cremerius, *Der Wahn und die Träume,* 164.

79. The importance of this last example will be discussed later.

80. The identification of the Gradiva with the sketchbook is further secured by the opening aside that it is "als ob der Künstler, statt wie in unsern Tagen mit dem Stift eine Skizze auf ein Blatt hinzuwerfen, sie [die Gradiva] auf der Straße im Vorübergehen rasch nach dem Leben in Tonmodell festgehalten habe" (23).

81. Recall again the image of Freud, poring over his German maps of Rome and Pompeii through the long Viennese winter, carefully imagining and orchestrating his lightning-quick excursions in the spring. How different, really, from Hanold? See Tögel, *Berggasse-Pompeji und zurück.*

82. See Urban and Cremerius, *Der Wahn und die Träume,* 164.

83. See the discussion of inheritance, stereotypes, and photographic *clichés* in chapter 1. Photographs and plaster casts were very much linked in nineteenth-century museum culture as related means for acquiring copies of widely scattered (and otherwise unavailable) original artworks and artifacts, a practice that in turn led to the development of typology. I should also add that the notion of identicalness (or of reproducible identicalness) in figural statues tended to support and fit in neatly with a contemporaneous ideology of racial purity.

84. Vogel, "Das pompejanische Phantasiestück," 96–97. Walter Benjamin dwells on this same anecdote in his radio piece on Pompeii; see Benjamin, *Nachträge,* 218.

85. Not for nothing is he subsequently chided by Zoë as *Schusterjunge* (80).

86. See also 26, 28, 47, 52.

87. The Gradiva's *Ruhe in Bewegung* also involves the play of life, death, and reanimation to Hanold's subsequent fantasy of Zoë as the Gradiva *rediviva;* in this respect, it is worth noting how Hanold conceives of the Bild

as possibly a *Gruftdenkmal* (29). All this resonates with topoi conventionally associated with the narrative strain of the "Ligeia impulse" mentioned earlier.

88. Catriona MacLeod points out how important it is in this context that the classical ideal of *Ruhe in Bewegung* is without clear origin or ascriptive authorship but is itself a recycled, free-floating coinage in Germany's nineteenth-century simulacric economy. She also stresses its particular application in critical discourse to the genre of *Reliefbilder* (personal communication).

89. We might contrast Hanold's *Anspruch* with the Gradiva's own reputed *Anspruchlosigkeit* (26): his claim requires her loss; his pretension, her unpretentiousness.

90. Of course, the mirror of narcissism produces not only likenesses but also reversals; see also Aschenbach and Tadzio in Mann's *Der Tod in Venedig*.

91. Freud does not mention the story's incest motif in his essay, although he suggests it in his *Nachtrag* (163); narcissism does not figure in his discussion at all. I should add that even as Hanold forces the resemblances between the German man and woman near the end, so too (as Jensen was at pains to express to Freud) does he force the resemblances between Zoë and the Gradiva throughout—itself a reflection of the equally enforced resemblances between the *Reliefbild* and Hanold himself. Ultimately, Zoë is embraced as a figural mirror of Hanold, as *his* double (and doubles are never real).

92. Hanold also translates "Zoë" out of the Greek into the German "Leben": over and again, we see that the story is as much concerned with lingual transformations as with material, artifactual ones, as much with classical *Sprachphilologie* as *Sachphilologie*.

93. Many German readers would no doubt be alerted to this name play by memories of Ludwig Tieck's *Der Blonde Eckbert*.

94. Theodor Fontane's *Frau Jenny Treibel* gives brilliant expression to the mobile and precarious class context within which professional classicists situated themselves; all of what is said in this paragraph about Jensen's novella is confirmed and more fully elaborated in Fontane's novel.

95. Porter, *Nietzsche*, 255.

96. It is worth stressing how, unlike even his father, Hanold is never depicted as actually employed or working: classics is for him primarily merely a form of the *vita contemplativa,* of leisure, as far removed from the base of real work as possible. The baselessness, the detachment from the "real world" of productive activity, also extends to Hanold's specialty within classics, namely, archaeology: never are we led to imagine that he ever held a spade in hand. That is, his classicism is always exclusively imaginary work, part of the same imaginary economy as his plaster cast repro-

duction.

97. This appropriation of the classical in the service of enhancing both social and self-identity is to some extent already performed or accomplished for August and Grete through their given names, which resonate with both the Goethean and classical ideals. This is even more the case with Zoë, whose father seems to have been motivated by the same impulse that led Schliemann to name his children Agamemnon and Andromache. It is a question well worth pondering: why should a Prussian professor (of biology) wish to name his child Zoë?

98. The obvious paradox here is that, to be authentic, desire must be mediated by art or, rather, artifice.

99. Hanold's dream raises the further question of why he expected the statues to speak Greek and not Latin.

100. The French are conspicuous in their absence from Jensen's tale: there is not a single French tourist in all of Italy, let alone Pompeii, and although Jensen's language is designed to reflect Hanold's linguistic erudition, there are none of the casual borrowings from French phraseology one might perhaps expect. That the exclusion of the Romanic from the German-classical bond is overlaid with an exclusion of the Catholic and its Latin culture is worth remembering: like his friend Raabe, Jensen tended to identify the German national cause with his own Protestant culture and Catholicism with foreign interests.

101. Consider Hanold's reason for removing himself from present-day Rome: "er war nur aus einer lärmvollen Steingrube in die andre geraten," only that "die dutzendfachen Ausrufe der Verkäufer noch weit schrilltöniger im Ohr [kreischten] als in seiner deutschen Heimat" (36).

102. Hanold's lack of contact with the real Greece is all the more remarkable for a young German archaeologist trained in the age of Schliemann and of the dig at Olympia.

103. Nietzsche, *Die Geburt der Tragödie*, in *Sämtliche Werke*, vol. 1 (section 20).

104. See how in the passage cited earlier, Hanold imagines the "Modelle der antiken Kunstwerke" away from the Italians, rendering them Hellenized "Olympians" and hence German too, or how in Hanold's dream (also cited earlier), the Venus and Apollo speak German and not, as Hanold expects, Greek—with Latin or Italian simply elided without further ado.

105. The elaboration of racial models for German identity and archaeology is even more evident in the work of Freud's (and Hanold's) contemporary, the notorious Gustav Kossinna; see Marchand, *Down from Olympus*, 180–87; see also Marchand's discussion of Carl Schuchhardt et al (349).

106. To a somewhat lesser extent, this is also true of the Germans' northern cousins, the English; see 43.

107. Zintzen, "Wilhelm Jensen's *Gradiva* im Kontext," 52–53.
108. I am not claiming that the investment in whiteness is the exclusive obsession of this particular period in German culture: we can find it already in Winckelmann, and as Andreas Huyssen points out, it reappears in the Bauhaus movement as well (personal communication). In all cases, however, whiteness and classicism remain closely associated in the German imaginary.
109. Do note the phrase "zur Reizung der Kauflust" in the same passage: the commercial and erotic as one.
110. This same metaphorical white rain appears at the end of the story as well, when "die ganze ausgegrabene Stadt erschien, statt mit Bimssteinen und Asche, von den wohltätigen Regensturz mit Perlen und Diamanten überschüttet" (85): not a coarse and dirty real world ("Pompeji selbst!") but a richly aestheticized one filled with noble wealth and reflecting *Glanz.*
111. The transformation of the sullied gray of the plaster cast into the pure white of the marmoreal Zoë is precisely equivalent to the transformation of the dirty gray of the Vesuvian ash into the snow-white of the northern storm: in the one case, the off-white meanness is German; in the other, Italian; but in both the achieved white is German.
112. The underworld motif of this literary topos is perhaps most readily identified with the myth of Orpheus and Eurydice. The silence of the beloved can be readily seen in such related works as Storm's *Viola tricolor* or Mann's *Der Tod in Venedig.*
113. See 45; the example concerns the tension between "die mit Mosaiksteinchen eingelegte Inschrift" proclaiming the purity and good taste of the ancient innkeeper's wine and the graffiti suggesting its actual dilution with water. For the association of water with the plebian, see 67–68.
114. From a more literary perspective, we might say that classical archaeology helps introduce much of the post-idealist realism, the *realia* that *Dichtung* was supposed to illuminate (*die verklärte Wirklichkeit*).
115. Following other scholars, I include graffiti—and more broadly, inscriptions—in this silent, nonverbal world of archaeology, insofar as they fall outside the narrative tradition and its sustained cultural transmission.
116. One could also say that the crisis is not really resolved at all. Rather, like so much else in the story, it is simply displaced in a manner that disguises its continuance: despite several gestures to the contrary, the *archäologische Anschauung* and *philologische Sprache* are never abandoned by Hanold.
117. Freud, *The Aetiology of Hysteria* (1896), in *Studienausgabe,* 6:54/*Standard Edition,* 3:192. He is quoting Lucian. This passage will be analyzed in detail in chapter 3.

118. This last point has a long history in German nineteenth-century thought, beginning with Schleiermacher's formulation of hermeneutics in 1816 as split between a grammatical and a technical interpretation, with the latter aiming to reach "the subjectivity of the one who speaks, the language being forgotten," and later replaced by the term "psychological interpretation"; see Ricoeur, "Task of Hermeneutics," 47.

119. See the initial characterization of the plaster cast as permeated by *etwas Durchgeistigtes* (26).

120. This shift to German as the language of archaeology is evident in both private correspondence and published scholarship; see Marchand, *Down from Olympus,* 101–2.

121. This rise in the stock of German is also evident in literature, in the emergence of a literary tradition—poetic realism—independent of classical models.

122. See Stray, *Classics Transformed,* on German science and inspiration.

123. See ibid., 102–10.

124. This is, of course, the opposite argument to that made by Freud: whereas he argues that it is the inner unconscious psyche of Hanold that transforms and insinuates itself into the external, supposedly conscious reality of his science, I am arguing that it is the external imaginary reality of his science that is transformed and installed as a supposedly unconscious psychology.

125. See also the motif of the "common" water at the two hotels (39) and in the wine (45).

126. An interesting parallel can be drawn with Keller's *Der Grüne Heinrich,* where the dead beloved, Anna, is imagined by the protagonist, Heinrich Lee, to be able to see his every thought, which he therefore strives to make as noble and worthy as possible. In other words, the mechanism for manufacturing a proper interior identity that we see here between Hanold and the Gradiva is a recognizable tool in the arsenal of Bildung; what is new, of course, is the figuring of the *Geisterseherin* as specifically classical.

127. It is, moreover, the same ennobling function or mechanism of subjectivized archaeology to which Zoë refers in her own subsequent deployment of the archaeological metaphor. She notes how the study of *Altertumswissenschaft* transformed Hanold into something "so *großartig* wie ein . . . ausgrabene[s] vorsintflutliche[s] Vogelungetüm . . . Nur daß dein Kopf eine ebenfalls so *großartige* Phantasie beherbergte . . . mich auch für etwas Ausgegrabenes anzusehn—das hatte ich nicht bei dir vermutet" (81). In the case of both Hanold himself and his projected fantasy of Zoë, the metaphorically archaeological is that which constitutes its subject as *großartig* in a reciprocal play of mirroring investments.

128. In other words, it is the linking of introjection with retrojection.

129. Recall Zoë's comment to her friend Gisa: "Ich sagte mir, irgend etwas Interessantes würde ich wohl schon allein hier ausgraben. Freilich, auf den Fund, den ich gemacht . . . hatte ich mit keinem Gedanken gerechnet" (75).

130. See Trigger, *History of Archaeological Thought,* 57–58.

131. See Freud, *Totem und Tabu,* in *Studienausgabe* 9:295 / *Standard Edition* 13:1. C. G. Jung had similar, and similarly disturbing, ideas, which often seem, like Freud's, to import James Frazier's British imperialist anthropology into the realm of the individual human psyche. Jung will be further discussed in chapter 3.

132. The application of postcolonial critique to psychoanalysis might begin with the questions, Are the psyche and the child the ultimate subalterns? Is either permitted to speak, other than in the language of the (conscious adult) master? Again, it is not an issue of colonialism being structured like the unconscious but of the unconscious being structured like colonialism. For some specific criticism leveled by Benjamin at the related attitude toward children implied by both psychoanalysis and the culture of Bildung, see the epilogue.

133. Even Freud concedes that the story provides no reason for Hanold to repress such a memory; see the earlier section, "Digging Freud." We might also emphasize that Hanold explicitly rejects Zoë's explanation, "Daß jemand erst sterben muß, um lebendig zu werden. Aber für die Archäologie ist das wohl notwendig" (82), and thus implicitly refutes both Freud's reading of a lost-and-then-recovered memory and its understanding of the intended parallel with archaeology.

134. The parallel between Norbert's attraction to Zoë qua Gradiva here and, in Hitchcock's *Vertigo,* Scottie's attraction to Judy qua Madeleine can perhaps throw the point into greater relief. Even though Judy "was" Madeleine to begin with, it is only insofar as she reproduces the fictitious Madeleine a second time that Scottie is attracted to her at all. It would be fatuous to argue that Scottie was originally in love with Judy, or finally so; and yet it is a strictly equivalent argument that Freud proposes for Norbert and Zoë.

135. Reprinted in Urban and Cremerius, *Der Wahn und die Träume,* 14.

136. There are other explicit examples of manufactured memories in the tale (e.g., 71, 72), all of them of a piece with the innkeeper's fabricated story of the love story behind the counterfeit brooch or, more broadly, with the simulacric economy of the story as a whole.

137. Porter, *Nietzsche,* 273–86.

138. See Urban and Cremerius, *Der Wahn und die Träume,* 16–17.

139. See Zintzen, "Wilhelm Jensen's *Gradiva* im Kontext," on the peculiarly

happy ending to Jensen's novella in comparison with other, related tales set in Pompeii; see also her speculations on why Freud should choose such a happy ending as his example.

Chapter 3

1. Walter Benjamin, *Berliner Chronik,* in *Gesammelte Schriften,* 6:465–519. All references to Benjamin's works referred to parenthetically in the text are to this edition; all references without a specified volume number are to volume 6 and refer exclusively to *Berliner Chronik.* English translations are based on Benjamin, *Selected Writings.* References in the text to the English edition are given after those to the German; all references to the English edition without a specified volume number are to volume 2 and refer exclusively to *Berlin Chronicle.*
2. For the Bibel-Babel controversy, see Marchand, *Down from Olympus,* 223–27.
3. See Ryan, *The Uncompleted Past.*
4. The same inadvertent reproduction of the very ideology he would oppose can be seen in the contemporary novel of Mann's friend Hermann Hesse, whose *Das Glasperlenspiel* (1943) ends with a most disquieting celebration of vitalist ideals.
5. See Assmann, *Moses the Egyptian,* 147.
6. For the reference to Galton, see Freud, *Studienausgabe,* 9:462/*Standard Edition,* 22:10. For more on the role of photography in the conceptual schema of this work, see Freud, *Studienausgabe,* 9:571/*Standard Edition,* 22:126; see also my discussion in chapter 1.
7. Freud, *Studienausgabe,* 9:459/*Standard Edition,* 22:7.
8. See Ibid., 9:506/22:57.
9. Ibid., 9:503–4/22:54.
10. See Freud's notion of the *archaische Erbschaft* discussed at length in the Moses book (*Studienausgabe,* 9:545–49/*Standard Edition,* 22:98–102).
11. For more on this particular essay of Freud's, see Reinhard, "The Freudian Things."
12. Jung, *Seelenprobleme der Gegenwart,* 326. Cited by Benjamin, *Das Passagenwerk* [K6, 1], 5:504.
13. See esp. Jung, *Archetypes.*
14. Benjamin, *Das Passagenwerk* [K6, 3], 5:505; see also Benjamin, "Über einige Motive bei Baudelaire," 1:608.
15. See Benjamin, *Gesammelte Schriften,* 1:1068–70.
16. Bachofen, *Das Mutterecht.* For Bachofen's influence on Freud's psychology, see my discussion in chapter 2.
17. See in particular "Geist und Seele" and "Vom Traumbewusstsein" in

Klages, *Sämtliche Werke*, 3:1–154 and 3:155–238.

18. Archaeology was traditionally linked to the image as opposed to the text-based culture of philology, and this common investment in the visual as opposed to the textual was an important part of the identity between photography and archaeology. Insofar as Klages linked images with the prehistoric and texts with reason, he seems to perpetuate the new, nineteenth-century binary of image and text introduced and sustained by archaeology.

19. Jaeger, "Introduction: The Place of the Greeks in the History of Education," in *Paideia*, xiii–xxix. See also Marchand, *Down from Olympus*, 319–30.

20. Jaeger, *Paideia*, xiii–xxix.

21. For the grace of Goethe, see Marchand, *Down from Olympus*, 327.

22. Jaeger, "Die geistige Gegenwart der Antike," 160; cited by Marchand, *Down from Olympus*, 324.

23. Marchand, *Down from Olympus*, 337; for the new emphasis on visuality and the culture of *Schönheit*, see Jaeger's discussion of the statues of the Olympic victors (*Paideia*, 25).

24. Rodenwaldt and Hege, *Die Akropolis*. See Marchand, *Down from Olympus*, 339. Szegedy-Maszak, in "True Illusions," and Hamilakis, in "Monumental Visions," both point out how the tradition of excluding both people and modern structures from photographs of the Acropolis in order to emphasize its timeless, mythical qualities was part of the aesthetic photographic tradition established by Felix Bonfils and William Stillman already in the late 1860s.

25. For Scholem's comments, see Benjamin, *Gesammelte Schriften*, 6:797.

26. For more on Benjamin's involvement in the Youth Movement, see Witte, *Walter Benjamin*, 22–39.

27. Benjamin, *Gesammelte Schriften*, 2:75–87/*Selected Writings*, 1:37–47.

28. See Witte, *Walter Benjamin*, 26; McCole, *Walter Benjamin*, 46.

29. See Benjamin's letter to Wyneken of March 9, 1915, renouncing his mentor, included in Benjamin, *Correspondence*, 75–76.

30. See also Benjamin's citation of Brecht's comment, "There is no longer any doubt—the struggle against ideology has become a new ideology," in Benjamin, "Conversations with Brecht," in *Reflections*, 217.

31. See Witte, *Walter Benjamin*, 16. Two good examples of the kinder, more erotically tinged tone of *Berliner Kindheit* can be seen in the vignettes "Das Fieber" and "Gesellschaft"; see also the wonderful reading of "Ein Gespenst" in Hamacher, "The Word *Wolke*," 149–51.

32. See Eiland and Jennings, *Walter Benjamin*, 2:637 (notes to *Berlin Chronicle*).

33. This echoes the more general claim Benjamin formulated in "Schicksal

und Charakter" (1919): "das Außen, das der handelnde Mensch vorfindet, kann in beliebig hohem Maße auf sein Innen, sein Innen in beliebig hohem Maße auf sein Außen prinzipiell zurückgefuhrt, ja als dieses prinzipiell angesehen werden" (2:173). Although Benjamin admits this claim is often a problematic one, he also says it is true of precisely those aspects of his own life he explores in *Berliner Chronik* (491–92) and, clearly, of those aspects of Goethe's life he explores in this essay.

34. See also Benjamin, "Der Erzähler": "Indem [der Bildungsroman] den gesellschaftlichen Lebensprozeß in der Entwicklung einer Person integriert, läßt er den ihn bestimmenden Ordnungen die denkbar brüchigste Rechtfertigung angedeihen" (2:443).

35. Benjamin, *Das Passagenwerk* [N2a, 4], 5:577.

36. Compare also the section "Tiefbau-Arbeiten" in the same work, describing an archaeological dig in the Weimar marketplace (4:101).

37. See the *Vorwort* to *Berliner Kindheit*, where Benjamin uses the image of immunization (*Impfung*) to characterize this sense of disaffection.

38. See also, "Wider ein Meisterwerk: Zu Max Kommerell, 'Der Dichter als Führer in der deutschen Klassik'" (1930; 3:252–59), which takes aim against the culture of classical Bildung and its present continuance more broadly.

39. It is perhaps even more like Barthes's idea of decomposition wherein Barthes says, "I remain within this [bourgeois] consciousness and proceed to dismantle it, to weaken it, to break it down on the spot," and "I agree to accompany such decomposition, to decompose myself in the process" (*Roland Barthes*, 63). For Benjamin's use of the term "decomposition," see *Das Passagenwerk* [Y7a, 1], 5:838–39.

40. See Buck-Morss, *Dialectics of Seeing*, 67–68.

41. As Benjamin writes, "Lange, jahrelang eigentlich, spiele ich schon mit der Vorstellung, den Raum des Lebens—Bios—graphisch in einer Karte zu gliedern." Christopher Wild points out how this tactic recalls the *Mnemotechnik* of the Greek poet Simonides, whose recollection of the seating arrangement of guests at a banquet just before the collapse of the building assisted him in the recovery work of the excavated bodies and led to his original discovery of the *ars memoriae* (personal communication). It is indeed worth noting Benjamin's recourse to such a notably archaic technique of recall and especially one that seems already to evoke a kind of primal archaeological scene for its practice.

42. "Sich in einer Stadt nicht zurechtzufinden—das mag uninteressant und banal sein . . . In einer Stadt aber sich zu verirren—das bedarf schon einer ganz anderen Schulung" (469).

43. He more directly takes issue with it in his essays on Naples and Pompeii.

44. Benjamin was well aware that this journey also always implies a Faustian theft of Helen and appropriation of the classical world for the German's own: see "Über einige Motive bei Baudelaire," 1:646.

45. For Benjamin and the museum director, Wilhelm Bode, see McIsaac, "Divide between Nature and Civilization"; Alexander, "Wilhelm Bode and Berlin's Museum Island," in *Museum Masters.* For Benjamin on the role of state museums in fashioning the (hated) public imaginary, see "Eduard Fuchs, Der Sammler und der Historiker," 2:465–505.

46. Benjamin further emphasizes this compounding of the classical and the Teutonic in Hessel's work when he describes "die deutsch-griechische Neigung zur Wortverbindung" such as *nordblond,* etc. (3:83).

47. Not surprisingly (nor insignificantly), the latter vignette incorporates much of both of Benjamin's Hessel reviews.

48. Benjamin, "Untergang von Herculanum und Pompeii," 7:214–20.

49. For classicism as the propping pillar for *allgemeine Bildung,* see *Das Passagenwerk* [Y4, 4], 5:831.

50. See *Berliner Kindheit,* 4:294–96.

51. Such classicizing can also be seen to contest such a nationalist cultural imaginary. Germany was poised between two self-conceptions at the time, balanced on either side of the archaeological fault line that ran through its territory and divided the Romano-Germanisch nation of the south from the "free" region of the north. This archaeological split in its past yielded different conceptions of its national identity in the present, pitting a more European-integrated image against a racially distinct one, a civilized heritage against a barbaric one or, conversely, a tainted, decadent heritage against a pure, uninfected one, etc. (The split was institutionally reinforced by the competing communities of archaeologists, the professional and classically trained practitioners of *Altertumswissenschaft,* and the amateur, most Germanophile pliers of *Altertumskunde.*) Within this context, the evocation of the Greco-Roman past, especially when juxtaposed with the north German setting of Berlin, could be highly charged in subversive ways. That is, the classical figuration of the Teutonic site could have a dual effect: on the one hand, it could lend the institutional splendor and authority of the classical to the still rather provincial homeland history; on the other, it could weaken the availability of Berlin's past (and artifacts) to support a separatist, racially "pure" non-European conception of the German. Benjamin seems to underscore this latter effect in his review of *Spazieren in Berlin* (and he does much the same thing in *Berliner Chronik*) by pairing Hessel's description of Berlin with those of Paris, and contrasting both with the traditional descriptions of Rome and its *nationalen Heiligtümer.* Whereas the latter pairing (Berlin/Rome) very much reinforces the institutional dreams of

German neoclassicism qua legitimated empire, the former (Berlin/Paris) tends to deflate such dreams, not least by keeping Germany part of a broader, more modern European identity. Compare Hitler's take on Paris and Berlin, described in Buck-Morss, *Dialectics of Seeing*, 328. Even more than Benjamin, Wilhelm Raabe exploits this classicizing affront to German nationalism; see especially his story "Keltische Knochen" and his novel *Das Odfeld*.

52. For another formulation of this project, see "Paris, die Hauptstadt des XIX. Jahrhunderts," 5:45–59, esp. 46–47. See also Lindner, "Das Passagenwerk."

53. See Benjamin, "Paris, die Hauptstadt des XIX Jahrhunderts," 5:54, 5:59.

54. See "Das Kunstwerk im Zeitalter seiner technischen Reproduzierbarkeit," 1:439; also Snyder, "Benjamin on Reproducibility," 164.

55. See Benjamin, "Paris, Hauptstadt" 5:54, 59. McCole, *Walter Benjamin*, 211.

56. McCole, *Walter Benjamin*, 217; see also Buck-Morss, *Dialectics of Seeing*, 463; Benjamin, "Solange es noch einen Bettler gibt, solange gibt es noch Mythos," *Das Passagenwerk* [K6, 4], 5:505.

57. McCole, *Walter Benjamin*, 208–9.

58. We find the same dusty landings and niches in *Berliner Kindheit*. For more on Benjamin and dust, and especially dust and archaeology, see the epilogue.

59. Consider "Abschied nehmen von das was noch anhielt, was dauerte" (468); "ob mein Alter schon weg sei" (475); "zu spät!" (494).

60. For example, in Benjamin, the city as labyrinth becomes the self as labyrinth (491); this will be discussed in more detail later.

61. "Rückkehr von den Courses de la Marche: 'La poussière a dépassé toutes les espérances. Les élégances retour de la Marche sont quasi ensevelies, à l'instar de Pompeï, et il faut les déterrer à coups de brosse, sinon à coup de pioche'" (*Das Passagenwerk* [D3a,5], 5:165).

62. See Benjamin, *Das Passagenwerk* [D1a,3], 5:158.

63. Benjamin specifies this temple as *mexikanisch*. For his 1916 studies in pre-Columbian culture, see Eiland and Jennings's chronology in Benjamin, *Walter Benjamin*, 1:500; Witte, *Walter Benjamin*, 34.

64. Richter, in *Walter Benjamin*, makes the ingenious suggestion "that the word [Mark-talle] seals within its disfiguration: the contemporary *Mark* and the historical currency, the *Thaler*" (212).

65. Other such words in *Berliner Chronik* include *Brauhausberg, Pfaueninsel, Stieglitz*, etc. See Hamacher's masterful analysis, "*The Word Wolke*"; see also Carol Jacobs on Stieglitz in Jacobs, *In the Language of Walter Benjamin*, 30–33.

66. These prostitutes are also mythologized, albeit in a negative way, referred

to as "gleichsam Laren dieses Kults des Nichts" (472). Benjamin's critical interest in the figure of the prostitute was extensive—see, e.g., Convolut O in *Das Passagenwerk*.

67. Buck-Morss, *Dialectic of Seeing*, 114–24.

68. This concern is also raised by McCole's study in a variety of different contexts, although he consistently argues that Benjamin avoids said complicity: I am not as sure.

69. As the earlier discussion of Goethe noted, this "outside to inside" movement is a major concern of Benjamin's early essay "Schicksal und Charakter" (2:171–79). For the mimetic faculty, see "Lehre vom Ähnlichen" (2:204–10) and "Über das mimetische Vermögen" (2:210–13).

70. Benjamin's belief that our shaping dreams are not in us, our psyches, but in our belongings, our artifacts, that the true locus of the archaic mythological dreamworld is not in the psychic interior of the bourgeois subject but in the domestic interior of his furnished home, and that only in the mimetic moment of chiastic introjection does it becomes his psychic interior as well is the reason for his analytical assault on the grandmother's abode, as the surest way to approach *der möbilierte Mensch, der neue Mensch,* who has been formed in his confrontation with the furniture from the second half of the nineteenth century and *its* embodiment of archaic dream forms and mythic consciousness—its caryatids, vases, and shades of Pompeii red, etc. It is similarly his reason for foregrounding the counterpart to this interior space, namely, the exterior urban architecture, especially neoclassical and Gothic, that projects its dreams of national identity onto the more publicly conceived bourgeois subject. Here too the real focus remains the mimetic construction of the subject via the moment of chiastic return. For *der mobilierte Mensch,* see "Traumkitsch" (2:622); see also McCole, *Walter Benjamin,* 218.

71. It is worth pointing out that, in this regard, the Jungian and Bachofen–based Klagesian psychologies are no different from the Freudian here discussed.

72. There have been many readings of this passage from *Berliner Chronik*, some more successful than others: see, e.g., Rugg, *Picturing Ourselves,* 157–58; Jacobs, *In the Language of Walter Benjamin,* 28–29; Richter, *Walter Benjamin,* 42–48. None seeks to place it against the background of similar archaeological metaphors of the time.

73. As Benjamin says of the crown molding in his school (and he says much the same about his first books, etc.), the reason he is able to recover this one broken and banal fragment when all the rest has been washed away is because "alles, was mir sonst ins Blickfeld kam, hat früher oder später irgendwie für mich von Nutzen sein [können], mit einem Gedanken, einen Handgriff sich verbunden, die ihn mit sich in das Meer des

Vergessens führten. Nur diese schmale Leiste, die der gesunde Wellenschlag des Alltags täglich unzählige Male wieder aufgeworfen, bis sie wie ein Muschel auf dem Sande an dem Strand meiner Träumerei liegen blieb" (509–10).

74. See Buck-Morss, *Dialectics of Seeing;* McCole, *Walter Benjamin,* 249–52.

75. This probing is to be done carefully, *tastend,* with a spade only and not Freud's shovel or pickaxe; the native respects his soil, almost tills it, in ways unknown to Freud's rational foreign traveler.

76. The emphasis on Bilder reappears decisively in the *Vorwort* to *Berliner Kindheit* as well.

77. See Weber, "Mass Mediauras."

78. Benjamin, *Das Passagenwerk* [N2a3], 5:577.

79. For more on Klages's concept of Bild, see his essay "Vom Traumbewußtsein" in Klages, *Sämtliche Werke,* 3:155–238.

80. This is something like but also more than T. S. Eliot's "We had the experience but missed the meaning, / And approach to the meaning restores the experience / In a different form" (from part 2 of "The Dry Salvages" in *Four Quartets*).

81. Benjamin describes this as a kind of reverse experience of déjà vu: not the present as an uncanny repetition of the past, but the past as an equally uncanny anticipation of the future (518).

82. Buck-Morss, *Dialectics of Seeing,* 71–72.

83. Benjamin, *Das Passagenwerk* [N2a, 4], 5:577; the passage follows immediately after the one contrasting archaic and dialectical images cited earlier.

84. Darby, "Photography, Narrative." Darby supports the parallel with the "tantalizing evidence" that Benjamin seems to have set several passages of *Berliner Chronik* in verse (220).

85. For the indebtedness of Benjamin's concept of Bild to Bergson's concept, see the review of Carol Jacobs's book by James McFarland. For Bergson's influence on modernist thought, see inter alia the discussion of Mann's *Der Zauberberg* in chapter 1; the influence on Eliot's *Four Quartets* seems equally patent. For the comparison with Klages and Jung and the designation of the latter pair as fascist, see Benjamin, *Gesammelte Schriften,* 1:608.

86. Jacobs, *In the Language of Walter Benjamin,* 9–14.

87. See also Benjamin, *Einbahnstraße,* 4:117.

88. See Benjamin's discussion of Proust's "Glücksidee" as "das ewige Nocheinmal, die ewige Restauration des ursprünglichen, ersten Glücks," in "Zum Bilde Prousts" (2:313).

89. See Darby's delightful elaboration of the connections between photography and railways in Benjamin's thought: Darby, "Photography, Narra-

tive," 215–16.

90. Benjamin, *Das Passagenwerk* [Y8, 1], 5:839.

91. Benjamin, *Das Passagenwerk* [Y4, 4], 5:831.

92. Mann appreciates Renger-Patzsch's photography for reasons that are very close to those for which Benjamin praises that of August Sander. For Mann on Renger-Patzsch, see chapter 1; for Benjamin on Sander, see below.

93. Benjamin, "Paris, Hauptstadt," 5:57: see Buck-Morss, *Dialectics of Seeing,* 90.

94. For the phantasmagoria of continuity, see Buck-Morss, *Dialectics of Seeing,* 67.

95. Rugg mentions Atget as a model for the literary technique Benjamin deploys in *Berliner Kindheit* (*Picturing Ourselves,* 158); for various reasons to be discussed, I find the applicability to *Berliner Chronik* far more apt.

96. See Buck-Morss, *Dialectics of Seeing:* "André Breton's novel *Nadja* (1928), Benjamin notes, is a book more about Paris than about the elusive heroine named in the title. Breton includes photographs of Paris empty of people that mark the narrated events as if transient experience could be made present within the material spaces of cafés and street-corners known to the reader" (33).

97. As John Szarkowski notes, in his over thirty years in Paris, Atget never photographed the Eiffel Tower, the Arch of Triumph, Granier's Opera, or the grand boulevards of Haussmann, all monuments to state ideology and, in part, of a specifically nineteenth-century bourgeois imaginary; See Szarkowski and Hambourg, *Work of Atget,* 1:13.

98. Hambourg, "The Structure of the Work," in Szarkowski and Hambourg, *The Work of Atget,* 3:15. Hambourg also comments on Atget's idiosyncratic filing system for his more than 4,000 pictures, which seems to anticipate Benjamin's practice in *Das Passagenwerk* (10).

99. Benjamin calls this "die Wirklichkeit abzuschminken" (2:377/2:518).

100. Hambourg, *The Work of Atget,* 3:15.

101. Ibid., 3:14–15, 3:12.

102. In discussing Dadaism and John Hartfield's photography in "Der Author als Produzent," Benjamin stresses that such tiny authentic fragments of daily life rupture time as well (2:692–93); as so often in Benjamin, the dimension of time and space are tightly interwoven.

103. See "Über einige Motive bei Baudelaire," 1:644–50. To my knowledge, this reversal in the sense of aura has gone mostly unremarked in the extensive critical literature. We might want to qualify the claim that this latter aura conveys a meaning by heeding Scholem's more cautious formulation that such fragments retain instead a "validity"; see Alter, *Nec-*

essary Angels. Even with this caveat, it should be clear that Benjamin is once again approaching the territory of Klages's vitalism and submerged images.

104. The review is of a book by Karl Bloßfeldt, *Urformen der Kunst: Photographische Pflanzenbilder*. Benjamin recapitulates some of his main points about Bloßfeld again in the "Kleine Geschichte" essay (2:372). Besides photo enlargements, Benjamin also discusses their temporal equivalents in slow-motion or time-lapse photography.

105. See Benjamin, "Das Kunstwerk im Zeitalter seiner technischen Reproduzierbarkeit," 1:498.

106. In the related passage in the "Kunstwerk" essay, Benjamin specifically mentions Freud's "Psychopathologie des Alltagslebens."

107. See Rugg, *Picturing Ourselves*, 133.

108. Kaiser and Kittler, *Dichtung als Sozialisationsspiel*. For books and Bildung, see also my discussion in chapter 1 and Winthrop-Young, "Magic Media Mountain."

109. For more on *Höfe* and aura, see Weber, "Mass Mediauras," 93.

110. The role of the grandmother in addition to the mother is foregrounded in the original version of *Wilhelm Meister, Die Theatralische Sendung* (and in *Dichtung und Wahrheit*).

111. In all fairness to both Goethe and Keller, we need to note that, in the latter, Heinrich Lee's first theater experiences are when he is dressed up to play just such a monkey on stage, and the play in which he performs is Goethe's *Faust*. So rather than choosing a point completely outside of the Bildung tradition from which to launch his critique, Benjamin can be shown to isolate out a detail embedded within it—as indeed his theory of the photograph would lead us to expect.

112. The occasion of this particular scene is a performance of Schiller's *Wilhelm Tell*, and we might well both recall the central role this play serves in *Der Grüne Heinrich* as part of Heinrich's Bildung (and socialization) and read the child Benjamin's barely suppressed—indeed only momentarily deferred—resentment and rebellion against tyrannical power here as an alternative internalization of the play: again, as in the case of the little monkey, finding a *winziges Fünkchen Zufall* embedded within the larger Bild as the image for his own "other" meaning.

113. Freud might call this cohering nexus the secondary revision, the narrative ordering—but also distorting and hiding—of the remembered Bilder.

114. Benjamin places great weight on these cards, claiming they represent the key to his *Lebensschicksale* (500).

115. See also Benjamin, *Das Passagenwerk* [Y6a, 6], 5:837. Of course, Benjamin's postcard also resembles one of those *Abbilder* whose mass pro-

duction exudes the sense of *Flüchtigkeit und Wiederholbarkeit* that works against the *Eimaligkeit und Dauer* so central to the establishment of aura and its corresponding social identity—from either perspective, as a vehicle of national identity or as a cheap and common postcard, a dirty picture.

116. Weber would seem to legitimate a reading of the *Höfe* in this passage as also traced through with suggestions of aura ("Mass Mediauras," 93–94).

117. The second passage is a citation from Lichtwark.

118. For Benjamin's *Verzicht* of the *Ich*, see 475–76.

119. I.e., photography helped develop typology in archaeology, but the typology developed in archaeology also came to determine the psychology behind much of the typology associated with photography.

120. For the privileged objectivity and authenticity of photography, see Benjamin, *Gesammelte Schriften*, 2:385. For its inherent reproducibility, and hence typology, see ibid., 2:379.

121. I.e., just as archaeology functions as both the method of excavation and as the site of excavation (in Mann, Jensen, Freud, and Benjamin himself), so too does photography serve not merely as a metaphor for the method of viewing memories but for the mode of recording them in the first place.

122. "Aus einer kleine Rede über Proust, an meinem vierzigsten Geburtstag gehalten" (2:1064–65). See also Hansen, "Benjamin, Cinema and Experience"; McCole, *Walter Benjamin*, 273.

123. In this respect, the literary equivalent of photomontage in *Berliner Chronik*, with its deliberate disruption of linear, coherent narrative, merely accentuates the effect that photography per se always wreaks on perception and experience and that Benjamin is working to achieve with each and every Bild.

124. This kind of memory is also a kind of forgetting, its *Glanz* a kind of obscurity, insofar as, by assimilating it to the *durée* of conscious experience, the object (or experience) is deprived of its otherness, its potential disruption. As Benjamin notes elsewhere, Freud claims an event cannot be both conscious and remembered at once: consciousness is a form of parrying memory, of not allowing it to happen, of preemptively absorbing the "shock" of experience by making sense of it.

125. See Benjamin, "Über einige Motive bei Baudelaire" in *Gesammelte Schriften*, 1:612–14. Such memories seem also to partake of a paradoxical status as both remembered and forgotten at once, albeit oppositely from that of conscious memory. Because they were never consciously registered, never *bewußt*, they remain *unbewußt*, unknown (unmastered, unassimilated), unseen, but for that very reason stored instead in mem-

ory. For more on the interchangeability of memory and forgetting and the "net" of consciousness, see Bahti, "Theories of Knowledge."

126. Recall the desire of the much-later viewer to catch the aslant or down-turned gaze of the photographed subject discussed in "Kleine Geschichte" (2:371).

127. Cf. the candle subsequently placed behind the picture postcard of the Halle Gate or the dream later snuck behind the memory to illuminate it.

128. This seems to be the approach of Rugg (see *Picturing Ourselves*, 137).

129. The same strange premise or conclusion seems operant in Bergson's schema in *Matière et Mémoire* as well.

130. We do know that in the psychological polemics of the time, the term "Chock" always indicates the (electrifying) impact of the external, specifically modern-urban-technological world on the individual psyche, in pitted contrast with vitalistic psychologies that would see the igniting impulses arising from within the isolated individual him- or herself. See Killen, "From Shock to Schreck."

131. An additional complication arises if we briefly foreground the interplay of photography and archaeology in this passage: for while the interplay is itself broadly prepared by modernist psychological models, what Benjamin does with it seems to play against, rather than within, that standard interplay. We note how Benjamin seems to introduce a stratification of the psyche into his photographic metaphor: he describes "ein tieferes Ich" and "ein tiefstes Ich," both of which, in their contrast with "unser waches taggerechtes Ich," seem consigned to some more or less unconscious, dark region beneath the concealing everyday: the evocation of spatial metaphors seems also implicitly to conjure up an archaeological model for the mnemonic subject (compare "an anderer Stelle" here and "an immer andern Stelle, in immer tieferen Schichten" earlier [487]). But we also note how Benjamin does not describe the "unzerstörbarsten Bilder" as themselves "deep" or "buried," erupting from some prehistoric mythical realm such as we find in Klages or Jung. Instead, they are described as actual images, from the actual and quite quotidian external world; see below.

132. The implicit resistance to the various *Lebensphilosophien* can be seen not only in the photographic, and hence technological, metaphor for memory but also in the subject that here evokes it. The particular hidden, forgotten, and recalled memory is of *die Krankheit Syphilis* (519): even as Mann linked photography and tuberculosis to explore his degenerating subject, so does Benjamin link photography and syphilis, working against the dangerously affirmative vision of myth and life with his own, equally disturbing vision of technology and disease.

133. Benjamin even adds "rechts mag die Männlichlichen einzeichnen, links

die weiblichen" (491), further stressing the traditional Bildung structure of his scheme.

134. See Jacobs, *In the Language*, 23.

135. In his earlier essay "Schicksal und Charakter," Benjamin seems to reject the latter claim *im großen;* here, *im kleinen,* he clearly accepts it, even quoting the same passage from Nietzsche to support that which, in the essay, he had quoted only to reject (2:173).

136. Jacobs notes that the name of the street on which these houses are set evokes the archaeological metaphor as well: Kupfergraben (*In the Language*, 38).

137. Karl Schinkel was a nineteenth-century architect best known for his adaptations of classical Greek forms to modern structure; see Eiland and Jennings, *Walter Benjamin: Selected Writings*, 2:636.

138. The *Vitrinen* might also be read as an interiorization of arcades, the eponymous subject of Benjamin's *Das Passagenwerk*.

139. See Benjamin's essay "Strenge Kunstwissenschaft," 3:363–69, here 3:365.

140. The term "Kostbarkeiten" links the artifacts here to the "Bilder, die aus allen früheren Zusammenhängen losgebrochen als Kostbarkeiten in den nüchternen Gemächern unserer späten Einsicht . . . stehen" (486) that Benjamin described in his memory-as-archaeology metaphor, further reinforcing both the archaeological and the self-regarding/interiorized nature of the present passage.

141. Riegl's book stresses the difference between the classicism of the "fine arts" and the craftsmanship of his usually overlooked subject matter, the quotidian ornaments such as Benjamin is here contemplating. In his essay "Strenge Kunstwissenschaft" (3:363–74), Benjamin links this with the attention paid to *das Unbedeutende* (3:366) that we have seen him embrace throughout. See Riegl, *Late Roman Art Industry*.

142. This too, perhaps even especially, can be linked with Benjamin's reference to Riegl's work, which insists on the abandonment of universalizing classical art studies and on the embrace of a rigorously historical approach instead (3:364–65). Moreover, the very notion of a *Kunstindustrie* does much the same to the aesthetic realm as the historical does to the classical. We might also wish to associate the *Etagenwohnung* of the *Antiquitätenhändler* that lies behind the classical facade with the notion of stratification as well.

143. The donor of the ring is Ernst S[choen] whose relationship with Benjamin's wife Dora forms part of the "Verflechtung" of "Urbekanntschaften" allegorized by Benjamin in his essay on Goethe's *Die Wahlverwandtschaften*.

144. Jacobs, *In the Language*, 38.

145. Jacobs also notes this gesture of distanciation but ascribes very different motives for it from those suggested here, none of which amounts to anything approaching a renunciation (ibid.).

146. On "mass," see Weber, Mass Mediauras," 88–96; see also section 19 of "Der Erzähler," where Benjamin describes the storyteller's ability to see in a ring gemstone "eine natürliche Prophezeiung der versteinerten, unbelebten Natur auf die geschichtliche Welt . . . in der er selber lebt" (2:463).

147. One of the peculiarities of Jacobs's reading of the last two rings is that she reverses their order of presentation so that she ends with the Medusa ring and so too with its emblematized ideals as the most decisive for understanding the poetics (and politics) behind *Berliner Chronik* in particular and Benjamin's work as a whole. This is to ignore not only the structure of Benjamin's composition but also its accompanying, and determinative, erotic logic. As Benjamin says in the opening pages of *Berliner Chronik,* the only thread through the labyrinth is *Liebe:* that is nowhere more clear than here, when he comes to discuss the *Mittelpunkt.*

148. Editors' notes tell us this is Julia Cohn, who figures heavily in the auto-biographical allegory of Benjamin's essay on *Die Wahlvervandtschaften.* Benjamin does not name her. She has her predecessors in the Bildungsroman tradition in figures such as Wilhelm's Natalie, Heinrich von Ofterdingen's Matilda, Heinrich Lee's Dorothea Schönfund, Hans Castorp's Clawdia, and Norbert Hanold's Zoë. She also has her predecessors in *Berliner Chronik* in the figures of the (also unnamed) aristocratic Luise von Landau, Benjamin's *Mitschulerin,* who (together with Pindar) inspires his first writing (an essay on nobility), and the (equally anonymous) occupants of a small brothel on the rue de la Harpe, "das ich mit Aufbietung meiner letzten Kräfte (und zum Glück nicht ohne den Faden einer Ariadne) betrat" (469).

149. Benjamin's *stumpf* here seems very much the same as Roland Barthes's notion of *matte,* which he defines as "insignificant, exempt from meaning," and adds that the more one succeeds in making images and memories *matte,* the better they escape the image-system: Barthes, *Roland Barthes,* 101. Interestingly, the opposite of *matte* for Barthes is the lustrous beauty of the Medusa (122).

150. Much as the *punctum* of an old photograph is only recognized after the art of the photographer has receded from view or as the "truth content" of Goethe's *Die Wahlverwandtschaften* is recognized, separated from its mythic material content, by Benjamin the critic, a century removed.

151. It should be noted that Riegl himself, with his notion of *Kunstwollen,* etc., plays into the vitalist tradition, especially in his polemics with the

"mechanistic" scheme of Semper. Benjamin counters this by approaching his (Riegl's) *Urformen* through the technological lens of the camera.

152. Even as, we note, Benjamin himself stands outside the charmed circle of marital relations that bind its figures to Goethe's novel(s), so too does he stand outside the official band of official culture, assuming instead the more modest, and troubled, role of lover.

153. Benjamin, *Gesammelte Schriften*, 2:452, 2:462–63.

154. For nature vs. myth, see Benjamin, *Gesammelte Schriften*, 2:458; for naive poetry, see 2:452; for *Entfaltung*, see esp. the essay "Franz Kafka," 2:420.

155. For *Keimkraft*, see Benjamin, *Gesammelte Schriften*, 2:446.

156. See Darby, "Photography, Narrative," 222; Rugg, *Picturing Ourselves*, 151.

Epilogue

1. See Buck-Morss, *Dialectics of Seeing*, 261–66; Mehlman, *Walter Benjamin for Children*.

2. Benjamin seems nowhere to have written of color photography nor of children and photography.

3. See Benjamin, "Alte vergessene Kinderbücher," 3:16–17.

4. References to Sebald's major works in the text will be to the following editions. All references without identifying a particular volume are to *Austerlitz;* other works are cited using the following abbreviations:

    | S | *Schwindel. Gefühle* (*Vertigo*) |
    | AU | *Die Ausgewanderten* (*The Emigrants*) |
    | RS | *Die Ringe des Saturns* (*The Rings of Saturn*) |
    | LL | *Luftkrieg und Literatur* ("Airwar and Literature") |

5. "Max Ferber" in the English translation by Michael Hulse. For Sebald's reasons for changing the character's name for the English translation, see McCulloh, *Understanding W. G. Sebald*, 41.

6. See *Die Ringe des Saturns* and its narrator's plan to give up teaching (218).

7. Sebald's is a notably male world, marked by an absence of significant female figures (the strangely vacuous figure of Maria in *Austerlitz* included) and especially of significant erotic relations (see the almost embarrassed description of the coupled couple on the beach in *Die Ringe des Saturns*). What erotically tinged relations there are in Sebald's work are almost all between men, and almost all are merely implicitly so, which perhaps partially explains Sebald's sympathy for the works of Thomas Mann. In any case, one gets a sense that, along with those of Bildung and psychoanalysis, the master narrative of sexual identity has

been lost in Sebald's world.

8. Sebald, *Die Ausgewanderten*, 32–35; Sebald, *Austerlitz*, 205–6.

9. This is all the more surprising in that Sebald himself chose to read classics rather than pursue the modern language track as a *Gymnasium* student (Gordon Turner lecture, Duke University, fall 2003).

10. In *Luftkrieg und Literatur*, Sebald does seem to diagnose all of postwar European civilization as afflicted by psychological trauma; he does not, however, ever look to psychology as offering any help or model for healing. In making this statement, I am somewhat disagreeing with a major thesis of J. J. Long, who argues for a Freudian "working-through" via the mechanism of narrative itself ("History, Narrative, and Photography"). For a competing view, see Garloff, "Emigrant as Witness," 92.

11. Sebald, "Mit den Augen des Nachtvogels," 315. The phrase "Unmeisterliche Wanderjahre" refers to the title of one of Améry's texts as well as to Goethe's novel.

12. See McColloh, *Understanding W. G. Sebald*, 133–34.

13. A major difference is that while Benjamin's landscape is consistently urban, Sebald takes his *flânerie* into the countryside as well, which leads to, or is symptomatic of, an extremely problematic reintroduction of the natural into the socio-historical world in Sebald's fiction; see the next note.

14. Two prime examples of the latter are the city of Dunwich in *Die Ringe des Saturn* and the village of Elias's childhood in *Austerlitz*, both of whose ruins now lie underwater. The equation of the destructions due to human history and to natural decay lend a notably Baroque atmosphere to Sebald's world, which in its way might also seem rather Benjaminian. But as we saw in chapter 3, Benjamin guards against the dangers implicit in equating historical conditions with natural ones, and Sebald's work shows why this is so important: the equation risks justifying political violence as no different from natural wear and tear and so ends by absorbing the singularities of human history into an almost mythical, generalized schema.

15. It should be emphasized that Sebald's use of exclusively black-and-white photographs, both in their content and their medium, runs a continual risk of falling prey to a kind of modernist nostalgia, a risk also inherent in the apparent imitation of Benjamin's program. While such nostalgia might well represent a strong part of Sebald's appeal—it is implicit in Susan Sontag's question "Is literary greatness still possible?" and her noting of Sebald's work as one of the "few answers still available"—it is crucial that it not be mistaken as part of his value. Only insofar as Sebald is able to register and explore the *lost* possibility of Benjamin and Atget, only insofar as he is able to instantiate the *problem* of Nach-bildung, does

he have a legitimate claim to our critical approbation.

16. The spectre of Rilke's Paris from *Die Aufzeichnungen des Malte Laurids Brigge* (1910) nonetheless is never far off, as indeed it haunts Benjamin's *Berliner Chronik* as well.

17. This is surely one of the meanings of Austerlitz's earlier claim, "irgendwo wüßten wir natürlich, daß die ins Überdimensionale hinausgewachsenen Bauwerke schon den Schatten ihrer Zerstörung vorauswerfen und konzipiert sind von Anfang an im Hinblick auf ihr nachmaliges Dasein als Ruinen" (32). They always carry the history of their own destruction within them, reproducing the archaeological ruins of the past in their very present structure, in a way that the future, at least, is sure to recognize.

18. For the *Wiederaufbau* as a *zweite Liquidierung*, see *Luftkrieg und Literatur*, 14–16.

19. Cf. Amir Eschel, "Against the Power of Time: The Poetics of Suspension in W. G. Sebald's Austerlitz," *New German Critique* 88 (Winter 2003): 71–96, which, however, takes a much more positive view of such timeless spaces overall; also McCulloh, *Understanding W. G. Sebald*, 119.

20. Buck-Morss, *Dialectics of Seeing*, 95.

21. We might identify this as a loss of faith in Kossinna's axiom about cultural areas. But we should also note how, as we explored in both chapters 2 and 3, Germans in the late nineteenth and early twentieth century frequently dug up "finds" that were not their own but with which they nonetheless identified and used as the foundation for their own identity formation, namely, "classical" finds. The difference in Sebald's postmodern world is that this bad-faith practice has become both anxiously self-conscious and so pervasive as to include almost all prewar experiences, even those—especially those—within German borders themselves.

22. E.g., "Ich [spürte] in zunehmenden Maß, daß die rings mich umgebende Geistesverarmung und Erinnerungslosigkeit der Deutschen, das Geschick, mit dem man alles bereinigt hatte, mir Kopf und Nerven anzugreifen begann" (AU 338); see also Austerlitz and the *Ordnungs- und Sauberkeitswahn* of the National Socialists (287).

23. The name Max that Sebald assigns to his artist figure here is also the name by which he himself was known to friends and family.

24. See the description of Janine Rosalind Dakyn's study at the beginning of *Die Ringe des Saturns* (17–18), whose accumulated layers of paper rival the strata of Aurach's paint.

25. For the theme of testimony in *Die Ausgewanderten*, see Garloff, "The Emigrant as Witness."

26. See the image at the end of "Dr. Henry Selwyn" of "ein Häufchen geschliffener Knochen und ein Paar genagelter Schuhe" that resurface

from under the glacial moraine after seven decades (AU, 37).

27. Another way of making this same point is to consider Hamburger's observation that "Meine Halluzinationen und Träume . . . spielen häufig in einer Umgebung, deren Merkmale teilweise auf die Weltstadt Berlin, teilweise auf das ländliche Suffolk verweisen" (214), a purely imaginary setting that can yield only a similarly imaginary self.

28. Sebald, "Mit den Augen des Nachtvogels," 316.

29. Janouch, *Gespräche mit Kafka.*

30. It is worth noting that this photography, especially in the case of Austerlitz but also for Sebald's authors/narrators, is also always part of their Atgetlike archaeological project focusing on the outmoded and abandoned to the modern world. Photography plays equally into the project of self-construction and archaeology.

31. It is one of the grave shortcomings of the otherwise excellent edition of Benjamin's *Selected Writings* by Harvard University Press that photographs are included in so many places—including especially *Berlin Childhood*—where Benjamin himself elected to leave photographs out. For a discussion of Benjamin's possible reasons for so doing and the concomitant travesty involved in their inclusion in the Harvard edition, see Rugg, *Picturing Ourselves,* 133–38.

32. Kracauer, "Die Photographie," 32.

33. For a more positive assessment of photographs in Sebald's work, see Harris, "The Return of the Dead."

34. See Sebald, "Mit den Augen des Nachtvogels," 316.

35. See also what Sebald says about the pictorial representation of great naval engagements, that they are always figments of the imagination, not least because "[die] Representation der Geschichte . . . berüht auf einer Fälschung der Perspektive" (RS 95; 152).

36. Recall Sebald's own practice, freely admitted in interviews, of doctoring the photos in his books.

37. Cf. Aurach's almost immediately following, and decidedly nonphotographic, memory of the last time he saw his parents (AU 279–80), a memory constructed much more along the model sketched out by Kracauer as authentic.

38. This is as true of old photos meant to recall the past as it is of old buildings converted into new, mnemonic institutions.

39. For Sebald on the nomadic quality of photographs, see the interview with Christian Scholtz, the interview with Michael Seeman, and the interview with Maya Jaggi. My thanks to Judith Ryan, Gordon Turner, and Heather Klomhaus for their generous help in tracking down these references.

40. Consider the narrator's question in *Die Ringe des Saturns:* "Wie kommt

es, daß man in einem anderen Menschen sich selber und wenn nicht sich selber, so doch seinen Vorgänger sieht?" (217–18).

41. One of the more perplexing features of this photograph, more evident on the novel's cover (the German edition, not the English translation) than in the smaller print included in the text, is a smudged scribble over the child's head—something of a dirty aura, obviously marking the picture itself as retouched. The version on the cover of the German edition is also, strangely, colored in.

42. Like Rembrandt's dissected body, the problem of Věra is inscribed into the character herself: e.g., "Seit ich nicht mehr gut aus dem Haus gehen kann und darum fast nichts Neues mir mehr begegnen, sagte Věra, kehren die Bilder, die uns damals so sehr erfreuten, in zunehmender Deutlichkeit, quasi als Phantasien in mir zurück" (231; see also 296–97).

43. Cited by McColloh, *Understanding W. G. Sebald*, 136–37.

Works Cited

Adam, Hans Christian. "Heinrich Schliemann und die Photographie." In *Das Land der Griechen mit der Seele suchen: Photographien des 19. und 20. Jahrhunderts,* 38–41. Cologne: Ausstellungskatalog des Agfa Foto-Historama im Römisch-Germanisch Museum, 1990.

Adorno, Theodor. *Minima Moralia: Reflexionen aus dem beschädigten Leben.* Vol. 4 of *Gesammelte Schriften.* Ed. Rolf Tiedemann. Frankfurt am Main: Suhrkamp, 1980.

Alexander, Edward. *Museum Masters: Their Museums and Their Influence.* Nashville: American Association of State and Local History, 1983.

Alter, Robert. *Necessary Angels: Tradition and Modernity in Kafka, Benjamin, and Scholem.* Cambridge, MA: Harvard University Press, 1991.

Améry, Jean. *Jenseits von Schuld und Sühne.* Stuttgart, 1977.

Armstrong, Nancy. *Fiction in the Age of Photography: The Legacy of British Realism.* Cambridge, MA: Harvard University Press, 1999.

Arnold, Bettina, and Henning Hassmann. "Archaeology in Nazi Germany: The Legacy of the Faustian Bargain." In *Nationalism, Politics, and the Practice of Archaeology,* ed. Philip L. Kohl and Clare Fawcett, 70–81. Cambridge: Cambridge University Press, 1995.

Assmann, Jan. *Moses the Egyptian: The Memory of Egypt in Western Monotheism.* Cambridge, MA: Harvard University Press, 1997.

Bachofen, Johann Jakob. *Das Mutterrecht.* Basel: B. Schwabe, 1948.

Bahn, Paul G., ed. *The Cambridge Illustrated History of Archaeology.* Cambridge: Cambridge University Press, 1996.

Bahti, Timothy. "Theories of Knowledge: Fate and Forgetting in Early Works of Walter Benjamin." In Nägele, *Benjamin's Ground,* 61–82.

Barthes, Roland. *Camera Lucida: Reflections on Photography.* Trans. Richard

Howard. New York: Hill and Wang, 1981.

———. *Roland Barthes*. Trans. Richard Howard. New York: Hill and Wang, 1977.

Baudelaire, Charles. *The Painter of Modern Life and Other Essays*. Trans. and ed. Jonathan Mayne. London: Phaidon, 1964.

Benjamin, Walter. *The Correspondence of Walter Benjamin*. Ed. Gershom Scholem and Theodor Adorno. Trans. Manfred R. Jacobson and Evelyn M. Jacobson. Chicago: University of Chicago Press, 1994.

———. *Gesammelte Briefe*. Ed. Cristoph Gödde and Henri Lonitz. Frankfurt am Main: Suhrkamp, 1997.

———. *Gesammelte Schriften*. Ed. Rolf Tiedemann and Hermann Schweppenhäuser. Frankfurt am Main: Suhrkamp, 1980.

———. *Walter Benjamin: Selected Writings*. Ed. Marcus Bullock, Howard Eiland, Michael Jennings, et al. Trans. Edmund Jephcott, Rodney Livingstone, et al. 4 vols. Cambridge, MA: Harvard University Press, 1996–2003.

Bergson, Henri. *Matière et Mémoire: essai sur relation du corps l'esprit*. Paris: Presses Universitaires de France, 1953.

———. "Le mécanisme cinématographie de la pensée et l'illusion mécanistique." In *L'évolution créatrice*, 272–368. Paris: Presses Universitaires de France, 1981.

Berman, Russell. *Enlightenment or Empire: Colonial Discourse in German Culture*. Lincoln: University of Nebraska Press, 1998.

———. *The Rise of the Modern German Novel: Crisis and Charisma*. Cambridge, MA: Harvard University Press, 1986.

Bernal, Martin. *Black Athena: The Afroasiatic Roots of Classical Civilization*. Vol. 1 of *The Fabrication of Ancient Greece, 1785–1985*. New Brunswick, NJ: Rutgers University Press, 1987.

Blüher, Hans. *Die Rolle der Erotik in der männlichen Gesellschaft. Eine Theorie der menschlichen Staatsbildung nach Wesen und Wert*. 2 vols. Jena: Diederichs, 1917–19.

Bronfen, Elisabeth. *Over Her Dead Body: Death, Femininity, and the Aesthetic*. New York: Routledge, 1992.

Brontë, Charlotte. *Jane Eyre*. London: Penguin, 2003.

Buck-Morss, Susan. *The Dialectics of Seeing: Walter Benjamin and the Arcades Project*. Cambridge, MA: MIT Press, 1991.

Cadava, Eduardo. "Words of Light: Theses on the Photography of History." In *Fugitive Images: From Photography to Video*, ed. Patrice Petro, 221–44. Bloomington: Indiana University Press, 1995.

Cohn, Dorrit. *Transparent Minds: Narrative Modes for Presenting Consciousness in Fiction*. Princeton: Princeton University Press, 1978.

Crary, Jonathan. *Techniques of the Observer: On Vision and Modernity in the*

Nineteenth Century. Cambridge, MA: MIT Press, 1990.

Daniel, Glyn. *A Hundred and Fifty Years of Archaeology.* Duckworth, 1975.

Darby, David. "Photography, Narrative, and the Landscape of Memory in Walter Benjamin's Berlin." *Germanic Review* 75, no. 3 (2000): 210–25.

Darwin, Charles. *On the Expression of the Emotions in Man and Animals.* New York: D. Appleton, 1896.

Derrida, Jacques. *Dissemination.* Trans. Barbara Johnson. Chicago: Chicago University Press, 1981.

Dickens, Charles. *Oliver Twist; or, The Parish Boy's Progress.* London: Penguin, 1985.

Downey, Helen M., trans. *Delusion and Dream: An Interpretation in the Light of Psychoanalysis of* Gradiva, *a Novel, by Wilhelm Jensen, Which Is Here Reprinted, by Sigmund Freud.* New York: Moffatt Yard, 1927.

Downing, Eric. *Double Exposures: Repetition and Realism in Nineteenth-Century German Fiction.* Stanford: Stanford University Press, 2000.

Doyle, Sir Arthur Conan. *The Case for Spirit Photography.* New York: George H. Doran, 1923.

———. *The Coming of the Fairies.* New York: George H. Doran, 1922.

Draaisma, Douwe. *Metaphors of Memory.* Cambridge: Cambridge University Press, 2000.

Dreyfus, Hubert L., and Paul Rabinow. "The Methodological Failure of Archaeology." In *Michel Foucault: Beyond Structuralism and Hermeneutics,* 79–103. Chicago: University of Chicago Press, 1982.

Eiland, Howard, and Michael Jennings. *Walter Benjamin: Selected Writings.* 4 vols. Cambridge, MA: Harvard University Press, 1996–2003.

Ernst, Barnard M. L., and Hereward Carington, *Houdini and Conan Doyle: The Story of a Strange Friendship.* London: Hutchinson, 1933.

Eschel, Amir. "Against the Power of Time: The Poetics of Suspension in W. G. Sebald's Austerlitz." *New German Critique* 88 (Winter 2003): 71–96.

Faulkner, William. *Absalom, Absalom!* New York: Random House, 1986.

Fontane, Theodor. *Frau Jenny Treibel.* In *Sämtliche Werke,* ed. Edgar Groß et al. Munich: Nymphenburger, 1959.

Foucault, Michel. *The History of Sexuality. Volume I: An Introduction.* Trans. Robert Hurley. New York: Random House, 1980.

Freud, Sigmund. *Delusion and Dream.* Trans. Helen M. Downey. New York: New Republic, 1927.

———. *Der Wahn und die Träume in W. Jensen's "Gradiva" mit dem Text der Erzählung von Wilhelm Jensen.* Ed. Bernd Urban and Johannes Cremerius. Frankfurt am Main: Fischer, 1973.

———. *Gesammelte Werke, chronologisch geordnet.* Ed. Anna Freud et al. Frankfurt am Main: Fischer, 1968–78.

———. *The Standard Edition Complete Psychological Works of Sigmund Freud.*

Trans. and ed. James Strachey. 24 vols. London: Hogarth Press, 1966.

———. *Studienausgabe.* Ed. A. Mitscherlich et al. Frankfurt am Main: Fischer, 1982.

Gabo, Naum, and Anton Pevsner. "The Realist Manifesto." In *Russian Art of the Avant Garde: Theory and Criticism, 1902–1934,* ed. John E. Bowit, 208–15. New York: Viking, 1976.

Galton, Francis. *Inquiries into Human Faculty and Its Development.* London: Macmillan, 1883.

Garloff, Katja. "The Emigrant as Witness: Sebald's *Die Ausgewanderten.*" *German Quarterly* 77, no. 1 (2004): 76–93.

Gernsheim, Helmut. *The Origins of Photography.* New York: Thames and Hudson, 1982.

Goethe, Johann Wolfgang. *Italian Journey.* Trans. W. H. Auden and Elizabeth Mayer. London: Penguin, 1970.

———. *Wilhelm Meisters Lehrjahre.* In *Werke in vierzehn Bänden,* ed. E. Trunz. Munich: Deutscher Taschenbuch Verlag, 1981.

Greenblatt, Stephen. *Shakespearean Negotiations.* Berkeley: University of California Press, 1988.

Gunning, Tom. "Phantom Images and Modern Manifestations: Spirit Photography, Magic Theater, Trick Films, and Photography's Uncanny." In *Fugitive Images: From Photography to Video,* ed. Patrice Petro, 42–71. Bloomington: Indiana University Press, 1995.

Hamacher, Werner. "The Word *Wolke*—If It Is One." In Nägele, *Benjamin's Ground,* 147–75.

Hambourg, Maria Morris. "The Structure of the Work." In John Szarkowski and Maria Morris Hambourg, *The Work of Atget. Volume 3: The Ancien Regime.* New York: Museum of Modern Art, 1983.

Hamilakis, Yannis. "Monumental Visions: Bonfils, Classical Antiquity and Nineteenth Century Athenian Society." *History of Photography* 25, no. 1 (2001): 5–12.

Hanney, Roxanne. "Proust and Negative Plates: Photography and the Photographic Process in *A La Recherche du temps perdu.*" *Romanic Review* 74, no. 3 (1983): 342–54.

Hansen, Miriam. "Benjamin, Cinema, and Experience: 'The Blue Flower in the Land of Technology.'" *New German Critique* 40 (1987): 179–224.

Harris, Stephanie. "The Return of the Dead: Memory and Photography in Sebald's *Die Ausgewanderten.*" *German Quarterly* 74, no. 4 (2001): 379–91.

Hello, Ernest. *L'Homme.* Paris: Victor Palmé, 1872.

Heyse, Paul. *Unvergeßbare Worte und andere Novellen.* Berlin: Wilhelm Hertz Verlag, 1883.

Holub, Robert. *Reflections of Realism: Paradox, Norm, and Ideology in Nine-*

teenth-Century German Prose. Detroit: Wayne State University Press, 1991.

Hörisch, Jochen. *Gott, Geld, und Glück: Zur Logik der Liebe in den Bildungsromanen Goethes, Kellers, und Thomas Manns*. Frankfurt am Main: Suhrkamp, 1983.

———. "Die deutsche Seele up-to-date." In *Arsenale der Seele: Literatur- und Medienanalyse seit 1870,* ed. Friedrich Kittler, 13–23. Munich: W. Fink, 1989.

Huysmans, J.-K. *A Rebours*. Gallimard, 1977.

Huyssen, Andreas. "The Vamp and the Machine." In *After the Great Divide: Modernism, Mass Culture, Postmodernism,* 65–82. Bloomington: Indiana University Press, 1986.

Jacobs, Carol. *In the Language of Walter Benjamin*. Baltimore: The Johns Hopkins University Press, 1999.

Jaeger, Werner. "Die geistige Gegenwart der Antike." In *Humanistische Reden und Vorträge*. 2nd ed. Berlin: De Gruyter, 1960.

———. *Paideia: The Ideals of Greek Culture*. Vol. 1 of *Archaic Greece, the Mind of Athens*. Trans. Gilbert Highet. Oxford: Oxford University Press, 1939.

Janouch, Gustav. *Gespräche mit Kafka: Aufzeichnungen und Erinnerungen*. Frankfurt am Main: Fischer, 1968.

Jung, C. G. *The Archetypes and the Collective Unconscious*. Trans. R. F. C. Hull. Princeton: Princeton University Press, 1968.

———. *Seelenprobleme der Gegenwart*. Zürich, 1932.

Kaiser, Gerhard, and Friedrich A. Kittler. *Dichtung als Sozialisationsspiel: Studien zu Goethe und Gottfried Keller*. Göttingen: Vanenhoeck und Ruprecht, 1978.

Keller, Gottfried. *Der Grüne Heinrich*. Ditzingien: Reclam, 2003.

Kevles, Bettyann Holtzmann. *Naked to the Bone: Medical Imaging in the Twentieth Century*. New Brunswick, NJ: Rutgers University Press, 1997.

Killen, Andreas. "From Shock to Schreck: Psychiatrists and Telephone Operators in Germany, 1900–1926." *Journal of Contemporary History* 38, no. 2 (2003): 201–20.

Kittler, Friedrich. *Aufschreibesysteme 1800/1900*. Munich: W. Fink, 1985.

———. *Discourse Networks, 1800/1900*. Trans. Michael Metteer, with Chris Cullens. Stanford: Stanford University Press, 1990.

———. *Grammophon, Film, Typewriter*. Berlin: Brinkmann and Bose, 1986.

———. "The Mechanized Philosopher." In *Looking After Nietzsche,* ed. Laurence Rickels, 195–207. Albany: SUNY Press, 1990.

Klages, Ludwig. *Sämtliche Werke*. Ed. Ernst Frauchiger et al. Bonn: Bouvier Verlag Herbert Grundmann, 1974.

Koc, Richard. "Magical Reenactments: Reflections on 'Highly Questionable'

Matters in *Der Zauberberg.*" *Germanic Review* 68, no. 3 (1993): 108–17.

Kofman, Sarah. *Camera Obscura of Ideology.* Trans. Will Straw. Ithaca, NY: Cornell University Press, 1999.

Kracauer, Siegfried. "Die Photographie." In *Das Ornament der Masse,* 21–39. Frankfurt am Main: Suhrkamp, 1977.

Kudszus, Winfried. "Understanding media: Zur Kritik dualistischer Humanität im *Zauberberg.*" In *Besichtigung des Zauberbergs,* ed. Heinze Saueressig, 55–80. Biberach an der Riss, 1974.

Kuspit, Donald. "A Mighty Metaphor: The Analogy of Archaeology and Psychoanalysis." In *Sigmund Freud and Art,* ed. Lynn Gamwell and Richard Wells, 133–51. New York: Abrams, 1989.

Lindner, Burkhardt. "Das Passagenwerk, die Berliner Kindheit, und die Archäologie des "Jüngstvergangenen." In *Passagen: Walter Benjamins Urgeschichte des neunzehnten Jahrhunderts,* ed. Norbert Bolz and Bernd Witte, 27–48. Munich: Fink, 1984.

Long, J. J. "History, Narrative, and Photography in W. G. Sebald's *Die Ausgewanderten.*" *Modern Language Review* 98, no. 1 (2002) 117–37.

MacLeod, Catriona. *Embodying Ambiguity: Androgyny and Aesthetics from Winckelmann to Keller.* Detroit: Wayne State University Press, 1998.

Mann, Thomas. *Briefe 1889–1936.* Ed. Erika Mann. Frankfurt am Main: Fischer, 1961.

———. *Gesammelte Werke in dreizehn Bänden.* Frankfurt am Main: Fischer, 1974.

Marchand, Suzanne. *Down From Olympus: Archaeology and Philhellenism in Germany, 1750–1970.* Princeton: Princeton University Press, 1996.

Marx, Karl, and Friedrich Engels. *The German Ideology.* Ed. R. Pascal. New York, 1963.

Mavor, Carol. *Pleasures Taken.* Durham, NC: Duke University Press, 1995.

McCole, John. *Walter Benjamin and the Antinomies of Tradition.* Ithaca, NY: Cornell University Press, 1993.

McCulloh, Mark R. *Understanding W. G. Sebald.* Columbia: University of South Carolina Press, 2003.

McFarland, James. Review of Carol Jacobs, *In the Language of Walter Benjamin. Colloquia Germanica* 34, no. 1 (2001): 88–91.

McIsaac, Peter. "The Divide between Nature and Civilization in Second Empire Anthropological and Archaeological Exhibitions." Unpublished manuscript.

McLuhan, Marshall. *Understanding Media: The Extensions of Man.* New York: McGraw-Hill, 1964.

Mehlman, Jeffrey. *Walter Benjamin for Children: An Essay on His Radio Years.* Chicago: University of Chicago Press, 1993.

Miller, D. A. *The Novel and the Police*. Berkeley: University of California Press, 1988.

Morris, Ian. *Archaeology as Cultural History*. Malden, MA: Blackwell, 2000.

———, ed. *Classical Greece: Ancient Histories and Modern Archaeologies*. Cambridge: Cambridge University Press, 1994.

Nägele, Rainer. *Benjamin's Ground: New Readings of Walter Benjamin*. Detroit: Wayne State University Press, 1988.

Nehamas, Alexander. "'Getting Used to Not Getting Used to It': Nietzsche in *The Magic Mountain*." *Philosophy and Literature* 5, no. 1 (1981): 73–90.

Newhall, Beaumont. *The History of Photography from 1839 to the Present*. Boston: Little, Brown, 1982.

———, ed. *Photography: Essays and Images*. New York, 1980.

Nietzsche, Friedrich. *Die Fröhliche Wissenschaft*. In *Sämtliche Werke: Kritische Studienausgabe in fünfzehn Einzelbände*, vol 3., ed. Giorgio Colli and Mazzino Montinari. Munich: Deutscher Taschenbuch Verlag, 1988.

Porter, James I. *Nietzsche and the Philology of the Future*. Stanford: Stanford University Press, 2000.

Proust, Marcel. *A la Recherche du temps perdu*. Paris: Gallimard [Bibliothèque de la Pléiade], 1954.

Reinhard, Kenneth. "The Freudian Things: Construction and the Archaeological Metaphor." In *Excavations and Their Objects: Freud's Collection of Antiquity*, ed. Stephen Barker, 57–80. Albany: SUNY Press, 1996.

Richter, Gerhard. *Walter Benjamin and the Corpus of Autobiography*. Detroit: Wayne State University Press, 2000.

Ricouer, Paul. "The Task of Hermeneutics." In *Hermeneutics and the Human Sciences*, ed. and trans. John B. Thompson, 43–62. Cambridge: Cambridge University Press, 1981.

Riegl, Alois. *Late Roman Art Industry*. Trans. Rolf Winkes. Giorgo Bretschneider, 1985.

Rodenwaldt, Gerhart, and Walter Hege. *Die Akropolis*, 2nd ed. Berlin, 1935.

Rohrwasser, Michael. "Wilhelm Jensens 'pompeijanisches Phantasiestück' und Sigmund Freud's Interpretation." In *Freuds pompeijanishe Muse*. Wien: Sonderzahl, 1996.

Ryan, Judith. *The Uncompleted Past: Postwar German Novels and the Third Reich*. Detroit: Wayne State University Press, 1983.

Rugg, Linda Haverty. *Picturing Ourselves: Photography and Autobiography*. Chicago: University of Chicago Press, 1997.

Said, Edward W. *Orientalism*. New York: Vintage, 1978.

Sante, Luc. *The Factory of Facts*. New York: Pantheon, 1998.

Scholem, Gershom, and Theodor W. Adorno, eds. *The Correspondence of Walter Benjamin*. Trans. M. R. Jacobson and E. R. Jacobson. Chicago: University of Chicago Press, 1994.

Schultz, Karla. "Technology as Desire: X-ray Vision in *The Magic Mountain*." In *A Companion to Thomas Mann's The Magic Mountain,* ed. Stephen Dowden, 158–76. Columbia, SC: Camden House, 1999.

Sebald, W. G. *Austerlitz*. Frankfurt am Main: Fischer, 2003. Translated by Anthea Bell as *Austerlitz* (New York: Random House, 2001. New York: Random House, 2001.

———. *Die Ausgewanderten: Vier lange Erzählungen*. Frankfurt am Main: Fischer, 1994. Translated by Michael Hulse as *The Emigrants* (New York: New Directions, 1996).

———. *Die Ringe des Saturns*. Frankfurt am Main: Fischer, 1997. Translated by Michael Hulse as *The Rings of Saturn* (New York: New Directions, 1998).

———. Interview with Maya Jaggi from St. Jerome Event with W. G. Sebald, recorded live from Queen Elizabeth Hall, London in September 2001.

———. Interview with Christian Scholtz, "Der Schriftsteller und die Fotografie," Manuskript des Radio Features, Erstsendung am 16.2.1999 im WDR, Köln.

———. Interview with Michael Seeman for the program *Kamer met Uitzicht,* produced by Netherlands TV, VPRO, first broadcast July 12, 1998.

———. *Luftkrieg und Literatur*. Frankfurt am Main: Fischer, 2001. Translated by Anthea Bell as "Airwar and Literature" in *On the Natural History of Destruction* (New York: Modern Library, 2003).

———. "Mit den Augen des Nachtvogels. Über Jean Améry." *Études Germaniques* 43, no. 3 (1988) 313–27.

———. *Schwindel. Gefühle*. Frankfurt am Main: Eichborn Verlag, 1998. Trans. Michael Hulse as *Vertigo* (New York: New Directions, 1999).

Sekula, Allan. "The Body and the Archive." In *The Contest of Meaning: Critical Histories of Photography,* ed. Richard Bolton, 342–89. London: MIT, 1989.

Shanks, Michael. "Photography and archaeology." In *The Cultural Life of Images: Visual Representation in Archaeology,* ed. Brian Leigh Molyneaux, 73–107. London: Routledge, 1997.

Smith, John H. "Cultivating Gender: Sexual Difference, Bildung, and the Bildungsroman." *Michigan Germanic Studies* 13 (1987): 296–32.

Snyder, Joel. "Benjamin on Reproducibility and Aura: A Reading of "The Work of Art in the Age of Its Technical Reproducibility." In *Benjamin: Philosophy, Aesthetics, History,* ed. Gary Smith, 158–74. Chicago: University of Chicago Press, 1989.

Sontag, Susan. *On Photography*. New York: Farrar, Straus & Giroux, 1977.

———. *Illness as Metaphor*. New York: Farrar, Straus & Giroux, 1977.

Storm, Theodor. *Viola tricolor*. In *Sämtliche Werke,* vol. 3. Ed. Albert Köster. Leipzig: Insel, 1919.

Stray, Christopher. *Classics Transformed: Schools, Universities, and Society in England, 1830–1960.* Oxford: Clarendon Press, 1998.

Szarkowski, John, and Maria Morris Hambourg. *The Work of Atget. Volume I: Old France.* New York: Museum of Modern Art, 1981.

Szegedy-Maszak, Andrew. "An Eye for Antiquity." *Archaeology* 43, no. 4 (1990): 54–57, 76.

———. "Sun and Stone: Images of Ancient, Heroic Times." *Archaeology* 41, no. 4 (1988): 20–31.

———. "True Illusions: the Early Photographs of Athens." *J. Paul Getty Museum Journal* 15 (1987): 125–38.

Tatar, Maria. *Spellbound: Studies on Mesmerism and Literature.* Princeton: Princeton University Press, 1978.

———. *Lustmord: Sexual Murder in Weimar Germany.* Princeton: Princeton University Press, 1995.

Tögel, Christfried. *Berggasse-Pompeji und zurück: Sigmund Freuds Reisen in die Vergangenheit.* Tübingen: edition diskord, 1989.

Traill, David A. *Schliemann of Troy: Treasure and Deceit.* London: John Murray, 1995.

———. "'Priam's Treasure': Schliemann's Plan to Make Duplicates for Illicit Purposes." In *Myth, Scandal, and History: The Heinrich Schliemann Controversy,* ed. William Calder and David Traill, 110–24. Detroit: Wayne State University Press, 1986.

Trigger, Bruce. *A History of Archaeological Thought.* Cambridge University Press, 1989.

Turner, R. Steven. "Historicism, *Kritik,* and the Prussian Professoriate, 1790 to 1840." In *Philologie und Hermeneutik im 19 Jahrhundert II.* Göttingen: Vandenhoeck and Ruprecht (1983) 450–78.

Urban, Bernd, and Johannes Cremerius, eds. *Der Wahn und die Träume in W. Jensen's "Gradiva" mit dem Text der Erzählung von Wilhelm Jensen,* by Sigmund Freud. Frankfurt am Main: Fischer, 1973.

Von Schrenck-Notzing, Freiherr Albert. *Materialisationsphänomene: Ein Beitrag zur Erforschung der Mediumischen Teleplastie.* Munich: Ernst Reinhardt, 1913.

Weber, Samuel. "Mass Mediauras, or: Art, Aura, and Media in the Work of Walter Benjamin." In *Mass Mediauras: Form, Technics, Media,* ed. Alan Cholodenko, 76–82. Stanford: Stanford University Press, 1996.

Weisinger, Kenneth. "Distant Oil Rigs and Other Erections." In *A Companion to Thomas Mann's Magic Mountain,* ed. Stephen D. Dowden. Columbia, SC: Camden House, 1999.

Wellbery, David E. Foreword to *Discourse Networks, 1800/1900,* by Friedrich Kittler, trans. Michael Metteer, with Chris Cullens, vii–xxxiii. Stanford: Stanford University Press, 1990.

Wickert, Lothar. *Das Deutsche Archäologische Institut: Geschichte und Dokumente*, in *Beiträge zur Geschichte des Deutschen Archäologischen Instituts 1879 bis 1929*. Mainz: Verlag Philipp von Zabern, 1979.

Winthrop-Young, Geoffrey. "Magic Media Mountain: Technology and the Umbildungsroman." In *Reading Matters: Narratives in the New Media Ecology*, 29–52. Ithaca, NY: Cornell University Press, 1997.

Witte, Bernd. *Walter Benjamin: An Intellectual Biography.* Trans. James Rolleston. Detroit: Wayne State University Press, 1991.

Woods, John E., trans. *The Magic Mountain: A Novel,* by Thomas Mann. New York: Knopf, 1995.

Zantop, Susanne. *Colonial Fantasies: Conquest, Family, and Nation in Precolonial Germany, 1770–1780*. Durham, NC: Duke University Press, 1997.

Zintzen, Christiane. "Wilhelm Jensen's *Gradiva* im Kontext: Archäologische, touristische und populäre Pompejana im 18. und 19. Jahrhundert." In *Freuds pompejanische Muse,* ed. Michael Rohrwasser et al. 43–90. Wien: Sonderzahl, 1996.

Freud, Sigmund (*continued*)
*Civilization and Its Discontents
(Das Unbehagen in der Kultur)*,
173–74; "colonialist" impulses
and ambitions, 104; concepts of
repression and compromise, 117;
consciousness and memory,
342n124; "Constructions in Psychoanalysis" ("Konstruktionen in
der Analyse"), 174; "Delusion
and Dreams in W. Jensen's
'Gradiva'" ("Der Wahn und die
Träuma in W. Jensens
'Gradiva'"), 4, 67, 108, 113–26,
134, 149, 153, 156, 158, 161,
163, 165–66, 173, 325n64,
326n69; equation of archaeology
and psychoanalysis, 173; *Introductory Lectures on Psychoanalysis*
("Widerstand und Verdrän-
gung"), 34; introjection of a
social imaginary, 214; on inversion, 56; lack of interest in Pompeii, 109; lifelong interest in
Schliemann, 8, 23; memory as
photography, 247, 250, 253;
model of latency, 31–32; *Moses
and Monotheism (Der Mann
Moses und die monotheistische
Religion)*, 31–32, 172–73; "A
Note on the Unconscious,"
32–33; notion of a repetition
compulsion, 39; and Oedipus,
14; and photography, 29, 31,
32–34, 245; psychoanalysis as a
kind of archaeological dig, 116;
racial models for constructing the
German, 143; "Resistance and
Repression," 34; "saxa loquuntur," 152; *Totem and Taboo
(Totem und Tabu)*, 173; on
trauma, 252
Frith, Francis, 88
Furtwängler, Adolf, 100

Gabo, Naum, 44

Galton, Francis, 6, 42, 89, 172, 245;
Mischphotographie, 40
George, Stefan, 175, 177
George circle, 201
German archaeology: "big dig" at
Olympia, 95; differentiation of
classical from Mediterranean
archaeology, 96, 98; Nazification
of, 98, 99, 125; shift from Italian
(and French and Latin) to German, 95; split within, 98–101
German culture: classical Bildung tradition, 90–91; dominance of
philhellenism, 90
Germania libera, 99, 100
German national identity: ancient
Greece as model for, 10, 95–96;
role of archaeology in the elaboration of, 92–93, 98, 99; role of
psychoanalysis in the elaboration
of, 125–26
Germany: Bismarckian nationalism,
106; founding of the Second
Reich, 104; investment in helping the Ottoman Turks, 96–97,
100–101; "scientific" archaeology, 154
Goethe, Wolfgang von, 2, 7, 11, 56,
67, 79; centennial celebration of
death, 169; model of classical
world, 90, 95, 108; model of
unfolding *(Entfaltung)*, 265;
notion of *das Urphänomen*, 187,
226, 237, 267; privileging of
Greeks over Romans, 176
Goethean Bildung, 90, 187, 265
Gounod, Charles-François, 81
Gradiva (Jensen), 104; archaeological
language, 152–53; Baedeker
guidebook, 127, 193; Bildung
deployment of classicism, 265;
fashioning of the classical as
"German," 140–43; Freud's
reading of, 4, 67, 108, 113–26,
134, 149, 153, 156, 158, 161,
163, 165–66, 173, 325n64,

CPSIA information can be obtained
at www.ICGtesting.com
Printed in the USA
BVHW040600200319

543125BV00010B/220/P